orientation to the theater

SECOND EDITION

orientation to the theater

Theodore W. Hatlen

University of California
Santa Barbara

PRENTICE-HALL, INC., Englewood Cliffs, New Jersey

Printed in the United States of America

ISBN: 0-13-642090-7

Library of Congress Catalog Card Number: 72-182139

10 9 8 7 6

TEXT AND PHOTOGRAPH ACKNOWLEDGMENTS

TEXT

3: "The Hollow Men" in *Collected Poems, 1909–1962* by T. S. Eliot, copyright, 1936, by Harcourt Brace Jovanovich, Inc. Copyright, ©, 1963, 1964 by T. S. Eliot. Reprinted by permission of the publishers.

4–8: Samuel Beckett, *Krapp's Last Tape and Other Dramatic Pieces,* reprinted by permission of Grove Press, Inc. Copyright © 1957 by Samuel Beckett; copyright © 1958, 1959, 1960 by Grove Press, Inc.

18–20, 86–87: *Antigone,* from *Oedipus the King and Antigone* by Sophocles. Trans. by Peter D. Arnott. Copyright © 1960. Reprinted by permission of Appleton-Century-Crofts, Educational Division, Meredith Corporation.

34–36: Copyright © 1958 by Maurice Valency. Reprinted from *The Visit,* by Friedrich Duerrenmatt, trans. by Maurice Valency, by permission of Random House, Inc. Act I, pp. 3-5.

47: Eugene O'Neill, *Anna Christie.* Copyright 1922 by Random House. Reprinted by permission of the publishers.

53–54: from *In the Matter of J. Robert Oppenheimer,* by Heinar Kipphardt, pp. 125-127. Originally published in German as *In der Sache J. Robert Oppenheimer.* © 1964 Suhrkamp Verlag, Frankfurt am Main. This translation © 1967, 1968 by John Roberts. Reprinted by permission of Hill and Wang, Inc.

(Acknowledgments continue on page 331.)

PRENTICE-HALL INTERNATIONAL, INC., *London*
PRENTICE-HALL OF AUSTRALIA, PTY. LTD., *Sydney*
PRENTICE-HALL OF CANADA, LTD., *Toronto*
PRENTICE-HALL OF INDIA PRIVATE LIMITED, *New Delhi*
PRENTICE-HALL OF JAPAN, INC., *Tokyo*

in appreciation of
three great teachers

ALEXANDER DRUMMOND
THOMAS WOODS STEVENS
HUBERT C. HEFFNER

contents

preface

The primary task in understanding the theater is to develop an appreciation of the drama, not merely as a way of telling a story, or as a vehicle of production, but as a special kind of artistic creation that combines its own particular methods with the universal values of all kinds of artistic creation. The basic premise of this book is that the theater is a means to an end—the appropriate and expressive interpretation of a play. Attention is placed on dramatic structure, dramatic techniques, and the various forms and modes of dramatic composition, always in context with theatrical production.

Like all works of art, a play is caused by the conditions of creation. In part, the final product represents the personal qualities of the artist and his way of looking at life. In part, the play is symbolic of the cultural milieu in which it was created. In part, the artist's method reveals the circumstances under which he worked—the availability of materials and the technical practices of his time. This is especially true in the composite art of dramatic production where the effect of the play may depend upon the size and shape of the physical theater, the conventions of the stage, the capacities of the actors, and the tastes of the audience. The interaction of these factors is a source of constant pressure that determines the way in which the playwright will create. The effect of these influences will be examined on a number of writers whose varied structures and techniques indicate the change in dramatic composition and theatrical production from age to age.

Dramatic art, like all genuine creative expression, is a reminder that a culture is not to be judged by its material accomplishments alone, but also by the ideals and aspirations that motivate human conduct, and the faiths by which men live. In dealing with the significant actions and choices of his characters, a dramatist has at his disposal special means of delineating the human condition. Thus, a play is more than an evening's diversion in the theater, more than pages of text; it is at once a personal statement of the dramatist and a clue to the culture that produced it. The objective of this book is to provide the student with the tools of analysis which will give him insight into the total imaginative process that makes up the art of the theater.

It is intended that *Orientation to the Theater* be used in conjunction with the reading of representative plays selected by the instructor from the great number now readily available. In my own course I have used *Antigone, Oedipus Rex, The Miser, Hamlet, The School for Scandal, An Enemy of the People, Ghosts, Miss Julie, Major Barbara, The Caucasian Chalk Circle, Waiting for Godot, The Glass Menagerie, Zoo Story,* and *The Leader.*

I wish to express my gratitude to William Reardon and Michael Addison, my colleagues in the Department of Dramatic Art at the University of California, Santa Barbara, and to my students over the years. I am grateful to the following persons and institutions for their cooperation in the preparation of this book: the Theater Collection of the New York Public Library; Werner Hecht of the Berliner Ensemble; Rudolf Joseph of the Stadtmuseum, Munich; Josef Svoboda and Jaroslav Anton of the Prague National Theater; Dr. Eckehart Nölle of the Theatermuseum, Munich; Jerzy Grotowski of the Polish Laboratory Theater; Jovan Cirilov of the Belgrade International Theater Festival; the British Museum; the Victoria and Albert Museum; Walter G. Silva; Jarka Burian; Martha Swing; Patricia Peters; Leanora Kirchner; Colleen Ellis, and Edna Hatlen.

T. W. H.

orientation to the theater

art and imitation

The theater is in revolt. It rocks with confusion and change as new voices clamor to be heard and old ones are drowned out. But ferment is nearly the normal condition of the theater, especially when the society it serves is in a state of upheaval. Are there dramatic principles that can accommodate such a wide range of offerings—from Greek tragedy to a rock festival, from a medieval religious play to a happening, from a Shakespearean tragedy to an absurdist play by Ionesco? And what about the experimental productions that reject the theater itself? Fortunately, dramatic art is resilient and versatile, and despite all manner of attacks it has thus far shown the capacity to survive.

In times of confusion, it helps to go back to fundamental principles. In drama this means turning back to Aristotle who, while much maligned and misunderstood these days, still speaks with insight and wisdom that we cannot ignore. For example, consider the following statement from his *Poetics*, written in the fourth century B.C.:

> . . . The instinct of imitation is implanted in man from childhood, one difference between him and other animals being that he is the most imitative of living creatures, and through imitation learns his earliest lessons; and it is also natural to delight in imitations. We have evidence of this in the facts of experience. Objects which in themselves we view with pain, we delight to contemplate when reproduced with minute fidelity: such as the forms of the lowest animals and of dead bodies. The cause

> of this again is that to learn gives the liveliest pleasure, not only to philosophers, but to men in general; whose capacity, however, of learning is more limited. Thus the reason why men enjoy seeing a likeness is that in contemplating it they find themselves learning or inferring, and saying perhaps, "Ah, that is he." For if you happen not to have seen the original, the pleasure will be due not to the imitation as such, but to the execution, the coloring, or some such other cause.[1]

In this statement from the *Poetics,* Aristotle lays the groundwork for dramatic imitation, or mimesis. Like the other arts, the function of drama is to give pleasure through learning. An object of imitation pleases us not only because of the information it provides, but also because we find aesthetic pleasure in the execution and in discovering relationships between the particular and the universal. Learning is a process of understanding the known through the unknown, and the artist makes use of this process in creating an imitative work.

Consider some uses of imitation.

While driving along the edge of the Mohave Desert one day, I stopped and took the photograph opposite. It is a casual snapshot without much concern about composition or lighting, just a black and white record of a typical desert scene. The photograph simply shows the kinds of vegetation and topographical details that make up the desert. The imitation is not a calculated statement of a point of view.

Now consider another view of a western desert in the next illustration, James Swinnerton's *Monument Valley.* The painter has used nature as the source of his imitation in a representational way. But the painting is much more selective than a photograph. Swinnerton has carefully composed his scene so that a pleasing relationship of line, shape, and color emphasizes the center of interest—the pinnacle rising sharply from the desert floor. The harsh, barren quality of the desert has been toned down and the dramatic lighting enhances the appealing aspects of the scene. The pleasure we gain from such a work comes from the skill of the execution, which enables us to recognize a pleasing representation of the desert. The painting, which is far more controlled than my snapshot, is also an imitation of actuality. Neither the snapshot nor the painting exploits the locale for symbolic meaning.

The poet imitates reality too, but he works in a different way than the representational painter. Although he may use images with a strong visual impact, he is likely to work indirectly. He implies qualities, that is, he prefers to establish relationships that suggest a feeling or idea. His concern is not with particulars alone but with the universals that unite and order experience.

1. S. H. Butcher, *Aristotle's Theory of Poetry and Fine Art* (London: Macmillan, 1907).

1 Scene in the Mohave Desert (photograph by the author).

2 Painting of the desert: James Swinnerton's *Monument Valley.*

At one point in "The Hollow Men," T. S. Eliot suggests a desert setting because it relates appropriately to the type of people he is depicting.

III

This is the dead land
This is cactus land
Here the stone images
Are raised, here they receive
The supplication of a dead man's hand
Under the twinkle of a fading star.

Is it like this
In death's other kingdom
Waking alone
At the hour when we are
Trembling with tenderness
Lips that would kiss
Form prayers to broken stone.

IV

The eyes are not here
There are no eyes here
In this valley of dying stars
In this hollow valley
This broken jaw of our lost kingdoms

In this last of meeting places
We grope together
And avoid speech
Gathered on this beach of the tumid river

Sightless, unless
The eyes reappear
As the perpetual star
Multifoliate rose
Of death's twilight kingdom
The hope only
Of empty men.[2]

Eliot uses the desert as the environment of spiritual aridity, nihilism, and hopelessness—a dead land of dead or dying men. His images and words go beyond the immediate scene to make a more universal point. In his "Literature and the Modern World" (in *American Prefaces*) Eliot wrote: "We are obviously at the end of an age, oppressed by the sense

2. T. S. Eliot, *Collected Poems, 1909–1962* (New York: Harcourt Brace Jovanovich, 1963).

of corruption and decay and fearful of the kinds of change which may come, since come change must."

Eliot's poem reveals in desert imagery his concern for the bareness of mankind in a fading world. Although the instinct to imitate was only his starting point, it leads to a more universal comment on the human condition. We experience pleasure in the perceptions he has provided.

When the playwright makes an imitation, he must go beyond appearance and words to give information and insight by showing men in action. We will discuss the nature of the dramatist's art more fully later, but at the moment let us see how one of the outstanding contemporary writers, Samuel Beckett, uses the desert as the scene for his little play, *Act Without Words, I.*[3]

Desert. Dazzling light.

The man is flung backwards on stage from right wing. He falls, gets up immediately, dusts himself, turns aside, reflects.

Whistle from right wing.

He reflects, goes out right.

Immediately flung back on stage he falls, gets up immediately, dusts himself, turns aside, reflects.

Whistle from left wing.

He reflects, goes out left.

Immediately flung back on stage he falls, gets up immediately, dusts himself, turns aside, reflects.

Whistle from left wing.

He reflects, goes towards left wing, hesitates, thinks better of it, halts, turns aside, reflects.

A little tree descends from flies, lands. It has a single bough some three yards from ground and at its summit a meager tuft of palms casting at its foot a circle of shadow.

He continues to reflect.

Whistle from above.

He turns, sees tree, reflects, goes to it, sits down in its shadow, looks at his hands.

3. Samuel Beckett, *Krapp's Last Tape and Other Dramatic Pieces* (New York: Grove Press, 1958).

A pair of tailor's scissors descends from flies, comes to rest before tree, a yard from ground.

He continues to look at his hands.

Whistle from above.

He looks up, sees scissors, takes them and starts to trim his nails.

The palms close like a parasol, the shadow disappears.

He drops scissors, reflects.

A tiny carafe, to which is attached a huge label inscribed WATER, descends from flies, comes to rest some three yards from ground.

He continues to reflect.

Whistle from above.

He looks up, sees carafe, reflects, gets up, goes and stands under it, tries in vain to reach it, renounces, turns aside, reflects.

A big cube descends from flies, lands.

He continues to reflect.

Whistle from above.

He turns, sees cube, looks at it, at carafe, reflects, goes to cube, takes it up, carries it over and sets it down under carafe, tests its stability, gets up on it, tries in vain to reach carafe, renounces, gets down, carries cube back to its place, turns aside, reflects.

A second smaller cube descends from flies, lands.

He continues to reflect.

Whistle from above.

He turns, sees second cube, looks at it, at carafe, goes to second cube, takes it up, carries it over and sets it down under carafe, tests its stability, gets up on it, tries in vain to reach carafe, renounces, gets down, takes up second cube to carry it back to its place, hesitates, thinks better of

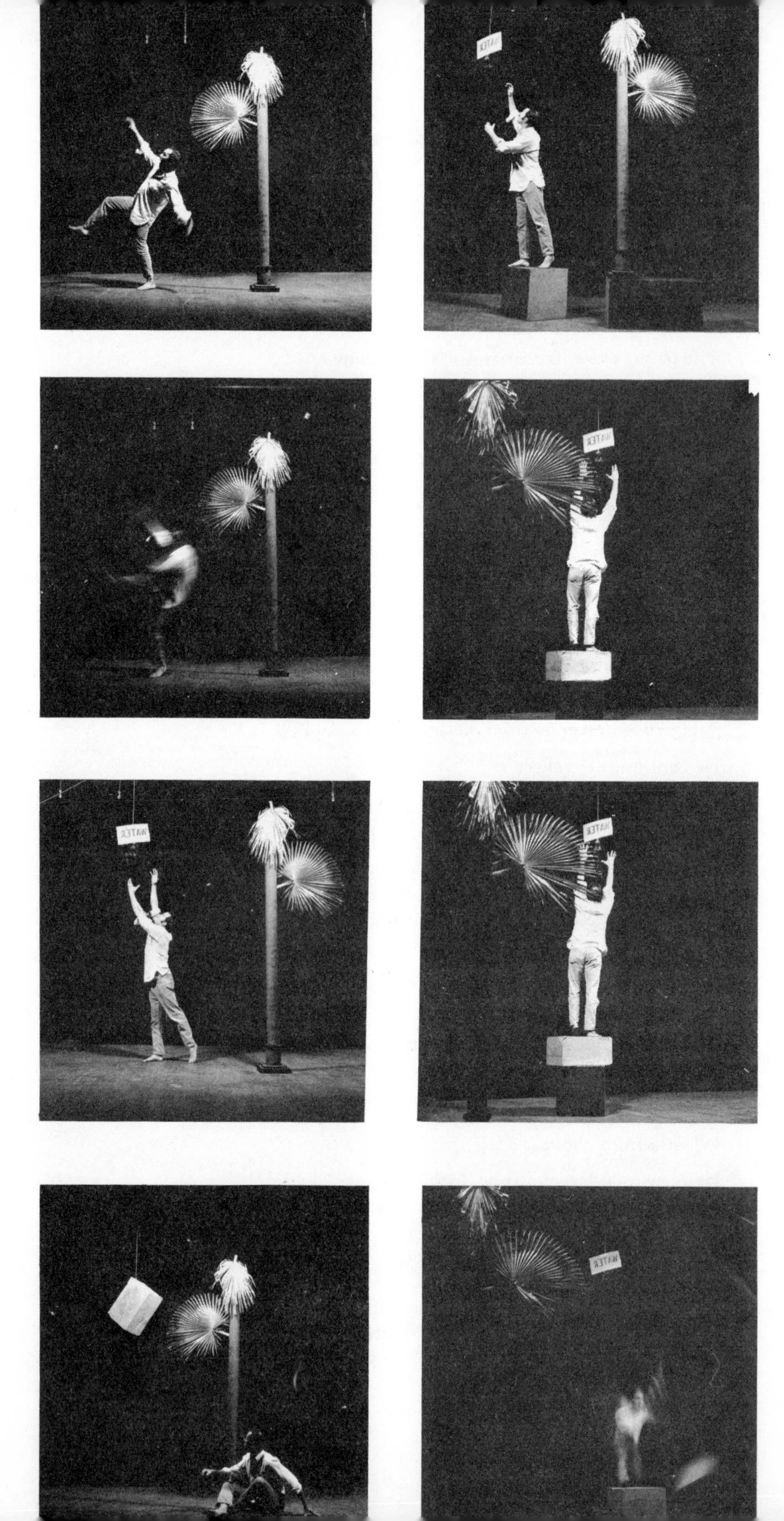
WATER

3 Actions from *Act Without Words, I.*

it, sets it down, goes to big cube, takes it up, carries it over and puts it on small one, tests their stability, gets up on them, the cubes collapse, he falls, gets up immediately, brushes himself, reflects.

He takes up small cube, puts it on big one, tests their stability, gets up on them and is about to reach carafe when it is pulled up a little way and comes to rest beyond his reach.

He gets down, reflects, carries cubes back to their place, one by one, turns aside, reflects.

A third still smaller cube descends from flies, lands.

He continues to reflect.

Whistle from above.

He turns, sees third cube, looks at it, reflects, turns aside, reflects.

The third cube is pulled up and disappears in flies.

Beside carafe a rope descends from flies, with knots to facilitate ascent.

He continues to reflect.

Whistle from above.

He turns, sees rope, reflects, goes to it, climbs up it and is about to reach carafe when rope is let out and deposits him back on ground.

He reflects, looks around for scissors, sees them, goes and picks them up, returns to rope and starts to cut it with scissors.

The rope is pulled up, lifts him off ground, he hangs on, succeeds in cutting rope, falls back on ground, drops scissors, falls, gets up again immediately, brushes himself, reflects.

The rope is pulled up quickly and disappears in flies.

With length of rope in his possession he makes a lasso with which he tries to lasso carafe.

The carafe is pulled up quickly and disappears in flies.

He turns aside, reflects.

He goes with lasso in his hand to tree, looks at bough, turns and looks at cubes, looks again at bough, drops lasso, goes to cubes, takes up small one, carries it over and sets it down under bough, goes back for big one, takes it up and carries it over under bough, makes to put it on small one, hesitates, thinks better of it, sets it down, takes up small one and puts it on big one, tests their stability, turns aside and stoops to pick up lasso.

The bough folds down against trunk.

He straightens up with lasso in his hand, turns and sees what has happened.

He drops lasso, turns aside, reflects.

He carries back cubes to their place, one by one, goes back for lasso, carries it over to cubes and lays it in a neat coil on small one.

He turns aside, reflects.

Whistle from right wing.

He reflects, goes out right.

Immediately flung back on stage he falls, gets up immediately, brushes himself, turns aside, reflects.

Whistle from left wing.

He does not move.

He looks at his hands, looks around for scissors, sees them, goes and picks them up, starts to trim his nails, stops, reflects, runs his finger along blade of scissors, goes and lays them on small cube, turns aside, opens his collar, frees his neck and fingers it.

The small cube is pulled up and disappears in flies, carrying away rope and scissors.

He turns to take scissors, sees what has happened.

He turns aside, reflects.

He goes and sits down on big cube.

The big cube is pulled from under him.
He falls. The big cube is pulled up and
disappears in flies.

He remains lying on his side, his face
towards auditorium, staring before him.

The carafe descends from flies and comes
to rest a few feet from his body.

He does not move.

Whistle from above.

He does not move.

The carafe descends further, dangles and
plays about his face.

He does not move.

The carafe is pulled up and disappears
in flies.

The bough returns to horizontal,
the palms open, the shadow returns.

Whistle from above.

He does not move.

The tree is pulled up and disappears in
flies.

He looks at his hands.

CURTAIN

In the painting of the desert we noted how the artist selected the most appealing aspects of the landscape. Beckett and Eliot have chosen to emphasize the negative qualities of the desert setting and to draw an analogy between desert aridity and human sterility. Beckett's single character is a stranger caught in a hostile situation from which he cannot escape, even in suicide. His attempts to gratify his desires are thwarted by an unseen presence that taunts and frustrates him until he surrenders. The playwright like the poet uses the desert symbolically to comment on the absurd condition of modern man. The imitation is expanded from the particular to the universal, and we find pleasure in the perceptions the writers give us.

Another aspect of imitation, not mentioned by Aristotle, is important in the study of drama—the use of imitation in ritual. Early in the twentieth century a group of British scholars interpreted the ritualistic origins of Greek drama in the light of anthropological discoveries. Sir James G. Frazer, in his widely influential *The Golden Bough,* explained how early man expressed his wants ritually through mythologies. He noted in nature a pattern of annual death and revival that was repeated in the death and resurrection of certain gods. The people identified the celebration of this cycle with the attainment of their primary needs, food for survival of the body and children for the survival of the race. At the core of these rites is imitation. The ritual pattern invented to insure fertility centered on a god-figure who annually died and was resurrected. Primitive man, ignorant of natural laws and causes, tried by imitation to propitiate the gods. His desires were enacted, demonstrated, rehearsed. This process, known to the anthropologist as *imitative magic* or *sympathetic magic,* makes use of impersonation and characterization. Man is an *actor* in the sense that he acts out his wants. Imitative magic may take such forms as a rain dance in which the performers beat on the drum to suggest thunder, rattle seeds in hollow gourds to suggest the patter of rain, and squirt water from their mouths to show falling rain. Cave paintings of ancient man depict the wounding and slaying of animals to insure success on the hunt.

These primitive rites and customs provided the means for communal sharing of significant action. Since primitive man used gesture and dance to communicate, he turned easily to acting out his important desires and reenacting those events he treasured.

The original spontaneous individual account becomes the property of the group and, through repetition, it is shaped into a fixed pattern. The particular exploits of an individual are joined to those of others to represent all exploits. A single combat symbolizes warfare in general. The original imitative gestures and movement are abstracted, set to rhythm, turned into chant and dance, and accorded the status of a tribal celebration.

The next step in development is significant because it marks the transition from a physical activity that exists for its own sake to an established religious rite. The warrior, recalling his previous success, reenacts his victory *before* he goes into battle in order to invoke the aid of supernatural forces in fulfilling his wishes. Since he is a doer, a man of action, the primitive man acts out his desires rather than his satisfactions. He imitates the action he wants to have happen. When the tribe employs *sympathetic magic* to assure victory in warfare, the ceremony is no longer a celebration for the joy of the activity. It becomes a serious religious ritual that expresses the deepest needs and longings of the people and associates them with the supernatural.

Man reenforces his strength with a weapon—a rock, a club, a spear, a gun, a rocket, a bomb. He does what he can to insure good crops—he tills the land, plants the seed, and irrigates the soil. Then, when he realizes that he is subject to forces beyond his control, he invokes divine intervention to provide him with a good harvest. He links himself to the present with his mate and children and the tribe; he projects himself beyond the grave with rites of passage, which will assure him of an afterlife.

Man's attempts to widen his experience and increase his power result from a complex cluster of motives—his need to communicate, to survive, to understand, to secure recognition and status. They represent his deepest longings, to which he gives expression in religious ceremonies often based on imitations of an action.

It is in such rituals that we find the basic elements of drama—music, song, dance, costuming, mimetic action, and communal performance. But not all ritual becomes drama. In most cultures the transition is never made. The rites continue as a functional activity, never attaining the detachment necessary to transform them into works of art that exist for their own sake. Or the ceremony may remain fixed in a simple repetitive form, never elevated through creative and interpretative expression. Drama cannot begin without the disciplined construction of an orderly sequence of words and actions representing a real or imaginary experience, to which impersonation is added. In Greece this remarkable transformation of ritual into drama took place.

The attempts of Gilbert Murray and others to trace the origin of Greek tragedy from primitive rites have appealed to many scholars because the plays were performed originally in a festival honoring Dionysus, god of wine, fertility, and vegetation. The legend of this god's rebirth as a young man is a symbolic representation of the calendrical cycle of the death of the seed as it is buried in the ground and of its rebirth with the coming of spring. But the case for the origin of Greek tragedy is not clear-cut, for no Greek tragedy now extant dramatizes the resurrection of a god or hero, nor do the plays involve the use of magical rites to gain supernatural powers. The plays were not written for the participants but for the spectators, and the questions raised were often a criticism of life rather than a celebration of it. Furthermore, despite the pervasiveness of fertility rituals, only the Greeks developed tragedy with its burden that wisdom lies not in aspiring to a godlike stature but in man "thinking mortal thoughts."

Drama and ritual are alike in that they are both ordered sequences of imitative action, a similarity that is reemphasized in our theater today. Art takes many forms, but often the impetus is the desire to imitate. When the artist makes a direct representation of nature, the audience's pleasure is in recognizing the likeness and in appreciating the skill of execution. But as the artist becomes concerned with significance beyond mere sensory stimuli, his imitation may lead to the most profound and complex expressions of man.

4 Dancing maidens and Dionysus. Greek vase painting.

5 Scene from *Oedipus Rex* with Oedipus surrounded by the Chorus, who look to the King as their savior from the plague. Stratford Shakespearean Festival, Ontario, Canada, 1954.

7 *Prometheus Bound* by Aeschylus at Stanford University showing Prometheus visited by Oceanus and the Chorus. Directed by Erik Vos, designed by Richard L. Hay.

8 Ancient performers in bird costumes. From a Greek vase painting, British Museum.

6 (opposite) Ancient Greek tragedy was a communal ritual. View through the entrance arch of the Theater of Epidaurus during a modern production of *Antigone*.

When we were children we not only learned by imitation but, through imaginative imitation, we extended the range of our experience. We engaged in daring adventures that enabled us to escape from the narrow borders of our immediate surroundings. We fought battles, became exotic creatures, soared aloft on the wings of imagination. This capacity for fanciful life continues with us into adulthood, for man always tries to extend himself beyond his physical attributes and circumstances. Sometimes man projects himself into the past by recalling his earlier experiences or by passing on the myths and legends of his ancestors. Sometimes he pursues adventure by making his way into the unknown—exploring strange waters, crossing into undiscovered country, scaling a precipitous mountain, shooting for the moon. As we have seen, sometime he attempts to gain strength and perhaps immortality by linking himself with supernatural powers.

Modern man's efforts to enlarge his scope of influence and action have led to interesting patterns of behavior. His work may confine him to a cubicle within cubicles where the scheme of organization takes its inspiration from the machine. He rides to and from work by machine, communicates with others through mechanical and electronic devices, simplifies his work through standardization of form and procedure. He may live in a mass-produced house, wear mass-produced clothing, and eat precooked dinners while his senses are bombarded with volleys of machine-projected words and images. His life is at least partially symbolized by the frustration he feels in his car. Underneath the gleaming hood and chrome, several hundred units of horsepower await the touch of his foot, but he is forced to crawl along in a snarl of city traffic until he finally escapes into the open countryside, only to find his speed and direction rigidly limited by flashing lights and warning signs confining him to a narrow concrete ribbon from which he may see only an occasional glimpse of the passing landscape. The dead level of sameness in this standardized world clashes sharply with his nervous system, for beneath his sanforized, wash-and-wear exterior flow the same elemental juices as those of Don Juan, Marco Polo, and Davy Crockett. Hence, modern man, like his forebears, finds it necessary as well as desirable to break through his restricting shell to find ways of extending himself.

Through art and literature man learns to share vicarious experiences and to catch a glimpse of something beyond the stiff confines of his everyday existence. He can feel the spirit of adventure that lifts him out of the deadening routine of the commercial or institutionalized world and invites him to participate in the imitation of actions more compelling and meaningful than his own. When the forms of art become rigid and standardized, when they lose their original creative impulse and no longer imitate the actions of the living, the time is ripe for a change. The search for continuing life characterized the arts during the last century.

Through experiment and innovation, dramatic art sought to assimilate the new ideas of the nineteenth century. Again, in our time, change is in the air. And again theater is desperately trying to find new purpose and meaning.

conventions in art

In the photograph of the desert, you saw a flat, small black-and-white image that is recognizable as a representation of reality, but the photograph is not reality itself. Each kind of imitation has its own conventions. That is to say, there are agreements as to how the game is to be played. In the painting of the desert, the artist applied pigment to a flat surface within a regular framework. T. S. Eliot's "The Hollow Men" employs words in a rhyme scheme with a measured cadence. An audience viewing *Act Without Words, I* is likely to sit in a darkened auditorium, while on a lighted stage an actor in modern clothes goes through a series of apparently realistic actions without a word of dialogue.

In the Greek theater outdoor performances were given in the daytime as public ceremonies. There were only three speaking characters onstage at one time, men played the female roles, there was little or no violence onstage, and actors wore masks and special footgear and headpieces. The plays, which dramatized ancient legends and myths, were written in verse, and were usually presented against a permanent setting. They had simple stories that took place in a short space of time. In the Elizabethan theater, as in the Greek, the roles were played by male actors in an outdoor theater in the daytime with little or no use of illusionistic scenery. The plays, written in verse, were different from the Greek drama in form and content. The plays were usually complicated, involving several plot lines, comic matter was mixed with serious, high-born characters with low, and the playwright ransacked history and literature for material that would tell an exciting story. The plays were performed by professional actors in theaters whose dimensions and arrangement placed the actor close to the spectator so that the subtleties of language could be exploited. The convention of the large unlocalized platform gave the dramatist a great deal of freedom in staging an animated and complicated narrative.

The conventions of realistic production that have dominated the theater since the latter part of the nineteenth century suggest actuality through lifelike representation of characters and setting. There was tacit agreement that performer and audience would remain separate from one another. The audience occupied the auditorium and the actor remained onstage. The separation of these two entities was facilitated by the darkened auditorium and the lighted stage, the architectural features of the raised stage that could be closed off by a curtain and the proscenium arch. There was also a psychological barrier known as the "fourth wall," a convention in which the actors pretended that the audience did not exist and avoided direct communication across the footlights. Dramatic structure was linear and tied to story. Scenery, which was designed to give the illusion of reality, was patently artificial and arranged to facilitate exits and entrances. Furniture was grouped to open out toward the house; lighting was arbitrary, and scenic materials conventionalized. It is essential to recognize these practices in evaluating any drama because of their pressure in shaping the play and its production.

Conventions in the art are constantly susceptible to change. Just as we had remarkable innovations in painting and music in the twentieth century, we have rebellion in the theater. The spectator at a current production may no longer be sure how much of the performance will be onstage and how much in his lap, nor can he be sure that the play has a clear beginning, middle, and end, or that he will be able to understand what the actors say and do. The modifications that take place in all the arts from time to time are not the result of some personal whim, or novelty for its own sake, but significant new experiments, which are rooted in valid aesthetic ground and the intellectual climate in which they are produced.

exercises

1. Analyze the motion picture as a form of imitation.
2. Describe the use of imitation in the learning process.
3. What are the limitations of photography as a form of imitation?
4. What authentic rituals exist today? What is their form and function?
5. What aspects of drama are found in ritual?
6. What is the function of sympathetic magic?
7. In what respects is a poem an imitation?
8. Compare the conventions of representational and nonrepresentational painting.
9. Aristotle considered dance and music as forms of imitation. Why?
10. Write an inversion of *Act Without Words, I,* in which the man gets everything.
11. Add a second character and dialogue to *Act Without Words, I* and perform it. Evaluate the effect of the changes.
12. How does the artist give us fresh perceptions?
13. To what extent do art forms depend for their effect on the appearance of reality?

14. Explain how the artist's skill in execution may give pleasure.
15. To what extent is the artist obligated to communicate his ideas and feelings?

suggested reading

Francis Fergusson, *The Idea of a Theatre,* 1949.
Edith Hamilton, *The Greek Way,* 1952.
Jane Ellen Harrison, *Ancient Art and Ritual,* 1913.
Carl G. Jung, *Man and His Symbols,* 1964.
H. D. F. Kitto, *The Greeks,* 1951.
Allardyce Nicoll, *The Development of the Theatre,* new rev. ed., 1966.
A. W. Pickard-Cambridge, *The Dramatic Festivals of Athens,* 1953.

play list

Everyman
Sophocles, *Oedipus Rex*
Thornton Wilder, *Our Town*

dramatic action

The painter defines his imitation in visual images, the musician in an arrangement of sounds, and the dramatist creates in action. In the study of drama it is unfortunate that often our first contact with a play is through the printed page. Understanding a play by its text is like trying to take a journey by looking at a map. The result is that we are apt to think of a play as a collection of words. We deliberately selected *Act Without Words, I* as the first dramatic material in this text in order to emphasize the point that drama is essentially action. In these days when nearly everything in the theater is under scrutiny, the importance of action in theatrical experience remains intact. Because dramatic action is fundamental, it is necessary to consider it in some detail.

Webster's New Collegiate Dictionary defines action as "the act or process of producing an effect. . . ." Synonyms are: "Action, act, deed meaning something done or effected. Action implies a process which takes time and involves more than one step. . . ." This definition is basic to our understanding of the various kinds of action in drama, for the word "drama" literally means "a thing done," and is derived from the Greek verb "to do." Painting, sculpture, and architecture are static, but drama is dynamic. A play is like a wheel—its true function is not realized until it is set in motion.

As the Roman critic Horace observed, "the mind is less actively stimulated by what it takes in through the ear than by what is presented

to it through the trustworthy agency of the eyes—something that the spectator can see for himself."

At least in part, the force of Horace's statement is realized by the audience's *empathic response. Empathy* comes from the Greek "feeling into." It may be defined as *imitative motor response.* Notice the word "motor." An empathic response is more than sympathy, more than an attitude of the mind; it involves physical identification and participation. When we escape into the countryside, part of our sense of relaxation is the result of feeling the lines of the wide horizon with our bodies. Conversely, when we are cramped down in a low-ceilinged cellar, our musculature responds to the environment. We have had the experience of listening to an unsure soprano trying desperately to hit a high note beyond her range, and have felt some of her tension in our own throats. When an actor forgets his lines, we may blush and perspire along with him, borrowing some of his humiliation. Our capacity to respond empathically to the actions of others is one of the reasons that farce and melodrama have such wide popularity, for they are built on frameworks of physical action that provide the audience with an ample opportunity to respond empathically to the visual stimuli. Films and television have a similar appeal because the images on the screen are in constant motion. Likewise, the largest audiences are attracted to those sporting events that involve vigorous physical action to which the spectator can respond empathically.

Another aspect of our way of responding to action is found in Francis Fergusson's term "histrionic sensibility"—the spectator's ability to perceive and discriminate actions and visual symbols, just as the trained ear discriminates sounds. We employ this histrionic sensibility when we judge behavior. For example, although we may not hear the dialogue between an umpire and an enraged baseball player, even at a considerable distance we understand the feelings of the two adversaries by their gestures. When we communicate with one another on important issues, we prefer face-to-face contact which enables us to judge the *way* things are said, as well as the words themselves. We constantly use this sensibility in evaluating others' responses to what we say or do. Histrionic sensibility is a part of the way we understand and appreciate the full content of a play in performance. The shrug of a shoulder, the lifting of an eyebrow, the tone of voice, the nod of the head, the atmosphere of the environment, the pace of the action constitute an eloquent vocabulary of a universal language. These forms of communication are essential to the dramatic experience although they may be so ephemeral that they vanish at the moment of creation. They are at the heart of the special resources of the theater because they stir the blood, awaken our memories, spur the imagination, set off chains of emotional reaction, engage our sympathies, and help to establish the validity and meaning of the action.

9 Helene Weigel, a character in action in Brecht's *Mother Courage* at the Berliner Ensemble.

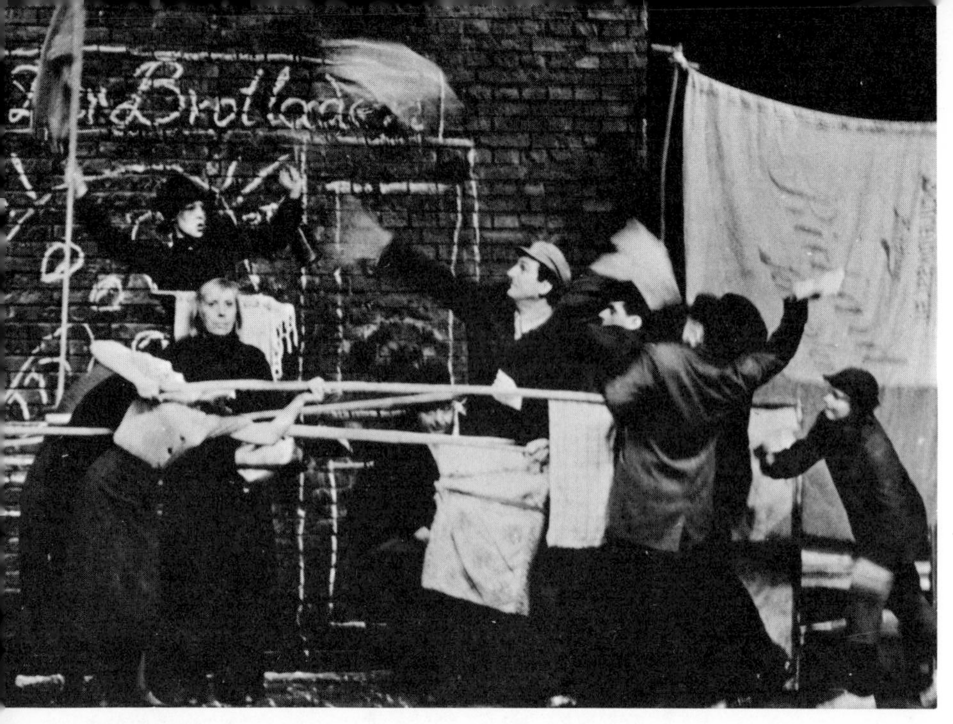

10 A climactic moment staged theatrically in the Berliner Ensemble production of *Der Brotladen*.

11 Psychological action in Brecht's *Die Mutter* at the Berliner Ensemble.

Thus we see that man has special capacities for responding to action: he is "eye-minded," he has the ability to enter empathically into the experiences of others, and he develops his histrionic sensibility as a means of interpreting behavior.

kinds of action

In the theater, there are at least four kinds of action which are important for our understanding.

1. In its simplest form, action refers to the actors' entrances and exits, the stage business of the characters, the larger movements of the ensemble, the quarrels, love scenes, struggles—all the overt action of the play.

The modern playwright usually specifies this kind of action in stage directions. For example, Beckett in his *Waiting for Godot* begins with this direction: "Estragon, sitting on a low mound, is trying to take off his boot. He pulls at it with both hands, panting. He gives up, exhausted, rests, tries again. As before."

The dramatists in previous eras did not write in their pieces of business. The actor took his cue for action from the lines themselves. In Antony's speech over the dead body of Caesar, note the essential actions.

> ANTONY: Nay, press not so upon me; stand far off.
> CITIZENS: Stand back! room! bear back!
> ANTONY: If you have tears, prepare to shed them now.
> You all do know this mantle; I remember
> The first time ever Caesar put it on;
> 'T was on a summer's evening, in his tent,
> That day he overcame the Nervii.
> Look! in this place ran Cassius' dagger through:
> See what a rent the envious Casca made. (act 3, scene 2)

Movement implied by the dialogue and necessary for understanding the plot is known as *inherent business*. It comes directly out of the playwright's text. When the director and actor put a play in rehearsal, they must decide just how each line and action is to be interpreted. For example, in the opening business of *Waiting for Godot*, how does Estragon sit, what direction does he face, how long does he attempt to take off his boot, and what does his action convey to the audience? What is the quality of his movement? When he tries a second time, is the action repeated exactly, or with more frustration or anger? Is he comical? baffled? exasperated? The interpretation of the script in production often leads to the invention of *imposed business*, action that was not visualized by the writer but is considered an appropriate extension of the play. Stage business both inherent and imposed must be as carefully controlled as the lines the actors speak, for it is a part of the total stimulus to which the audience responds. Many of the most telling moments of the theater are those provided by the performer's actions when, through gesture, posture, and facial expression, he gives tangible evidence of an idea or emotion: Grusha's escape over the bridge in *The Caucasian Chalk Circle;* Jean's transformation into an animal in Ionesco's *The Rhinoceros;* Charlotte Corday's whipping of de Sade with her hair in *Marat/Sade.* These pieces of business indicate how drama is created in visible action.

2. Dramatic action is also psychological. It is mental and emotional as well as physical. When the psychologist analyzes behavior, he searches for clues to inner motivation expressed in a person's overt actions. Similarly, the playwright devises signs that give the audience insight into a character's inner life, that explain the turbulence beneath a deceptive facade.

Although *Act Without Words, I* has an undeniable theatrical impact, dependence on external movement is a limiting factor. A play about a solitary, mute figure lacks the scope possible in plays in which dialogue extends the meaning of the action, and the presence of two or more actors offers the opportunity for interaction and reaction. But despite the lack of specific delineation, Beckett's character is involved in a psychological experience. He changes from an aggressive, striving character to one who no longer reacts. Frustration has taken its emotional toll.

Psychological action has been a major concern in most significant Western drama, and until recent times the serious playwright has taken the pains to develop his characters from the inside out. As a contrast to Beckett's character, who is known to us only by his external movements, let us look at the action in a more traditional play in which characters' motivations are more fully revealed. Consider the first episode of *Antigone,* one of the most popular tragedies in the fifth century B.C. Sophocles dramatizes the events of a Theban saga in which Antigone defies her uncle Creon's edict that the body of the rebel Polyneices remain unburied. The episodes of the play are a series of strong conflicts beginning with the clash between the two sisters over the decision whether or not their brother should be buried.

ANTIGONE: Ismene, my dear, my mother's child, my sister,
What part of Oedipus' sad legacy
Has Zeus not laid in full on us who live?
There is nothing bitter, nothing of disaster,
No shame, no humiliation I have not seen
In the number of your sufferings and mine.
And now what is this order which they say
Our leader has announced throughout the city?

Do you know? Have you heard? Or do I have to tell you
That what has happened to our enemies
Is threatening to fall upon our friends?
ISMENE: I have heard no word of friends, Antigone,
To bring me comfort or to bring me pain
Since the time we two were robbed of our two brothers,
Dead in one day, and by each other's hand.
And now the Argive army overnight
Has disappeared, I am no nearer knowing
Whether my luck has changed for good or bad.
ANT: I know, too well. That is why I wanted to bring you
Outside the courtyard, to talk to you alone.
ISM: What is it? Trouble, you do not need to tell me.
ANT: What else, when Creon singles out one brother
For a hero's grave, and lets the other rot?
They are saying he has laid Eteocles in the ground
With every rite and custom that is fitting
To give him honor with the dead below.
But Polyneices' body, that was killed
So pitifully, they say he has commanded
Should not be mourned or given burial
But lie unburied and unwept, a feast
For passing birds to gorge on at their pleasure.
And so, the rumor runs, has our good Creon
Decreed for you and me—for me, I say!
And is on his way here now, to spell it out
To those who have not heard. He does not take
This matter lightly. Anyone who disobeys
In any way will die by public stoning.
So there you have it. Now we shall soon find out
If you are a true-born daughter of your line,
Or if you will disgrace your noble blood!
ISM: But, my poor sister, if things are as you say,
What ways and means have I to set them straight?
ANT: Ask yourself, will you work with me, help me do it?
ISM: What adventure is this? What do you have in mind?
ANT: Will you help this hand of mine to lift the dead?
ISM: You mean to bury him? Against the law?
ANT: Bury my brother? Yes—and bury yours,
If you will not. No-one shall call me faithless.
ISM: You would not dare, when Creon has forbidden it!
ANT: He has no right to keep me from my own.
ISM: Oh sister, think of how our father died,
Hated, despised, and driven by the sins
He had himself laid bare, to turn his hand
Against himself, and strike out both his eyes.
And then his mother, wife—which shall I call her?
Knotted a noose, and took away her life.

Then the final blow, two brothers in one day,
Unhappy pair, each shedding kinsman's blood,
Lay hands on each other, and made one in death.
Now we two are alone. Think how much worse
Our deaths will be, if in despite of law
We brave the king's commandment and his power.
Let us not forget two things—that we were born
Women, and so not meant to fight with men;
And then, that we must do what our masters tell us—
Obey in this, and other things far worse.
I, then, will ask the kingdom of the dead
To pardon me; since I am no free agent,
I will yield to the powers that be. There is no sense
In meddling in things outside our sphere.
ANT: I shall not persuade you. You would not be welcome
To help me now, even if you wanted to.
Be what you want to be; but I intend
To bury him. It is a noble way to die.
I shall lie with him for love, as he loved me,
A criminal, but guiltless; for the dead
Have longer claims upon me than the living.
There is my lasting home. If you think fit
To dishonor the god's commandments, then you may.
ISM: I mean them no dishonor; but when it means
Defying the state—I am not strong enough.
ANT: Let that be your excuse. Now I shall go
To heap the earth on my beloved brother.
ISM: Antigone, no! I am so afraid for you!
ANT: You need not fear for me. Look after yourself.
ISM: At least tell no-one what you mean to do.
Keep it a secret, I shall do the same.
ANT: Oh no, denounce me! You will be in far worse trouble
For keeping silence, if you do not tell the world.
ISM: You have a hot heart where you should be shivering.
ANT: I know I am giving pleasure where I should.
ISM: Yes, if you can. But you ask much of yourself.
ANT: When I have no more strength, then I shall stop.
ISM: No point in starting when the cause is hopeless.
ANT: Go on like this and you will make me hate you,
And the dead will hate you too; you give him cause.
Leave me alone with my stupidity
To face this dread unknown; whatever it is,
Anything is better than to die a coward!
ISM: Then if your mind is made up, go. You are a fool,
And yet your own will love you for it.[1]

1. *Oedipus the King and Antigone by Sophocles*, trans. Peter D. Arnott (New York: Appleton-Century-Crofts, 1960).

12 Antigone and Ismene in a dramatic clash during the opening scene of a modern Greek production of *Antigone.*

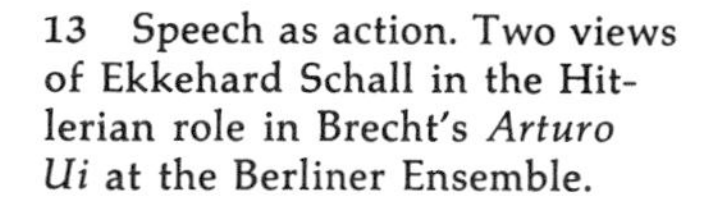

13 Speech as action. Two views of Ekkehard Schall in the Hitlerian role in Brecht's *Arturo Ui* at the Berliner Ensemble.

14 An eighteenth-century production of *Hamlet* showing a number of the important actions.

15 Bruckner's *Die Verbrecher* at the Schiller Theater, Berlin, showing simultaneous actions in a multiple set. Usually the playwright concentrates on a single action at a time.

16 A scene from Meierhold's *Turandot* in Moscow, 1925, showing the whole stage in action.

17 A recent Czechoslovakian production of Gorki's *The Last Ones,* designed by Josef Svoboda, showing the action onstage accompanied by projections of actions on the background.

Sophocles' dramatic method in *Antigone* is different from Beckett's in *Act Without Words, I.* Beckett's play is all physical action with no speech; this episode is mostly speech with little physical movement. Aside from the entrance and exit of characters, there is no business, no movement, not a single stage property indicated. And yet the scene is dynamic—something happens. Emotions are intensified and the drama goes forward, but through psychological action.

In Beckett's pantomime no explanatory material is provided nor is there any attempt to probe into character. The episode from *Antigone* reveals two distinctly different characters. Sophocles' problem was to establish Antigone as a character at the outset so that the actions that follow are credible to the audience. Within a hundred lines of dialogue he provides the background of the characters as members of an ill-fated family who have already suffered humiliation as their "sad legacy." As in Beckett's play, we begin with an active protagonist who is striving toward an objective but is thwarted by a higher power. In Sophocles' play, the central figure continues to struggle, and the reasons for her struggle are given in her character. The presence of Ismene as a second character enables the playwright to externalize in concrete statements their different points of view and characters. This interaction of character sets up a clash of motivations and defines the rift between the sisters.

Antigone is more than a story about an illegal burial and the suicides that follow it. What really matters is the testing of the characters' convictions. The decision we see Antigone make does not come from external pressures—quite the contrary. Ismene, like the man in Beckett's play, yields to pressure from above, but Antigone's behavior is explained from within. The episode is important for its psychological action.

An interesting way of looking at a play is to consider the psychological distance the characters travel from the beginning to the end. Many plays show a radical change in character that may take the form of psychological destruction. Take, for example, Creon, Antigone's adversary. At his first appearance, the confident King tells the people:

> Gentlemen, the state is in troubled waters,
> But now the gods have set us back on course. (lines 156–57)

Contrast this speech with Creon's lines at the end of the play:

> I do not know
> Which way to take, where to lean;
> My hands can do nothing right;
> I am crushed beneath my fate. (lines 1266–68)

Similar examples of psychological ruin are to be found in *Macbeth, Phèdre, A Streetcar Named Desire,* and *Hedda Gabler.*

The psychological action may be one of maturation rather than destruction, as for example, in Ibsen's *A Doll's House,* in which our first impression of Nora changes from that of a childlike character to a mature woman. London audiences that first saw John Osborne's pivotal play, *Look Back in Anger,* in 1956, were outraged by Jimmy Porter's behavior when he insults his companions and strikes his pregnant wife. But as the play develops, the playwright gradually reveals the protagonist's personal agonies so compellingly that Jimmy comes to be regarded with compassion by the time the final curtain falls.

The psychological action need not define a change in fortune; it may simply serve as a process of revelation and intensification. In Edward Albee's *Who's Afraid of Virginia Woolf?* we come to understand the nature of George's and Margaret's strange attachment for one another. Chekhov is sometimes criticized because of the apparent lack of action or purpose in his plays. On closer acquaintance, he emerges as a past master in suggesting the rich inner life of his characters through subtle details or fragments of dialogue and internal action. Antigone, unlike Creon and Ismene, does not change psychologically during the play. She is the same character at her final exit as at her initial entrance, but we are now keenly aware of her inner motivation.

Drama is usually strong in emotional content. The actions and words of the dramatis personae are rooted in feeling. Most plays deal with a set of characters at the most critical moment in their careers, and the events that they experience are generally rich in psychological action.

3. Speech itself is a form of action. It is a way of doing, a part of the process of producing an effect. Notice how limited the playwright is in *Act Without Words, I* compared to Sophocles. In the first episode of *Antigone,* the dialogue reveals the contrasting characters, explains their motives, and intensifies the emotional expression. The episode is an active process of persuasion, a tug-of-war of words as each states her point of view. Their speech is more than narration or recitation; it is a way of characterizing two opposing people by having them make decisions that profoundly affect their futures.

Implicit in most dramatic dialogue is an underlying pattern of action as the character strives toward a goal, seeks to influence the behavior of others, justifies his position, and searches for the meaning of his experience. Consider the full range of implied movement in a typical passage from Shakespeare. In *Richard III,* the King is visited by the ghosts of those whom he has murdered. He awakens from his guilty nightmare and cries out:

> Give me another horse: bind up my wounds.
> Have mercy, Jesu!—Soft! I did but dream.

O coward conscience, how dost thou afflict me!
The light burns blue. It is now dead midnight.
Cold fearful drops stand on my trembling flesh.
What do I fear? Myself? There's none else by:
Richard loves Richard; that is, I am I.
Then fly. What, from myself? Great reason why:
Lest I revenge. What, myself upon myself? (act 5, scene 3)

Words are spoken in context; they find their source in the dramatic situation and enable the character to articulate his feelings and ideas. They are an integral part of the action. In the Antigone–Ismene conflict, the language is a pulsing force whose pressure increases as the characters speak. No pantomimist can convey the total emotional burden of the scene. In the theater, the speaking character is a character in action.

Many contemporary innovators attack the "tyranny of the word" and the restrictions of the text, but theater without speech is incomplete. Those who insist on returning to primitive ritual because of its emotional impact through symbolic action should remember that language is symbolic, too. It is an effort to recapture the archetypal feelings and urges of man but, as Freud demonstrated to the world, the inner life of fears, dreams, and desires is revealed through external signs, and not the least of these is the spoken word. Drama may have begun in ritualized gesture and dance, but the theater reached maturity only after it found its voice, and those who have given stature to drama have been poets, not the priests of esoteric rites. And these poets have understood the word as action.

4. You will recall in the dictionary definition cited earlier the statement: "Action implies a process which takes time and involves more than one step." This kind of action, this step-by-step process, is the play itself, referred to by Aristotle as a "system of actions."

action as ordered progression

Drama, like ritual, presents an ordered progression of action as, for example, a church wedding follows a set pattern leading to the ultimate union of a couple. *Act Without Words, I* is a skillfully articulated sequence of incidents showing the transition of an active man to a passive one. Each minor action within the framework leads to the next action that in turn leads to the final result. The character's frustrated efforts to satisfy his needs must precede his unsuccessful attempts at suicide, which in turn must precede his resignation. Eliminate any one of the incidents, or change the sequence of them, and the play is distorted. Reverse the order, and begin with a passive figure who reaches for various objects and continues to struggle at the end, and the effect of the play is radically changed. While Beckett's little play is as long as a single episode, it nevertheless illustrates the sequential pattern of dramatic action. In its construction it resembles a motion picture in which the editor has gone through the photographed footage, selected the number of frames of various shots he wishes to use, and spliced them together so that the relationship of image to image in the overall series achieves the result he desires.

Similarly the plot of a play is made up of a number of incidents, each adding to the development of the total effect. As we have seen, the Antigone–Ismene clash begins the main action, provides the essential background of character and situation, and propels the situation forward to the succeeding events. In the initial incident the emotion builds up through a clash of wills to Antigone's final outburst:

> Leave me alone with my stupidity
> To face this dread unknown; whatever it is,
> Anything is better than to die a coward! (lines 97–99)

Antigone is an organized "system of actions" in which, episode by episode, the emotional momentum gathers its force until the final catastrophe. As in Beckett's play, each incident, placed in its proper order, is an integral part of the cumulative process. The development of a play is not only dependent on keeping the story elements clear, but also on creating a "structure of feeling," in Raymond Williams' phrase.

> The more one looks at the text of the play, the more one realizes that a simple, yet radical pattern, a controlling structure of feeling, has been clearly isolated and designed in the writing. And then if one looks at the performance, one sees that this design is being continually enacted, in the parts of the whole. For it is a design made for performance; the purpose of the play is not report, not description, not analysis, but enactment of a design. The structure of feeling is the formal written structure, and also the structure of performance. The conflict and resolution are not a story, a telling of things past, but are always present in words and movement.[2]

While traditional drama is organized around a pattern of action, playwrights have not always adhered to a strict formula. During the Renaissance, French and Italian neoclassicists attempted to follow prescribed rules. However, even they had their differences. Among the Greek playwrights, the shape of the action in the works of Euripides is not at all like that of Aeschylus, and the comedy writer Aristophanes is markedly different in structure from the Greek tragic writers. Even a

2. Raymond Williams, *Drama in Performance* (London: F. Muller, 1954).

single playwright's practice may vary from play to play. Ibsen's scheme of action in *Peer Gynt* is entirely different from that of his *Ghosts.* O'Neill's structure for *The Hairy Ape* is in sharp contrast to that of *Desire Under the Elms* or *Strange Interlude.* The critics of structured drama give the impression that it is hidebound; hardly true, as a representative sample of the plotting practices of playwrights in nearly any anthology will confirm.

On the other hand, most dramas show certain comparable characteristics. Plays are imitations of men in action, and this action has some kind of unifying principle. The structure is made up of a meaningful series of incidents calculated to elicit audience response. The plot usually follows a linear arrangement and centers on a few characters caught in moments of crisis. The action gathers momentum with increasing involvement until tension is released and equilibrium is restored. Note that this general format is not the basis for judging a play. What really counts is the effect it makes on the audience. Playwrights have discovered that one way of making the desired impact is through a well-organized structure. The reason that pattern is so persistent is not because it is admired by critics as a literary technique, but because it works.

Currently we are witnessing all manner of experiments seeking new forms of theater—a valid objective as we shall see later. Concern with traditional drama is being replaced by emphasis on the creative act itself, on ritual, on spontaneous participation, on sensitivity, on nonverbal communication. It is fashionable to rebel against the neatly plotted play, but the one essential that experimentalists have been unable to discard is action—and whenever action is present, some basis of organization can be found. Random action is in itself a kind of sequence with an intended purpose. Chaos makes its own kind of statement. Strictly speaking, a plotless play is as impossible as nonvisual painting or soundless music.

A nonrepresentational painter does not create an image that tells a story, but his painting is, nevertheless, carefully organized. The avant-garde playwright may place undifferentiated characters on stage performing miscellaneous tasks for no apparent reason; but his decision to work nonsequentially is an act of construction that characterizes his kind of plot. True, he is non-Aristotelian and unconventional and perhaps as nonlinear as he is noncurvilinear, but he cannot avoid the basic ingredient —a system of action.

the effect of dramatic action

We have emphasized here that drama is essentially an imitation of men in various forms of action. Now we need to return to the definition of action as "a process of producing an effect." This raises the question, what is the effect of dramatic action and on whom? To assess dramatic action in this sense is to determine what attitudes and opinions we as audience are to assume and what emotions we are to feel. The playwright creates the action to gain our concern. Unless our attention is really engaged and our emotions are truly involved, the play does not fulfill its intended purpose. But in life no effect occurs without a cause, and in the theater, no action without a reason. To create a heroic character, the dramatist must show us heroic actions. Sophocles could not simply describe his protagonist as a "courageous young woman." The audience insists: "Show us the evidence. Then we will believe; then we will care."

All forms of dramatic action are intended to produce appropriate effects. In the past, these effects cluster about two terms—pleasure and emotional response. We take pleasure in learning, and we enjoy being moved.

In its simplest and most popular form, drama pleases its audience on the game level. It exists only as amusement and diversion. Unlike the two plays of Beckett and Sophocles we have been discussing, drama at its most simple lacks secondary or residual meaning, declines to sharpen our perception, and fails to arouse our deeper emotions. If the play holds our favorable attention, arouses laughter, suspense, or excitement, the intended effect is achieved. Many theatergoers insist only on this level of appeal. Most drama is thus concerned with the surface aspects of make-believe and does not examine life. The dominant attitude that shapes such theater seems to be the complaint: "This world has enough unhappiness without my having to suffer in the theater. When I go to a show, I want to forget my troubles." While this point of view is not conducive to the elevation of drama as a significant form of art, it does represent the prevailing outlook of motion picture and television audiences, and even a good deal of the professional theater audience.

Where are the satisfactions in this kind of drama? In part, pleasure comes from the emotional release of taking a mental holiday from one's daily cares, from an escape into a world less demanding than our own. In part, pleasure comes from the skill of execution that an accomplished performer can give.

Another appeal of more serious forms of the theater is to give us pleasure through learning by affording us the opportunity to extend the scope of our experiences, to expand our capacity for understanding and compassion. Consider how much you learn from your experiences outside the college classroom. We are all collectors of experience. Some of us live within a narrow range of familiar people and places; others seem to have an insatiable desire for adventure. Many of you, no doubt, welcome the opportunity to explore a foreign country on a shoestring and your thumb, but an older generation prefers a known way, the assurance of good food and lodging, and predictable situations. But for all of us drama becomes a means of enlarging our experience. Often a play enables us to probe into the depths of character and situations that contribute to our understanding. We become aware of the complexity of motivation, the results of minor conflicts and repression, the varied ways people respond to one another, the rationale behind social conduct. We observe the factors that may cause suffering or satisfaction; we witness the origin and growth of an emotional event in its entirety, the beginning, middle, and end and from several points of view; we become aware of the potentials of power and passion, the importance of communication and connections of affection; we discover the common humanity that makes it possible for us to find an interest and meaning in actions as diverse as a twentieth-century pantomime and an ancient Greek tragedy.

A deeper kind of learning and emotional effect comes from serious drama, which in the past occupied a central position in the culture. The great works of drama depict great characters exploring the great issues of life. As Aristotle wrote, tragedy deals with serious imitations of men in action effecting a catharsis—a purging away, a cleansing of the ignoble, the mean, the base. Such drama exalts and elevates mankind. The chorus in *Antigone* sings: "Wonders are many, and none is more wonderful than man." In the masterpieces of drama, good and evil are ruthlessly examined, choices are made, and judgments rendered that indicate the distilled wisdom of the race. Man's loftiest ideas and aspirations have been the significant content of the drama. The theater in times past has been an institution of edification and spiritual stimulation. Today there are voices in the wind that call for us to return to a theater that will once again function through myth and ritual to reestablish the communal experiences that bind us together.

exercises

1. What art forms are static? dynamic?
2. Which art forms need an interpreter? What is the effect of the interpreter in the creative process?
3. Cite three examples of "histrionic sensibility."
4. Make up examples of each kind of action.
5. Make up three examples of stage business to indicate: 1. place, 2. character, 3. atmosphere, 4. mental state.
6. As a group, improvise actions to establish a bus station, a doctor's waiting room, a roadside cafe, a country store.
7. Invent a single incident that will show a character undergoing a psychological change.

8. Create a scene in which Haemon attempts to dissuade Antigone from burying Polyneices.
9. Write a speech for Antigone to give to the class in which she justifies her actions and asks for support.
10. Edit the speeches in the Antigone–Ismene scene to eliminate the emotional content.
11. Devise examples of stage business, with or without dialogue, to establish the character traits of a hero, a coward, a militant, a stranger, a crook.
12. Improvise scenes of the offstage action in *Antigone,* such as the guards on duty, the burial, and the suicides.
13. Trace the psychological change in a character in a play, noting the steps the playwright provides.
14. Analyze a play on the basis of its effect on an audience. What is the total effect? How is it achieved? Note the effect of each incident.
15. Discuss the variety of possible effects of dramatic action in the theater.
16. Devise a skeletal plot composed of several episodes as a "system of actions" dramatizing a strong character with a specific objective. Arrange the action to achieve emotional intensification.
17. Describe the pleasure of learning.
18. Describe how as spectators we "act out the play for ourselves."

suggested reading

Rudolph Arnheim, *Art and Visual Perception,* 1954.
Bernard Beckerman, *Dynamics of Drama,* 1970.
Eric Bentley, *The Life of the Drama,* 1967.
Francis Fergusson, *The Idea of a Theater,* 1949.
Allardyce Nicoll, *The Theatre and Dramatic Theory,* 1931.
Ronald Peacock, *The Art of Drama,* 1957.
Raymond Williams, *Drama in Performance,* 1954.

play list

Edward Albee, *The Zoo Story*
Jean Anouilh, *Antigone*
Samuel Beckett, *Waiting for Godot*
Henrik Ibsen, *Hedda Gabler*
John Osborne, *Look Back in Anger*
Harold Pinter, *The Birthday Party*
Sophocles, *Antigone*

the elements of drama

So far we have discussed drama as the imitation of men in action. We need now to consider the shape of that action and the various theories and principles pertaining to it. Few people have written good plays by following theory. Very often the practitioner has no clearly defined theory, or he may, as some playwrights seem to do, talk about theory one way and write another. In the theater the acid test has always been, how will it play before an audience? So the theorist needs to make his judgments on the practical aspects of production. Fortunately, the fountainhead of classical theory, Aristotle's *Poetics,* was written by a man who examined plays on the basis of their theatrical effectiveness.

The *Poetics,* written a century after the golden age of drama, is chiefly concerned with Sophoclean tragedy. Aristotle seems to draw many arbitrary conclusions from insufficient evidence. Indeed, it is not certain whether Aristotle's work concerning poetry, at least as it has come down to us, is a set of lecture notes prepared by one of his students or a compact lecture outline devised by the master himself. In addition, critics find other ample grounds to disagree over the precise meaning of his language and ideas as well as their origin in and applicability to the drama and the theater of his time. His observations and terminology

chapter 3

serve, nevertheless, as useful starting points. With all of the admitted limitations of his treatise, to discuss dramatic theory and practice, then and now, without serious consideration of Aristotle is to talk about relativity without referring to Einstein or about twentieth-century painting without mentioning Picasso. By using Aristotle's ideas as important points of reference, we will thus examine in this chapter the dramatic theory and practice that characterize most of our drama. In a later chapter, we will discuss the departures from tradition.

Although the *Poetics* is primarily an investigation of tragedy, many of its principles apply to other forms of drama. Aristotle argued that a play is separable for purposes of analysis into six elements, which are listed here in order of the importance he gave them:

1. Plot
2. Character
3. Thought
4. Diction
5. Music
6. Spectacle

We will use this hierarchy as a convenient framework throughout the book. Hence, familiarity with these elements and their component parts is necessary for the discussions that follow. Many of Aristotle's terms have special meanings that differ significantly from everyday use.

1. *plot*

Aristotle's first element, *plot,* is a complex one that includes the twelve aspects involved in the construction of a play:

A. Exposition
B. Discovery
C. Reversal
D. Point of attack
E. Foreshadowing
F. Complication
G. Climax
H. Crisis
I. Denouement
J. Unity of time
K. Unity of place
L. Unity of action

These plot materials may be identified in most plays, although the parts of plot are sometimes not separate entities. For instance, the climax and crisis may occur at the same time, or exposition may be used for foreshadowing.

Aristotle regarded plot as the chief part of drama. He said that plot is "the life and soul of tragedy." Plot is the formal element of the play in the sense that it gives the action its form. Plot is to the playwright what composition is to the painter and musical form is to the composer. Plot is not synonymous with story. In a play that tells a story, the plot is the *shape* of the story, the organization of its incidents. In *Act Without Words, I,* the plot is Beckett's arrangement of the action: the man's attempt to escape at the sides of the stage, his attempts to reach the carafe of water, his futile effort at suicide, and his submission. The plot is made up of a series of instances selected and arranged to establish the man's frustration and his eventual inability or unwillingness to respond.

In the episode from *Antigone* discussed in chapter 2, we saw only the first of a connected chain of episodes leading to disaster. The opening incident establishes the probability of the succeeding action and creates a tension. Plot, then, is many actions dependent on one another, like scoring a run in baseball or moving the football down the field in a planned series of maneuvers toward a calculated goal. The playwright makes a plot out of dialogue and action to suit his purpose. He decides what evidence he will present, just as Heinar Kipphardt did when he wrote *In the Matter of J. Robert Oppenheimer.* From three thousand typewritten pages of testimony before the Atomic Energy Commission, he selected the cogent incidents, which became a play of a hundred pages.

The two plays we have just referred to, *Act Without Words, I* and *Antigone,* follow the usual linear sequence that has until recently characterized much of Western drama. In some forms of drama where there is much activity, the incidents may not be obviously connected, but they are always *related.* Medieval drama, which sometimes involved hundreds of actors and dozens of incidents, was not causally tied by incidents, but the action was related by the theme—often the gospel of salvation. Chronicle plays, the epic drama of Brecht, and the Kabuki plays of Japan have this kind of organization in common: the incidents are related to the whole rather than hooked together in a tight sequence. When Strindberg set out to create an unreal atmosphere in *The Dream Play,* he devised a plot of disconnected and bewildering images and incidents. The point is that the playwright chooses the form of action that suits his purpose. Whether the form is tightly knit, circular, loose, or even chaotic, *the form is the plot.* Regarded in this sense, then, there is no such thing as a plotless play.

Western dramatists have followed the Aristotelian preference for a system of actions organized in a "necessary and probable" order to elicit the proper emotional response. As a consequence, most of our plays involve human beings caught in decisive moments of struggle, suffering, and conflict. Tension is increased as the drama moves toward a climax and an ultimate decision. In other words, the plot may be regarded as a *structure of feeling.*

The Greeks used such plots very early in their dramas. A typical Greek tragedy is built around a character involved in a situation that requires a choice. As we have seen in *Antigone,* once the protagonist makes a decision, pressure is brought to bear on her, but the tragic figure will not be diverted from her course of action, and the catastrophe occurs.

A typical Greek "old comedy" also shows a leading character embarking on a plan of action, usually an extravagant and impracticable one. For example, in the *Acharnians,* a private citizen decides to negotiate a personal peace treaty with Sparta. Opposition is set up against his plan and the issues are contested. The idea is tried out and the results shown. The comedy ends in revelry. In both of these early forms of drama, the plot results from a character making a decision that he attempts to put into action against opposition. This essential pattern has been the characteristic dramatic structure ever since.

A play is composed of a series of units. Major divisions are the acts, which may be divided into scenes, and these may be separated still further by a director into a series of "beats." "Scenes" in the French sense refers to any new groupings of characters. "Beats" are a director's rehearsal device for separating small units of action, such as the appearances of the ghost in the first scene of *Hamlet,* Kate's final speech in *The Taming of the Shrew,* or Romeo's suicide in *Romeo and Juliet.* An examination of the structure of any play reveals these various units. For example, *Oedipus Rex* consists of a series of eight or nine episodes involving two or three speaking characters—Oedipus and Creon, Oedipus and Teiresias, Oedipus and the Herdsman. Between each of these episodes, which are of only a few minutes' duration, the Chorus chants lyric passages. In a modern play, the structure of each act or scene is composed of various groupings of characters, such as Nora and Mrs. Linden, Nora and Torvald, Nora and Krogstad. Each of these scenes of groupings is designed by the playwright for specific dramatic purposes. In *Acts Without Words, I,* the man makes seven attempts to reach the carafe of water. Each of these beats is different and each one intensifies the effect of frustration.

The plot is devised to produce a cumulative effect; it is plot that gives the play its tension and emotional momentum. In addition, the plot provides the explanation and meaning of the sum total of the parts. What are the events that cause the transition from Oedipus, the heroic king, to Oedipus, the blinded exile? What happens to Nora in between the time she makes her first gay entrance in her "doll's house," and the end of the play when she walks out on her husband and children? The plot answers these questions by providing the salient incidents which account for the changes that occur. The plot charts the course of action and carries with it the increasing burden of emotion.

A. EXPOSITION

When the curtain rises on a play, the dramatist faces the problem of capturing his audience's attention and providing the spectator with the necessary background so that he can follow the subsequent action. Letting the viewer know who the characters are, what their relationship to one another is, what motivates them, and what their world is like is the task of *exposition.* You will recall how much information Sophocles provides in the first episode of *Antigone* so that very shortly we understand the characters' background, their differences in temperament and motivation, and their present situation. The information comes to us out of a character clash so that the speeches and actions seem probable. Standard expository devices are "feather-duster" scenes of two minor characters bouncing information off each other to the audience, narrators, confidants, dumb shows, choruses, asides, soliloquies, prologues, and all kinds of visual aids. The stage setting is, of course, a means of providing environmental material.

Henrik Ibsen, regarded as the father of modern drama and a master realist, gives us a good example of the skillful use of unobtrusive exposition in the opening scene of *A Doll's House:*

(NORA *enters, humming gaily. She is in outdoor dress, and carries several parcels, which she lays on the right-hand table. She leaves the door into the hall open, and a* PORTER *is seen outside, carrying a Christmas tree and a basket, which he gives to the* MAIDSERVANT *who has opened the door.)*

NORA: Hide the Christmas tree carefully, Ellen; the children must on no account see it before this evening, when it's lighted up. *(to the* PORTER, *taking out her purse)* How much?

PORTER: Fifty öre.

NORA: There is a crown. No, keep the change.

(The PORTER *thanks her and goes.* NORA *shuts the door. She continues smiling in quiet glee as she takes off her outdoor things. Taking from her pocket a bag of macaroons, she eats one or two. Then she goes on tip-toe to her husband's door and listens.)* Yes; he is at home. *(She begins humming again, crossing to the table on the right)*

HELM: *(in his room)* Is that my lark twittering there?

NORA: *(busy opening some of her parcels)* Yes, it is.

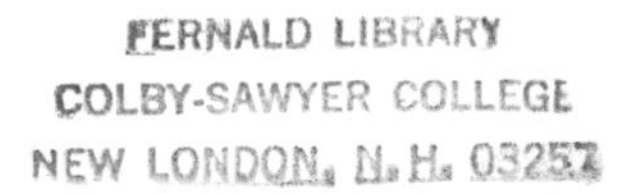

HELM: Is it the squirrel frisking around?

NORA: Yes!

HELM: When did the squirrel get home?

NORA: Just this minute. *(hides the bag of macaroons in her pocket and wipes her mouth)* Come here, Torvald, and see what I've been buying.

HELM: Don't interrupt me. *(a little later he opens the door and looks in, pen in hand)* Buying, did you say? What! All that? Has my little spendthrift been making the money fly again?

NORA: Why, Torvald, surely we can afford to launch out a little now. It's the first Christmas we haven't had to pinch.

HELM: Come, come; we can't afford to squander money.

NORA: Oh, yes, Torvald, do let us squander a little, now—just the least little bit! You know you'll soon be earning heaps of money.

HELM: Yes, from New Year's Day. But there's a whole quarter before my first salary is due.

NORA: Never mind; we can borrow in the meantime.

HELM: Nora! *(he goes up to her and takes her playfully by the ear)*[1]

Notice that Ibsen begins the play with his two major characters and immediately establishes their relationship to one another through dialogue and business. As a contrast to Ibsen's unobtrusive exposition, consider the forthright manner of handling exposition in act 1 of *The Visit.*

A railway-crossing bell starts ringing. Then is heard the distant sound of a locomotive whistle. The curtain rises.

The scene represents, in the simplest possible manner, a little town somewhere in Central Europe. The time is the present. The town is shabby and ruined as if the plague had passed there. Its name, Güllen, is inscribed on the shabby sign-board which adorns the façade of the railway station unit, left. This edifice is summarily indicated by a small house and a wooden platform facing the audience, beyond which one imagines the rails to be. The THIRD MAN *leans on a baggage truck standing Down Left. In the station wall is a door with a sign:* Eintritt Verboten. *This leads to the station master's office. Left of the station is a little house in grey stucco, formerly whitewashed. It has a tile roof, badly in need of repair. Some shreds of travel posters still adhere to the windowless walls. A shingle hanging over the entrance Left reads:* Männer. *On the other side the shingle reads:* Damen. *And under this a torn timetable marked* Fahrplan *hanging on two nails. Along the wall of the little house there is a wooden bench, backless, on which two* MEN *are lounging cheerlessly, shabbily dressed, with cracked shoes. The*

1. Henrik Ibsen, *A Doll's House*, trans. William Archer (New York: Scribner, 1906).

PAINTER *is busied with paint-pot and brush Down Left. He is kneeling on the ground, painting a strip of cloth with the words,* Welcome, Clara. THE SECOND MAN *is seated on a wooden box near the station master's office. The warning signal rings uninterruptedly while the sound of the approaching train comes closer and closer. The* STATION MASTER *issues from his office, advances to the Center of the platform and salutes. The* TRAIN *thunders past in a direction parallel to the footlights, between them and the audience, and is lost in the distance. The* MEN *on the bench follow its passing with a slow movement of their heads, from Left to Right.*

FIRST MAN: The "Emperor." Hamburg-Naples.

SECOND MAN: Then comes the "Diplomat."

THIRD MAN: Then the "Banker."

FOURTH MAN: And at 11:27 the "Flying Dutchman." Venice-Stockholm.

FIRST MAN: Our only pleasure—watching trains.

(The station bell rings. The STATION MASTER *comes out of his office and salutes the train. The* MEN *follow its course, Right to Left.)*

FOURTH MAN: Once upon a time the "Emperor" and the "Flying Dutchman" used to stop here in Güllen. So did the "Diplomat," the "Banker" and the "Silver Comet."

SECOND MAN: Now it's only the local from Kaffigen and the 12:40 from Kalberstadt.

THIRD MAN: The fact is, we're ruined.

FIRST MAN: What with the Wagonworks shut down.

SECOND MAN: The Foundry finished.

FOURTH MAN: The Golden Eagle Pencil Factory all washed up—

FIRST MAN: It's life on the dole.

SECOND MAN: Did you say life?

THIRD MAN: We're rotting.

FIRST MAN: Starving.

SECOND MAN: Crumbling.

FOURTH MAN: The whole damn town—

THIRD MAN: Once we were a centre of industry.

THE PAINTER: A cradle of culture.

FOURTH MAN: One of the best little towns in the country.

FIRST MAN: In the world.

SECOND MAN: Here Goethe slept.

FOURTH MAN: Brahms composed a quartet.

THIRD MAN: Here Berthold Schwarz invented gunpowder.

THE PAINTER: *(Rises, moves to* FIRST MAN.) And I who once got first prize at the Dresden Exhibition of Contemporary Art—What am I doing now? *(Station bell rings.)* Painting signs!

(STATION MASTER *comes out, throws away cigarette. All rush;* THIRD MAN gets cigarette and sits Center smoking. FIRST MAN moves back to bench, stands, others remain standing around THIRD MAN.)

FIRST MAN: Well, anyway, Madame Zachanassian will help us.

FOURTH MAN: *(Moves back to bench.)* If she comes.

THIRD MAN: *(Moving toward trolley.)* If she comes.
SECOND MAN: Last week she was in France. She gave them a hospital.
FIRST MAN: *(Sits on bench.)* In Rome she founded a free public nursery.
THIRD MAN: In Leuthenau, a bird sanctuary.
THE PAINTER: *(Crosses Center.)* They say she got Picasso to design her car.
FIRST MAN: Where does she get all that money?
SECOND MAN: An oil company, a shipping line, three banks and five railways—
FOURTH MAN: And the biggest string of geisha houses in Japan. *(Laugh.)*[2]

Exposition is a part of the general discovery process, but it deals primarily with background material, while discovery includes events that may happen in the course of the play onstage, as, for example, Nora's discovery of the true character of her husband, Jason's discovery of Medea's slaughter of their two sons, and the doctor's discovery of Lady Macbeth's madness.

B. DISCOVERY

The playwright is obligated to impart a steady stream of information to the audience. He must reveal his characters' motivations and objectives, their relationships, and their feelings. The most satisfactory kind of *discovery* is that which comes from the characters themselves. As the protagonist discovers the truth, the audience shares the experience of his discovery, as in *Oedipus* and *Ghosts.* In these plays, the spectator gains the impression of an actual happening. A skillful playwright possesses the ability to invent and organize a series of interesting and compelling discoveries. For instance, notice the number and variety of effective discoveries in *Hamlet:* the ghost's revelation of the murder, the guilt of Claudius, the madness and death of Ophelia, the pirates' attempt to slay Hamlet, the death of Polonius, and the poisoned sword and drink.

Discovery scenes may be those of recognition. For example, in Aeschylus's *Libation-Bearers,* Electra recognizes her brother, Orestes, by a lock of his hair and by their matching footprints. In Sophocles' *Electra,* Orestes is recognized by his father's signet ring, and in the Euripidean version, a tutor recognizes Orestes by a scar. In classic comedy, recognition scenes between long-lost relatives and lovers were effected very often by signs and symbols such as rings, lockets, and distinguishing physical markings.

Discovery is often accompanied by *anagnorisis* (recognition). The truth is realized in the recognition of the difference between appearance

2. Friedrich Duerrenmatt, *The Visit,* adapted by Maurice Valency (New York: Random House, 1958).

18 The Russian actress Nazimova as Nora in the opening expository scene of Ibsen's *A Doll's House*.

Mrs Abingdon, Mr King, Mr Smith, and Mr Palmer, in the Characters of Lady Teazle, Sir Peter Teazle, Charles and Joseph Surface.

19 (opposite, top) Alfred Lunt and Lynne Fontanne in the New York production of Duerrenmatt's *The Visit.*

20 (opposite, bottom) The "Screen Scene" from *The School for Scandal,* showing a comic discovery scene that results in a reversal.

21 A scene of foreshadowing preparing for Julie's suicide in Strindberg's *Miss Julie.*

and reality, between what is expected and what actually occurs. In serious drama, this may be self-discovery; for example, throughout *Hamlet* the protagonist submits himself to introspective analysis. And in *Oedipus Rex* the tragic hero gradually discovers the awful truth about himself. In the second episode of *Antigone,* Creon discovers the burial of the body, then the guilt of Antigone. Later, through the messenger (a widely used device in classic drama), Creon learns of the death of Antigone, his son and his wife, and at the end he recognizes his guilt in the catastrophes. The art of playwriting is in part the art of creating effective discoveries.

C. REVERSAL

Many plays follow the pattern described by Aristotle as "a change of fortune in the action of the play to the opposite state of affairs." The protagonist seems headed on a course of action only to have a sudden change in direction lead to disaster. When the messenger arrives to help Oedipus, the news he brings has exactly the opposite effect from the one intended; his discovery of the king's true identity brings catastrophe. King Lear's intended division of his kingdom is reversed when his daughter Cordelia is unable and unwilling to compete with her sisters to flatter her father. The *reversal* from good fortune to calamity is a characteristic of most tragedies, which show the fall of a high character, such as Oedipus, Macbeth, or Lear. Comedy most often uses reversal in the opposite direction: the little man achieves status, or the lovers overcome opposition in such plays as *The Inspector General,* where an impostor is mistaken for an official, or *The Doctor in Spite of Himself,* where a woodcutter becomes the court physician.

Reversals often come as a surprise, but the traditional playwright usually takes care to create a background of probability. Aristotle particularly admired the reversal in *Oedipus Rex* because it was combined with discovery.

D. POINT OF ATTACK

Once the playwright has provided sufficient background to hold the audience's attention, he begins the chain of events that constitutes the main action. The *point of attack* refers to that moment in the play in which the precipitating force sets the mechanism in motion—the first pitch is thrown, the football is kicked off, the first blow is landed, the battle is joined. The point of attack is the first complication. A disequilibrium is created, resulting in change that continues until a new equilibrium is established. The point of attack initiates the process of change. One common form is the arrival of a major character: Madame Zachanassian in *The Visit;* King Agamemnon in *Agamemnon;* Blanche DuBois in *A Streetcar Named Desire;* and Anna in *Anna Christie.* Another is the making of a decision: Antigone decides to bury Polyneices; Oedipus promises to rid the kingdom of the plague; Grusha saves the child. Still another is the making of an important discovery: Horatio sees Hamlet's father's ghost; Nora learns of Krogstad's threat; the Madwoman of Chaillot is told of the plot to drill for oil. In Beckett's pantomime the point of attack begins with the very first action, as the man is hurled back when he tries to leave the stage.

The location of the point of attack in the story relates directly to the physical theater and its conventions. The more flexible the stage, the freer the dramatic form and the greater the opportunity for an early attack and the presentation of a great deal of action. For example, medieval and Elizabethan playwrights exploited the freedom provided by their stages to tell complicated stories with many scenes and characters, while the Greek dramatists felt obliged to begin their plots as near as possible to the major crisis. If Shakespeare had dramatized *Oedipus Rex,* he might have presented the original warning of the oracle and proceeded to show Oedipus clashing with his father, solving the riddle, and marrying his mother. In most realistic plays, playwrights use a late point of attack in order to concentrate on a few characters in an intense situation. Those who work with freer forms and wish to cover a wider range of action, such as the expressionists and Brecht, often use an early point of attack. As our present drama becomes more flexible, is less tied to one locale, and encompasses more characters and more social action, the dramatist often pushes the attack back to enable him to give a wider view, as in such plays as Brecht's *The Caucasian Chalk Circle* and Shepard's *Operation Sidewinder.*

E. FORESHADOWING

In the exposition, we have observed how the playwright must furnish the audience with background material. He also has the task of preparing the spectator for future developments. He does this by *foreshadowing,* that is, he makes the subsequent action credible by supplying clues that he carefully inserts in early parts of the play. Everyone is familiar with the techniques of foreshadowing or "planting" employed by a mystery-story writer when he takes pains to drop hints that the butler is left-handed, that his revolver is hidden in the desk drawer, and that the chauffeur has an assumed name. The dramatist is likewise obliged to prepare for the audience's acceptance of the developments of the action by foreshadowing.

Foreshadowing has several purposes. It makes the event appear believable, it builds suspense, and it creates tension. It may reveal character, and it aids in the development of climaxes, crises, and complications. Foreshadowing may also prepare for an entrance and create atmosphere.

Within the first thirty lines of *Hamlet*, several references are made to the "dreaded sight" that has appeared twice before, as a means of preparing for the ghost's entrance and of providing the appropriate atmosphere. In *A Doll's House*, Nora's deception with the macaroons on her first appearance prepares for the discovery of her larger deception in forging her father's signature, and Helmer's treatment of her as a child symbolizes his view of Nora. In *The Visit* the playwright quickly sets the background for the action by contrasting the past with the present, and then thrusts the interest forward to the coming of the wealthy Madame Zachanassian so that we are intrigued to know why she is returning to this miserable town.

The playwright values suspense more than he does surprise, and the traditional practice is to establish the background of an action, as in the first scene of *Antigone*. On the other hand, many writers today regard life as alogical and incomprehensible and reflect this view in their plays. Dramatists such as Pinter, Frisch, and Duerrenmatt have written striking plays in which the action reflects a nameless dread, an overpowering sense of unidentified evil. A favorite device of the iconoclast is to build anticipation deliberately, and then to reverse expectations. For example, many plays begin with the act of waiting: the soldiers of the watch and Horatio wait for the ghost; the watchman waits for sign of Agamemnon's return; Electra waits for the coming of Orestes. The person expected usually arrives, but Beckett inverts this old device to make his point. Estragon and Vladimir wait for Godot but he never comes.

F. COMPLICATION

The point of attack is the first *complication*. A complication is any new force introduced into a play that affects the direction of the course of action. Once the playwright has selected his characters, determined his theme, and planned the beginning and end of the play, he constructs the plot through a series of complications. Kenneth Macgowan considers complications so important that he says they are "the lifeblood of ninety-nine and ninety-nine hundredths per cent of a play."

Let us consider for a moment the analogy of a three-stage rocket. It is prepared for launching, its course is charted, and its destination determined. The mechanism is fired and the rocket is projected into space, but the initial impetus is insufficient to keep it moving; additional thrusts are needed from second- and third-stage firings to send the rocket soaring on its trajectory. In a similar way, the dramatist decides on his objective and sets his course of action. He precipitates the initial motion by means of a complication (the point of attack), but the plot, like the rocket, needs additional force to keep the tension moving forward and upward. Like the rocket's secondary and tertiary firings, additional complications accelerate and increase the action until the play reaches its highest point. The play has a pattern of increasing intensification from the introduction of the first complication to the major crisis when the fate of the protagonist is settled. Complications are used by the playwright to create a "straining forward of interest," in George Pierce Baker's apt phrase. Their purpose is to intensify the emotions, arouse suspense, provide the building blocks of the play's structure, and illustrate and determine what happens to the characters.

Romeo falls in love with Juliet, but the situation is complicated by the enmity between the two families. This hostility is aggravated when Romeo slays Tybalt, causing a new complication, the banishment of Romeo. Another complication is raised when Juliet's father insists that she marry Paris immediately. In order to avoid the marriage, a plan is devised for Juliet to feign death through the use of a magic potion. But the letter to Romeo disclosing the plan is not delivered, further complicating the action. Romeo learns of Juliet's apparent death, goes to her, and takes poison. Juliet awakens to find her lover dead—another complication. She joins him in death. Shakespeare, like most playwrights, begins with a character trying to reach an objective, but complications intervene and require the character to readjust as the play gathers momentum and intensity. It is through complications that the playwright constructs his plot.

G. CLIMAX

The *climax* is the culmination of a course of action, "the maximum disturbance of the equilibrium," "the moment of the most intense strain," "the crisis of maximum emotion and tension." The nineteenth-century German critic Gustav Freytag sees the structure of the play as a pyramid with five steps: (1) introduction, (2) rise, (3) climax, (4) return or fall, and (5) catastrophe. While drama does not generally conform to such a balanced and arbitrary pattern, Freytag was right in representing the climax as the apex of the triangle, the highest point of the structure.

Actually, a play is a series of climaxes, with moments of stability and adjustment in between. The action surges forward and upward in mounting tension through minor climaxes until the major climax, when the emotional impact of the play is strongest. The structure, in this respect, resembles a boxing match between two opponents of similar strength and skill. In each round, there are moments of climactic action with first one fighter gaining the advantage and then the other. In between the peaks of action, there are relatively quiet moments and rest periods between the rounds. In the frantic last round, the major climax is reached when one boxer succeeds in knocking the other one out.

Dramatic climaxes are the result of an arrangement of actions and events of increasing tension, as, for example, the climaxes of Ibsen's *A Doll's House:*

Krogstad threatens to reveal Nora's secret.
Nora pleads unsuccessfully with Helmer to retain Krogstad.
Krogstad writes his damning letter to Helmer.
Nora dances the tarantella to keep Helmer from reading the letter.
Helmer reads the letter and berates Nora.
Kragstad's second letter saves Helmer's reputation.
Nora tells Helmer of her decision to leave him.

Each of the climaxes is organically related to the central action, providing a unified effect and cumulative intensification of emotion.

Until recently it was felt that a good play was required to present an "obligatory scene" of climactic action leading to a resolution, but modern plays have been successful without this device, most notably such absurdist plays as *Waiting for Godot, The Bald Soprano,* and *Endgame,* which, like *Act Without Words, I,* make an appeal to the intellect rather than to the emotions.

H. CRISIS

Although the terms *crisis* and *climax* are sometimes used interchangeably because they may occur at the same time, we shall consider a crisis to mean a time of decision, a turning point, a crossroads. After an accident (which may be a climax), a patient hovers between life and death. He is at a moment of crisis. A batter steps to the plate with the score tied and the bases loaded. The count reaches three balls and two strikes. The game is at a point of crisis. (It is probably at the climax, too.)

A crisis involves a clash of interest. The protagonist is faced with alternatives that will determine his fate. Hamlet, sword in hand, must decide whether or not to slay the praying Claudius; Juliet must decide whether or not to take the sleeping potion; Nora must decide whether or not to leave her husband.

Sometimes a character makes his own decisions; sometimes they are thrust upon him. A crisis may lead to good fortune or catastrophe, depending on the nature of the play and the author's intent. Plays are usually made up of a series of crises growing out of a series of complications. The major crisis toward the end of the play determines the outcome of the action.

A dramatist creates situations that dramatize his characters at critical moments of their careers. For a while the outcome is in doubt. The protagonist teeters on the brink of success or failure. A decisive action occurs that settles the fate of the hero. The moments of decision are the crises.

22 (opposite, top) A climactic moment in Brecht's *St. Joan of the Stockyards* at the Berliner Ensemble.

23 (opposite, bottom) A scene of crisis in the Berliner Ensemble production of Brecht's *The Caucasian Chalk Circle.*

24 The strike scene that serves as the denouement of Odets's *Waiting for Lefty* at the Group Theater, 1935.

25 (opposite) *In the Matter of J. Robert Oppenheimer*, Mark Taper Forum, Los Angeles, directed by Gordon Davidson.

26 Scene from Ibsen's *Ghosts* at the Munich Kammerspiele. The action has become discussion.

Many plays have a series of crises occurring within the incidents. Ismene and Antigone are at a moment of crisis in the first scene as each decides her course of action. In Greek drama the character has some freedom of choice, but many recent playwrights, who are determinists, have dramatized characters with no more chance to assert themselves than the man in Beckett's pantomime.

I. DENOUEMENT

The *denouement* is the part of the play from the major crisis to the final curtain. It is the end of the play, the final resolution of difficulties that have been raised. In *Act Without Words, I,* the man gives up; Antigone and Haemon are dead, and Creon realizes his tragic error; the blinded Oedipus goes into exile; Romeo and Juliet are united in death; Oswald loses his mind; Godot does not come; Hedda commits suicide. The denouement is the untying of the knot which the complications have formed. It indicates the ultimate disposition of the protagonist. The function of the denouement is to restore order, to unify and complete the course of action, and to provide an ending that seems necessary and probable.

The denouement of the play is a fairly good indication of the skill and integrity of the dramatist. It must be credible in terms of the characters themselves and their previous actions. The inept playwright may find his characters in an inextricable situation and resort to an implausible suicide or some other violent action in the mistaken notion that these acts in themselves are dramatic, or he may use an outside force to intervene and unsnarl the entanglements. The hero, incapable of working out his own salvation, must be rescued by the Marines, the Coast Guard, the Air Force, the king, or a miracle from on high. Another weak denouement occurs when the playwright violates his characters in a sudden change of direction, in order to shock or surprise. Still another questionable, though sometimes amusing, denouement is the indeterminate ending. Pirandello in *Right You Are If You Think You Are* makes an acceptable use of this device, but ordinarily the spectator likes to have the major questions answered before he goes home.

The denouement of comedy usually shows the protagonist successful in overcoming obstacles to reach the land of his heart's desire; the denouement of tragedy often shows disaster. The denouements of both comedy and tragedy frequently involve a reversal of the hero's status.

The modern playwright who rejects the traditional format may not provide a clear-cut denouement but may leave the resolution ambiguous or up to the audience, as in Beckett's *Endgame* and Brecht's *The Good Woman of Setzuan;* or he may reverse the expected ending, as in Ionesco's *The Leader* and *The Chairs.* Still another device is to come full circle to the beginning, as in Beckett's *Waiting for Godot* and Ionesco's *The*

Bald Soprano. (Incidentally, Ionesco's original ending called for the author to appear on stage and shoot the audience; his second thought was to end the play as it began. His third thought, after the hundredth performance, was to begin with the same dialogue but to substitute Mr. and Mrs. Martin for Mr. and Mrs. Smith.)

the unities

Most dramatists have sought some means of creating unity in their plays by character, thought, or mood—some way of providing a central focus. Aristotle suggested unity in an interlocking arrangement of the incidents with "a beginning, middle, and end." During the Renaissance, scholars insisted on imposing on the dramatist the "classical" unities of time, place, and action. Actually, Aristotle mentions only time and action. Moreover, he does not set down rules for dramatic composition, but rather his observations record the practices of the Greek playwrights of the preceding century. Aeschylus, Sophocles, and Euripides did not write according to rules, but constructed their plays to meet the conventions of the theater and their own imaginations. They did not regard drama as a fixed and unchangeable form, but created their plays and the methods of presentation to suit themselves. The notion that playwrights must observe rules or conform to the unities has historically found little acceptance outside the neoclassical drama of seventeenth-century France. In general, playwrights have written for popular approval rather than for academic acceptance.

J. UNITY OF TIME

Aristotle wrote: "Tragedy endeavors, as far as possible, to confine itself to a single revolution of the sun, or but slightly to exceed this limit." Italian Renaissance scholars interpreted *unity of time* to mean a maximum of twelve hours, but preferably only as long as the action of the play. The Greek playwrights usually were close to Aristotle's observation, although several of their plays represent events taking place over a longer time span. Greek dramatists were not concerned with strict adherence to real time, their interest lying in the actions and ideas of their characters rather than in the lapse of time. Dramatists in other periods have felt free to use all the time needed to encompass the action. However, because of the compact nature of drama, playwrights usually restrict action to a relatively short time period.

K. UNITY OF PLACE

Aristotle said nothing about *unity of place,* although it was customary for Greek tragic writers to use a single locale or, at the most, two. Perhaps the continual presence of the chorus influenced this practice. Perhaps the fact that drama originated in a performance in a single locale set a precedent. Perhaps the outdoor, daylight performances without shifts of scenery conditioned the playwriting. But more likely, it was the play's structure, which, centered on a few characters shown in the climactic and critical stages of their careers, required no change of scenic background. Renaissance Italians attempted to restrict the action of a play to a single building or, at the most, to a single city.

For the most part, playwrights have ignored the Renaissance scholars' dictum regarding place and have moved around freely in space as their plots required and as the physical equipment or conventions of the theater permitted. While numerous plays require freedom to move from place to place, dramatists usually concentrate their action in order to keep the focus clear.

L. UNITY OF ACTION

Unity of action means that the drama deals with a single course of events that involves little or no extraneous material, no mixture of comic and serious matter. Aristotle said that the plot should be simple enough to be held easily in the mind of the spectator. The most important condition for unity is the organic interrelation of parts. Aristotle wrote: "The structural unity of the parts is such that, if any one of them is displaced or removed, the whole will be disjointed and disturbed. For a thing whose presence or absence makes no visible difference is not an organic part of the whole." Greek writers of tragedy usually created simple, well-articulated plots.

The history of drama reveals that playwrights often have ignored the unity of action as Aristotle defined it, particularly in Elizabethan England where the physical theater with its unlocalized platform permitted the use of complicated stories and actions, and where the medieval tradition of mixing comedy with serious drama was an accepted practice. Japanse Kabuki drama also moved freely in time and space, with complicated plots that ranged from elaborately stylized battle scenes, employing full use of the revolving stage and the flower walk, to long static scenes of domestic life in which two characters sit and talk over their tea or saki. But even in "panoramic drama" dramatists have been conscious of the need to find some means of unifying the effect. Christopher Marlowe achieved unity of character by focusing all the action on a central figure. Others have sought a unity of idea by selecting only those characters and incidents germane to the development and projection of their theme. Still others have ignored structural unity and achieved a unity of atmosphere. Most dramatists have striven to suggest a singleness of purpose or effect in order to clarify and organize their creative efforts.

2. *character*

By placing *character* as his second element, Aristotle started an argument that continues to this day. Many modern playwrights and critics insist that character is the most important element of drama, while others insist with equal firmness that character is further down the scale. The controversy is a fruitless one since valid arguments can be made on both sides. Furthermore, plot and character both work together in practice; as Aristotle quite rightly points out, actions in drama create character. If the playwright wants to portray a hero, some action must indicate his heroism, just as Molière, in *The Miser*, gives concrete evidence of the protagonist's miserliness in the treatment of his children, servants, and guests. We can state that "plot is character in action." The sequence of events is rooted in the characters' wills, desires, and objectives, which are revealed by skillful selection and organization.

The nature of the dramatic method and the conditions and conventions of the physical theater have exerted important influences on characterization. Unlike the novelist, who can demonstrate character by a wide range of incidents over many years and under many conditions, and can show either directly or obliquely the secret thoughts coursing through the heads of his creatures, the playwright must select a few key incidents in a short space of time and in a few locales, and he must reveal character by speech and behavior. The dramatist has no means of commenting directly on character. Only the designers of the stage setting, costumes, and makeup have some opportunity for direct comment (though in visual terms). As a result, the character in plays must be simplified, their qualities made clear in a few telling scenes. Because of the compression of the medium, characterization in drama often becomes one-dimensional, especially in farce, melodrama, and in the minor roles of most plays.

Like other aspects of drama, characterization has varied with fashion. In Greek, Elizabethan, and Japanese drama, the roles of women were played by men. Medieval drama often made use of allegorical figures representing single attributes of character, such as Wisdom, Greed, and Gluttony. High tragedy has dealt primarily with men "as better than they are," and low comedy with men "as worse than they are." Medieval characters ranged from God to the Devil, from purest saint to most abject sinner. Some characters have been drawn on a heroic scale, masters of their fate, working out their destinies by dint of their own resources; other characters have been treated as hapless victims of an unfortunate heredity and environment, incapable of taking action, defeated, frustrated, and resigned. Modern dramatists of realistic and naturalistic persuasion have endeavored to create the illusion of complicated character by piling up a wealth of physical details, by capitalizing on the significant trifle, and by searching for the psychological meaning beneath the act. The expressionists have experimented with split personalities, or have effaced from characters all aspects of individuality, reducing them to X or Mr. Zero. Dramatic literature is filled with a wide variety of portraits.

During the last quarter of the nineteenth century, developments in scientific method and psychology led playwrights to delineate characters with rich inner lives and complex motivations. Ibsen, Strindberg, and Chekhov were particularly successful in creating figures authentically alive. Here is Ibsen's account of his method of working with character:

> When I am writing I must be alone; if I have eight characters of a drama to do with I have society enough; they keep me busy; I must learn to know them. And this process of making their acquaintance is slow and painful. I make, as a rule, three casts of my dramas, which differ considerably from each other. I mean in characteristics, not in the course of treatment. When I first settle down to work out my material, I feel as if I have to get to know my characters on a railway journey; the first acquaintance is struck up, and we have chatted about this and that. When I write it down again, I already see everything much more clearly, and I know the people as if I had stayed with them for a month at a watering place. I have grasped the leading points of their characters and their little peculiarities.[3]

Many twentieth-century plays depend for their appeal on solid characters whose motivations reveal the findings of contemporary psychology. Great stress has been placed not on defining the complexities of the individual but also often on exploiting the *interaction* of characters and on exposing the tensions and turbulence that result from interrelationships. Many modern writers and theorists now reject this kind of drama in favor of plays that emphasize philosophical or political content and subordinate the individual identity to the larger social scene. In these instances, character is not defined at all (as in *Act Without Words, I*), or no attempt is made to create credible people. Some plays mix three-dimensional characters with obvious theatrical figures, or utilize one actor to play several roles. In such plays, the playwright is interested in the character's function rather than his personality. But in general, because the traditional drama has dealt with the fate of the individual protagonists, dramatists have usually taken great care to create characters whom we recognize as genuine.

While he is restricted in scope, the playwright's use of selection and emphasis gives clarity and directness to his figures. Since the dramatist

3. Henrik Ibsen, quoted in George Brandes, *Ibsen and Björnson* (London: Heinemann, 1899).

is confined to a few events, he places great weight on them and thus brings his characters into sharp focus because all their behavior appears significant onstage. He avoids thereby the diffuseness of real life and the rambling indirectness of many novels. Onstage all is relevant.

Character may be delineated in four ways. First, character is established by appearance. The actor's physical qualities give an immediate stimulus to the audience. Many modern playwrights have a specific image in mind and describe the character's appearance in considerable detail. For example, Luigi Pirandello in *Six Characters in Search of an Author* describes the Father as

> . . . a man of about 50: hair, reddish in color, thin at the temples; he is not bald, however; thick moustache, falling over his still fresh mouth, which often opens in an empty uncertain smile. He is fattish, pale, with an especially wide forehead. He has blue, oval-shaped eyes, very clear and piercing. Wears light trousers and a dark jacket. He is alternately mellifluous and violent in his manner.[4]

The playwright frequently builds a character's entrance in order to place special attention on his initial appearance. Notice the care O'Neill has taken with the first entrance of his major character in *Anna Christie:*

> *There is a ring of the family entrance hall.* (LARRY *[the bartender] comes to the door and opens it a trifle—then with a puzzled expression, pulls it wide.* ANNA CHRISTOPHERSON *enters. She is a tall, blond, fully developed girl of twenty, handsome after a large, Viking-daughter fashion but now run down in health and plainly showing all the outward evidences of belonging to the world's oldest profession. Her youthful face is already hard and cynical beneath its layers of make-up. Her clothes are the tawdry finery of peasant stock turned prostitute. She comes and sinks wearily in a chair by the table, left front.)*
>
> ANNA: Gimme a whiskey—ginger ale on the side. *(Then, as* LARRY *turns to go, forcing a winning smile at him.)* And don't be stingy, baby.[5]

Second, character is revealed by speech. The kind of language employed by the person, his manner of speaking, his voice quality, his inflection pattern, pitch, rate, and general vitality all say something about him. The dramatist takes great care to write dialogue that makes an immediate statement about the characters. In the first few lines of *The Glass Menagerie,* Tennessee Williams gives us a clear portrait of Amanda:

4. Luigi Pirandello, *Six Characters in Search of an Author,* English version by Edward Stover from *Naked Masks,* ed. Eric Bentley (New York: Dutton, 1922).

5. Eugene O'Neill, *Anna Christie* (New York: Random House, 1922).

AMANDA *(to her son):* Honey, don't *push* with your *fingers.* If you have to push with something, the thing to push with is a crust of bread. And chew—chew. Animals have sections in their stomachs which enable them to digest food without mastication, but human beings are supposed to chew their food before they swallow it down. Eat food leisurely, son, and really enjoy it. A well-cooked meal has lots of delicate flavors that have to be held in the mouth for appreciation. So chew your food and give your salivary glands a chance to function![6]

Until the realistic and naturalistic theater of the late nineteenth century, the dramatist was able to use asides and soliloquies to reveal his characters' private thoughts to the audience. Contemporary playwrights rarely employ these devices because they destroy the illusion of reality. However, some playwrights use them occasionally, and they also use long speeches of reminiscence as a means of conveying information or a state of mind so that the audience will understand a character's condition. Many of the speeches in Chekhov's plays fulfill these functions. His characters often speak to themselves out of context so that the dialogue is a series of disconnected monologues. At times, playwrights give their characters long passages in which they express their thoughts and emotions. Conspicuous examples are found in the plays of Sartre, Ionesco, Beckett, Gorki, Ugo Betti, Tennessee Williams, and in almost all expressionistic plays. Whatever the form or function of the dialogue, the playwright ordinarily makes an effort to use his speeches to depict characters.

Third, character is established by action. Sometimes the playwright delineates his characters by their initial actions. For example, Ferenc Molnár opens *Liliom* with a prologue in which he shows his protagonist characteristically working as a barker in an amusement park:

Liliom stands at the entrance, a cigarette in his mouth, coaxing the people in. The girls regard him with idolizing glances and screech with pleasure as he playfully pushes them through the entrance. Now and then some escort resents the familiarity, whereupon Liliom's demeanor becomes ugly and menacing, and the cowed escort slinks through the entrance behind his girl or contents himself with a muttered resentful comment.[7]

A character's external actions gives us clues to his inner motivations. His role in the root-action of the play is revealed by the culmination of

6. Tennessee Williams, *The Glass Menagerie* (New York: Random House, 1945).

7. Ferenc Molnár, *Liliom,* trans. Benjamin Glazer, in S. M. Tucker, ed., *Modern Continental Playwrights* (New York: Boni and Liveright, 1929).

the plot, but the small detailed business of characterization helps the audience to build up a composite portrait. Sometimes, the playwright may deliberately give the audience a misleading or ambiguous impression of a character at the beginning of the play and then gradually reveal the truth as the play progresses. In the opening scene of Ibsen's *A Doll's House* (pp. 33–34), Nora's initial appearance and actions suggest a doll-like character, but our first impression is changed by her subsequent action. In John Osborne's *Look Back in Anger*, the audience is perplexed and even alienated by the protagonist's sadistic behavior, but as they come to know the reason for his suffering, they reach an understanding of his conduct. Action is a fundamental technique for depicting character.

Fourth, a character may be revealed by what others say about him, and the way they react to him. Sometimes the playwright uses comment about an absent character as a method of revealing the truth about him. For example, the true character behind the blustering, swaggering barker, Liliom, is indicated by Julie's line: "It is possible, dear, that someone may beat you, and beat you, and beat you—and not hurt you at all." Willy Loman in *Death of a Salesman* is a man who never saw himself or his motivations accurately. His son Biff expresses the truth about Willy when he says, "He had the wrong dreams. All, all wrong. . . . The man didn't know who he was."

The playwright may deliberately mislead or perplex the spectator by having characters say ambiguous or controversial things. Molière begins *Tartuffe* with a domestic quarrel in which he exposes two entirely different points of view about his leading character. Pirandello delighted in making the point time and again in his plays that it is difficult, if not impossible, to really comprehend the character of another. Hence, his plays are filled with conflicting statements about the characters. In some plays, the writer intends to leave the audience in a state of confusion. However, more usually, the dramatist reveals the genuine nature and background of his characters through the speech of another.

The sharpness of a character's image is in part dependent on the structure of the drama. Plays written for a theater that permits most of the essential action to appear onstage gives the playwright a greater opportunity to create more vivid, complex characters than plays that are confined to a minimum of action. For example, one reason that Hamlet is such a rich and interesting character is the number of eyes we see him through—the Ghost's, Horatio's, Ophelia's, Gertrude's, Polonius's. When we contrast this variety of character exposure to that of Agamemnon or Orestes or Antigone, we realize how limited the Greeks were in delineating complex characters. Some playwrights, notably Shakespeare, possess the ability to sketch memorable characters in a very few lines, but most dramatists develop their characters' roles at length in order to create distinctive and believable personalities.

The credibility of character is enhanced by the presence of the actor. The personal attributes of the performer add to the play a dimension that is difficult to describe and often impossible to predict in advance. In the hands of some actors, villains have become heroic, heroines insipid, comic characters dull, and minor roles have taken over the play. It is a commonplace of the theater that flat, pedestrian material has, on occasion, been made by the actor to seem rich and captivating stuff; that talented performers have taken superficial parts and infused them with the warmth and glow of life. The playwright's conception of character is at the mercy of the actor. It is to the latter's credit that he very often extends and enlarges the original sketch into a fully rounded portrait.

In most drama the purpose of showing men in action is to enlist our interest and involve our emotions in the fortunes of the characters. To accomplish his purpose, the dramatist creates characters with whom we have some kind of bond, either through temperament, condition, or destiny. If we cannot connect with them, we remain passive and indifferent, and the action does not fulfill its function. Hence, it is important for us to believe in the characters. That is why Aristotle emphasized the need for actions that were "necessary and probable." Some characters leave us cold. Their motivations and sense of values seem incredible; they are confused and incomprehensible; they make no effort to decide their fate; they are too self-centered, or too shortsighted. But a playwright can kindle our interest and sympathy in nearly any kind of character if he gives us understanding.

3. *thought*

The third Aristotelian element is *thought*, or *dianoia*. In his analysis of Aristotle's work, Ingram Bywater offers this definition of thought:

> *Dianoia* in the sense it bears in the *Poetics*, like *ethos* [character], is an element in the personality of the *dramatis personae*. It is their intellectual capacity, as evinced in their language (or it may be in their actions), and it is to be seen whenever they argue or make an appeal to the feelings of their hearers; in other words when they reason or plead with one of the other *dramatis personae* in the same sort of way as a rhetor might do.[8]

Thought is more than intellect, since the reasons for a character's behavior are bound up with his emotions. Plays are not objective debates,

8. Ingram Bywater, trans., *Aristotle on the Art of Poetry* (Oxford: Clarendon, 1920).

mere presentations of factual data and logical arguments leading to a clear decision. Characters in drama make subjective decisions under pressure, enmeshed in webs of conflicting emotions. In this respect, dramas are like the experiences of life with all their complicating networks of feeling and meaning beyond the immediate moment. It is relatively easy to make a list of the arguments advanced by Nora and Helmer leading up to Nora's departure in *A Doll's House.* But in order for the audience to grasp the significance of her decision, Ibsen had to prepare for the scene with more than two acts of background material that would place the husband's and wife's conflict in appropriate emotional context. While dramatic characters often make their choices on emotion and impulse, there is usually a rational background for their actions. This constitutes the thought of individual characters.

In presenting dramatic conflicts, the dramatist frequently presents both sides. The medieval playwright found it necessary to show the Devil as well as God, vices as well as virtues. Hence, in most plays, the dramatist presents a variety of thoughts. He shows the case for the antagonist as well as for the protagonist. Creon and Ismene advance cogent arguments against Antigone, and expose the rationale for their points of view. Willy Loman's attitude toward life is contrasted with that of Biff and Charley, Marchbanks' with Morell's, Blanche's with Stella's and Stanley's. The reasoning process, which includes the characters' motivations, constitutes one aspect of what Aristotle referred to as thought.

In addition to the rationale of individual characters, thought also concerns a play's theme—a kind of "golden text" that summarizes the moral and indicates the symbolic meaning of the play as a whole, such as "love conquers all," "murder will out," and "niceness pays." But drama does not always lend itself to such neat copybook maxims. A given play may convey a variety of interpretations to an audience. Most of Ibsen's contemporaries were profoundly shocked at Nora's decision to leave her husband and children, although her action is entirely credible to most of us today. Some people regard Antigone as headstrong and foolish in openly defying Creon and thus deliberately choosing to die. In the notes he wrote while directing *A Streetcar Named Desire,* Elia Kazan clearly shows that he intended to express Williams's point of view: "If we don't watch out, the apes will take over." But in production, the impression conveyed to many spectators as a result of the actors' performance was that Blanche threatened the Kowalski home, and Stanley was justified in treating her brutally. The ideas of great dramas have, of course, been sources of endless academic contention. What is the true interpretation of *Hamlet?* Is Shylock a comic or tragic figure? Is the tragedy of *Antigone* really the tragedy of Creon? Varied interpretations of a play's meaning indicate that the dramatist has not been explicit in stating his theme. A drama's significance remains the subject of personal interpretations. Inevitably the individual reader and spectator is challenged to search his own mind and experience in evaluating the action.

On the other hand, some dramatists have set about to illustrate a theme. For example, the medieval drama, which was a sort of visual aid designed to frighten people into salvation, patently stated the point of the story. In the best known of all medieval plays, *The Moral Play of Everyman,* a Messenger prepares the audience to receive the moral in the prologue. At the end of the play a Doctor appears to reemphasize it in these words:

> This moral men may have in mind;
> Ye hearers, take it of worth, old and young,
> And forsake Pride, for he deceiveth you in the end,
> And remember Beauty, Five Wits, Strength and Discretion
> They all at the last do Everyman forsake,
> Save his Good-Deeds, these doth he take.
> But beware, and they be small
> Before God, he hath no help at all.

One of Ibsen's most important contributions to drama was his concern with dramatic themes that would provoke thought and discussion. His approach to the thought element of a play is evident from the preliminary notes he made while contemplating *A Doll's House.* These are Ibsen's "Notes for a Modern Tragedy":

> There are two kinds of spiritual law, two kinds of conscience, one in man and another, altogether different, in woman. They do not understand each other; but in practical life the woman is judged by man's law, as though she were not a woman but a man.
>
> The wife in the play ends by having no idea of what is right or wrong; natural feeling on the one hand and belief in authority on the other have bewildered her.
>
> A woman cannot be herself in the society of the present day which is an exclusively masculine society, with laws framed by men and with a judicial system that judges feminine conduct from a masculine point of view.
>
> She has committed forgery, and she is proud of it; for she did it out of love for her husband, to save his life. But this husband with his commonplace principles of honour is on the side of the law and regards the question with masculine eyes.
>
> Spiritual conflicts. Oppressed and bewildered by the belief in authority, she loses faith in her moral right and ability to bring up her children. Bitterness. A mother in modern society, like certain insects who go away

> and die when she has done her duty in the propagation of the race. Here and there a womanly shaking-off of her thoughts. Sudden return of anxiety and terror. She must bear it all alone. The catastrophe approaches, inexorably, inevitably. Despair, conflict and destruction.[9]

Although Ibsen acknowledges that he began with a clearly stated theme when working on a play, he also took considerable pains to present his thought by implication and innuendo rather than by direct statement. As a consequence, the spectator is not overly conscious of Ibsen's themes. Unlike the medieval writers, Ibsen did not point to clear-cut solutions to the problems he raised. His purpose was to provoke thought rather than to persuade the audience to adopt a plan of action. Following Ibsen's example, many modern playwrights have found their source material in the problems of our day. The content of today's plays is often a reflection of today's thought, as the playwright weighs the values and motives by which men live, seeks for individual fulfillment, or searches for reality. An interesting example of the playwright's concern with thought is contained in Oppenheimer's final speech to the audience after the Atomic Energy Commission hearing has decided to deny him security clearance:

> As I was thinking about myself, a physicist of our times, I began to ask myself whether there had not in fact been something like ideological treason, a category of treason Mr. Moffat proposed should be considered here. It has become a matter of course to us that even basic research in the field of nuclear physics is top secret nowadays, and that our laboratories are financed by the military and are being guarded like war projects. And when I think what might have become of the ideas of Copernicus, or the discoveries of Newton, under present-day conditions, I begin to wonder whether we were not perhaps traitors to the spirit of science when we handed over the results of our research to the military, without considering the consequences. Now we find ourselves living in a world in which people regard the discoveries of science with dread and horror, and go in mortal fear of new discoveries. And meanwhile there seems to be very little hope that people will soon learn to live together on this ever smaller planet. We, the physicists, find that we have never before been of such consequence, and that we have never before been so completely helpless. I ask myself, therefore, whether we, the physicists, have not sometimes given too great, too indiscriminate loyalty to our government, against our better judgment—in my case, not only in the matter of the hydrogen bomb. We have spent years of our lives in developing ever sweeter means of destruction, we have been doing the work of

9. Henrik Ibsen, "Notes for a Modern Tragedy," *The Works of Henrik Ibsen*, (New York: Scribner, 1911.)

> the military, and I feel in my very bones that this was wrong. We have been doing the work of the devil, and now we return to our real tasks. We must devote ourselves entirely to research again. We cannot do better than keep the world open in the few places which can still be kept open.[10]

When a playwright represents men in action, he dramatizes their significant behavior and decisions and thus provides insight into the ways by which men live and move and have their being. In tragedy, the dramatist is concerned with the profoundest problems and the most elevated concepts of mankind, which involve the relation of his characters to their gods, the meaning of justice, and a probing into good and evil. In comedy, the playwright may exploit the ridiculous aspects of human conduct. In some forms of drama, notably farce and melodrama, the dramatist may have little or no interest in the secondary meaning of the actions of his characters. Persons in his plays are concerned only with action itself, not with the meaning of action. In creating this kind of drama, the playwright has little reference to actuality, except to require the external appearance of real life. He freely manipulates his characters according to the exigencies of his plot and excuses the absence of thought and motivation on the grounds that he is concerned only with theatrical values. He is essentially dishonest.

Whatever the purpose of the playwright, the action of significant drama is as meaningful as an experience of life itself. The choices that the characters make, their behavior and motivation, and the sequence of the events of the play are all rewarding subjects for investigation. The attitude of the playwright is inferred from his treatment of plot and character. He may be humane and sensible like Shakespeare and Molière; he may write with the scathing satire of Ben Jonson, the detachment of Congreve, the compassion of Chekhov and Hauptmann, the zeal of Eugène Brieux and the early Clifford Odets, the incisive and perplexing probing of Pirandello, the bleak pessimism of Sartre and Beckett, the comic audacity of Shaw, or the cynical objectivity of Brecht. A play, then, is more than a passing diversion unrelated to life. It is a revelation of the human condition.

As we shall see later, modern drama grew out of the nineteenth-century realism, in which serious playwrights reflected the changing thought and behavior of their times. Now the realistic playwright has given way to one who frequently is more concerned with the thought than with individual personalities. Current drama protests—sometimes against our life style, and always against man's loss of philosophic roots

10. Heinar Kipphardt, *In the Matter of J. Robert Oppenheimer* (New York: Hill and Wang, 1968).

or orientation. Another avenue of current experimentation is the attempt to find expression of the archetypal experiences and connections of man in a nonverbal theater of ritual and myth.

4. diction

Aristotle's fourth element is *diction,* by which is meant the language of the play, the words the actors speak.

The function of the diction is to provide a means for communicating the thoughts and feelings of the characters, and ultimately to convey the playwright's total meaning to the audience. As John Howard Lawson says, "Speech puts the actual impact of events into words: it dramatizes forces which are not seen." In modern drama, the dramatist's lines must, as someone has suggested, "advance the plot, delineate character, or get a laugh." Good dialogue is a means to an end, not an end in itself, for the real merit of the drama does not reside so much in wording as in its solid structure, in the sequence of the plot, in the integrity and vividness of the characterization, and in the meaning of the action behind the facade of language.

Discourse in drama must be clear, since the language must be immediately apprehended by the listener; in the theater, there is no turning back the page, no pausing to weigh and consider a line before continuing to the next. The dialogue must be interesting despite the need for simplicity and economy. It should capture the spirit of life and character. As the Irish playwright J. M. Synge put it: "In a good play, every speech should be as fully flavored as a nut or an apple." The diction must be appropriate for the character and the situation. Lines do not exist in the theater as separate entities. They are always in context, growing out of the emotionally charged incidents of the plot. The language of drama must be dynamic. As we have already suggested, speech is a form of action. Dialogue shows the character's relationship to others, reflects the progression of the action, indicates what is happening inside the characters, reveals their suffering, growth, or decline. It is a means of articulating the clash of wills and conflicting motivations. In high comedy, verbal wit may substitute for physical movement.

The dramatist needs the poet's feeling for language—a rich imagination, a facility with provocative imagery, an awareness of the weight, texture, and arrangement of words. Dramatic dialogue is not contemplative or static; it is harnessed to action and change. Even in the Japanese Noh dramas, which are often plays of reminiscence, the dialogue pulses with life of the remembered event. Finally, good dialogue must be suited for oral expression. The lines must give the actor a basic pattern for performance. They must reveal fully the character's emotions and motivations as the actor interprets them before the audience.

Much of the serious drama before the nineteenth century was linked to poetry. The Greek and Elizabethan masters of drama were poets as well as playwrights. Their works, therefore, have an added literary value, and their use of verse seems particularly appropriate for their elevated tragedies of highborn characters. In modern times poetry has given way to prose when the naturalist and realist bring onstage commonplace figures in the everyday pursuits of life. Many people have lamented the absence of poetry in the modern theater; attempts have been made to recapture some of the enrichment of the poetic speech, notably by Maxwell Anderson, Christopher Fry, Bertolt Brecht, T. S. Eliot, and Federico García Lorca. While modern drama lacks elevated language, it would be a mistake to think that all plays written in the poetic form were successful. Indeed, the use of verse in the past was often puerile and ostentatious. Many poets had no sense of dramatic form or theatrical awareness. Oftentimes, their preoccupation with the language retarded the action and filled their plays with linguistic clutter that made the drama unstageworthy.

The use of prose in the modern theater has often resulted in stage speech that is flat and pedestrian and filled with the clichés of commonplace conversation. On the other hand, the current emphasis on functional speech has brought gains in directness and clarity. In the hands of some modern playwrights, the dialogue is often vivid and evocative. The Irish drama is especially filled with the juice of life. Here is a typical fragment of Sean O'Casey's *The Plough and the Stars:*

(FLUTHER *coughs.* MRS. GOGAN, *who has wandered from the chest of drawers, down L., to the fireplace, where she is fingering Peter's shirt, turns to look at* FLUTHER, *as soon as she hears the cough.)*

MRS. GOGAN: *(with an ominous note in her voice)* Oh, you've got a cold on you, Fluther.

FLUTHER: *(carelessly)* Oh, it's only a little one.

MRS. GOGAN: You'd want to be careful, all th' same. I knew a woman, a big lump of a woman, red-faced an' round-bodied, a little awkard on her feet; you'd think, to look at her, she could put out her two arms an' lift a two-storied house on th' top of her head; got a ticklin' in her throat, an' a little cough, an' th' next mornin' she had a little catchin' in her chest, an' they had just time to wet her lips with a little rum, an' off she went. *(She begins to look at and handle the shirt)*

FLUTHER: *(a little nervously)* It's only a little cold I have; there's nothing derogatory wrong with me.

MRS. GOGAN: *(warningly)* I dunno; there's many a man this minute lowerin' a pint, thinkin' of a woman, or pickin' out a winner, or doin' work as you're doin', while th' hearse dhrawn be th' horses with the black plumes is dhrivin' up to his own hall door, an' a voice that he doesn't hear is muttherin' in his ear, "Earth to earth, an' ashes t' ashes, an' dust to dust."

FLUTHER: *(faintly, affected by her talk)* A man in th' pink o' health should have a holy horror of allowin' thoughts o' death to be festerin' in his mind, for *(with a frightened cough)* be God, I think I'm afther gettin' a little catch in me chest that time—it's a creepy thing to be thinkin' about. (FLUTHER *sits weakly in chair L. of table)*

MRS. GOGAN: It is, an' it isn't; it's both bad an' good. . . . It always gives meself a kind o' thresspassin' joy to feel meself movin' along in a mournin' coach, an' me thinkin' that, maybe, th' next funeral'll be me own, an' glad, in a quiet way, that this is somebody's else's.

FLUTHER: *(very frightened)* An' a curious kind of a gaspin' for breath—I hope there's nothin' derogatory wrong with me.

MRS. GOGAN: *(examining the shirt)* Frills on it, like a woman's petticoat.

FLUTHER: *(panic-stricken)* Suddenly gettin' hot, an' then, just as suddenly gettin' cold.

MRS. GOGAN: *(holding out the shirt towards* FLUTHER) How would you like to be wearin' this Lord Mayor's nightdress, Fluther?

FLUTHER: *(vehemently)* Blast you an' your nightshirt! Is a man fermentin' with fear to stick th' showin' off to him of a thing that looks like a shinin' shroud?[11]

As George Bernard Shaw points out, the modern drama has gained in what he calls the "discussion" element. Modern playwrights have tended to center their attention on dramatic experiences in which characters analyze and describe the forces at work on them. They do not pass through a series of adventures without cerebration. They talk over the issues and expose points of view. Nora and Helmer thrash out their differences; Mrs. Alving, Manders, and Oswald articulate their attitudes; even in Chekhov, where characters often are frustrated or crushed by the forces about them, they speak their minds and discuss the circumstances which have affected their lives. Shaw, of course, was especially fond of ventilating controversial issues, and his plays are full of shafts and barbs about all manner of problems.

Over the years dramatists have used a variety of dialogue devices. One of the most interesting, devised by the Greeks, is called *stichomythia,* which means dialogue, usually short, delivered in alternating lines. The Greek dramatist employed stichomythia as a method of building tension much as a motion picture editor uses rapid intercutting of film clips to increase intensity.

In the seventeeth-century French theater, Molière broke lines of dialogue into short, interrupted bursts of speech through the device of

11. Sean O'Casey, *The Plough and the Stars* (New York: Macmillan, 1926).

stichomythia. You will find an example of this in the scene between Toinette and Argan, *Le Malade Imaginaire* (pp. 121–122).

In *The Great White Hope,* Howard Sackler uses stichomythia for what would be in a film the shots that show the offstage action of the big fight. A man has climbed a ladder so he can see into the arena. He is describing the fight to the other men. (The "Kid" is Jack Jefferson's opponent.)

MAN 6: Kid, won't let him—
MAN 1: All he's got,
he's workin' like a butcher—
MAN 2: No—
MAN 7: He's gotta—
MAN 5: Kid—Kid—
MAN 9: Kid—
MAN 1: Hookin him
sluggin—Oh that eye—
MAN 6: Ride him out—
MAN 7: Kid—
MAN 6: Bust your hand, you—
MAN 1: Murder, it's murder—
MAN 4: No more—
MAN 2: Clinch him—
MAN 1: Ref—
MAN 6: Clinch him, dummox
MAN 2: No more—
MAN 1: Ref—
MAN 5: Stop it—
MAN 2: Ref, ya—
NEGRO BOY: Eh! Eh! Eh! Eh!
MAN 1: He's
on the ropes, he can't see, he's rollin,
he's punchy—
MAN 2: How the hell does he—
Roar.
MAN 6: Is he—
MAN 1: No, it's a bell, lemme down . . . lemme down . . .[12]

One of Shakespeare's favorite linguistic devices was the soliloquy, a solo speech used generally to analyze introspectively or to examine and weigh a future course of action. "To be or not to be" is, of course, the most familiar example. Playwrights used the convention of the soliloquy as a means of revealing the workings of a character's mind. The French neoclassicists often replaced the soliloquy with confidants for each of the

12. Howard Sackler, *The Great White Hope* (New York: Dial Press, 1968).

leading characters so that private thoughts could be bounced off the ears of servants, friends, and duennas to the audience. In popular melodrama, the soliloquy often was used as an expository device to reveal information to the audience as well as to delineate character.

The use of extended narration for recounting offstage or antecedent action has been used from the time of the Greeks to the present day. Effective examples are the Second Messenger's description of the death of Jocasta in *Oedipus Rex,* the Nurse's account of the burning of the magic gown in *Medea,* the sergeant's report of Macbeth's victory in battle, and Rodrique's unabashed 65-line description of his valor in repulsing Turks in *The Cid.* Although lengthy speeches were more widely used in dramas of the past, they are still employed occasionally today. Examples are Blanche's extended speech in which she relates the death of her sixteen-year-old lover in *A Streetcar Named Desire,* and the brutally vivid account of one of the addicts in *The Connection,* in which a single character holds the stage by himself for at least twenty minutes.

In recent times, the expressionists have revived the use of the soliloquy primarily in order to reveal character and character relationships. In Elmer Rice's *The Adding Machine,* both Mr. and Mrs. Zero speak soliloquies several pages long. An ingenious adaptation of this device is seen in Beckett's one-act *Krapp's Last Tape,* in which a single character contrasts his old age with his life some thirty years ago by listening to and commenting on a tape recording of his own voice. O'Neill and Andreyev, two twentieth-century playwrights, have used what amounts to soliloquies and asides in experimental plays to contrast a character's inner thoughts with his spoken ones. But in general, the soliloquy and the aside are rejected as inappropriate for realistic drama.

A number of recent new playwrights have refused to conform to the established techniques and conventions of the theater. These so-called absurdists are of special interest. They reject dramatic structure in order to create a new kind of dialogue. Beckett, Ionesco, and Harold Pinter, in particular, have written stage speech that, while intentionally pedestrian and hackneyed, is remarkably evocative. Their use of clichés in short segments of sound, which are combined with frequent pauses, is strangely expressive in performance. At times, this kind of dialogue is used to satirize the vacuity of commonplace conversation. At other times the very flatness of the language can serve as a kind of desperate cover to conceal the fear of silence.

The following passage of dialogue indicates Pinter's remarkable ability to create theatrical effects with the colloquial idiom. In *The Birthday Party,* Stanley has sought refuge at a seaside resort, but he has been followed by two unidentified, sinister strangers who undermine and destroy him. As they are about to take him away in their long black car, this dialogue occurs:

MC CANN: He looks better, doesn't he?
GOLDBERG: Much better.
MC CANN: A new man.
GOLDBERG: You know what we'll do?
MC CANN: What?
GOLDBERG: We'll buy him another pair. *(They begin to woo him, gently and with relish. During the following sequence,* STANLEY *shows no reaction. He remains with no movement, where he sits.)*
MC CANN: Out of our own pockets.
GOLDBERG: It goes without saying. Between you and me, Stan, it's about time you had a new pair of glasses.
MC CANN: You can't see straight.
GOLDBERG: It's true. You've been cockeyed for years.
MC CANN: Now you're even more cockeyed.
GOLDBERG: He's right. You've gone from bad to worse.
MC CANN: Worse than worse.
GOLDBERG: You need a long convalescence.
MC CANN: A change of air.
GOLDBERG: Somewhere over the rainbow.
MC CANN: Where angels fear to tread.
GOLDBERG: Exactly.
MC CANN: You're in a rut.
GOLDBERG: You look anaemic.
MC CANN: Rheumatic.
GOLDBERG: Myopic.
MC CANN: Epileptic.
GOLDBERG: You're on the verge.
MC CANN: You're a dead duck.
GOLDBERG: But we can save you.
MC CANN: From a worse fate.
GOLDBERG: True.
MC CANN: Undeniable.
GOLDBERG: From now on, we'll take the hub of your wheel.
MC CANN: We'll renew your season ticket.
GOLDBERG: We'll take twopence off your morning tea.
MC CANN: We'll give you a discount on all inflammable goods.
GOLDBERG: We'll watch over you.
MC CANN: Advise you.
GOLDBERG: Give you proper care and treatment.[13]

Other dialogue devices have been used from time to time in the theater, such as choral speeches; antiphonal passages between a leader and a group; staccato, telegraphic fragments of speech in expressionistic plays; extensive monologues, prologues, and epilogues for exposition, foreshadowing, or commenting on the action; bits of poetry, and in-

13. Harold Pinter, *The Birthday Party* (New York: Grove Press, 1959).

volved conceits and epigrams. But the primary form of diction in most drama is compressed dialogue, which, despite its conventions, gives to the listener the impression of natural conversation.

5. *music*

Aristotle's fifth element is *music*, which refers to all of the auditory material of a play. It includes sound effects and the tonal pattern of the spoken word. Music encompasses all aspects of sound—pitch, rate, quality, duration, volume, and rhythm. We remember that Greek drama had its origin in dithyrambs, and that music, chanting, and dancing were integral parts of the performance. The speech of the Athenian playwrights was created in rich patterns of verse in which the sound, texture, and cadence of the language were significant. In the Oriental theater, music continues to play an essential part in the total effect. The language of the Elizabethans often was rich in lyricism that broke out into song. Melodrama was originally linked to music, and even though the spoken word came to dominate the genre, musical backgrounds were used to accompany exits and entrances of major characters and to reinforce the mood of emotionally loaded scenes.

Although the motion picture has always exploited the evocative power of music to heighten its effects, naturalistic and realistic drama has rejected music as an artificial intrusion. But even in realistic drama, playwrights have used sound to enhance the mood of their plays. For example, Chekhov was very conscious of the use of sounds in *Uncle Vanya.* In the final act of the play a melancholy atmosphere is reinforced by the click of the counting beads, the scratch of the pen, the churring of a cricket, the tapping of the night watchman's cane, the soft strumming of a guitar, and the bells of the carriage as Dr. Astrov makes his departure. Other modern dramatists with a keen ear for the expressiveness of sound are O'Neill, Williams, Maeterlinck, García Lorca and O'Casey.

The nonrealistic playwrights, particularly the expressionists, have freely introduced music into their plays. Brecht, with his lyrical gifts, made notable use of music in novel ways—often to oppose the mood of the adjoining scenes. Of course, America's major theatrical innovation, the musical comedy, is frequently a musical exploitation of a successful play. Occasionally the musical moves away from light comedy and makes its own valid statement as drama, as in *Fiddler on the Roof, West Side Story,* and *Man of La Mancha.* Many playwrights today are intrigued with the rediscovery of ritualistic elements of the theater and their productions include a considerable amount of music and sound. An entertaining example of a ritualized version of the present-day scene is the

27 Engraving showing the lavish use of spectacle in an eighteenth-century theater in Naples.

28 (opposite, top) Hamlet confronts his father's ghost. Leslie Howard as Hamlet. Setting designed by Donald Oenslager.

29 (opposite, bottom) The final climactic scene in *Hamlet*, the duel, which leads to the denouement. Royal Shakespeare Theatre, 1961.

"tribal rock" *Hair*. Another recent development is multimedia theatrical productions, in which action, speech, visual images, music, and sound are all used at once, often not in relationship to one another but as separate entities.

6. *spectacle*

The sixth Aristotelian element of drama, *spectacle*, refers to all the visual aspects of production—scenery, lighting, costume, makeup, and the business and movement of the actors. A glance at the openings of *A Doll's House* on page 33 and *The Visit* on page 34 indicates the visual quality of drama. In the chapter on the stage designer, we will discuss at some length the nature and function of scenery, and in the chapters on forms and styles of drama, we will consider the particular contribution of spectacle to different types of plays.

The kind and amount of spectacle have varied throughout theatrical history. In the Greek, Elizabethan, and Japanese Noh plays, virtually no representation of locale is required except that supplied by the architecture itself. Nonetheless, these plays are rich in spectacle, particularly in the use of striking costumes and in the action of the performers. The use of the chorus in Greek plays, the use of dance in Noh and Kabuki drama, and the use of the entire ensemble in panoramic movement in Elizabethan plays enhance the visual appeal of the performances. With the development during the Renaissance of the proscenium arch over the stage, a taste was cultivated for pictorialism in the theater and elaborate use was made of complicated settings. The realistic and naturalistic movements in the late nineteenth century gave spectacle a new importance in production because of the scientifically inspired concern with environment as a conditioning force in determining behavior. Hence spectacle came to assume an organic, psychological role in the theater by reinforcing the meaning of the play and serving as an expository device to relate character to the social milieu. Although this view of the function of spectacle is the current one, complete and factual representation of actuality is usually tempered in practice by increasing the setting's simplicity and theatricalism.

While at times spectacle has dominated the stage, dwarfing or competing with the actor for the audience's attention, our current attitude is that the legitimate function of the visual aspects of theatrical production is to provide the appropriate psychological and physical environment for the drama, to create atmosphere, and to serve the actor's needs as he performs the play. Inasmuch as a play is intended to be acted, the action and the environment of that action contribute heavily to the impact of the play in the theater. This is spectacle.

The opening scene from *Hamlet* that follows illustrates the work of a master playwright in full command of his materials. Notice the application of the elements we have been discussing. There is skillful use of exposition as Shakespeare establishes the atmosphere of the scene and the relationship of the characters. He adroitly integrates the immediate situation with background material in such a way as to carry the action forward.

Scene I—Elsinore. A platform before the castle.
(FRANCISCO *at his post. Enter to him* BERNARDO.)

BERNARDO: Who's there?
FRANCISCO: Nay, answer me: stand, and unfold yourself.
BERNARDO: Long live the king!
FRANCISCO: Bernardo?
BERNARDO: He.
FRANCISCO: You come most carefully upon your hour.
BERNARDO: 'Tis now struck twelve; get thee to bed, Francisco.
FRANCISCO: For this relief much thanks: 'tis bitter cold, (1)
And I am sick at heart. (2)
BERNARDO: Have you had quiet guard?
FRANCISCO: Not a mouse stirring.
BERNARDO: Well, good night.
If you do meet Horatio and Marcellus,
The rivals of my watch, bid them make haste. (3)
FRANCISCO: I think I hear them. Stand, ho! Who is there?
(*Enter* HORATIO *and* MARCELLUS) (4)
HORATIO: Friends to this ground.
MARCELLUS: And liegemen to the Dane.
FRANCISCO: Give you good night.
MARCELLUS: O, farewell, honest soldier:
Who hath relieved you?
FRANCISCO: Bernardo hath my place.
Give you good night.
(Exit)
MARCELLUS: Holla! Bernardo!
BERNARDO: Say.
What, is Horatio there?
HORATIO: A piece of him.
BERNARDO: Welcome, Horatio; welcome, good Marcellus. (5)
MARCELLUS: What, has this thing appear'd again to-night? (6)
BERNARDO: I have seen nothing.
MARCELLUS: Horatio says 'tis but our fantasy,
And will not let belief take hold of him
Touching this dreaded sight, twice seen of us:
Therefore I have entreated him along
With us to watch the minutes of this night,
That if again this apparition come,
He may approve our eyes and speak of it. (7)

(1) Names and occupations of guards given and the time established.
(2) Question is raised by Francisco's feeling "sick at heart."

(3) Prepares for the entrance of Horatio and Marcellus.

(4) Entrance and identification of Horatio and Marcellus.

(5) Friendly character relationship indicated.
(6) Introduces the reason for the visit. Has "this thing" appeared again?

(7) Horatio's skepticism is established about the "dreaded sight" that guards have seen twice. Builds suspense and raises the question—will the ghost appear?

HORATIO: Tush, tush, 'twill not appear. (8)
BERNARDO: Sit down a while;
And let us once again assail your ears,
That are so fortified against our story,
What we have two nights seen.
HORATIO: Well, sit we down,
And let us hear Bernardo speak of this.
BERNARDO: Last night of all,
When yond same star that's westward from the pole
Had made his course to illume that part of heaven
Where now it burns, Marcellus and myself,
The bell then beating one,— (9)
(*Enter* GHOST) (10)
MARCELLUS: Peace, break thee off; look, where it comes again!
BERNARDO: In the same figure, like the king that's dead.
MARCELLUS: Thou art a scholar; speak to it, Horatio.
BERNARDO: Looks it not like the king? mark it, Horatio.
HORATIO: Most like it: it harrows me with fear and wonder. (11)
BERNARDO: It would be spoke to.
MARCELLUS: Question it, Horatio.
HORATIO: What art thou, that usurp'st this time of night,
Together with that fair and warlike form
In which the majesty of buried Denmark
Did sometimes march? by heaven I charge thee, speak!
MARCELLUS: It is offended.
BERNARDO: See, it stalks away.
HORATIO: Stay! speak, speak! I charge thee, speak! (12)

(*Exit* GHOST) (13)
MARCELLUS: 'Tis gone, and will not answer.
BERNARDO: How now, Horatio! you tremble and look pale:
Is not this something more than fantasy?
What think you on't?
HORATIO: Before my God, I might not this believe
Without the sensible and true avouch
Of mine own eyes.
MARCELLUS: Is it not like the king?
HORATIO: As thou art to thyself:
Such was the very armor he had on
When he the ambitious Norway combated;
So frown'd he once, when, in an angry parle,
He smote the sledded Polacks on the ice. (14)
'Tis strange.
MARCELLUS: Thus twice before, and jump at this dead hour,
With martial stalk hath he gone by our watch. (15)
HORATIO: In what particular thought to work I know not;
But, in the gross and scope of my opinion,

8) Horatio, the scholar, voices his skepticism.

(9) Bernardo describes previous encounters. Prepares for ghost's entrance.
(10) Ghost's entrance destroys Horatio's skepticism and raises the questions—Who is the ghost? Why does it appear? First complication and point of attack.

(11) Discovery. The ghost is recognized as King Hamlet. Establishes credibility of the ghost and makes the question more specific and compelling—what is the meaning of the ghost reappearing? "Fear and wonder" emotional response.

(12) Ghost acts as if it would speak. Unsuccessful attempts to question it add suspense.
(13) Exit of ghost delays answer. Strengthens question—why does the ghost of the dead king reappear? What does it want to say?

(14) Recognition reasserted. Emotions aroused; suspense and atmosphere established.

(15) Repetition of antecedent experiences adds to anxiety.

MARCELLUS: Good now, sit down, and tell me, he that knows,
Why this same strict and most observant watch
So nightly toils the subject of the land,
And why such daily cast of brazen cannon,
And foreign mart for implements of war;
Why such impress of shipwrights, whose sore task
Does not divide the Sunday from the week;
This bodes some strange eruption to our state. (16)
What might be toward, that this sweaty haste
Doth make the night joint-laborer with the day:
Who is't that can inform me? (17)
HORATIO: That can I;
At least the whisper goes so. Our last king,
Whose image even but now appear'd to us,
Was, as you know, by Fortinbras of Norway,
Thereto prick'd on by a most emulate pride,
Dared to the combat; in which our valiant Hamlet—
For so this side of our known world esteem'd him—
Did slay this Fortinbras; who by a seal'd compact
Well ratified by law and heraldry,
Did forfeit, with his life, all those his lands
Which he stood seized of, to the conqueror:
Against the which, a moiety competent
Was gaged by our king; which had return'd
To the inheritance of Fortinbras,
Had he been vanquisher; as, by the same covenant
And carriage of the article design'd,
His fell to Hamlet. Now, sir, young Fortinbras,
Of unimproved metal hot and full,
Hath in the skirts of Norway here and there
Shark'd up a list of lawless resolutes,
For food and diet, to some enterprise
That hath a stomach in't: which is no other—
As it doth well appear unto our state—
But to recover of us, by strong hand
And terms compulsatory, those foresaid lands
So by his father lost: and this, I take it,
Is the main motive of our preparations,
The source of this our watch and the chief head
Of this post-haste and romage in the land. (18)
BERNARDO: I think it be no other but e'en so:
Well may it sort, that this portentous figure
Comes armed through our watch, so like the king
That was and is the question of these wars. (19)
HORATIO: A mote it is to trouble the mind's eye.
In the most high and palmy state of Rome,
A little ere the mightiest Julius fell,

(16) Apprehension expressed for the state.

(17) Marcellus asks the meaning of the preparations for war. Are they related to the appearance of the ghost of Hamlet?

(18) Horatio provides exposition and sketches the political background. Provides the frame of reference of the social situation. Notice that Shakespeare first captures the attention, builds atmosphere and suspense, and then provides this lengthy explanation.

(19) Search for meaning of the ghost's appearance as an armed figure.

The graves stood tenantless, and the sheeted dead
Did squeak and gibber in the Roman streets:
As stars with trains of fire and dews of blood,
Disasters in the sun; and the moist star,
Upon whose influence Neptune's empire stands,
Was sick almost to doomsday with eclipse:
And even the like precurse of fierce events,
As harbingers preceding still the fates
And prologue to the omen coming on,
Have heaven and earth together demonstrated
Unto our climatures and countrymen. (20)
(*Re-enter* GHOST) (21)
But soft, behold! lo, where it comes again!
I'll cross it, though it blast me. Stay, illusion!
If thou hast any sound, or use of voice,
Speak to me:
If there be any good thing to be done,
That may to thee do ease and grace to me,
Speak to me:
If thou art privy to thy country's fate,
Which, happily, foreknowing may avoid,
O, speak!
Or if thou hast uphoarded in thy life
Extorted treasure in the womb of earth,
For which, they say, you spirits oft walk in death,
Speak of it: stay, and speak! (22) (*The cock crows*) (23)
Stop it, Marcellus.

MARCELLUS: Shall I strike at it with my partisan?
HORATIO: Do, if it will not stand.
BERNARDO: 'Tis here!
HORATIO: 'Tis here!
(*Exit* GHOST) (24)
MARCELLUS: 'Tis gone!
We do it wrong, being so majestical,
To offer it the show of violence;
For it is, as the air, invulnerable,
And our vain blows malicious mockery. (25)
BERNARDO: It was about to speak, when the cock crew.
HORATIO: And then it started like a guilty thing
Upon a fearful summons. I have heard,
The cock, that is the trumpet to the morn,
Doth with his lofty and shrill-sounding throat
Awake the god of day, and at his warning,
Whether in sea or fire, in earth or air,
The extravagant and erring spirit hies
To his confine: and of the truth herein
This present object made probation.

(20) Atmosphere of foreboding is reinforced by vivid imagery.
(21) Second appearance of ghost strengthens question and builds suspense further. Will it speak? Notice that this entrance follows a static sequence and thrusts the action forward again.

(22) Scene rises to a climax and crisis as Horatio repeatedly asks the ghost to speak.
(23) Cock crows, deferring the ghost's answers to questions.

(24) Ghost's exit adds further emphasis to suspense and purpose of the ghost. Carries tension forward when the meaning is still in doubt.

(25) Awe and wonder at the "majestical" ghost.

MARCELLUS: It faded on the crowing of the cock.
Some say that ever 'gainst that season comes
Wherein our Saviour's birth is celebrated,
The bird of dawning singeth all night long:
And then, they say, no spirit dare stir abroad,
The nights are wholesome, then no planets strike,
No fairy takes nor witch hath power to charm,
So hallow'd and so gracious is the time.
HORATIO: So have I heard and do in part believe it.
But look, the morn, in russet mantle clad,
Walks o'er the dew of yon high eastward hill:
Break we our watch up; and by my advice,

Let us impart what we have seen to-night
Unto young Hamlet; for, upon my life,
This spirit, dumb to us, will speak to him:
Do you consent we shall acquaint him with it,
As needful in our loves, fitting our duty? (26)
MARCELLUS: Let's do't, I pray; and I this morning know
Where we shall find him most conveniently.
(Exeunt) (27)

(26) Guards and Horatio search for meaning. Daylight comes. They plan for future action. Will the ghost speak to Hamlet?

(27) Their exit carries the suspense and questions forward into the play. Builds up tension and anticipation for the meeting between Hamlet and his father's ghost.

exercises

1. Distinguish between plot and story.
2. Write three scenes of discovery.
3. Compare the opening scene of *Hamlet* with that of *Antigone*.
4. What are the characteristics of dramatic dialogue?
5. Write out a summary of the plot incidents of a play or film.
6. Record a sample of overheard dialogue and compare it with that of a play.
7. Devise a statement for the thought element suitable for a play and devise a series of complications to develop it.
8. How do the so-called classical unities affect dramatic structure?
9. Contrast the spectacle of a Greek play with that of a modern drama.
10. Create a dramatic character and indicate the various methods of delineating his qualities.
11. Using *The Visit* as a model, create the opening exposition for an original play.
12. Distinguish between suspense and surprise and give an example of each.
13. Discuss the playwright's methods for building emotional climaxes.
14. Discuss the uses of reversal in dramatic structure.
15. Cite examples of foreshadowing in *Antigone* and *Hamlet*.
16. Write a short biography of an imaginary character. Describe his basic motivations and describe some means by which you would make his inner life clear to the audience.

suggested reading

Bernard Beckerman, *Dynamics of Drama*, 1970.
Eric Bentley, *The Life of the Drama*, 1967.
Hubert C. Heffner, Samuel Selden, and Hunton D. Sellman, *Modern Theatre Practice*, 4th ed., 1959.
H. D. F. Kitto, *Form and Meaning in Drama*, 1956.
John Howard Lawson, *Theory and Technique of Playwriting*, 1936.
Kenneth Thorpe Rowe, *The Theater in Your Head*, 1959.
J. L. Styan, *The Dramatic Experience*, 1965.
Alan Reynolds Thompson, *The Anatomy of Drama*, 1942.

play list

Friedrich Duerrenmatt, *The Visit*
Henrik Ibsen, *A Doll's House*
Eugène Ionesco, *Chairs*
Heinar Kipphardt, *In the Matter of J. Robert Oppenheimer*
Eugene O'Neill, *Anna Christie*
Tennessee Williams, *The Glass Menagerie*

tragedy

One of the most perplexing human phenomena is the paradox of deriving pleasure through pain. What satisfaction can we obtain from watching the undeserved punishment of a well-intentioned heroine like Antigone? What is the aesthetic justification for involving ourselves in Hamlet's ordeal in an alien world? How can we find enjoyment in the decline and fall of a powerful king like Oedipus? In an attempt to answer these questions we need to consider the nature of tragedy.

The idea of tragedy is man-made. There is no ideal of tragedy—only a small collection of plays that (with more or less agreement) we call tragedies. Of the original Greek tragedies fewer than ten percent are extant, so we have only very small sampling. Even among the Greeks, there was no one typical tragedy. Moroever, tragedies from other periods, such as the Elizabethan and the French neoclassic times, differ markedly from those of the Greeks.

In addition to the plays, we have a body of critical theory about tragedy that is even more diverse and contradictory than the plays themselves. The seminal work on tragedy was written for Greeks about Greek drama by the Greek Aristotle. Therefore, to us, his views are very restricted, since obviously life and thought have changed astonishingly since his time. Aristotle set a pattern, followed by so many critics since, of making generalizations from carefully selected examples that supported his view. He based most of his theory on Sophocles, and although

he refers to Euripides as the "most tragic of poets," he devotes little attention to him or to the other great writer of Greek tragedy, Aeschylus. Neither of these dramatists wrote in a way that satisfied Aristotle. As for the neoclassicists, they wrote in rigid conformity to Aristotle's "rules," but they distorted and misunderstood his thought. The Elizabethans, Shakespeare and his contemporaries, wrote for their audiences and, except for Ben Jonson, paid no attention to theory.

It is apparent, then, that tragedy has a varied background and that, in both theory and practice, it is susceptible to many interpretations. Despite these difficulties, the quest for the tragic spirit is worth pursuing, remembering that ultimately tragedy is a quality of experience which each one must come to know for himself.

aristotle's definition of tragedy

Let us turn our attention to Aristotle's very significant definition of tragedy and then examine his terms: "Tragedy, then, is an imitation of an action that is serious, complete, and of a certain magnitude; in language embellished with each kind of artistic ornament, the several kinds being found in separate parts of the play; in the form of action, not of narrative; through pity and fear effecting the proper purgation of these emotions."[1]

The origin of the word tragedy is a matter of conjecture. "Tragos" in Greek means goat; "oide" means song. The exact connection of goat-song to drama is not clear, although three hypotheses are advanced: (1) a goat was sacrificed as part of the original improvised ritual honoring Dionysus; (2) the chorus wore goatskins for costumes; and (3) a goat was offered as a prize in the early choral contests. In any case, tragedy was associated with goat-song or goat-singer in its early stages. The terms "tragic" and "tragedy" as we use them in everyday speech have little to do with "tragedy" as a form of drama. A person may speak of the "tragic" death of a small girl in an automobile accident. While tragedy usually involves catastrophe, it is not the calamity itself on which attention is focused in drama. Death may even seem incidental, as in *Hamlet* or *Romeo and Juliet* when it occurs to such secondary characters as Polonius, Paris, or Tybalt. The validity of genuine tragedy is not concerned with the act of violence, but with what that act says about life—the struggle of the protagonist, the issues at stake, the effect of his suffering.

Tragedy has been called the drama of *high seriousness.* It deals with the most profound and universal problems of man—his purpose

1. Ingram Bywater, trans., *Aristotle on the Art of Poetry* (Oxford: Clarendon, 1920).

30 Greek tragic mask.

31 Scene from *Oedipus Rex* at the National Theater, Prague. Designed by Josef Svoboda, directed by M. Machacek.

32 José Ferrer in *Oedipus Rex* at the University of Utah. Directed by Byron McGrath, designed by Vern Adix.

and destiny, the nature of good and evil, a man's relationship to forces greater than himself, the consequences of individual responsibility. Tragedy is never frivolous, trivial, or mean. It goes far beyond diversion or amusement to investigate spiritual values and struggles.

Tragedy attains *magnitude* in the heroic stature of its characters, in the use of poetry, in the universality of its meaning, and in the loftiness of its ideas. Tragedies are elevated; they possess scale and scope far beyond the petty vicissitudes of daily existence. Magnitude of character is realized in tragedy through the use of highborn characters, persons of nobility and prominence who occupy "exposed positions"; people who as Aristotle said "are better than we are."

A tragedy is *complete;* it has a beginning, a middle, and an end—and each of these parts is causally related, thus creating a unified effect because the plot is a well-articulated structure with no extraneous material. The course of action is a "necessary and probable" linking of antecedents and consequents. Such unity and wholeness are fundamental to the Greek aesthetic view of life.

By *language with each kind of artistic ornament,* Aristotle explains, "I mean that with rhythm and harmony or song superadded; and by *the kinds separately,* I mean that some portions are worked out with verse only, and others in turn with song."

The chief difference between the *dramatic* and *narrative form* is a result of the manner of presentation. A narrative may be written or told; drama must be presented with impersonation and action—it is "a thing done." The dramatic form puts the creative work of the playwright before an audience in the theater by means of the actors' performance.

Pity, fear, and *catharsis* are terms that have perplexed and intrigued scholars and critics for generations. Because tragedy aims to produce this special effect, it will be discussed at length later in the chapter. For a preliminary statement let us realize that pity goes beyond mere pathos to include the compassion that accompanies shared grief, and that fear transcends sheer fright to convey a sense of anxious concern and profound reverence. Catharsis suggests purgation and purification—a release of emotional tension that results in tranquility.

With Aristotle's definition in mind, and acknowledging its shortcomings due to his limited basis for observation, let us consider some important principles that characterize tragedy.

plot

Are there aspects of plot that apply exclusively to tragedy? Aristotle felt that the tragic effect was achieved through structure, and he specified the "necessary and probable" arrangement of the incidents, the preferred kinds of recognitions, reversals, and denouements, in addition to the qualities of the tragic hero. Note then a basic Aristotelian concept: *the form of the action determines its effect.*

Susanne K. Langer in advancing her perceptive theory of the tragic rhythm stresses the form:

> Dramatic acts are analogously connected with each other so that one directly or indirectly motivates what follows it. In this way a genuine rhythm of action is set up. . . . That rhythm is the "commanding form" of the play; it springs from the poet's original conception of the "fable," and dictates the major divisions of the work, the light or heavy style of its presentation, the intensity of the highest feeling and most violent act, the great or small number of characters, and the degrees of their development. The total action is a cumulative form and because it is constructed by a rhythmic treatment of its elements, it appears to *grow* from its beginnings.[2]

Yet Aristotle's tenet of unity of action—a plot simple enough to be held easily in the mind of the spectator—does not apply to Elizabethan drama. Moreover, Shakespeare and his contemporaries disregarded unity in their combination of comic and serious material, their high- and low-born characters, their mixture of verse and prose, their plots and subplots that rambled about freely on the flexible Elizabethan stage.

Tragedy does not depend on the Aristotelian form. It may be achieved by any system of actions that succeeds in creating the emotional effects of tragedy.

There are certain generalizations, however, that apply to the treatment of dramatic materials. Tragedy usually deals with a positive and active protagonist caught in sharp conflict with opposing forces. In the ensuing struggle, he suffers greatly and goes to disaster. Tragic conflicts are of a particular kind. The struggle is ethical, spiritual. Often the tragic hero is placed in a situation in which the courses of action open to him are at war with the moral order that he has accepted. Tragic tension is built on inner conflicts that test the protagonist's integrity.

In the organization of the incidents, the playwright must solve the customary problems of plot construction; he must create climaxes, crises, reversals, discoveries, etc., but always with a view as to what the events reveal about the hero. The interest is not in the incidents themselves, but what is going on inside—the effect on the protagonist's soul. When the dramatist reverses this point of view and makes the external action his primary concern, he writes melodrama. This is precisely what happened in English drama after Shakespeare, when Beaumont and Fletcher, Ford, Massinger, and Tourneur filled the stage with grisly and violent action.

2. Susanne K. Langer, "Tragic Rhythm," from *Feeling and Form* (New York: Scribner, 1953).

The writer of genuine tragedy constructs a plot that emphasizes "inwardness."

Because tragedy is relentlessly honest, the dramatist does not contrive a denouement to save the hero from catastrophe, or to spare him from suffering. Orestes is rescued from the Eumenides by divine intervention because Aeschylus was expressing his concern about institutionalized justice. Oedipus lives on after his crimes are revealed, but not as a concession to the sentimental satisfaction of the audience. Orestes and Oedipus both undergo excruciating suffering. When Corneille worked out a happy ending for the lovers in *The Cid,* he made his play a tragicomedy instead of a tragedy. In most tragedy, the catastrophic denouement is the "necessary and probable" outcome of the conflict.

Scenes of discovery or recognition are very important to the tragic plot. Aristotle admired discoveries which resulted in reversals, as in *Oedipus Rex.* Writers of tragedy demonstrated great skill in devising effective discoveries, such as Electra's recognition of Orestes, the ghost in *Hamlet,* Creon's discovery of the burial of Polyneices, and Sophocles' consummate craftsmanship in exposing Oedipus's guilt through a gradual revelation of the past. But far more important than these plotting devices are the scenes of self-discovery, when characters examine their actions and motives against the background of their moral codes. These "moments of truth" are singularly characteristic of great tragedy. One thinks of Phaedra's and Macbeth's horror when they realize the full import of their actions; of Hamlet's agonizing self-analysis when he tries to square appearance with reality; of Creon's and Othello's bitter suffering when their worlds tumble about them; of the self-torture of Oedipus when his crimes are known. Such discoveries contribute to the feelings of pity and fear, because they cause the audience to generalize from the individual experience of the tragic hero to a universal application. As the protagonist makes his discovery, we discover something of ourselves.

the tragic hero

Another Aristotelian concept of fundamental importance to the understanding of tragedy is the nature of the tragic hero. In his analysis of suitable figures to play the heroic role, Aristotle rejects three kinds of men before arriving at the most suitable one. Notice that the basis for his selection is the effect on an audience:

> It follows, therefore, that there are three forms of Plot to be avoided. (1) A good man must not be seen passing from happiness to misery or (2) a bad man from misery to happiness. The first situation is not fear-inspiring or piteous, but simply odious to us. The second is the most

> untragic that can be; it has no one of the requisites of Tragedy; it does not appeal either to the human feeling in us, or to our pity, or to our fears. Nor, on the other hand, should (3) an extremely bad man be seen falling from happiness into misery. Such a story may arouse the human feeling in us, but it will not move us either to pity or fear; pity is occasioned by undeserved misfortune, and fear by that of one like ourselves; so that there will be nothing either piteous or fear-inspiring in the situation. There remains, then, the intermediate kind of personage, a man not pre-eminently virtuous and just, whose misfortune, however, is brought upon him not by vice and depravity but by some error of judgment.[3]

The tragic hero is a good man, but not free from blemish—"an intermediate kind of personage" who, while not preeminently virtuous, is not depraved. His flaw is an error in judgment. This flaw (*hamartia*) has been the source of considerable controversy since it is not uniformly applicable to all tragedies, nor does it appear consistent with the variety of characters involved in catastrophes.

Aristotle seems to suggest that all tragic heroes should have about the same moral qualities, which is not the case at all. How does one equate the suffering of Prometheus with that of Oedipus? Antigone or Hippolytus with Medea? Hamlet with Macbeth, Lear with Romeo and Juliet? The degree of guilt seems to have little or nothing to do with justice. All tragic figures suffer, regardless of their degree of guilt or responsibility. Sometimes their fall seems to proceed not so much from crime and punishment as from cause and effect. Pity is not related to vengeance, but to "undeserved misfortune." Our attention then as we look at the hero is not on his guilt or innocence, but on the quality of his spirit. How does he respond to these "boundary situations" when he is tested to the limit? What is the effect on him of evil and injustice?

Northrop Frye gives us the image of the tragic hero at the top of the wheel of fortune, above humanity and below something greater in the sky, who acts as a "conductor" of power from above. "Tragic heroes are wrapped in the mystery of their communion with that something beyond which we can see only through them and which is the source of their strength and their fate alike."[4]

Susanne K. Langer sees the "tragic rhythm" transferred from natural activity to the sphere of human action in its pattern of growth, maturation and decline. The action of the play shows the hero's "self-realization" as, under increasing pressure, he reaches the limit of development and the final relinquishment of power—in "the vision of life as accomplished . . . the sense of fulfillment that lifts him above his defeat."[5]

3. *Aristotle on the Art of Poetry.*
4. Northrop Frye, "The Mythos of Autumn: Tragedy," from *The Anatomy of Criticism* (Princeton: Princeton University Press, 1957).
5. Langer, *Feeling and Form.*

tragedy deals with significant content

Tragedy achieves significance because it is concerned with the deep and abiding questions and problems that have perplexed man throughout the ages. As Allardyce Nicoll says, tragedy puts us in "contact with infinity. If we are religious, we shall say it is in contact with forces divine; if we are aesthetic, we shall say it is in contact with the vast illimitable forces of the universe. Everywhere in tragedy there is this sense of being raised to loftier heights."[6]

Henry Alonzo Myers asserts that "tragedy best expresses its conceptions of the orderly and absolute nature of values"; and Francis Fergusson observes that tragedy "celebrates the mystery of human nature and destiny with the health of the soul in view." Tragedy is oriented toward man's spiritual nature. It confronts suffering and evil with relentless honesty in such a way as to reveal both the weakness and nobility of man, his strength of will, and his capacity for suffering without breaking in the face of inevitable doom. Tragedy is not the drama of small souls bedeviled by the minor irritations of humdrum life. It does not concentrate on man's physical environment or welfare, nor with his getting and spending, his thing-collecting. On the contrary, tragedy lifts our vision beyond petty cares and mundane anxieties by forcing our attention on the great issues of life that affect our spiritual welfare. Clytemnestra is caught between avenging the death of her daughter and her duty to her husband; Antigone between her sacred obligation to the dead and obedience to the king; Hamlet between the necessity of avenging the death of his father and his moral sensibilities; Lear between sympathy and pride; Macbeth between ambition and conscience. Tragedy deals with matters of great consequence.

The significant content of tragedy gives this form of drama a sense of universality. The effect of the play goes beyond the particular characters and the immediate circumstances to achieve an atmosphere of broad application. If even kings may suffer, how vulnerable are we? To the Greeks and Elizabethans the fate of the ruler was connected directly with that of his subjects. There is implicit in genuine tragedy not only an elevation of life, but also an acute awareness of our common frailty and humanity. Thus the suffering and struggles of the tragic hero become a part of the universal experience of those who share the play.

In its magnitude and elevation, however, we must recognize that tragedy is removed a step from life. To perceive its great scope and grandeur, we need a certain amount of distance and perspective. In high tragedy there is a sense of aloofness and detachment, which in its most severe expression threatens to throw a chill of austerity over the drama

6. Allardyce Nicoll, *The Theory of Drama* (New York: Crowell, 1931).

and the characters. On the other hand, the universality of the problems and the degree of suffering draw us into the action.

tragedy produces a catharsis

The most significant element that distinguishes tragedy from other forms of drama is the tragic effect. Just what it is in tragedy that gives pleasure through pain is difficult to determine. Schlegel felt that the tragic tone was one of "irrepressible melancholy" as the audience is consoled and elevated through witnessing human weakness, exposed to the vagaries of fate and natural forces. Schopenhauer saw the meaning of tragedy as resignation and renunciation in the face of a miserable and desolate existence. On the other hand, Myers sees evidence of a just order in tragedy:

> Since it is positive and affirmative, great tragic poetry satisfies our deepest rational and moral inclinations. As rational beings, we are always looking for patterns, for order, for meaning in experience; as moral beings, we can be satisfied only by discovering in the realm of good and evil the special kind of pattern or order which we call justice. Tragedy reconciles us to evil by showing us that it is not a single, separate phenomenon but one side of change of fortune, and makes us feel that the change of fortune of a representative man is just.[7]

From these opposing statements, it is clear that what constitutes the tragic effect is capable of many interpretations. The effect is complex and highly personalized, arrived at through one's own contacts with life. In such plays as *Hamlet* and *Oedipus Rex*, we perceive values beyond the story and stage action as we seek to interpret the play with our experience and with our attitudes about life. Thus, the events of the play are raised to a universal level and move us, as Alan Thompson says, "to the impassioned contemplation of ultimates."

In any discussion of the tragic effect it is necessary to keep Aristotle's words "fear and pity" before us. What did he mean by them? Pity is not simply pathos, a soft sentiment of sorrow for one who is weak or unworthy. Pity is not contemptuous or patronizing. Tragic pity implies an equality, a sharing of grief. We enter into the experience of another through our sympathy and our fellow-feeling. Our pity for the tragic hero is an act of compassion.

Aristotle's concept of fear extends beyond sheer fright or terror to include anxious concern, solicitude, awe, reverence, and apprehension. In tragedy, fear is not merely a hair-raising, spine-tingling reaction of

7. Henry Alonzo Myers, *Tragedy: A View of Life* (Ithaca: Cornell University Press, 1956).

the nervous system; it is an emotion that warms the heart and illuminates the mind. Fear carries a sense of wonder. The terms fear and pity, therefore, must be universalized into a general concern for others, rather than remaining a private and personal identification with disaster.

What arouses fear and pity? Aristotle suggests that they are aroused by the suffering of a good but flawed man, involved in a fearful deed committed in ignorance, affecting persons who are close relatives or friends. He said that the good man is the best type of hero because a bad man evokes no pity (he gets what he deserves), and the suffering of a perfect man violates our sense of justice. He said that the fearful deed affecting someone close to the hero must be committed in ignorance, because if it were done knowingly, the hero would not be a good man. The commission of the deed in ignorance sets up the plot mechanism of recognition that Aristotle admired so much. Interestingly enough, the tragic deed he regarded as the "best" was a discovery made before the deed was perpetrated, as in *Iphigenia in Tauris* where Orestes is rescued in time by the recognition of his sister. Aristotle's view of the tragic deed is too narrow and does not apply to many tragedies, among them *Antigone, Hamlet, King Lear, Othello,* and the *Oresteia.*

Fear and pity are not the automatic result of following a dramatic formula. We have the capacity for compassion for many kinds of people, good and bad, in many kinds of situations, provided that we have understanding. Our sympathies can go out to foolish and evil characters like Lear and Macbeth; it is easier for us to understand the guilty passion of Phèdre than the self-righteousness of Hippolytus. What really counts is our ability to enter into the suffering of the characters as they are tested, and to find within ourselves an echo of their frailty and their flaws.

A. C. Bradley makes an interesting and valid contribution by pointing out his belief that in the catharsis of tragedy pity and fear unite with a profound sense of mystery and sadness due to the impression of waste.[8] In the catastrophe, something of value is destroyed. Important and worthwhile connections are broken. This is perhaps one of the reasons the layman speaks of the "tragedy" that occurs through some accident to a person of promise, who had a potential, a future before him. We do not have this same response to one along in years who has lived out his life. In the grief that accompanied the assassination of the Kennedys and Martin Luther King, there was the feeling of great waste. Bradley's view may also help to explain how there may be a kind of catharsis in dramas that deal with characters of small stature because of the sense of waste that their careers give to us. Blanche DuBois in *A Streetcar Named Desire,* Willy Loman in *Death of a Salesman* and Mother Courage in Brecht's play possess admirable potential which their society does not allow them to realize, and in their suffering we feel a sense of loss.

8. A. C. Bradley, *Shakespearean Tragedy* (London: Macmillan, 1957).

33 *Hamlet*, the play within the play. Stratford Shakespeare Festival production, Ontario, Canada.

34 *Mother Courage,* directed by Bertolt Brecht at the Munich Kammerspiele, 1950. Setting designed by Teo Otto.

35 (opposite, top) Modern production of *Romeo and Juliet* at the National Theater, Prague. Directed by O. Krejca, setting by Josef Svoboda.

36 (opposite, bottom) Final scene from Henry Irving's nineteenth-century English production of *Romeo and Juliet.*

37 The same scene from a German production. Note the romanticism in the staging.

38 Shakespeare's *Troilus and Cressida* produced at UCLA, directed by Henry Goodman, designed by Donald Crabs.

39 A climactic moment from Eugene O'Neill's *Desire Under the Elms*, a modern tragedy. Photo © Arnold Newman.

There is another interesting ramification of the notion that tragedy severs valuable connections. Most criticism centers on the main figures in the tragic deed but it also seems true that most if not all of the important connections are destroyed. For example, *Hamlet* not only suffers a break with his parents, but also with Ophelia, Laertes, Rosencrantz, Guildenstern and, at the end, Horatio. In *Antigone* connections are broken between the heroine and Haemon and Ismene, and between Creon, Haemon, and Eurydice. Macbeth suffers the loss of all his valued connections. It appears then that a part of the emotional force of tragedy comes from a general disintegration of valuable ties.

This emotional response to tragedy is a complex one. It must be broad enough to encompass a variety of experiences and extensive enough to include shades of feeling such as the heartbreak at the end of *King Lear, Phèdre, Romeo and Juliet,* and *Oedipus Rex;* the sense of triumph at the end of *Hamlet, The Crucible,* and *Antigone;* and the appalling sense of waste at the end of *Macbeth, Ghosts,* and *Othello.* Aristotle obviously intended that the catharsis should be therapeutic, a purging of the spectator's fear and pity, resulting in a sense of release and tranquility. He is cleansed and exhilarated when he is liberated from his own emotional entanglements, his disturbing passions. Fear gives way to certainty, even though that certainty is death. Pity goes beyond feeling and becomes understanding. The spectator leaves the theater "in calm of mind, all passion spent." The end result is, as Northrop Frye suggests, that the audience experiences a "kind of buoyancy." Or again, in Edith Hamilton's words, "the great soul in pain and death transforms and exalts pain and death." Myers universalizes the meaning more explicitly:

> These are the main features of the tragic spirit. It lifts us above self-pity and reconciles us to suffering by showing that evil is a necessary part of the intelligible and just order of our experience. It lifts us above the divisive spirit of melodrama by showing that men are neither naturally good nor inherently evil. It saves us all from the pitfalls of utopianism and fatalism. It teaches moderation by showing that the way of the extremist is short, but at the same time it shows the man of principle that an uncompromising stand is not without its just compensations. And most important, it teaches us that all men are united in the kinship of a common fate, that all are destined to suffer and enjoy, each according to his capacity.[9]

tragedy is positive

Although tragedy involves suffering, evil, and death, it is a positive statement about life. As Nicoll says, "Death never really matters in

9. Myers, *Tragedy.*

tragedy. . . . Tragedy assumes that death is inevitable and that its time of coming is of no importance compared with what a man does before his death."[10]

Death may overtake the protagonist, but he is spiritually victorious. He is not an abject, craven victim of fate who goes cowering to his doom. The principles for which he lived and died survive his passing. The hero dies; heroism lives on. We admire the audacity of the man who, disregarding human fraility, reveals an astonishing capacity for suffering in matters of the spirit. His action is an affirmation of life. He sustains our faith in mankind.

tragedy is honest

The writer of tragedy is unflinchingly honest. He shows life as it is, not as one wishes it might be. He has the courage to confront the terrors and perplexities of life; he acknowledges man's frailties. His plots are not manipulated to spare the protagonist; the hero goes relentlessly to his catastrophe. Nor does tragedy demonstrate poetic justice in which the virtuous are rewarded and the wicked punished. Instead, the dramatist shows the clash between our desire for justice and what really happens. He presents the evil along with the good. In the treatment of character, the protagonist is not the white-washed, idealized hero of romanticism or the black-hearted villain of melodrama. He is a mixture of clay and stardust. He is an admirable character, but he usually possesses a flaw, and his imperfection links him to us. Tragedy rests on a solid basis of integrity, making no concessions to the wish-fulfillment desires of the audience. In Anouilh's modern version of *Antigone* the chorus makes this cogent statement about tragedy:

> Tragedy is clean, it is firm, it is flawless. It has nothing to do with melodrama—with wicked villains, persecuted maidens, avengers, gleams of hope and eleventh-hour repentances. Death, in melodrama, is really horrible because it is never inevitable. The dear old father might so easily have been saved; the honest young man might so easily have brought in the police five minutes earlier. In a tragedy, nothing is in doubt and everyone's destiny is known. That makes for tranquility. Tragedy is restful; and the reason is that *hope*, that foul, deceitful thing, has no part in it. There isn't any hope. You're trapped. The whole sky has fallen on you, and all you can do about it is to shout. Now don't mistake me: I said "shout": I did not say groan, whimper, complain. *That*, you cannot do. But you can *shout* aloud; you can get all those things said that you never thought you'd be able to say—or never knew you had it in you to say. And you don't say these things because it will do any good to say

10. Nicoll, *Theory of Drama.*

them: you know better than that. You say them for their own sake; you say them because you learn a lot from them. In melodrama, you argue and struggle in the hope of escape. That is vulgar; it's practical. But in tragedy, where there is no temptation to try to escape, argument is gratuitous: it's kingly.[11]

diction

The elevated style of tragedy with its characters and themes of great magnitude required poetic language, and tragedy is characterized by the grandeur of the diction. But like all good language for the stage, it is functional—as an appropriate level of speech for the dramatic situation, not as a separate element of the play. In general, tragedy has been written by men with poetic gifts who have the ability to combine dignity with clarity, who speak with an eloquence that is free from bombast or self-conscious display. Their verse gives a lift to the drama through the use of images and rhythms that have the essential quality of being eminently speakable. The language is a form of dramatic action and has a special evocative power to suggest a meaning beyond the sound and image. Like tragedy itself, it has the quality of universality. Note the full range of one of Sophocles' choral odes from *Antigone:*

The world is full of wonderful things,
But none more so than man,
This prodigy who sails before the storm-winds,
Cutting a path across the sea's gray face
Beneath the towering menace of the waves.
And Earth, the oldest, the primeval god,
Immortal, inexhaustible Earth,
She too has felt the weight of his hand
As year after year the mules are harnessed
And plows go back and forwards in the fields.
Merry birds and forest beasts,
Fish that swim in the deep waters,
Are gathered into the woven nets,
Of man the crafty hunter.
He conquers with his arts
The beasts that roam in the wild-hill country;
He tames the horses with their shaggy manes
Throwing a harness about their necks,
And the tireless mountain bull.

Speech he has made his own, and thought
That travels swift as the wind,

11. Jean Anouilh, *Antigone*, trans. Lewis Galantière (London: Van Loewen, 1946).

40 Nineteenth-century German staging of *King Lear*.

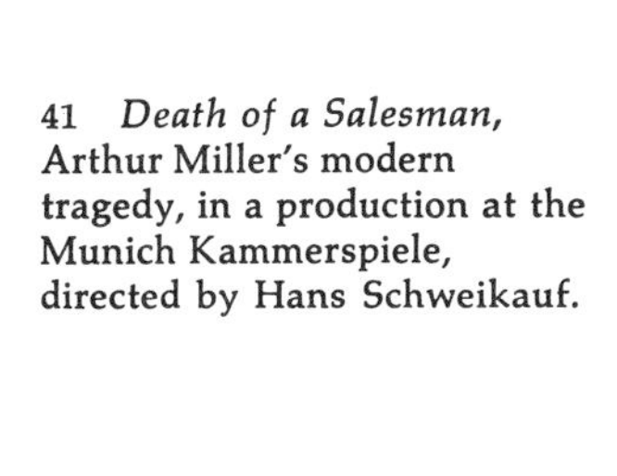

41 *Death of a Salesman,* Arthur Miller's modern tragedy, in a production at the Munich Kammerspiele, directed by Hans Schweikauf.

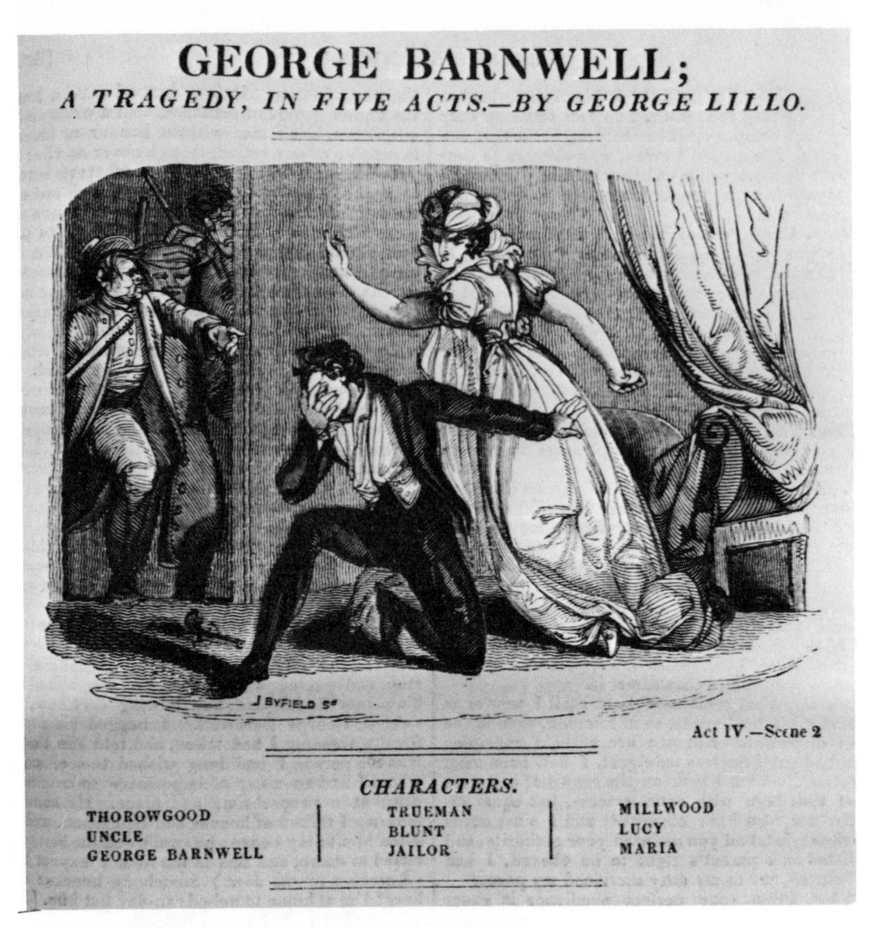

42 Scene from George Lillo's eighteenth-century English domestic tragedy, *George Barnwell, the London Merchant.*

And how to live in harmony with others
In cities, and how to shelter himself
From the piercing frost, cold rain, when the open
Fields can offer but a poor night's lodging.
He is ever resourceful; nothing that comes
Will find him unready, save Death alone.
Then will he call for help and call in vain,
Though often, where cure was despaired of, he has found one.

The wit of man surpasses belief,
It works for good and evil too;
When he honors his country's laws, and the right
He is pledged to uphold, then city
Hold up your head; but the man
Who yields to temptation and brings evil home
Is a man without a city; he has
No place in the circle of my hearth,
Nor any part in my counsels.[12]

an aesthetic pleasure

In returning to the question of how pain brings pleasure, we need to return to our first quotation from Aristotle (pages 1–2) where he says, "Objects which in themselves we view with pain, we delight to contemplate when reproduced with minute fidelity: such as the forms of the lowest animals and of dead bodies. The cause of this again is that to learn gives the liveliest pleasure." What learning does the suffering in tragedy provide? Moral philosophers and many critics have insisted that the function of drama is to teach morality, but efforts to use tragedy as moral preachment have proved futile.

The learning pleasure that tragedy affords is not moral but aesthetic. We enjoy the grandeur of conception, the ability of the dramatist to create significant action around great themes. And we also enjoy the "insight experiences" he gives us, showing us injustice and evil, excessive pride and passion, the effects of violence and tyranny—and showing us how, in the face of adversity and calamity, man's spirit and integrity remain intact. As Kenneth Burke puts it, the experience is one of Purpose, Passion, and Perception. The tragic hero's purpose is defeated, his passion is agonizing, but he comes to terms with his fate through perception. And from that imitation we learn—we attain a clearer awareness of the mystery of our own nature, and we are enriched by the intensification of our perception of life. As Langer suggests, there is aesthetic pleasure

12. *Oedipus the King and Antigone by Sophocles*, trans. Peter D. Arnott (New York: Appleton-Century-Crofts, 1960).

in seeing the tragic rhythm completed, the expectation fulfilled and, within the tragic rhythm, man's ultimate dignity achieved.

As a part of the universality of tragedy there are those who see in it a way of connecting us to the latent experiences of myth and ritual that have absorbed the attention of Jung and his followers—experiences that are "deeply implanted in the memory of the race." Gilbert Murray describes the phenomenon in these terms:

> In plays like *Hamlet* or the *Agamemnon* or the *Electra* we have certainly fine and flexible character-study, a varied and well-wrought story, a full command of the technical instruments of the poet and the dramatist; but we have also, I suspect, an undercurrent of desires and fears and passions, long slumbering yet eternally familiar, which have for thousands of years lain near the root of our most intimate emotions and have been wrought into the fabric of our most magical dreams. How far into the past ages this stream may reach back, I dare not even surmise; but it seems to me as if the power of stirring it or moving with it were one of the last secrets of genius.[13]

exercises

1. What is the function of tragedy?
2. Give examples of actions that cause fear and pity.
3. What are the characteristics of the tragic hero?
4. To what extent is the tragic hero responsible for his fate?
5. Describe the atmosphere of tragedy. How is it created?
6. After reading a tragedy, discuss the means by which your emotions were involved by the action.
7. Describe a potential modern tragic hero.
8. Explain your concept of catharsis.
9. Why does tragedy involve suffering?
10. What makes the tragic hero admirable?
11. What is the relation of tragedy to morality? Does it teach a lesson?
12. Is romantic love appropriate for tragedy?
13. Contrast tragic drama with accidental disaster.
14. Explain the relationship of tragedy to catastrophe.
15. What are the difficulties of writing tragedy in the modern world?
16. What is the cause of tragic events?
17. Evaluate Langer's theory of the "tragic rhythm."
18. How can witnessing painful events give pleasure?
19. Since all drama is artificial, how can it be said that tragedy is "honest"?

13. Gilbert Murray, "Hamlet and Orestes," in *The Classical Tradition in Poetry* (Cambridge, Mass.: Harvard University Press, 1927).

suggested reading

A. C. Bradley, *Shakespearean Tragedy*, 1932.
Northrop Frye, *The Anatomy of Criticism*, 1957.
Edith Hamilton, *The Greek Way*, 1952.
H. D. F. Kitto, *Greek Tragedy*, 2nd ed., 1950.
Joseph Wood Krutch, *"Modernism" in Modern Drama*, 1953.
Susanne K. Langer, *Feeling and Form*, 1953.
Herbert Muller, *The Spirit of Tragedy*, 1956.
Henry Alonzo Myers, *Tragedy: A View of Life*, 1956.
Elder Olson, *Tragedy and the Theory of Drama*, 1961.

play list

Aeschylus, *Choephori*
Bertolt Brecht, *Mother Courage*
Euripides, *Hippolytus; Medea*
George Lillo, *The London Merchant*
Arthur Miller, *The Crucible; Death of a Salesman*
Jean Racine, *Phèdre*
William Shakespeare, *Hamlet; Romeo and Juliet*
Sophocles, *Oedipus Rex; Electra*
J. M. Synge, *Riders to the Sea*

melodrama

In the previous chapter we considered tragedy, the loftiest and rarest form of drama. We come now to melodrama, a form nearly antithetical to tragedy because the dramatists of these two types have held two entirely different points of view. Tragedy examines values; melodrama exploits action. Tragedy confronts good and evil with unblinking honesty; melodrama escapes from life. Tragedy considers eternal spiritual problems; melodrama deals with the transitory, the material, the physical. Tragedy evokes fear and pity; melodrama arouses suspense, pathos, terror, and sometimes hate. However, melodrama is not mere ineffectual tragedy. As a matter of fact, a well-written melodrama may be superior to an inept tragedy. The point is that the two forms of drama are different. They are similar only in that they both *seem* serious. Like tragedy, melodrama may involve suffering and painful aspects of life—death and dishonor. But in melodrama the seriousness is a pretense because the writer is concerned only with theatrical values. Outwardly, melodrama appears to show real people in genuine jeopardy, but melodrama rigs the consequences of actuality in manipulating the plot toward escape, reprieve, or rescue, and culminates in a happy ending.

For the past two centuries, many dramatists have written for the middle-class audience that increasingly has captured the theater from the aristocracy. This new audience did not care much about tragedy or literate drama. Catering to its taste, playwrights created works of strong

action and sentiment. Their plays were variously called tragicomedy, "domestic" or "bourgeois" tragedy, "tearful" comedy, melodrama, and *drame*. We will arbitrarily employ the last two terms in this chapter, attempting to distinguish between them, and noting their special qualities.

It is a common fallacy to associate melodrama exclusively with such nineteenth-century plays as *East Lynne, Under the Gaslight,* and *Ten Nights in a Bar-Room*. While it is true that such thrillers flourished up until the end of the century, it is also true that melodrama remains today, along with farce, our most popular form of theatrical entertainment. The outward appearances of melodrama have changed throughout the years but the basic appeals that brought our great, great grandparents to the theater are the same in kind as those that appear tonight on our television and motion-picture screens.

Frank Rahill, in his excellent study of the form, defines melodrama this way:

> Melodrama is a form of dramatic composition in prose partaking of the nature of tragedy, comedy, pantomime and spectacle, and intended for a popular audience. Primarily concerned with situation and plot, it calls upon mimed action extensively and employs a more or less fixed complement of stock characters, the most important of which are a suffering heroine, or hero, a persecuting villain and a benevolent comic. It is conventionally moral and humanitarian in point of view and sentimental and optimistic in temper, concluding its fable happily with virtue rewarded after many trials and vice punished. Characteristically it offers elaborate scenic accessories and miscellaneous divertissements and introduces music freely, typically to underscore dramatic effect.[1]

The term melodrama combines two Greek words meaning music and drama. At one time the word was literally synonymous with opera. Melodrama was first allied with music in Italy and France. In Germany, it referred to dialogue passages spoken to orchestral accompaniment. The modern connotation of the word, however, stems from the late eighteenth-century French theater and its subsequent development, especially in England and America. Up until 1791, the Comédie Française and the Italian Comedians enjoyed monopolistic control over the legitimate theaters of Paris. Ingenious managers circumvented governmental restrictions by contriving a kind of entertainment based on pantomime accompanied by dance, song, and dialogue, which elicited a popular fol-

1. Frank Rahill, *The World of Melodrama* (University Park: Pennsylvania State University Press, 1967).

lowing due to its sensational qualities. When freedom of production was granted to all theaters, the word *melodrame* was attached to the pantomime with dialogue and music.

The French playwright Pixerécourt became the foremost playwright of the new form, which exactly fitted the taste of the lower classes. He made a careful study of his audiences until he perfected the machinery that was to dominate melodrama from that time to this and to make him one of the most popular playwrights who ever lived. He wrote nearly sixty melodramas, which played more than 30,000 performances in France alone. His plots were based on exciting action, surprise and suspense, the sharp contrasts of vice against virtue, the comic and the pathetic, and he thrilled his audiences with spectacular scenes such as fires, floods, and collisions. Although he wrote his plays rapidly, he worked with them in the theater personally, taking great pains to produce them exactly as he intended. The success of his efforts caused him to be known as "the Napoleon of the Boulevard."

Before Thomas Holcroft returned from France to London to introduce melodrama in his *A Tale of Mystery* (1802), the popular taste for its mood and action had been set in gothic novels, in sentimentalized, long-suffering dramatic heroines, and in the introduction of spectacular effects on the stage. "Monk" Lewis's *Castle Spectre,* three years earlier, contained much of the machinery of melodrama in its plot about an orphan girl, Lady Angela, ensnared by the wicked Lord Osmond, who has slain her father and taken over his property. The setting is a castle haunted by the ghost of the girl's mother. Thanks to the efforts of Earl Percy, disguised as a farmer, the villain is foiled and all comes to a happy ending.

Melodrama was introduced into America in 1804 in Turnbull's *Riddap; or, The Robbers of Calabria.* It became the most popular form of theater fare although most of it was imported from France and England. It was only later that American playwrights learned to exploit the native scene for plays of big city life, firemen plays, and finally our most successful contribution to melodrama, plays of the wild west.

Melodramatic scenes and situations were, of course, known in drama from almost the beginning of the theater. Euripides teetered precariously on the edge of melodrama in several of his plays, and Seneca fell over the brink and wallowed in sensational and horrible material. The Elizabethan "tragedies of blood" employed much of the machinery of melodrama with scenes of horror and violence. Jacobean playwrights delightly in grisly scenes of exciting action. The early eighteenth-century "she-tragedies" of Nicholas Rowe, with their sentimentalism and overwrought emotions, were in the melodramatic vein. Schiller's *The Robbers* capitalized on the fugitive situation so dear to the heart of writers of melodrama. August von Kotzebue, the late eighteenth-century German playwright, enjoyed an enormous popularity and commercial success in his plays, which possessed much of the flavor of melodrama, notably *The Stranger,* and *The Spaniards in Peru.* In the first half of the nineteenth century in France, Eugène Scribe turned out superficial, but "well-made" contrivances that were skillfully constructed and theatrically exciting. In England, the way had been prepared for melodrama by the gothic novels of Mrs. Radcliffe and "Monk" Lewis. In 1829, Douglas Jerrold made a phenomenal hit in London with his *Black-Eyed Susan,* which set the endlessly copied pattern of the machinations of the villain against a long-suffering heroine and a manly hero rescued at the last moment by a reprieve.

At first melodrama owed its popularity to its story appeal. Its pattern was a series of strong actions performed by clear-cut characters demonstrating the triumph of simple virtues and the ultimate defeat of villainy. The characters were sometimes credible because of the skillful performance of actors who added to the original bare outline the force of their own personalities. To satisfy the tremendous demand for new material, hack playwrights ground out new plays like our television writers, and like their modern counterparts, most writers followed well-established formulas.

As the nineteenth century progressed, efforts were made to create more realistic melodramas. The easiest way to accomplish this was through the external aspects of production—especially the stage scenery. Toward the end of the century, the theater technician ran away with the show. New and spectacular effects became a prime source of audience appeal. The stage mechanic was called upon to represent on stage not only accurate replicas of familiar landscapes, buildings, and monuments, but also to reproduce all manner of sensational effects. Melodrama tended to become simply a scenario for exciting action. As a result of its elaboration of the visual aspects of production and its demand for strong stories and movement, nineteenth-century melodrama brought about its own destruction and played directly into the hands of the development of the motion-picture industry.

By the end of the nineteenth century the stage melodrama had run its course with the increasing sophistication of the audience and the changes in the world outside. As drama moved toward realism, the old formulas and characters of melodrama gave way. Even when the theater aimed at the popular audience it was necessary to make plots more credible, to include more kinds of characters on stage and to give them more depth, to capture the impression of more normal speech. As for one of the major appeals of melodrama—the sensation scenes—the new medium of the film offered potentialities for spectacle far beyond the capacities of the limited stage.

43 Action in an early nineteenth-century melodrama, Pocock's *The Miller and His Men.*

A TALE OF MYSTERY;

A MELO-DRAME, IN TWO ACTS.—BY THOMAS HOLCROFT.

44 Typical action from Holcroft's hit, *A Tale of Mystery.*

45 Scene from Monk Lewis's popular melodrama, *The Castle Spectre.*

THE CASTLE SPECTRE;

A DRAMATIC ROMANCE IN FIVE ACTS.—BY M. G. LEWIS.

appeal of melodrama

Melodrama has been one of man's favorite ways to escape from the the real world to a land more in keeping with his heart's desire. Its enormous popularity at the beginning of the nineteenth century was a direct response to the audience's love of action, sentimentality, and spectacle. Melodrama appealed to the lower stratum of society—the ignorant and underprivileged, who found not only escape from the drudgery of a mean existence, but also an outlet for their repressed hatred of the villain who often symbolized for them the power of corrupt authority.

Melodrama appeals to the wide audience with a hunger for excitement and adventure. It awakens strong responses by its familiar black-and-white conflicts and escapades, which have a basic pattern of vigorous action. Its by-products are thrills and tears. Its machinery includes chases, escapes, reprieves, conflicts, and struggles—all kinds of situations in which there is physical danger and jeopardy. Melodrama does not face problems; it avoids thought or controversy by the simple expedient of eliminating the troublemaker. It aims at maximum identification with the audience.

Melodrama is a drama of mediocrity, since it can be written and performed by mediocre people, and its appeal is to a broad, undiscriminating audience that prefers its entertainment on the level of simple action with no intellectual overtones or disturbing aftermaths. As Thompson suggests, "The playwright's art here lies in a melodramatic golden mean between no response and painful response." Melodrama does not aspire to the austere elevation of tragedy nor does it pretend to come to grips with social problems and their conditioning effects on behavior. It is quite content to deal with effects and ignore causes.

Melodrama purges the softer emotions with its strong sentimental appeal. It is concerned with what Thompson refers to as "the pink section of the emotional spectrum." Melodrama usually deals with a story of wish-fulfillment in which dreams come true, virtue is rewarded, evil is punished, and pure and brave hearts are united. The writer makes use of such emotionally loaded devices as a suffering heroine, a sick child, a wounded horse or dog, a tortured hero, a heartless and brutal villain, and love of motherhood, country, and babies.

The audience of melodrama must yield its critical faculties to the action. There is little solace for the skeptic. Any resemblance of the character or situations to reality is superficial. While the spectator for the duration of the play may find himself emotionally involved in the plot and identified with the hero, as Cleanth Brooks and Robert Heilman point out,[2] this kind of participation is on a game level—like an inter-

2. Cleanth Brooks and Robert Heilman, *Understanding Drama* (New York: Holt, Rinehart and Winston, 1948).

ested fan carried away momentarily by an exciting ball game. One leaves the theater with a sense of relief at the outcome and a feeling of being emotionally spent by suspense and excitement, but untroubled by the conditions which caused the suffering and conflict of the play.

While melodrama no longer occupies the same central position in the legitimate theater as it did in the nineteenth century, it continues its wide popular appeal in motion pictures and television as well as in occasional plays such as *Detective Story, The Mousetrap, Desperate Hours,* and *The Little Foxes.* Although most of the discussion which follows is concerned primarily with nineteenth-century drama, you will recognize its application to contemporary plays and the general relationship to our mass-entertainment media.

plot

The writers of melodrama were not men interested in the literary aspects of drama; they were men of the theater, experienced in production who knew all the tricks of the stage, and who possessed the know-how to squeeze all the excitement and suspense possible out of their scripts. They were not literary artists interested in "fine writing." They were skilled manipulators of characters and situations much like our present writers of "B" pictures and television plays, whose approach to writing is grounded on the idea that anything is legitimate that works.

The plot of melodramas relied heavily on story value. The audience did not come to probe character, to listen to bright parlor talk, or to consider perplexing social problems. They came to see familiar type characters involved in stories told in scenes of clear and vigorous action. They preferred those dramatic situations that showed characters struggling against fearful odds, trapped or marooned—holding out until help comes—the last bullet—the last drop of water—the last bite of food—the last cent. (Their souls were never a source of contention except perhaps in the "temperance plays.") The art of playwriting, therefore, became the art of devising scenes of excitement. Melodrama exaggerated climaxes and crises so that the structure of the play was a series of peaks of action rather than a well-knit steady progression of logically related events. A typical scene of climax from Boucicault's great favorite, *The Colleen Bawn* (1860) illustrates not only the kind of situation, but also the major emphasis on action:

> Music, low storm music. . . . Myles sings without then appears U.E.R. on rock. . . . Swings across stage by rope. Exit U.E.L.H. Music, boat floats on R.H. with Eily and Danny. Eily steps on to Rock C. (Danny) stepping onto the rock the boat floats away unseen. . . . Music. Throws her into

> water, L.C. She disappears for an instant then reappears clinging to Rock C. . . . Thrusts her down. She disappears. . . . Shot heard U.E.L.H. Danny falls into water behind C. Rock. Myles sings without. . . . Swings across by rope to R.H., fastens it up, then fishes up Double of Eily—lets her fall. Strips, then dives after her. Eily appears for an instant in front. Then double for Myles appears at back and dives over drum. Myles and Eily appear in front of Center Rock. Tableau. Curtain.

This kind of physical action is, of course, the standard material of melodrama, made appealing to nineteenth-century audiences by novel effects. It is interesting to note the use of character "doubles" in order to keep the scene moving. Other elements in this scene of special interest are the music for reinforcing the atmosphere and the use of the tableau at the end of the act. The writer of melodrama depended on all kinds of coups de théâtre for releasing strong feelings. He utilizes big curtains such as in the scene above, literally as "clap traps." While he may have succeeded in jolting the audience, the use of such techniques violated the tenets of good playwriting by calling attention to the trickery of the staging rather than concentrating the audience's attention on character and the play.

The playwright, mindful of the break in the continuity of his narrative because of the multiplicity of his episodes and the emphasis on a series of climactic actions, made an attempt to bind the scenes together by a variety of techniques. Changes of scenery were covered by music or special lighting effects. Often, the scenes were changed in view of the audience. Sets were devised for the use of simultaneous or parallel action. Still another practice was that of shifting the locale from one place to another while the action continued. The following example from *A Race for Life* indicates this device, which anticipates cinematic practice:

> Officers fire. Convicts rush on, struggle with officers. Shots outside; Gaspard seizes Jacques—is thrown off. Officer seizes Jacques, he throws him off when Holmes struggles off with Brady R.H. Men and officers struggle off R. and L. when all clear. Sound Change Bell.
>
> Rocks drawn off R. and L. Prison double set center revolves to old Light House and comes down stage. Jacques and Brady come on in boat, Men work sea cloth. Patty throws rope from light house window. Brady catches it. Picture. Slow curtain.

The plot of melodrama is essentially dishonest. It is rigged like a "fixed" fight. Actually the outcome is never in doubt. This does not mean, however, that the playwright takes no pains to give the illusion of actuality. The good writer of melodrama is a skilled craftsman with a shrewd sense of pace, rhythm, and a feeling for climactic action. He is an adept storyteller and showman. He not only knows the potentialities of the stage, but he also understands the audience for which he writes. Logic does not interest him so long as his play gives the impression of credibility which he achieves by keeping his narrative moving, and by creating the illusion of actuality through the use of realistic backgrounds, appropriate costuming, good casting, and dialogue that suggests the speech of everyday life.

Realism ultimately made its impact on melodrama, although up until 1900, most American plays were written as vehicles for the exploitation of a star or for the theatrical possibilities of staging. In the early part of the twentieth century, the motion picture began to attract a popular audience. Porter's films, *The Life of an American Fireman* and *The Great Train Robbery,* taught movie makers that their medium was ideally suited for narratives with bold and vigorous action. The motion picture quickly captivated the public fancy and assimilated melodrama as its staple product, which has continued to find favor ever since. A glance at recent newspaper advertisements makes this evident in such blurbs as these: "Overwhelming as the elements!" "Desires at a fever pitch under a blazing sun!" "Dramatic dynamite!" "This is a shocker! Good for thrills and a provocative psychological premise!"

The motion pictures and television have performed a distinct service to the legitimate stage by removing a good deal of the puerile material which formerly appeared on it. But melodrama is not dead in the theater. It often changes its external appearance, takes on greater surface reality, deals more credibly with character and dialogue—but nevertheless, it is still melodrama in its exaggerated emphasis of excitement and emotion for their own sake. The characteristic appeals continue to be exploited in such plays as *Gas Light, The Bad Seed, Dial "M" for Murder, Suspect, Wait until Dark, Conduct Unbecoming,* and *Night Must Fall.* In addition, there are any number of modern dramas which make free use of melodramatic material although they exhibit skillful craftsmanship and adroit plotting. The external action has been replaced by psychological tension, and there may be a measure of social significance in the action, but the flavor of melodrama still persists in such works as *The Children's Hour, Command Decision, Key Largo, The Traitor, Time Limit, Darkness at Noon,* and *Sleuth.*

character

Myers in his book *Tragedy: A View of Life* makes an interesting statement about character when he says: "In the black-and-white world of melodrama men are divided into two sharply opposed classes, represented by the unblemished hero and the unspeakable villain. . . . The first premise of melodrama is that there are two distinct kinds of men:

the first premise of tragedy is that all men are essentially the same."[3] Nineteenth-century melodrama and our contemporary motion-picture and television plays of action testify to the validity of Myers' observation. Characters are generally stamped-out, good or bad one-dimensional figures who pursue their objectives in a straight line without thought, development, or psychological complexity. They do not think, they act and as a result of their thoughtlessness, they become involved in all sorts of absurd entanglements such as being caught on a train trestle at midnight without a lantern or match, lost in the snow barefoot, or trapped in the villain's net because they misjudge the character of their adversary. The writer of melodrama has little or no concern with delineating characters as substantial individuals conditioned by their environment and past experiences, responding to the events in which they participate as individuals. Melodramatic characters are simple in heart and mind; they are objects of desire with whom the audience can readily identify itself.

Many characters from melodrama are types, especially the comic ones, who give the illusion of being drawn from life, but who are really comic devices exploited for their eccentricities or picturesqueness, rather than substantial, fully-rounded characters. Some leading roles in melodrama provided exceptional opportunities for actors who became so identified with the characters that they gave the impression of reality. For example, James O'Neill played the *Count of Monte Cristo* for 5,817 performances, and Denman Thompson appeared in *The Old Homestead* more than 7,000 times.

Nineteenth-century melodrama was the popular entertainment of the masses, and since maximum identification was the playwright's aim, he used characters from the ordinary walks of life. Heroes were not the elevated figures of the past; they were firemen, private soldiers, sailors, the farm boy, the hired hand. Very often the bad characters of the play were drawn from high society to show that hypocrisy and sham permeated the upper circle. Picturesque figures were copied from life, so that the drama in this country showed native characters as heroes and heroines, combatting the tradition of importing our dramas and characters from abroad. In all things, the common denominator prevailed.

thought

Most melodramas end with arbitrary scenes of poetic justice in which couples are paired off, and rewards and punishments are parceled out according to the actions of the characters in the play. As the final curtain descends, the audience is reassured that virtue will triumph,

3. Henry Alonzo Myers, *Tragedy: A View of Life* (Ithaca: Cornell University Press, 1956).

murder will out, and the wages of sin is death. A typical heart-throb ending occurs in the astonishingly popular *Uncle Tom's Cabin.*

> (GEORGE SHELBY *enters, supporting* TOM.—*Music. They advance to front and* TOM *falls, C.*)
>
> GEO: Oh! dear Uncle Tom! do wake—do speak once more! look up! Here's Master George—your own little Master George. Don't you know me?
>
> TOM: *(opening his eyes and speaking in a feeble tone)* Mas'r George! Bless de Lord! it's all I wanted! They hav'nt forgot me! It warms my soul; it does my old heart good! Now I shall die content!
>
> GEO: You shan't die! you mustn't die, nor think of it. I have come to buy you, and take you home.
>
> TOM: Oh, Mas'r George, you're too late. The Lord has bought me, and is going to take me home.
>
> GEO: Oh! don't die. It will kill me—it will break my heart to think what you have suffered, poor fellow!
>
> TOM: Don't call me, poor fellow! I *have* been poor fellow; but that's all past and gone now. I'm right in the door, going into glory! Oh, Mas'r George! *Heaven has come!* I've got the victory. The Lord has given it to me! Glory be to his name! *(Dies.)*
>
> *(Solemn music.*—GEORGE *covers* UNCLE TOM *with his cloak and kneels over him. Clouds work on and conceal them, and then work off.)*

Characters were motivated by conventional morality. Heroines were long-suffering, self-sacrificing, dutiful, and pure. The home was the center of their lives, and motherhood their crowning achievement. Heroes were upright, manly, brave and noble who revered womanhood and their country, and stood steadfastly for justice and honor. Villains were lustful, greedy barbarians who chased women, preyed on widows, and searched relentlessly and unscrupulously for dishonest gain. One could generally spot the villain by his scarred or unshaven face, his dark looks, his foreign dialect, or he might appear in just the opposite way as too well-dressed, too soft-spoken, too mannerly. His smooth and suave exterior belied the cold, hard glint in his eye, and the itching palm beneath the velvet glove.

Duty and self-sacrifice were the ennobling virtues of the lower classes. Whatever misfortunes befell, the honorable person performed his duty, confident that in the end justice would be meted out, in the next world if not here and now. Dozens of heroines declaimed such sentiments as the following passage from Daly's highly successful hit, *Under the Gaslight.*

> LAURA: Let the woman you look upon be wise or vain, beautiful, or homely, rich or poor, she has but one thing she can really give or refuse—her

46 Scene from a melodrama as depicted by Daumier.

47 Poster for an English melodrama showing the highlights of the action.

48 Scene from a Drury Lane production of *The Whip*, 1909. One of the main appeals of melodrama was in staging such scenes.

heart! Her beauty, her wit, her accomplishments, she may sell to you—but her love is the treasure without money and without price. She only asks in return, that when you look upon her, your eyes shall speak a mute devotion; that when you address her, your voice shall be gentle, loving and kind. That you shall not despise her because she cannot understand all at once, your vigorous thoughts, and ambitious designs: for when misfortune and evil have defeated your greatest purposes—her love remains to console you. You look to the trees for strength and grandeur—do not despise the flowers, because their fragrance is all they have to give. Remember—love is all a woman has to give; but it is the only earthly thing which God permits us to carry beyond the grave.

diction

The language of melodrama was singularly undistinguished. Since common characters carried the burden of the plot, playwrights attempted to suggest the everyday idiom on stage. This effort performed some service in undermining the bombast and extravagance of romantic diction, although the writer of melodrama was not entirely immune from flowery language. In moments of strong emotion, characters spouted such purple passages as that cited above from *Under the Gaslight*. But by and large, the playwright's emphasis on common characters, involved in scenes of violent action, led toward dialogue that suggested the texture of ordinary speech. As a result of his attempt to imitate the language of life, some playwrights endeavored to copy the dialects and provincialism of specific locales, which was a move toward increased realism.

The writer of melodrama made free use of such technical devices as asides and soliloquies, which not only aided him in the difficult problems of exposition imposed by episodic structure, but also gave him the opportunity to reveal character and motivation. In general, however, soliloquies were used for technical purposes rather than for high-sounding passages of well-worn rhetoric.

music

Melodrama, originally linked with music, continued that association. As the excerpts from *The Colleen Bawn* and *Uncle Tom's Cabin* have already indicated, music was an important accompaniment to the action. When the motion pictures took over melodrama, it was soon learned that sound was extremely useful for eliciting emotional response. Silent films were accompanied by appropriate scores for piano or pipe organ. For more ambitious productions such as *The Birth of a Nation,* a complete orchestral accompaniment was written and played for the showing of the picture. In our present motion pictures and television dramas, music continues as an indispensable element of production to establish atmosphere, bridge the action, or generate excitement.

Nineteenth-century melodrama made another interesting use of music. The entrances and exits of leading characters were accompanied by special musical themes suitable for their roles. But music in melodrama was an adjunct of production, rather than an organic part of the structure itself. Nevertheless, it was often a stronger source of emotional impact than the performance of the actors and the drama itself.

spectacle

In the first half of the century, almost all theaters made use of two-dimensional stock pieces consisting of backdrops and wings, on which were painted a variety of backgrounds such as a kitchen, a palace, a prison, a grotto, a woodland glade. This system possessed two virtues—it was economic and it made shifting rapid and easy. To change to a new setting, the backdrop was raised to reveal another one behind it, while wings slid along the grooves to uncover the new ones for the following scene. Throughout the country, theaters were equipped with stock sets so that a touring company needed to bring only its special effects and costumes along. But as the taste for sensational novelties grew, productions became increasingly elaborate and expensive. Metropolitan stages became more complicated with bridges, traps, elevators, moving platforms, and all kinds of paraphernalia for producing fires, floods, explosions, and all manner of astounding displays. The two-dimensional scenery was replaced by built-up solid pieces making the sets substantial and difficult to move. Belasco actually bought pieces of buildings and moved them intact onto the stage. Playwrights were obliged to create scenes calculated to exploit visual sensations. The following scene from *Pauvrette: or, Under the Snow* shows the kind of effects required:

> The summit of the Alps. Rocks and precipices occupy the stage. A rude hut on one side in front. A bridge formed by a felled tree across the chasm at the back. The stone-clad peaks stretch away in the distance. Night. . . . Storm, wind. She (Pauvrette) throws her scarf around her, and hastily ascends the rock—utters a long wailing cry—listens. . . . Descends to her hut. Maurice cries for help. Takes her alpenstock and a coil of rope, and reascends the rock. The wind increases—the snow begins to fall. She crosses the bridge and disappears off left. Bernard appears below on the rocks, L. He climbs up the path. . . . Pauvrette appears on the bridge, leading Maurice. . . . They cross the bridge. . . . They descend and enter the hut. . . . Large blocks of hardened snow and masses of rock

> fall, rolling into the abyss. Pauvrette falls on her knees. . . . Pauvrette enters the hut. The avalanche begins to fall—the bridge is broken and hurled into the abyss—the paths have been filled with snow—and now an immense sheet rushing down from the R. entirely buries the whole scene to the height of twelve or fifteen feet swallowing up the cabin and leaving above a clear level of snow—the storm passes away—silence and peace return—the figure of the virgin (in window) is unharmed—the light before it still burns.

It should be kept in mind that while sensational scenery called attention to itself, it was also used for more than pictorial representation. The setting was functional in that it served the actor's needs in a particular scene. A waterfall was not simply shown as an enlarged calendar picture for its visual appeal. It became a factor in the action when the hero struggled to save the heroine from plunging to her death. A railroad trestle was set on stage not merely for the novelty of showing a train, but also as a weapon of the villain who tied the hero to the tracks while the approaching light and whistle of the train were seen and heard. The setting was an essential part of the action. Hence, a considerable amount of ingenuity was required by the stage mechanic to devise effects which were not only visually credible, but also utilitarian enough to be used in chases, fights, and escapes. Incidentally, the actor had to be something of an athlete to dive from burning buildings, scale steep cliffs, and chase or be chased through a canvas jungle, and then recite lines. (It is no wonder that doubles were often used to keep the action continuous.)

One device by which melodrama sought to create the illusion of reality was through the use of actual and authentic properties on stage. Some playwrights and producers cluttered the stage with endless detail to make the stage picture seem real. Often a real property, such as a rowboat, made an incongruous contrast with the obviously painted backdrop of the sea. On the other hand, the use of genuine and homely objects on stage enhanced the realism of the acting by giving the actors an opportunity to create business and pantomime. James A. Herne, a successful writer of melodrama who attempted to emulate the new realism in his plays, was very fond of filling his scenes with the everyday objects and actions of life. In some of his plays he brought on dogs, chickens, a horse, geese, and live babies. He showed a shipyard in operation during which a boat was painted each evening. In another play, a flour mill actually worked. But perhaps his favorite device was his dinner scenes in which complete meals were eaten on stage. The following excerpt from *Sag Harbor* is typical:

> Susan enters with a smoking hot clam pie in a deep dish. She is greeted with a round of applause in which everybody at the table joins with the

exception of Freeman. Susan sets the pie in front of Ben, who helps himself to it. During the next scene, Susan busies herself waiting at the table, passing tea, bread and butter, and coming and going with food. Martha pours the tea, and Elizabeth helps applesauce from a dish which is placed in front of her. They all eat heartily, and there is a general atmosphere of good cheer.

As the elaboration of scenery progressed, it became increasingly difficult for a road company to tour since many of the outlying theaters could not accommodate the special scenery because of the lack of size or equipment, not to mention the increased cost of the touring production. The increasing solidity and complexity of scenery also affected playwriting. It meant that scenes could not be shifted as rapidly as previously. The result was to reduce the number of scenes in the play so that there were fewer locales and episodes. Under these conditions, the dramatist was forced to use less physical action, the narrative lost some of its fluency, and there was a tendency toward fuller development of character and dialogue.

Most serious modern playwrights have not aspired to scale the heights of tragedy, nor have they been content to confine themselves to sheer melodrama. They have tended to write middle-class plays for a middle-class audience dealing with contemporary man in commonplace circumstances. This vast body of dramatic literature defies definition because of its great diversity, its technical experimentation in dramaturgy and production, and because of its mixture of several forms of writing at once. Some critics simply use the general term drama, but we prefer, as a lesser evil, the French term *drame*, by which is meant those plays of serious intent usually dealing with contemporary life. Just as realism has been the dominant mode of modern drama, so the drame has been the preponderant form used by such writers as Henrik Ibsen, Anton Chekhov, Maxim Gorki, Sean O'Casey, Eugene O'Neill, Luigi Pirandello, Jean Anouilh, Clifford Odets, Arthur Miller, and Tennessee Williams.

Drame is allied to melodrama in that the playwright often attempts to involve the spectator in the action by identification with the characters and by creating suspense and tension. Drame differs from melodrama in that it may be interested in the realm of ideas, with sociological and philosophical issues at stake. Characters may be involved in genuinely significant action, provoking thought and discussion after the curtain has gone down.

Drame is allied to tragedy in its seriousness of purpose, in its relentless honesty of treatment, in its concern with the meaning of human conduct. Drame differs from tragedy in its narrowness of vision—with its emphasis often on material, temporary, or local conditions that deny it universality—with its mechanistic or deterministic sense of values, and with its general lack of elevation. Frequently, the writer of drames is fascinated by the psychological complexities of character. His dramatis personae are not the stock characters of melodrama; they are individuals with subtle and complicated motivations. They are not the tragic heroes of great stature who fall from high places, but ordinary people painfully searching for meaning and security in a baffling world of shifting values.

exercises

1. What are the emotional effects of melodrama?
2. In what ways is melodrama "dishonest"?
3. Compare the playwright's treatment of character in melodrama and tragedy.
4. Analyze the functions of different kinds of action in melodrama.
5. Contrast the treatment of violence and suffering in melodrama with that of tragedy.
6. Compare the use of spectacle in melodrama and drame.
7. How important is thought in melodrama?
8. After watching an "action" film, describe its melodramatic aspects.
9. What are the appeals of melodrama?
10. Describe the characteristics of a melodramatic hero.
11. How does melodrama achieve a realistic effect?
12. How is drame allied to tragedy?
13. How important is the thought element in drame?
14. Describe the audience response to melodrama.
15. What is the relation of melodrama to morality?
16. In what ways is melodrama like a game?
17. Does drame achieve more emotional response because it is closer to our own experience?

suggested reading

Eric Bentley, *The Life of the Drama*, 1964.
Maurice Disher, *Blood and Thunder: Mid-Victorian Melodrama and Its Origins*, 1949.
Alexander Lacey, *Pixerécourt and the French Romantic Drama*, 1928.
Richard Moody, *America Takes the Stage: Romanticism in American Drama and Theatre, 1750–1900*, 1955.
Frank Rahill, *The World of Melodrama*, 1967.
Nicholas A. Vardac, *Stage to Screen*, 1949.

play list

Dion Boucicault, *The Colleen Bawn*
Agatha Christie, *The Mousetrap*
Barry England, *Conduct Unbecoming*
Lillian Hellman, *The Little Foxes*
Sidney Kingsley, *Detective Story*
Frederick Knott, *Wait Until Dark*
Anthony Shaffer, *Sleuth*
Harriet Beecher Stowe, *Uncle Tom's Cabin*
Tom Taylor, *Ticket of Leave Man*
Emlyn Williams, *Night Must Fall*

comedy

Comedy wears many masks and appears in many guises—the ill-fitting tattered rags of the drunken hobo, the elegant evening clothes of the most sophisticated aristocrat, the overdressed finery of the fop. Comedy evokes many responses—a belly-laugh, warm and sympathetic general laughter, a well-concealed smile. Its armor includes such a variety of weapons as the rapier, the slapstick, the barbed shaft, and the custard pie. Comedy speaks many languages—epigrams, conceits, puns, obscenities, bon mots, wisecracks, insults, double entendres, hard and ruthless derision. The field of comedy is broad enough to encompass many variations—the romantic comedy of Shakespeare's *As You Like It;* the high comedy of Congreve's *The Way of the World;* a musical comedy like *Fiddler on the Roof;* a bedroom farce such as Feydeau's *Keep an Eye on Amélie;* an intimate revue like *Beyond the Fringe;* a Latin intrigue, *The Pot of Gold;* a political satire, *The White House Murder Case;* an Aristophanic thrust, *Lysistrata;* a Shavian comedy, *Man and Superman* and a "tribal rock" musical, *Hair.* Comedy also includes the prefabricated formula television fare of nightclub monologists and family situations built around the bewildering behavior of adolescents and the antics of their parents.

the nature of comedy

To define comedy is first to acknowledge the difficulties and hazards of definition. What makes one person laugh may make another grieve. The lively oak of comedy cannot be crammed into a flower pot of simple definition when one considers all its roots and branches, its variegated fruits and foliage. We usually refer to those plays as comedy that end happily, and those with an unhappy ending as tragedy. But even this broad generalization breaks down in some instances: Euripides chose to end *Alcestis* happily, and Dante called his great work with its elevated theme and treatment *The Divine Comedy.* While classicists and neo-classicists kept tragedy and comedy separate, many playwrights, notably the English, blended comic and serious matter, as in *Hamlet, Dr. Faustus,* and *Macbeth.* Aristotle in his *Poetics* makes an important distinction in saying that in tragedy men are shown as "better than they are" and in comedy as "worse than they are." As Northrop Frye has pointed out, the qualifying words that Aristotle uses for good and bad are *spoudaios* and *phaulos,* which have a figurative connotation of weighty and light. The lightness of touch is certainly one of the hallmarks of comedy.

Perhaps it is sufficient to say that comedy has as its purpose to delight, entertain, or regale an audience through the presentation of characters, situations, and ideas in the spirit of fun. As tragedy achieves its catharsis through fear and pity, so comedy aims in its special catharsis through laughter and amusement to keep man close to sanity and balance, to remind us of our human frailties, and to keep us humbly mindful of what we are rather than what we might wish ourselves to be.

kinds of comedy

The problem of classification is especially acute in comedy. Playwrights have a way of ignoring arbitrary pigeonholes, mixing various kinds of comic matter to suit their dramatic purposes without regard to academic convenience. For example, Aristophanes frequently uses all manner of obscenities and physical humor characteristic of farce, but he blends this material with satirical thrusts at the ideas of his contemporaries, filling his comedies with political and philosophical ramifications. The perplexed scholar in an attempt to catalogue this variety has been forced to use the label of "Aristophanic" comedy. Shakespeare is similarly difficult to categorize since he writes in a variety of ways—farcical, romantic, and "dark" comedies—sometimes mixing different styles in the same play.

Alan Thompson, in an effort to regularize the concept of different kinds of comedy, devised a comic ladder which takes this form:[1]

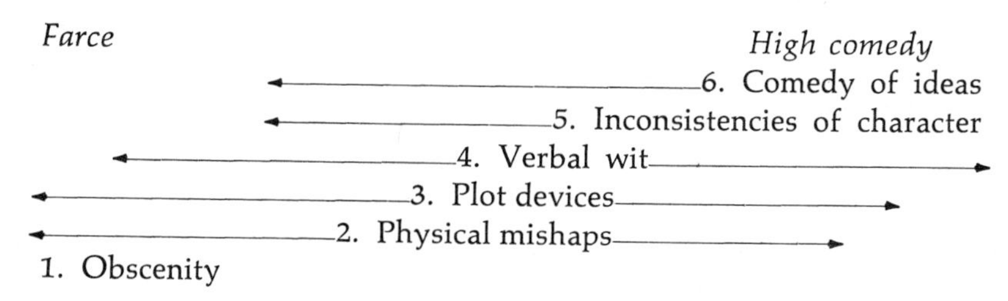

Allardyce Nicoll, in a similar effort, suggests five categories of comedy:[2]

> In general, there are five main types of comic productivity which we may broadly classify. Farce stands by itself as marked out by certain definite characteristics. The comedy of humours is the second of decided qualities. Shakespeare's comedy of romance is the third, with possibly the romantic tragicomedy of his later years as a separate subdivision. The comedy of intrigue is the fourth. The comedy of manners is the fifth, again with a subdivision in the genteel comedy.

Both Thompson and Nicoll place low or physical comedy at one end of the scale and the comedy of manners or ideas at the other end—and this seems like a logical arrangement, but the problem with the gradations in between, as well as with the two extremes is, as we have already noted, that they are not mutually exclusive. Moreover, playwrights have compounded plays of all of the elements blended in various fashions which defy neat schematic compartmentalization. The juices of comedy have a way of bubbling over, penetrating all kinds of chinks and crannies. They are difficult to cork up in logic-tight containers. The safest conclusion seems to be that comedy ranges between high and low, between the physical and intellectual, and that it differs in kind according to the playwright's purposes from play to play. Perhaps the most essential ingredient for all kinds of comedy is a point of view which we shall discuss subsequently as the comic attitude.

laughter

Since the nature of comedy is linked to the sources of laughter, some measure of the complexity of the subject may be suggested by the

1. Alan Reynolds Thompson, *The Anatomy of Drama* (Berkeley: University of California Press, 1942).
2. Allardyce Nicoll, *The Theory of Drama* (New York: Crowell, 1931).

various points of view exposed in the following observations by thinkers who have given serious thought to comedic material:

> Laughter is the indication of an effort which suddenly encounters a void. (Herbert Spencer)
>
> Laughter is the result of an expectation which of a sudden ends in nothing. (Immanuel Kant)
>
> . . . what either in the words or sense of an author, or in the languages or actions of men, is awry or depraved does strangely stir mean affections, and provoke for the most part to laughter. (Ben Jonson)
>
> . . . laughter almost ever cometh of things most disproportioned to ourselves and nature. (Sir Philip Sidney)
>
> The real cause would appear to lie in the sense of liberation which the laugh itself involves. It is the liberation of the natural man from the ties and conventions of society. In the same way, we may explain the laughter which greeted in the Middle Ages the appearance of the Devil-character of the mystery plays. (Allardyce Nicoll)
>
> The dignified, solemn and stately attributes of things require in us a certain posture of rigid constraint; and if we are suddenly relieved from this posture, the rebound of hilarity ensues, as in the case of children set free from school. (Alexander Bain)
>
> The comic is that side of a person which reveals his likeness to a thing, that aspect of human events which, through its peculiar inelasticity, conveys the impression of pure mechanism, of automatism, of movement without life. (Henri Bergson)
>
> . . . gratification of repressed tendencies. (Sigmund Freud)
>
> The essence of the laughable is the incongruous, the disconnecting of one idea from another, or the jostling of one feeling against another. (William Hazlitt)

While there is considerable structural lumber in these well-turned phrases, there is not much immediate shelter because one becomes conscious of their shortcomings when applying them to specific examples. There are, however, two points of general agreement. First, comedy implies a contrast in the juxtaposition of the normal and the abnormal, the expected and the unexpected. Second, comedy involves a sudden change. It will be helpful to keep these points in mind as we consider some of the comic theories whose root-ideas are to be found in the quotations which have just been cited. But before sketching the theories, we may gain some insight into our subject by glancing briefly at the functions of comedy.

49 Ancient Greek comedy showing Achilles watching his elderly tutor being pushed up the steps to a temporary stage. From a vase painting, British Museum.

50 Shakespeare's romantic comedy *As You Like It* at the Royal Shakespeare Theatre, 1961.

51 Comedy used as a weapon by El Teatro Campesino in connection with their strike program.

52 (opposite) Aristophanes' *Lysistrata* in a modern German production, Schlosspark Theater, Berlin, 1960.

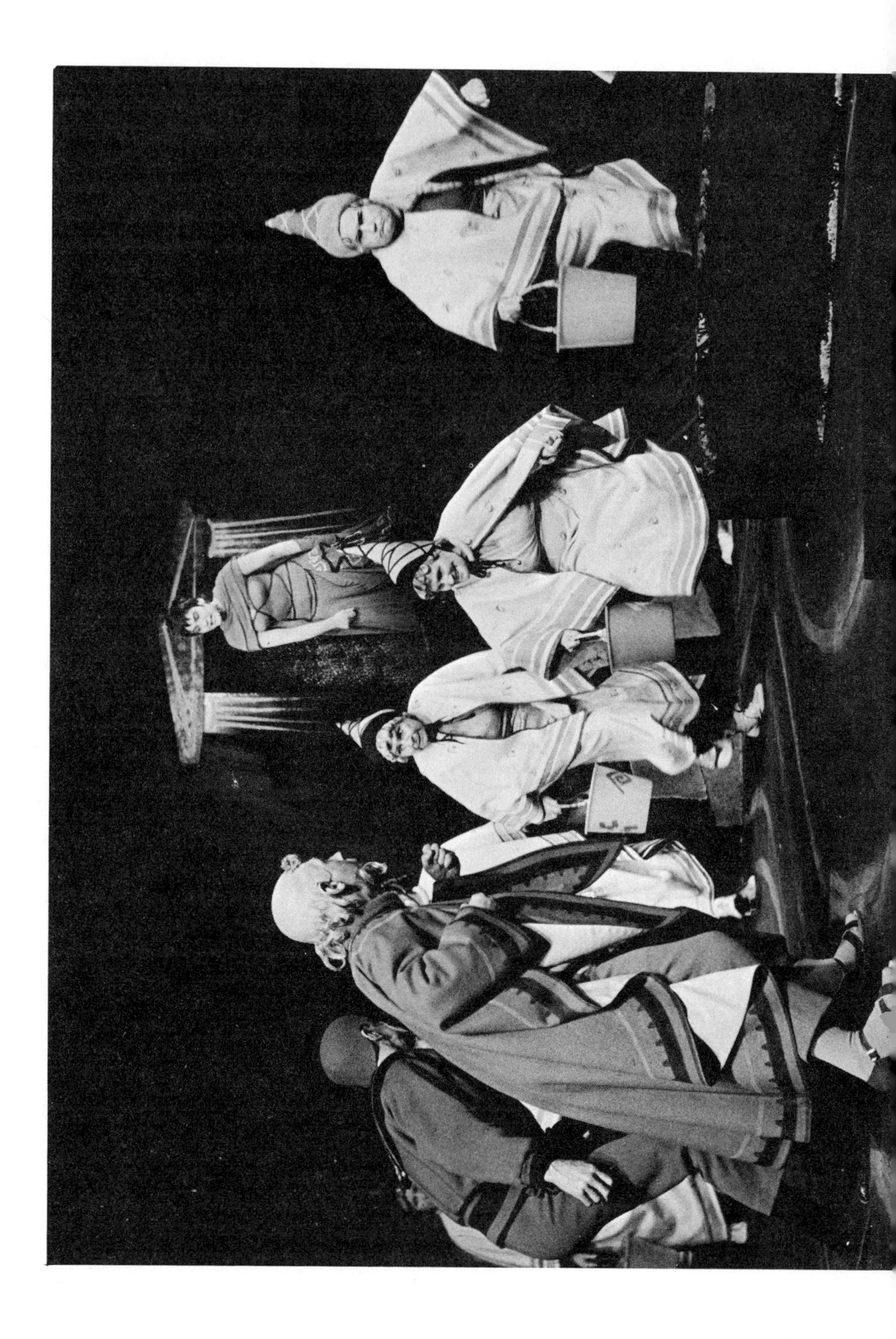

purposes of comedy

Many thinkers consider comedy to have a utilitarian basis. Goldoni regarded comedy as a means "to correct faults and foibles"; Hazlitt, "to unmask ignorance and deceit"; Meredith, "to vindicate reason, common sense, rightness and justice, for no vain purpose ever"; Shaw, "for the correcting of pretensiousness, of inflation, of dullness." The French philosopher Henri Bergson in his entertaining book *Laughter* summarizes this function of comedy as the drama of criticism in these words: "Laughter is, above all, a corrective. Being intended to humiliate, it must make a painful impression on the person against whom it is directed. By laughter, society avenges itself for liberties taken with it."[3]

When comedy serves such a purpose, the object of laughter is usually unsociable. This has little to do with morality since we are inclined to laugh at a character's eccentricities rather than at his vices or virtues, except insofar as they make him ludicrous. A comic character's deviation from the norm in speech, manners, or appearance causes us to laugh to keep him in line. This corrective use of laughter is, of course, not confined to the theater, inasmuch as the fear of ridicule is one of the primary forces in causing the members of society to conform. Hence, in comedy, the butt of the joke, by implication, suggests the sin of antisocial behavior.

But the purpose of comedy is not always critical. There is shared laughter in those situations when we laugh *with* a character rather than *at* him—a character who may be fully aware of his weakness, yet is appealing because we are reminded of our common human inconsistency. As instances of this kind of comic appeal, we think of characters caught in circumstances when they are embarrassed, fearful, and confused. Our laughter often becomes a bond of sympathy, not of ridicule. We do not isolate such characters from our approval; we share with them our universal experience as human beings. While the purpose of some comedy is critical, it also exists on the level of sheer entertainment and delight, serving only secondarily as a means of releasing tensions and inhibitions, although Freud saw in this the primary reason for the phenomenon of laughter.

Two modern critics, Northrop Frye and Susanne K. Langer, view comedy in a broad social context. In examining the "new comedy" of the Greeks, Frye finds a pattern that is remarkably pervasive in the comedies of Ben Jonson, Molière, the English Restoration, and even in our modern motion pictures. Speaking of new comedy he says:

3. Henri Bergson, *Laughter*, trans. Cloudesley Brereton and Fred Rothwell (New York: Macmillan, 1917).

> Its main theme is the successful effort of a young man to outwit an opponent and possess the girl of his choice. The opponent is usually the father *(senex)* and the psychological descent of the heroine from the mother is also sometimes hinted at. The father frequently wants the same girl, and is cheated out of her by the son, the mother thus becoming the son's ally. The girl is usually a slave or courtesan, and the plot turns on a *cognito* or discovery of birth which makes her marriageable. Thus it turns out that she is not under an insuperable taboo after all but is an accessible object of desire, so that the plot follows the regular wish-fulfillment pattern. . . .
>
> In all good New Comedy there is a social as well as an individual theme which must be sought in the general atmosphere of reconciliation that makes the marriage possible. As the hero gets closer to the heroine and opposition is overcome, all right-thinking people come over to his side. Thus a new social unit is formed on the stage, and the moment that this social unit crystalizes is the moment of the comic resolution. In the last scene, when the dramatist usually tries to get all his characters on the stage at once, the audience witnesses the birth of a renewed sense of social integration. In comedy as in life the regular expression of this is a festival, whether a marriage, a dance, or a feast.[4]

You will recall Langer's concept of the tragic rhythm; in comedy she sees "the motion and rhythm of living" that enhances our vital feeling—"the essential comic feeling, which is the sentient aspect of organic unity, growth and self preservation. . . ."

> Comedy is an art form that arises naturally whenever people are gathered to celebrate life, in spring festivals, triumphs, birthdays, weddings, or initiations. For it expresses the elementary strains and resolutions of animate nature, the animal drives that persist even in human nature, the delight man takes in his special mental gifts that make him lord of creation; it is an image of human vitality holding its own in the world amid the surprises of unplanned coincidence. What justifies the term "Comedy" is not that the ancient ritual procession, the Comus, honoring the god of that name, was the source of this great art form—for comedy has arisen in many parts of the world, where the Greek god with his particular worship was unknown—but that the Comus was a fertility rite, and the god it celebrated a fertility god, a symbol of perpetual rebirth, eternal life.[5]

Frye and Langer are describing a basic human activity—that of making important and valuable connections. Just as primitive man through sacrifice and sympathetic magic sought contact with the secret powers of the universe, as the religious man strives for communion with the

4. Northrop Frye, "The Argument of Comedy," from *English Institute Essays* (New York: Columbia University Press, 1948).
5. Susanne K. Langer, *Feeling and Form* (New York: Scribner, 1953).

ultimate, in a similar way social man cherishes his connections with his family, his associates, perhaps with organizations and activities. Comedy celebrates union and reunion, the restoration of health, the healing of wounds, the spirit of togetherness. Frye ties the comic process to social integration; Langer associates the comic spirit with the rhythm of life. Both are describing the phenomenon of man caught in a strange world, conscious of his frailty threatened by alienation, and seeking the communal warmth and strength of connections that make him whole.

the comic attitude

The question of pain and pleasure arises in comedy as well as in tragedy, for laughter and ridicule can be dangerous weapons. Molière, who was frequently in hot water for satirizing the law, medicine, and the church, observed that people do not mind being wicked, but "they object to being made ridiculous." And Ludovici tells us that "a laugh is a man's way of showing his fangs." Many critics view comedy as a corrective force. Those who favor the status quo use it as a means of making people conform, of punishing those who deviate from the accepted norm. Those who oppose the established society regard comedy as a device for deflation and exposure. Comedy becomes aggressive and easily leads to abuse and to the destruction of its essential lightness of spirit. Teasing turns into torment, mischief into vandalism. The trick is to create and retain the comic atmosphere.

Aristotle saw the problem clearly: "The ludicrous consists in some defect or ugliness which is not painful or destructive." As an example, he cites the comic mask which may be ugly and distorted, but gives no pain. Cicero echoed his idea by saying that comedy should show blemishes but they must be "nicely managed."

Let us see how the comic atmosphere is established in the opening minutes of Feydeau's *Keep an Eye on Amélie.*

The scene is laid in an elegant Paris apartment, with a grand piano, handsome furniture, paintings, objets d'art, potted plants, and a tray of liqueurs.

At the rise of the curtain AMELIE *is standing by the piano, entertaining her guests with the music of the gramophone.* BIBICHON, *cigar in mouth, is seated on the sofa between* YVONNE *and* PALMYRE. PALMYRE *is perched on the arm of the sofa.* VALCREUSE, *back to the audience, and* BOAS, *facing the audience, are on opposite sides of the card table, playing cards. The gramophone is playing a Caruso record: "Di quella pira" from Il Trovatore. For the most part the guests listen enraptured, nodding ecstatic approval. (The curtain should be lowered when the music begins to play. Curtain rises slowly on the eighth measure of recitative with the words: "Marse avvanpo.")*

YVONNE *(after an upsurge of Caruso's at about the thirteenth or fourteenth measure):* Ah!! Incredible!
ALL *(entranced):* Ah-h!!
AMELIE *(with utter refinement):* Can you believe it?
ALL: Ah-h! *(They all listen attentively.)*
BIBICHON *(at about the seventeenth measure of the aria):* Who is the loudmouth anyway? Is it Caruso?
AMELIE *(moving toward him):* "Loudmouth!"
BIBICHON: Well, who's doing the singing? He's got lots of talent.
YVONNE: Sssh! Be quiet!
BIBICHON: What they call a "God-given" voice.
ALL: Sssh-sssh!
BIBICHON: All right, all right.
Religious silence. The ladies are in seventh heaven. As Caruso approaches a climactic note at abou the twenty-ninth or thirtieth measure, BIBICHON *joins in, singing in a forced falsetto.*
BIBICHON: Ah! Ah! Ah! Ah!
ALL *(hissing him):* Sssh! Oh, no! Not you! Be quiet!
BIBICHON: Huh?
PALYMRE: One Caruso at a time!
YVONNE: You haven't any God-given voice!
BIBICHON: I was only helping him out.
PALYMRE: He doesn't need any help from you.
YVONNE: We want to listen.
BIBICHON: Who's stopping you? Not me.
ALL: Idiot! That's enough. Shut up! Quiet!
BIBICHON: I was right on key too. Listen. *(Singing.)* Ah! Ah![6]

The playwright has carefully created an elegant atmosphere by the visual aspects of the setting, the guests in a cultured surrounding of art and music; and as the guests listen appreciatively to a climactic moment in the music, he destroys the entire structure with Bibichon's first line. An attempt is made to restore the original mood, but Bibichon disrupts it again by joining in with his falsetto. This initial blast is enough to tell us we are in the atmosphere of comedy. The explosion is harmless—no one is really hurt, there is no genuine pain, the consequences are entirely social. The farcical atmosphere created assures us that we are to see a series of such antics, and sure enough within a few lines, Bibichon pinches the girls, a young man enters in an ill-fitting military outfit, the valet is caught drinking the wine by Amélie who slaps his face; he responds by staggering her with a wallop to the jaw.

Feydeau knew what all good writers of comedy must know, that it is important to create the appropriate climate for the enjoyment of the action to follow. The mood must establish a contagious sense of fun that

6. Georges Feydeau, *Keep an Eye on Amélie* (London: Van Loewen, 1958).

invites the spectator to drop his guard and his critical objectivity so he can enter into the action. This is the "general elation" that Bentley speaks of, which is "more important than any punch line."

Max Eastman has devoted considerable attention to analyzing the conditions essential for the "enjoyment of laughter" in his book of the same title. He has observed that humor depends on the existence of a favorable circumstance, and he concludes that "the condition in which joyful laughter most continually occurs is that of play." Laughter is not aroused by those situations where feelings run violent or deep. As a part of his evidence, Eastman cites the native response of a child who may welcome shock and disappointment as a pleasurable experience providing that an atmosphere of play has been established. If the child is teased, however, when he is tired or hungry, the fun is over: the atmosphere of play has been destroyed. Eastman's point of view is pertinent to our understanding of the comic attitude. How much emotional involvement should the audience be made to feel during a comedy? What is the basis for the comic attitude?

In Shakespeare's romantic comedies, the sentimental plays of Sheridan and Goldsmith in the eighteenth century, and in many of our contemporary works, the spectator is invited to enter into the emotions of the characters. We become concerned about the fortunes of the protagonist, our sympathies and hostilities are aroused by the playwright's treatment of his characters, we take pleasure in seeing the hero achieve his objective, usually accompanied by the jingle of money and wedding bells. The characters may be laughable, may at times appear foolish and weak, but the playwright does not criticize them. He treats them with tolerance and indulgence. Examples of comedies that involve our sympathies are *As You Like It, The Rivals, She Stoops to Conquer, They Knew What They Wanted, Born Yesterday,* and *Juno and the Paycock.* We laugh with their characters, rather than at them; there is no malice in our laughter.

On the other hand, Bergson argues that "laughter has no greater foe than emotion. . . . Its appeal is to the intelligence, pure and simple." Myers supports Bergson in this view saying: "Without detachment, we cannot realize the effect of comedy, which transforms the frustrations of reason into laughter." This point of view is well taken, especially at the extremes of the comic scale—low comedy and high. In most farce, our enjoyment stems from the action itself, the momentary laugh, the sudden release. We recognize that farce is a form of playing; we do not take its actions seriously. These are prefabricated characters racing through the convolutions of plot; they are not real people. No one experiences any genuine pain; the feelings do not penetrate the grease paint. Thus detachment is achieved because we consciously watch the actions of an artificial world.

Troisiéme Journée.
Le Malade imaginaire, Comédie representée
Dies tertius.

53 (opposite) Molière's *The Imaginary Invalid* performed at Versailles during the 1670s.

54 Petruchio teases his bride Kate in the Royal Shakespeare Theatre production of *The Taming of the Shrew*, 1960.

55 A more somber wedding scene in Shakespeare's comedy *Much Ado About Nothing* at the Royal Shakespeare Theatre, 1961.

High comedy has a different basis for objectivity. Its appeal is intellectual. The reaction to it arises out of perception and insight, rather than emotion. Sentiment is fatal to the aesthetic attitude required for intellectual wit and satire. Occasionally, the playwright lashes out too vigorously at his characters, stirring up an undertone of bitterness that destroys the comic effect. When Ben Jonson laid bare the human follies of his time in *Volpone* and *The Alchemist,* his unmerciful treatment of the brutality and viciousness of his characters threatened to dissipate the spirit of laughter by its savagery. The character of Shylock presents a perplexing challenge to the actor because of the wide range of his emotions; he is at once an object of ridicule and a human being whose deep suffering intrudes on the comic atmosphere. A recent example of bitterness that clashed with its intended comic tone is the bedroom scene in *The Waltz of the Toreadors,* in which Anouilh depicts the wife as so spiteful and rancorous in her attack on her husband that the attitude of detachment is undermined by pain.

The comic attitude requires a just sense of proportion so that the essential lightness of spirit is achieved, as Eastman suggested in play with the child. The audience of comedy cannot be pushed too hard in any direction. Excessive sentimentality, bitterness, depravity, exaggeration—any conspicuous straining for effect, any flat dullness or heavy-footed plodding upsets the niceness of balance so necessary for comedy, making it the most difficult of all the forms of drama to perform. The comic attitude is described effectively by Hegel in these words: "Inseparable from the comic is an infinite geniality and confidence, capable of rising superior to its own contradiction, and experiencing therein no taint of bitterness nor sense of misfortune whatever. It is the happy frame of mind, a hale condition of the soul, which, fully aware of itself, can suffer the dissolution of its aims."

An interesting aspect of the comic attitude is in connection with the absurdists with whom we will be dealing in chapter 9. They make use of all the comic and farcical devices discussed in this chapter and the next, yet their purpose is not comic. *Act Without Words, I* follows a standard comic pattern of an unfulfilled expectation, and the man's repeated efforts to reach the water are a good example of Bergson's comic theory of a man behaving mechanically. The absurdists' plays are filled with misunderstandings, and with unexpected turns and twists; language is broken down and made ridiculous; the characters use bits of comic business right out of vaudeville. Furthermore, the absurdists' plays may arouse a good deal of laughter—but it is apt to be uncertain, nervous laughter, not the relaxed enjoyment of genuine comedy. What then is missing? Essentially, the absurdist plays lack the comic atmosphere. The playful spirit is not created; the incongruities have an undercurrent of menace. The playwrights are in earnest, playing with deadly weapons. And their serious intent is too close to pain.

SOURCES OF LAUGHTER

The sources of comic effect have given scholar, critic, philosopher, and psychologist endless stimulation for speculation, and although their efforts have resulted in no uncontroversial conclusions, we may find some sustenance in their ideas. Among the various comic theories, some of which were suggested by the nine excerpts on page 110, let us briefly examine three which Allardyce Nicoll cites as the most prominent in his *The Theory of Drama*, realizing that a good deal of their validity depends on personal interpretation and careful selection of examples. The three theories are derision, incongruity, and automatism. You will recognize immediately the tendency of the theories to overlap because of the mercurial nature of comedy.

Derision. Aristotle's observation that comedy deals with men as "worse than they are" implies a comic theory of derision or degradation. It is ordinarily used as a form of criticism to combat pretentiousness or ignorance. Its objective is to keep man humble, balanced, and human. The legitimate targets of derision are pomposity, hypocrisy, and sanctimoniousness. As in life, laughter is used to keep people in line, to insure conformity to a socially acceptable code of behavior. Certainly Aristophanes was fully aware of the possibilities of derision as he ranged far and wide in his jibes against his contemporaries. Not even the audience was safe from his wit. For example, in *Peace*, Trygaeus after his ascent looks at the spectators and jeers at them:

> Ah! it's a rough job getting to the gods!
> My legs are as good as broken through it.
> *(to the audience)* How small you were to be
> sure, when seen from heaven! You all had the
> appearance too of being great rascals, but
> seen close, you look even worse.

Ben Jonson used his wit as an instrument of mockery against his fellow Elizabethans as he indicated when he stated the purpose of his comedy: "to strip the ragged follies of the time." Molière likewise brought low those who were guilty of excess, deriding those who were too ambitious in *Le Bourgeois Gentilhomme*, those who were too clever in *Les Précieuses Ridicules*, too exacting in *Le Misanthrope*, and too gullible in *Tartuffe*. The satirist has always regarded comedy as a salutary scourge to castigate awkward behavior.

Greek comedy ridiculed physical deformities as well as those of conduct. Comic characters were intentionally distorted and misshapen in appearance through the use of masks, phallic symbols, and padded costumes. A man's attempts to rise above himself were often counteracted by the reminder of his biological needs. Aristophanes delighted in mocking men and gods by exhibiting them in all kinds of embarrassing physical situations. He was ruthless in aiming his shafts of wit at all levels of life. The pattern of derision continues throughout dramatic literature to the present time, especially in farce, employing all manner of physical humor, coarse gags, barbed insults, and eccentric behavior. The satirist exploits situations in which characters are debased and reduced to objects of scorn by such formula devices as physical beatings, bodily functions—situations in which man is caught off-balance, red-handed, under the bed, in the closet, in his underwear—in any of the circumstances of life in which he is exposed, his dignity punctured, his flaw revealed, reminding everyone of his kinship with the animal world. Even the most serious moments of life are not free from the threat of derision. For example, the sacred liturgy of the church was burlesqued by medieval performers in their *Feast of the Asses*. In a contemporary film, *Mr. Hulot's Holiday*, Jacques Tati reduces the solemnity of a funeral to shambles when his leaking inner tube is mistaken for a wreath, hissing and writhing during the somber ceremony.

Degradation of character often involves a reversal of status. The deviate from normal social behavior, the inflated person is brought down off his pedestal. Such stock offenders against common sense and decent humanity as fools, fops, hypocrites, bumpkins, louts, misers, philanderers, braggarts, bores, and battle-axes are ridiculed into limbo because of their deformed behavior, their lack of wit or excess of ambition, greed, lust, or stupidity. The satirist uses barbs of derisive laughter to prick the inflated reputation of entrenched authority, often a popular form of comic appeal since the common man finds release and enjoyment in the discomfiture of those above him.

The dialogue of degradation may be an insult calculated to reduce the status of the recipient. The wisecrack has been a particular favorite device in American humor as the example from *The Man Who Came to Dinner* on pages 146–147 illustrates. An ancient example comes from Aristophanes' *Wasps* in the scene in which three dancers enter disguised as crabs. Two characters spy them and say:

PHILOCLEON: What's this? A shrimp or a spider?
XANTHIAS: It's a crab—a hermit crab, the smallest
of its kind; it writes tragedies.

The comic theory of derision is especially effective when the dramatist is treating ideas and characters critically. Although physical degradation, eccentric characters, and insulting language are confined mostly to farce, the satirist bent on attacking ideas also makes use of ridicule. Shaw's mockery of the established order of things kept an entire generation on edge; Aristophanes, Molière, and Jonson alienated many of their contemporaries by their attacks on politicians, the clergy, the law, and medicine. Derision is an effective weapon of criticism in the theater and a suitable source of laughter, but because it is critical and carries the overtones of contempt, it often ruffles those who are laughed at, and may beget bitterness and retaliation unless it is confined to those who have no power or status.

Incongruity. Perhaps because it is the most elastic and extensive theory of comedy, the idea of incongruity has the widest application. Incongruity is the result of the tension or dissonance set up by the juxtaposition of two objects or people that expresses a risible contrast, such as a large, fat woman matched with a small, skinny man, or a person out of place with his surroundings—in a bathing suit at the opera or in formal clothes at the beach. The contrast usually depends on the establishment of some kind of norm so that discrepancy is emphasized. There is a gap between the expected and the unexpected, between the intention and the realization, between the normal and the abnormal, which results in comic discord and inconsistency.

Incongruity may take several forms—situation, character, and dialogue. The comic situation based on incongruity presents a contrast between the usual or accepted behavior and the unusual or unacceptable. A typical pattern is to place a character in unfamiliar surroundings that reveal his social incongruity, such as a country bumpkin in polite society, the socially elite in bucolic surroundings, an intellectual among barbarians, a clown or an inebriate in a dignified gathering, a sailor in a harem, a coed in a men's dormitory, a tramp in the mayor's bed. Some examples of incongruous situations are the mismatched sword-fight between Viola and Aguecheek in *Twelfth Night,* the two duelists striking one another with musical instruments in *Squaring the Circle,* and the English professor engaging the football star in a fist fight in *The Male Animal.* Another version of the incongruous situation occurs when carefully laid plans go awry, often having the opposite effect than that intended, such as the dinner party that turns into a fiasco in *You Can't Take It with You* and the chaotic reception of the deputation team in Chekhov's *The Anniversary.* A classic example occurs in *The Taming of the Shrew* when Petruchio destroys the dignity of the marriage ceremony with his ragged attire and his raucous behavior which culminates when

> . . . he took the bride about the neck
> And kissed her lips with such a clamorous smack
> That at the parting all the church did echo.

Incongruity of character involves a contrast between the ideal and the real, or between appearance and actuality. This may be seen in such situations as Parolles' professed bravery and his actual cowardice when confronted with danger in *All's Well That Ends Well,* Malvolio's grotesque costuming and simpering when he attempts to create a favorable impression on Olivia in *Twelfth Night,* the depiction of Dionysus, the revered Greek god, as a cringing weakling in *The Frogs.* An aspect of incongruity of character that also fits Bergson's automatism is the inflexible character whose one-track mind separates him from the norm. We think of such examples as Molière's Alceste, whose exaggerated desire for frankness makes him socially bizarre and of Jonson's Morose, whose oversensitivity to noise sets him up as the butt of an elaborate joke.

Incongruity of language occurs when the dialogue is in sharp contrast to the social context, such as the sudden interjection of vulgarity into a polite conversation, or when the language has the opposite effect of that intended by the speaker. Still another use of incongruous language is in the use of speech which is unexpected or inappropriate to the characters, such as refined epigrams spoken by rustics, or wise sayings in the mouths of babes.

Incongruity in its various forms suggests imbalance and disproportion; there is the implication of an upset equilibrium, "the disconnecting of one idea from another, or the jostling of one feeling against another."

Automatism. One of the most imaginative and provocative theories of comedy was that advanced by Bergson in his book *Laughter,* in which he contends that the essence of the laughable is automatism—"something mechanical is encrusted on the living." Man becomes an object of laughter whenever he becomes rigid and machinelike, or whenever he loses control of himself or breaks contact with humanity.

Automatism of character occurs when an individual loses his human flexibility, and his behavior becomes mechanical in its repetition, or when a man becomes a puppet, no longer in control of his actions. The gist of Bergson's thinking is indicated by these representative statements about comedy and character: "We laugh every time a person gives us the impression of being a thing." "Any individual is comic who automatically goes his own way without troubling himself about getting in touch with the rest of his fellow beings." "Rigidity, automatism, absent-mindedness, and unsociability are all inextricably entwined, and all serve as ingredients to the making up of the comic in character." Bergson's point of view on one-sided characters is similar to that of Ben Jonson's comedy of "humours" in which he ridiculed those characters who were guilty of some imbalance, some excess:

> As when some one peculiar quality
> Doth so possess a man, that it doth draw
> All his effects, his spirits, and his powers
> In their confluctions, all to run one way
> This may be truly said to be a humour.

In such plays as *Epicene, Volpone,* and *The Alchemist,* Jonson makes comic figures of those who have lost control and succumbed to some individual trait of character causing eccentric and antisocial behavior. Such characters fit neatly in Bergson's theory of automatism.

Automatism of situation is often based on repetition. Characters are caught in the grip of circumstances and subjected to mechanical domination. Chaplin made use of this device in his famous mechanized corn-on-the-cob eating sequence, and his hilarious shaving pantomime to the accompaniment of a Brahms Hungarian Dance. Repeated patterns of behavior have been used very often as the framework for comedy as in the series of medical examinations in *Dr. Knock,* the alternating love scenes in *Squaring the Circle* and *The Love of Four Colonels,* and the repetition of the palm tree device in *Mister Roberts.* The skillful playwright in employing repetition adds new and unexpected twists to make the pattern more interesting. As an example of ingenious variety, refer to the scene from Aristophanes' *The Frogs* on pages 141–143. Meierhold in directing his interpretation of three Chekhov farces found thirty-eight references to fainting, which he exploited as a recurrent leitmotif in production. In musical revues, repeated variations of a comic piece of business are used in what is called a "running gag." A typical example used by Olsen and Johnson was that of an "escape artist" who, bound hand and foot, is given half a minute to free himself, but at the end of the allotted time is still securely tied. Every now and then he is shown as he continues his unsuccessful struggle. At the end of the performance, when the audience makes its exit through the lobby, the hapless escape artist is on the floor continuing his efforts.

Automatism of dialogue takes several forms. For example, Bergson says, "Inadvertently to say or do what we have no intention of saying or doing, as a result of inelasticity or momentum is, as we are aware, one of the sources of the comic." Inelasticity, of course, implies repetition, a standard form of comedy, as for example Slender's expression of his love in *The Merry Wives of Windsor* when he sighs every now and then, "Oh, sweet Ann Page." In a recent play to mock the monotonous dullness of ordinary social conversation, Ionesco in *The Bald Soprano* uses the phrases "That is curious, how bizarre, what a coincidence," in various forms more than two dozen times in four pages of dialogue. One of the most successful uses of automatism of language occurs in Molière's *Le Malade Imaginaire* when Toinette, a pert maid-servant, is pretending to be a physician examining her hypochondriac master, Argan:

TOINETTE: Let me feel your pulse. Come, come, beat properly, please. Ah! I will soon make you beat as you should. This pulse is trifling with me. I see that it does not know me yet. Who is your doctor?

ARGAN: Mr. Purgon.

TOINETTE: That man is not noted in my books among the great doctors. What does he say you are ill of?

ARGAN: He says it is the liver, and others say it is the spleen.
TOINETTE: They are a pack of ignorant blockheads; you are suffering from the lungs.
ARGAN: The lungs?
TOINETTE: Yes; what do you feel?
ARGAN: From time to time great pains in my head.
TOINETTE: Just so; the lungs.
ARGAN: At times it seems as if I had a mist before my eyes.
TOINETTE: The lungs.
ARGAN: I feel sick now and then.
TOINETTE: The lungs.
ARGAN: And I feel sometimes a weariness in all my limbs.
TOINETTE: The lungs.
ARGAN: And sometimes I have sharp pains in the stomach, as if I had the colic.
TOINETTE: The lungs. Do you eat your food with appetite?
ARGAN: Yes, Sir.
TOINETTE: The lungs. Do you like to drink a little wine?
ARGAN: Yes, Sir.
TOINETTE: The lungs. You feel sleepy after your meals, and willingly enjoy a nap?
ARGAN: Yes, Sir.
TOINETTE: The lungs, the lungs, I tell you. What does your doctor order you for food?
ARGAN: He orders me soup.
TOINETTE: Ignoramus!
ARGAN: Fowl.
TOINETTE: Ignoramus!
ARGAN: Veal.
TOINETTE: Ignoramus!
ARGAN: Broth.
TOINETTE: Ignoramus!
ARGAN: New-laid eggs.
TOINETTE: Ignoramus!
ARGAN: And at night a few prunes to relax the bowels.
TOINETTE: Ignoramus!
ARGAN: And, above all, to drink my wine well diluted with water.
TOINETTE: *Ignorantus, ignoranta, ignorantum.*

It is apparent that Bergson's theory is an interesting extension of the idea of incongruity, the jostling together of the human and the mechanical. By his ingenuity and persuasiveness, Bergson makes quite a plausible case for automatism, especially for the comedies of Molière, but like other comic theories, automatism does not explain all of the sources of laughter, nor is it appropriate to all kinds of comic effect. Nevertheless, automatism must be recognized as one of the explanations for the phenomenon of laughter, and we are indebted to Bergson for his stimulating analysis.

From the preceding discussion of representative theories of comedy, it is apparent that a case can be made for derision, incongruity, and automatism. It should also be obvious that it is impossible to fix comedy in a single rigid mold although recurrent patterns and mechanisms show through the diverse forms. This will be increasingly evident as we consider the structure and content of comedy.

plot

Good comedy requires skillful plotting. A comedy is not simply a loosely knit accumulation of situations and gags. Laughs must be carefully timed and built, situations contrived and an appropriate atmosphere established. A comedy playscript is a score for playing, and just as the composer must be fully cognizant of the possibilities of his music in the hands of musicians, in a similar way, the writer of comedy must be fully aware of the techniques and resources of the actor which will animate his material. The comic writer is acutely concerned with man in his social environment. Basic patterns of comedy depict a character who deviates from the norm or who is out of place with his surroundings. The implicit contrasts and conflicts require adroit delineation of the social milieu in order to expose the laughable elements of conduct. Tragic writers may concentrate on heroic figures, isolated from other characters and unaffected by their behavior, but comedy exploits the interaction of characters, the human scene, the group situation, the juxtaposition of characters. Comedy is more involved with the particular than with the universal. Its emphasis is on the here and now, not the long perspective. The playwright frequently develops timely allusions, local references, and contemporaneous characters. His material must have a sense of crispness and spontaneity. Comedy must not smell of the museum or the dead past. Hence, it is difficult for comedy to survive its time and place of origin because many of its most telling referents are gone.

A typical Aristophanic plot shows how the leading character becomes inspired with a ridiculous idea which is vigorously opposed by others. The idea is tried out and the results are demonstrated. The play ends in revelry. In the subsequent development of comedy, the original pattern persists. A character strives for an objective but he is thwarted because his goal is an impossible one, or he misjudges his objectives and his opposition, or he fights with the wrong weapons. His problem is finally solved when misunderstandings are cleared up and the truth emerges. The play ends happily, often with the lovers united in an embrace, a vestigial reminder of the orgiastic celebration of Greek "old comedy." In any case,

56 Scene from a *commedia dell'arte* performance. Note the varied comic business of the performers.

57 (opposite) Type characters from the Italian popular comedy, the *commedia dell'arte.*

DONNA PETRONELLA.
DONNA MARTINA.
LALAGE.
SIEUR ANSELMO.
SIEUR GERONTE
LUCINDE.
BRIGELLA.
LE MESETIN.
LE ARLEQUIN BERGAMASEO.
LE SCAPINE.
DONNA ANGELICA
LISETTE
Turba levis lepidos risus spectanda theatris
Excitat; ast caveat, seria quisquis amat.
Dem eitlen Sinn macht offt ihr Schertz u. Spiel viel Lachen,
Wer aber ernsthafft ist, der meydet ihre Sachen.
Cum Pr. Sac. Caes. Maj.
Mart: Engelbrecht excud. A.V.

IL DOTTORE
SCATALON BOLOGNESE.
MADLE. LUCINDE, fille de GERONIE.
IL CAPITANEO SPAVENTO NAPOLITANO.
MADLE. ARLEQUINE.
IL ARLEQUIN.
MADLE. COLUMBINE.
MONSR. OCTAVIO.
LA DONNA IULIA
LA CORINNE
LE SCARAMOUCHE
LE SIEUR PANTALON
Non oculos modo, sed loculos quoq; Comicus arte
Haud raro petulans vexat et evacuat.
Scarmuz und Arlequin kan manches klug ergötzen
Dabey Sie auch daß Hertz und Beutel offt verletzen.
Cum Pr. Sac. Caes. Maj.
Mart: Engelbrecht excud. A.V.

the comic plot usually involves an imbalance caused by the presence of some ridiculous element through error, ignorance, or ambition. The resultant conflicts and contrasts create comic tension which is released in laughter.

The plots of most comedies are made up of sharp complications which require careful craftmanship in the use of exposition, climaxes, crises, discoveries, and the denouement. The tangled threads of action must be kept clear to the audience, which is tricky business in plays of rapid action, mixups, and misunderstandings. In previous centuries, the playwright's task was made much easier by the conventions of the aside and the soliloquy, which allowed the playwright to communicate directly with the audience in informing them of the schemes and tricks of the plot and the disparity between truth and pretense. The climaxes and crises of comedy demand technical mastery because the high points of the action often involve a social situation in which a number of people are caught in the same net, obliging the playwright to deal with complex materials. Frequently, the emotional peaks are those of action and discovery, which require that the playwright have a strong sense of visual humor. Climaxes must be built and sustained without prolonging them beyond the limits of the material. The playwright's touch must be deft and sure to keep the pace rapid and to create the special climate of comedy which will insure laughter.

The materials from which comedies are made are venerable ones, as old as the theater itself. The sources of comic effect, which the classic playwrights Aristophanes, Plautus, and Terence used to delight the audiences of Athens and Rome, are still the stock in trade which you can see on your television or motion-picture screen tonight. Someone has suggested that, after all, there are only seven jokes: (1) the insult; (2) the pun; (3) sex; (4) family life; (5) reversal; (6) odd combinations; and (7) news. This may not be all-inclusive but the list is surprisingly universal. Similarly, the devices of comedy that the playwright uses are well established. Let us consider three very common devices for evoking laughter, realizing that these are representative examples and by no means an exhaustive list. Several other devices will be cited in the chapter on farce.

comic devices

One of the most reliable comic devices is that of teasing, which may take a variety of forms such as the delay of news which Shakespeare employs when the Nurse withholds Romeo's message from Juliet. Similarly in the Russian comedy, *Squaring the Circle,* Emilian, the letter-bearer, keeps the message from Abram's missing sweetheart until he performs a dance. Another version of the teasing device occurs in the opera *The Night Bell,* when the elderly groom, who has married a young bride, is interrupted frequently on his wedding night by the untimely entrances of his young rival who appears in a variety of disguises. Another form of teasing occurs when characters are intentionally placed in embarrassing or awkward situations. Elmire in *Tartuffe* deliberately teases Orgon by encouraging the hypocrite's attentions while her husband observes the scene from his hiding place underneath a table. Tony Lumpkin in *She Stoops to Conquer* teases his mother by driving her around her own garden in a carriage at night pretending that they are beset by robbers. In *The Taming of the Shrew,* Petruchio exposes Katherine to a series of teasings before she is finally tamed. He tests her in the following scene when he and Kate, accompanied by Hortensio, are on the road toward home:

PETRUCHIO: Come on, i' God's name; once more toward our father's
Good Lord, how bright and goodly shines the moon!
KATHERINE: The moon! the sun: it is not moonlight now.
PETRUCHIO: I say it is the moon that shines so bright.
KATHERINE: I know it is the sun that shines so bright.
PETRUCHIO: Now, by my mother's son, and that's myself,
It shall be moon, or star, or what I list,
Or ere I journey to your father's house.
Go on, and fetch our horses back again.
Evermore cross'd and cross'd; nothing but cross'd!
HORTENSIO: Say as he says, or we shall never go.
KATHERINE: Forward, I pray since we have come so far,
And be it moon, or sun, or what you please:
An if you please to call it a rush-candle,
Henceforth, I vow it shall be so for me.
PETRUCHIO: I say it is the moon.
KATHERINE: I know it is the moon.
PETRUCHIO: Nay, then you lie: it is the blessed sun.
KATHERINE: Then, God be blessed, it is the blessed sun:
But sun it is not, when you say it is not;
And the moon changes even as your mind.
What you will have it named, even that it is;
And so it shall be so for Katherine.

Another familiar plot mechanism of comedy is inversion. The entire play may be based on the turnabout of a down-trodden character who ultimately achieves a dominant position as in such plays as *The Solid Gold Cadillac,* and *Born Yesterday.* The reversal may be a temporary one with the characters temporarily thrown out of their usual milieu, only to return to their customary status as in *Jeppe of the Hills,* when the drunken ne'er-do-well is placed in the mayor's bed, treated royally for a day, and then returned insensible to the gutter where he was found. Similarly, in *The Admirable Crichton,* a butler assumes control of a household when the family is marooned on an island, but at the conclusion of the play he resumes his former servile position. A very successful use of reversal occurs in *Master Pierre Pathelin,* when the trickster is himself tricked by his own device. Inversion is used when female characters assume dominant roles, as in *Lysistrata, The Warrior's Husband,* and *The Queen's Husband.*

Another well-worn comic device is the use of the unfamiliar. A character or group of characters is placed in new surroundings, or they are engaged in unaccustomed activities. One form of this device is the process of teaching an inexperienced and often inexpert person, such as the English lesson in *Henry V*, the fencing lesson in *Everyman in His Humour* and the dancing lesson in *Le Bourgeois Gentilhomme.* The humor may be heightened by the additional twist of having the instructor as ignorant as his pupil. The awkward, embarrassed, or shy person making an adjustment to a new experience or surroundings is used again and again for comic effect, such as the love scenes in *Ah, Wilderness!,* the girls' first night in their basement apartment in *My Sister Eileen,* and the wedding night episode in *The Fourposter.*

Perhaps these three devices are sufficient to indicate some of the mechanisms of comedy. You will notice that among these devices and those cited in the chapter on farce, there are patterns of action which are also employed in tragedy. For example, the reversal formula of comedy is likewise utilized in tragedy: a highborn character who occupies an elevated position at the beginning of the play and falls to his catastrophe, as in *Hamlet, Agamemnon,* and *Antigone.* In comedy, the reversal often goes in the other direction. The little person, ignored and beaten down, emerges at the end of the play in a dominant position, as in *Three Men on a Horse* and *Beggar on Horseback.* The complications of mistaken identity used for comic purposes by Shakespeare in *A Midsummer Night's Dream, Twelfth Night,* and *Comedy of Errors* are utilized for tragic effect by Sophocles in *Oedipus Rex.* The nature of the mechanism does not determine the response, but more significant is the manner in which the playwright uses it, the spirit of the play. This point is brought forcibly home by comparing the plot mechanisms of *Romeo and Juliet* and the Pyramus and Thisbe episode in *A Midsummer Night's Dream.* The plots are strikingly similar, but one is used for comedy, the other for tragedy.

character

Because comedy wears many guises, there is great variation in character. Not only is there a difference in kind, but there is a difference in treatment. A comic character may be the unconscious butt of the joke, such as Hodge in *Poetaster* or Orgon in *Tartuffe*. Sometimes, a character may be conscious of his plight or absurdities, and shares his discomfiture with the audience as Falstaff does in *Henry IV*. Again, a comic character may, through his wit and insight, direct the laughter toward an idea or situation as Mirabell does in *The Way of the World* or as many Shavian characters do in mocking contemporary ideas and institutions. Sometimes a character may be comical because of his reversal from a downtrodden nobody to a person of status, as in *The Inspector General* and *The Doctor in Spite of Himself*. A character may arouse laughter by another kind of reversal—the pompous or inflated character who is humbled as the imposter is in *Tartuffe*, Kate in *The Taming of the Shrew*, and the Captain in *Mister Roberts*. A character may be comical because of his eccentric behavior, his lack of wit or judgment, his peculiar cast of mind, his delightful facility with language, his engaging animal spirits, his charming manner, or his buoyant attitude toward life.

Comic characters tend to be stock types. The playwright frequently is more concerned about developing the intricacies of plot than he is about revealing depth of character. Hence he sketches his figures lightly or else resorts to readily recognizable types. The dramatist may deliberately create one-sided roles to suit his comic purpose as a means of showing their inhumanity in their fixations and inflexibility. Again, he may purposely keep his characters in the simple mold of stock figures in order to prevent excessive emotional attachment that might destroy the light atmosphere of comedy. As character becomes more genuine and complex, drama moves away from comedy. As an example of how a type character may evolve into a sympathetic and complex human being, thus altering the flavor of the play, we may consider the case of the braggart soldier. As Lamachus in Aristophanes' *Acharnians*, Miles Gloriosus in Plautine comedy, and the Capitano in commedia dell'arte, he is an elementary source of comic effect because of the disparity between his pretended bravery and his cowardice in the face of danger. As Shakespeare's Falstaff, the character is vastly enriched as he rollicks his way through *The Merry Wives of Windsor*, and then is developed into such a complete personality in *Henry IV* that Hardin Craig referred to Falstaff as "the first great synthetic character in modern drama."

The writer of comedy is closer to surface reality than the writer of tragedy. The comic dramatist is more concerned with the immediate, the temporal, the commonplace. Hence, despite the fact that characters in comedy may be types in that they are psychologically simple, they may give a superficial effect of actuality to an audience, especially when acted by consummate comedians whose personal attributes enlarge and deepen the original image of the playwright to give the impression of credible, complex figures such as Joseph Jefferson's *Rip Van Winkle*.

Furthermore, the very nature of comic material is rooted in action, which gives to the actor license and latitude to transform a spare outline into a full figure.

Bergson describes the comic character as one who is "generally comic in proportion to his ignorance of himself. The comic person is unconscious." Such a character has a blind side that causes him to react in a ludicrous fashion. He is seen again and again as the victim of his ignorance: Malvolio in *Twelfth Night*, Orgon in *Tartuffe*, and Jeppe in *Jeppe of the Hills*. But Bergson's point of view is too narrow for universal application. All comic characters are not unconscious or ignorant of their shortcomings. As we have suggested earlier, there is laughter that is shared with the character when we borrow some of his humiliation as the inept lover, the raw recruit, the bashful swain, and the shy maiden. Falstaff's follies infect us all. We do not laugh at him to punish him or change him; we laugh because of the Falstaff in us. Laughter stems from sympathy as well as ridicule. It is true that numerous comic characters, especially those from classic and neoclassic comedy, fit neatly into Bergson's theory, but there are also scores of comic roles, particularly in English and American plays, which arouse our sympathy and affection, such as Rosalind in *As You Like It*, Viola in *Twelfth Night*, Billie in *Born Yesterday*, Marlow in *She Stoops to Conquer*, Professor Turner in *The Male Animal*, Charles Surface in *The School for Scandal* and Tony in *They Knew What They Wanted*. The kind of response which a character elicits from an audience varies with the playwright's purpose. It may be either critical or sympathetic.

thought

Most comedy does not bear a heavy burden of thought. The playwright is much more concerned with satisfying the needs of those spectators who come to the theater for diversion—who wish to avoid facing someone else's serious problems—spectators who have no immediate interest in intellectual stimulation in the theater. They want to have a good time—to laugh and forget themselves. Because this attitude represents the dominating taste of those who come to see a comedy, the comic writer's efforts are concentrated on interesting the audience in a series of lighthearted actions and sympathetic characters whose involvements are not taken seriously. While the basis for laughter in such comedy may imply an accepted code of behavior, and a system of values, the attention is not centered on weighing the merits of conventional morality, except insofar as it serves as a frame of reference for displaying incongruity. In most comedy, the playwright is not questioning values, he is exposing ridiculous behavior. For his purposes, the comic action is important rather than the meaning of the action.

There is a particular kind of comedy, however, which reverses this point of view, and makes of it a drama of criticism in which the appeal of the play is intellectual. This is known as high comedy.

High comedy, social comedy, or the comedy of manners is a special form of drama with its own particular emphasis and techniques. It is the very antithesis of farce or low comedy in that its appeal is to a limited, cultivated audience rather than a general undiscriminating public, and its stress is on dialogue rather than on action. High and low comedy possess one similarity—they both require an attitude of detachment, a freedom from emotional involvement.

High comedy is written for an audience that is urbane and sophisticated, with a commonly accepted code of behavior that is a matter of manners, not morals. Indeed, the Restoration audience was notorious for its immorality and licentiousness, and yet the period is the most brilliant one of high comedy in English literature. It was the purpose of the high comedies of Congreve, Wycherly, and Vanbrugh to mock those who violated its manners. The objects of laughter were the gauche, the outsiders, the pretenders whose absurd or awkward behavior caused them to lose their sense of balance. Ridicule was not a moral indictment, but a reproof for antisocial conduct. In other periods of theater history, writers of high comedy have directed their criticism at more universal targets—the foibles and follies of their age. Aristophanes scorned the militarists, Molière attacked hypocrisy and pretense, Shaw delighted in exposing the sham behind the sentimental and rigid precepts of Victorian behavior. High comedy is therefore a social weapon. Its implications extend beyond the immediate chuckle; its aim is to evoke thoughtful laughter; it is intended to have a residue of meaning. S. N. Behrman, a most successful American writer of high comedy commenting in the *New York Times*, sums up the playwright's point of view in this statement: "What makes the essence of high comedy is not the furniture of the room where the action takes place, but the articulateness of the characters, the plane on which they talk, the intellectual and moral climate in which they live. . . . One of the endless sources of high comedy is seriousness of temperament and intensity of purpose in contrast with the trivality of the occasion."

As Behrman suggests, the techniques of high comedy rely most heavily on language. Since it is addressed to an intellectual and cultivated audience, this kind of comedy employs bright repartee, conceits, epigrams, double entendres and all the refinments and subtleties of which the writer has command. The excerpt from Congreve's *The Way of the World* (pp. 131–133) exemplifies this style of writing. As a result of the preoccupation with dialogue, high comedy sometimes is deficient in plot and characterization, as Nicoll observed: "Wit, therefore, we may say, although it is one of the highest type of comic expression, when presented in an exaggerated form, kills the play in which it appears. It carries the artificiality which is present in all high comedy to a point of absurdity, so that we can feel in no way the connection between the figures on the stage and real life."[7]

High comedy is an esotric form of drama created for a particular kind of audience and demanding a special style of playing that is facile, suave, and artificial in keeping with the hothouse atmosphere of the play itself.

diction

Comedy employs a wide variety of language devices for its effect, from cleverly turned conceits and bon mots to crude puns, insults, vulgarisms, and deformed words. We have already observed some of its comic uses in derision, automatism, and incongruity. Most successful comic writers have excellent ears for dialogue and they take apparent delight in their verbal skill. The Elizabethans were especially fond of exploiting language for comic effect. We remember the rich texture of the rustic's speech in *A Midsummer Night's Dream,* the word-play of the doorkeeper in *Macbeth* and the grave diggers in *Hamlet.* Ben Jonson similarly took pains to create earthy and lively dialogue as this excerpt from *Every Man in His Humour* illustrates:

MATTHEW: I think this be the house. What ho!

COB: Who's there? Or, Master Matthew! Gi' your worship good morrow.

MATTHEW: What, Cob! How does thou, good Cob? Dost thou inhabit here, Cob?

COB: Ay, sir, I and my linage ha' kept a poor house here in our days.

MATTHEW: Thy linage, Monsieur Cob! What linage? What linage?

COB: Why sir, an ancient linage, and a princely. Mine ance'try came from a king's belly, no worse man; and yet no man either (by you worship's leave, I did lie in that), but herring, [A cob is a young herring] the king of fish (from his belly I proceed), one o' the monarchs of the world, I assure you. The first red herring that was broiled in Adam and Eve's kitchen do I fetch my pedigree from, by my harrot's books. His cob was my great-great-mighty-great grandfather.

MATTHEW: Why mighty, why mighty, I pray thee?

COB: O, it was a mighty while ago, sir, and a mighty great cob.

MATTHEW: How knows't thou that?

7. Nicoll, *Theory of Drama.*

COB: How know I? Why, I smell his ghost ever and anon.
MATTHEW: Smell a ghost? O unsavory jest! And the ghost of a herring cob?
COB: Ay, sir. With favor of your worship's nose, Mr. Matthew, why not the ghost of a herring cob as well as the ghost of Rasher Bacon?
MATTHEW: Roger Bacon, thou wouldst say?
COB: I say Rasher Bacon. They were both broiled o' the coals; and a man may smell broiled meat, I hope? You are a scholar; upsolve that now.
MATTHEW: O raw ignorance!

The writer of high comedy, of course, is especially concerned with dialogue since repartee becomes the drama's chief appeal, the animation of language and the nimbleness of wit replacing the physical action. The problem in writing such dialogue is to create an external sparkle and shine that masks the labor beneath it. Congreve, the Restoration playwright, was an acknowledged master of brilliant repartee as the following excerpt from the famous marriage discussion in *The Way of the World* exhibits:

MIRABELL: Do you lock yourself up from me, to make my search more curious, or is this pretty artifice contrived to signify that here the chase must end and my pursuits be crowned? For you can fly no further.
MRS. MILLAMANT: Vanity! No—I'll fly, and be followed to the last moment. Though I am upon the very verge of matrimony, I expect you should solicit me as much as if I were wavering at the grate of a monastery, with one foot over the threshold. I'll be solicited to the very last—nay, and afterwards.
MIRABELL: What, after the last?
MRS. MILLAMANT: Oh, I should think I was poor and had nothing to bestow, if I were reduced to an inglorious ease and freed from the agreeable fatigues of solicitation.
MIRABELL: But do you not know that when favors are conferred upon instant and tedious solicitation, that they diminish in their value, and that both the giver loses the grace, and the receiver lessens his pleasure?
MRS. MILLAMANT: It may be in things of common application; but never, sure, in love. Oh, I hate a lover that can dare to think he draws a moment's air, independent of the bounty of his mistress. There is not so impudent a thing in nature as the saucy look of an assured man, confident of success. The pedantic arrogance of a very husband has not so pragmatical an air. Ah! I'll never marry unless I am first made sure of my will and pleasure.
MIRABELL: Would you have 'em both before marriage? or will you be contented with the first now, and stay for the other till after grace?
MRS. MILLAMANT: Ah! don't be so impertinent.—My dear liberty, shall I

58 Comedy performed at the Park Theatre, New York, 1822.

59 Eighteenth-century Danish production of Holberg's *Jeppe of the Hills.*

60 Modern high comedy scene from Bernard Shaw's *Major Barbara.*

leave thee? My faithful solitude, my darling contemplation, must I bid you then adieu? Ay-h adieu—my morning thoughts, agreeable wakings, indolent slumbers, all ye douceurs, ye sommeils du matin, adieu.—I can't do 't, 'tis more than impossible.—Positively, Mirabell, I'll lie abed in the mornings as long as I please.

MIRABELL: Then I'll get up in the morning as early as I please.

MRS. MILLAMANT: Ah? Idle creature, get up when you will—and d'ye hear, I won't be called names after I'm married; positively, I won't be called names.

MIRABELL: Names!

MRS. MILLAMANT: Aye, as wife, spouse, my dear, joy, jewel, love, sweetheart, and the rest of that nauseous cant, in which men and their wives are so fulsomely familiar—I shall never bear that. Good Mirabell, don't let us be familiar or fond, nor kiss before folks, like my lady Fadler and Sir Francis; nor go to Hyde Park together the first Sunday in a new chariot, to provoke eyes and whispers, and then never to be seen there together again, as if we were proud of one another the first week, and ashamed of one another ever after. Let us never visit together, nor go to a play together; but let us be very strange and well-bred. Let us be as strange as if we had been married a great while, and as well-bred as if we were not married at all.

MIRABELL: Have you any more conditions to offer? Hitherto your demands are pretty reasonable.

MRS. MILLAMANT: Trifles—as liberty to pay and receive visits to and from whom I please; to write and receive letters, without interrogatories or wry faces on your part; to wear what I please, and choose conversation with regard only to my own taste; to have no obligation upon me to converse with wits that I don't like, because they are your acquaintance: or to be intimate with fools, because they may be your relations.—Come to dinner when I please; dine in my dressing room when I'm out of humour, without giving a reason. To have my closet inviolate; to be sole empress of my teatable, which you must never presume to approach without first asking leave. And lastly, wherever I am, you shall always knock at the door before you come in. These articles subscribe, if I continue to endure you a little longer, I may by degrees dwindle into a wife.

MIRABELL: Your bill of fare is something advanced in this latter account. —Well, have I liberty to offer conditions—that when you have dwindled into a wife, I may not be beyond measure enlarged into a husband?

MRS. MILLAMANT: You have free leave. Propose your utmost; speak and spare not.

MIRABELL: I thank you.—Imprimis then, I convenant that your acquaintance be general; that you admit no sworn confidante or intimate of your own sex—no she-friend to screen her affairs under your countenance, and tempt you to make trial of mutual secrecy. No decoy-

> duck to wheedle you—a fop scrambling to the play in a mask—then bring you home in pretended fright, when you think you shall be found out—and rail at me for missing the play and disappointing the frolic which you had, to pick me up and prove my constancy.

MRS. MILLAMANT: Detestable imprimis! I go to the play in a mask!

comedy in performance

More than other forms of drama, comedy depends upon performance for its full effect. The timing of the actor, his ability to play a piece of business, to project a laugh line, to bring out the risible qualities of situation and character without destroying the light atmosphere—these are special requisites for the complete realization of comedy.

One of the most puzzling aspects of the performance of comedy is in the variety of response from audience to audience. A comic line or piece of business may arouse boisterous laughter from one audience while the next performance may be greeted by a cold and stony silence. Friday and Saturday night audiences invariably outlaugh a Monday or Tuesday night one. Young spectators are more demonstrative than older ones. A scattered audience is less susceptible to laughter than a closely packed one. Within a given audience there are often individuals who are convulsed with laughter throughout, while others remain aloof and unamused.

In general, social facilitation helps create the climate for comedy. Laughter is a social gesture; it is contagious, but the audience must be in a light mood, easily susceptible to the courtship of comedy. Spectators must be wooed and won, not coerced. The comedian can lose the comic sympathy of his audience by making them conscious of his efforts to be funny. When someone says, "I am going to tell you a very funny story," he immediately doubles his difficulties in getting a laugh because the listener's critical faculties have been aroused, and he is aware of the means rather than the end. Let one performer in a comedy strain for effect by being "consciously cute," and he is likely to alienate the audience for the production as a whole.

Comedy is a framework for action. The inanimate script is brought to life by the performer, but his skill is dependent upon the craftsmanship of the playwright. As Thorndike says:

> Comedy finds its purpose aided by skillful use of words as well as by gesture and mimicry. It avails itself of the arts of the theatre and of literature. It delights in song as well as dance, in epigram as well as grimace, in paradox as well as slap-jack, and it can stoop to pruning as readily as to buffoonery. Whatever can be used in verse or fiction to

amuse and delight can be employed in the drama with the additional advantage of impersonation. It combines the humor of words and voice, of the audible and visible. Its form and movement, construction and texture, person and speeches, are all dependent on literary art. Its greatest creative triumphs are won by the pen.[8]

exercises

1. What is the effect of emotion on comedy?
2. How can comedy be used as a weapon?
3. Devise a comic scene based on incongruity or automatism.
4. What kind of catharsis does comedy produce?
5. Devise three comic entrances.
6. Create the atmosphere for the opening moments of a comedy.
7. Make a check mark for each place in *Keep an Eye on Amélie* where you would expect an audience to laugh. Explain the bases for the comic effect.
8. Devise three pieces of comic action based on Freud's theory of comedy.
9. Using a normally serious situation, convert it into a comic one.
10. Analyze the comic aspects of six cartoons.
11. Describe a sympathetic comic character *with* whom we laugh. Contrast him with an unsympathetic one *at* whom we laugh.
12. Describe the "comic attitude."
13. What are the characteristics of high comedy?
14. Discuss the absurdist's use of comedy.
15. To what extent does the comic effect depend upon the performer?
16. What causes laughter?

suggested reading

Henri Bergson, *Laughter,* trans. Cloudesley Brereton and Fred Rothwell, 1917.
Max Eastman, *Enjoyment of Laughter,* 1942.
John J. Enck, Elizabeth T. Forter, and Alvin Whitley, *The Comic in Theory and Practice,* 1960.
Marvin Felheim, *Comedy, Plays, Theory and Criticism,* 1962.
Paul Lauter, *Theories of Comedy,* 1964.
George Meredith, *Essay on the Idea of Comedy and the Uses of the Comic Spirit,* 1918.
Athene Seyler and Stephen Haggard, *The Craft of Comedy,* 1946.

8. Ashley H. Thorndike, *English Comedy* (New York: Macmillan, 1929).

play list

Jean Anouilh, *The Waltz of the Toreadors*
Aristophanes, *The Frogs; Lysistrata*
Jean Giraudoux, *The Madwoman of Chaillot*
Ben Jonson, *Volpone*
Garson Kanin, *Born Yesterday*
Molière, *The Miser; Tartuffe*
William Shakespeare, *A Midsummer Night's Dream; Twelfth Night*
George Bernard Shaw, *Major Barbara; Pygmalion*
Richard Sheridan, *The School for Scandal*
Thornton Wilder, *The Matchmaker*

farce

This chapter on farce is an extension of our discussion of comedy. Just as the counterpart of tragedy is melodrama, the counterpart of high comedy is farce. As a form of drama, farce is very old, and as for its universal appeal, it has been and continues to be, along with melodrama, our most popular kind of mass entertainment.

The purpose of farce is to entertain; the appropriate response to it is continuous and unrestrained laughter. Farce has little intellectual content or symbolic significance, is not concerned with presenting a message, makes no pretense of demanding serious consideration, has slight residue of meaning. In the journalistic fare of the theater, farce is the comic strip of the *Zam-Bang-Powie* school. Its appeal is simple, external, and spontaneous.

Farce may involve a complete play such as *The Comedy of Errors* and *Charley's Aunt*, or its techniques may be injected piecemeal into other forms of drama as in *Twelfth Night* and *The Frogs*. While critics may disparage farce as a degraded form of drama that "though it make the unskillful laugh, cannot but make the judicious grieve," nevertheless, it is a matter of fact that farcical devices and characters have been employed not only by dramatic hacks, but also by some of the most preeminent playwrights, including Shakespeare, Molière, and Aristophanes.

The script of farce must be regarded as a scenario for action. The distinctive essence of farce can be realized only in performance by ac-

complished comedians before a live audience. The gags, tricks, and devices that seem so absurd and flat in print may, in the hands of talented performers, move an audience to gales of laughter from which even the most sophisticated theatergoer does not remain aloof, even though, on later reflection, he may wonder at his lack of judgment in responding to such stuff.

Because the enjoyment of laughter is one of man's favorite diversions, farce is the most popular of all forms of comedy. It demands no intellectual insight, no awareness of a social norm, no linguistic sensitivity in finding nuances of meaning—all of which are necessary for understanding other forms of comedy. The response to farce is immediate and direct, offering no strain to the mind. Hence, this kind of laughing matter has a very wide appeal. The language barriers are slight because the performer in farce often expresses himself in the universal vocabulary of gesture and action. The enacted story is itself a kind of language which finds a ready audience.

plot

Farce is usually the comedy of situation. A good farcical plot provides a maximum opportunity for a series of complications, even though it is obvious that it has been contrived and manipulated by the playwright. The structure of farce is a framework for vigorous, rapid, and exaggerated action in which the characters move, rather than think, and where evoking laughter justifies nearly any means. Once the engine has been cranked up and set in motion, the speed is accelerated, and by unexpected blowouts, backfirings and explosions, the mechanism careens crazily through space, gathering momentum until it finally lurches to an awkward but happy ending in a cloud of steam with all of the parts still spinning; and while there has been a whirlwind of activity, the machine has not really moved an inch in any direction.

The skill of plotting farce is determined by the dramatist's ingenuity in inventing a variety of entanglements that will give the comedian a chance to play for laughs. The playwright usually exploits a basic situation which is highly improbable and atypical: a woodcutter reluctantly consents to become a court physician to cure the king's daughter of a feigned illness; two long-lost twin brothers, whose servants are another pair of twins, strive for reunion; two young Communists sharing a one-room apartment fall in love with each other's newly-wed wives; a shy greeting-card verse writer becomes involved with a gang of race track touts because of his skill in predicting the winners; a young man wagers that he can tell the complete truth for twenty-four hours; a genial husband undertakes the precarious responsibility of simultaneously maintaining two separate wives and families in Wilmington, Delaware, and Philadelphia, Pennsylvania. These are characteristic plot situations employed by writers of farce. Inventing a farcical plot requires ingenuity in manipulating situations, plus a shrewd sense of the theater. The playwright must know precisely how, when, and where to tickle the audience. An example of a plot which illustrates the materials and organization that characterize this kind of comedy is the medieval farce, *Master Pierre Pathelin.*

An impoverished lawyer, Pierre Pathelin assures his wife, Guillemette, that he has a plan for procuring some cloth. He visits the draper's shop, where he flatters the shopkeeper into giving him a piece of cloth. The draper is wary about parting with the cloth on credit, but Pathelin allays his fears by inviting him to visit his house where the draper will get his money and share a roast goose dinner. The scene ends when Pathelin walks off with the cloth leaving the draper to gloat over the price.

Pathelin brings the cloth home to his delighted wife. When his dinner guest arrives, Pathelin climbs into bed, and his wife informs the hapless draper that her husband could not possibly have purchased any cloth—he has been seriously ill for some weeks. The draper goes away, but returns immediately to find Pathelin feigning a ranting fit of madness. The draper becomes convinced that the devil has hoodwinked him. Another facet of the story now develops when the draper brings a shepherd into court, accused of having eaten several sheep belonging to the draper. The shepherd engages Pathelin to defend him, who feigning a toothache, masks his face until the draper makes his accusation. When Pathelin suddenly reveals his identity, the draper loses his wits and attacks the lawyer for stealing his cloth. The case becomes hopelessly lost in the confusing tangle of the two arguments. The bewildered judge tries to restore order by questioning the shepherd, who following Pathelin's counsel, answers all questions by bleating like a sheep. The judge abandons the trial; Pathelin has succeeded. The distraught draper dashes off saying to Pathelin: "I am going to your house to see if you are here or there." When Pathelin demands his fee from his client, the shepherd's only reply is continued bleating. The trickster is himself the victim of his own trick.

comic devices

In the chapter on comedy, three representative theories of comedy were cited—derision, incongruity, and automatism, and three characteristic devices were discussed—teasing, inversion, and the unfamiliar. These theories and devices are also applicable to farce, although their use is generally on an elementary level. Low comedy exploits the physical aspect of man. His body, its desires, and functions are a primary source for comic material. Farcical situations usually depend on visual humor—man is shown as the victim of his biological nature; not only sex, but any drive, appetite, or situation that makes him appear ridiculous causes him to lose his balance, his control of himself or his circumstances. Farcical characters move in an active physical world; they are out of place in the rarefied atmosphere of intellectual cerebration.

With this background in mind, let us consider some characteristic forms of farcical behavior from several entertainment media. A generation or two ago when vaudeville was popular entertainment, comedians relied very heavily on visual gags for their humor. George M. Cohan, one of America's best-loved comedians and playwrights, was once asked to make a list of his most successful pieces of comedy business. These were the first eight items on his list in an article "The Mechanics of Emotion," *McClure's Magazine*, November, 1913:

1. Whack on the back for friendship. Repeat three times.
2. Whack woman on back absent-mindedly thinking she is a man.
3. Step on a man's sore foot.
4. Person leans on elbow for support, slips and falls.
5. Mimicking walk of another person who can't see mimic.
6. Stumble over rug. Dignified person doubles the laugh.
7. Man takes a drink in one big gulp.
8. Two argue. One leaves and anticipates kick by bending his body forward. No kick.

In the days of the silent motion picture, farce was exceedingly popular in the slapstick comedies created by Mack Sennett, Charlie Chaplin, and Buster Keaton. The basic requirement for silent pictures was action—hence, it was a medium ideally suited for farce. Comedians tumbled their way through crazy situations at breakneck speed—wildly improbable situations, full of violence set off by the slightest provocation, and usually ending in a chase that annihilated all the canons of time and space. Some examples of typical farcical business: Harold Lloyd, playing a book salesman, approaches a tough customer and is thrown out. He returns a dozen times accelerating the pace. On another occasion he serves as a practice tackling-dummy for a football squad. He makes a speech at a dance with a kitten crawling inside his sweater. Buster Keaton chases butterflies in the countryside, completely oblivious to a band of wild Indians who pursue him. In another picture he sits on a hot stove, then sits on a cake of ice which melts rapidly. Ben Turpin, a cross-eyed explorer, surrenders to a stuffed lion.

That these familiar farcical patterns are still in use today may be seen by consulting the log of television programs where you will find such comic situations as these:

61 Farcial action and characters in an English burlesque opera, *The Dragon of Wantley.*

62 French and Italian farceurs. Comédie Française.

63 Feydeau's nineteenth-century farce *A Flea in Her Ear,* at the Hilberry Theater Repertory Company, Wayne State University. Directed by Richard Spear, setting designed by William Rowe.

64 Typical antics in an English farce, Arthur Murphy's *The Citizen.*

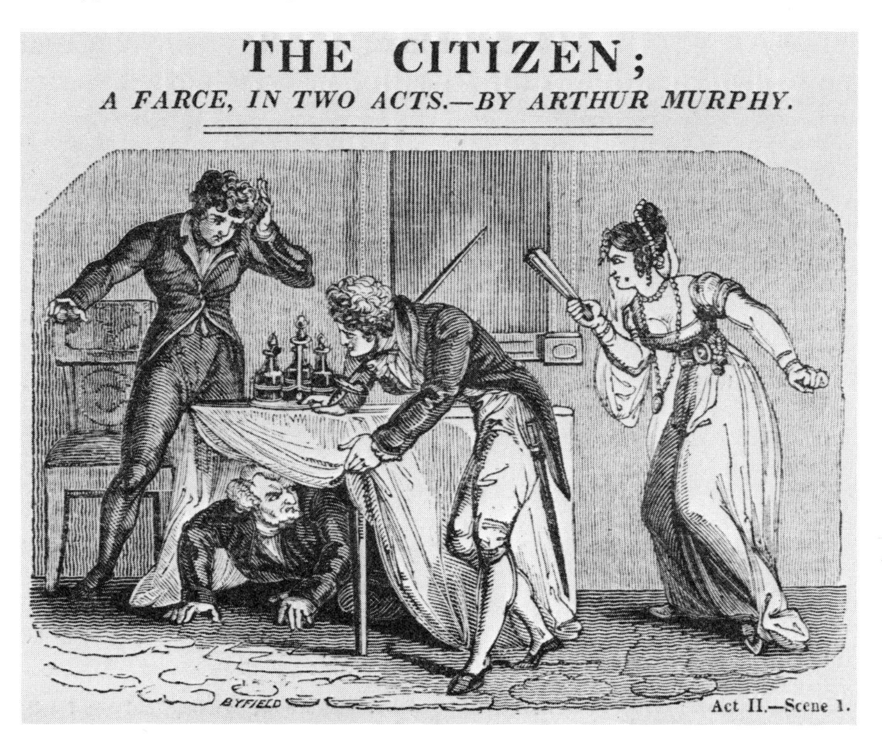

> The Honeymooners visit sunny Spain, where Ralph rushes to the rescue of a lovely senorita—and finds himself entangled in a blackmail plot.
>
> Jed locks Shorty in a bear cage so he can't run away from marriage any longer.
>
> Two college boys who think the Munster home is vacant decide it's just the place to hold a fraternity initiation.
>
> Don Hollinger injures his back demonstrating ski safety in Ann's apartment and is staying there—on doctor's orders—when Ann's father arrives for a visit.

These examples from vaudeville, motion pictures, and television indicate the comedian's approach to his material when his purpose is to arouse immediate laughter from a wide and undiscriminating audience. Similarly, in the legitimate theater, the devices of farce rely on visual humor centering on physical activities and usually involve complicated misunderstandings. Let us consider two typical farcical devices, physical violence and mistaken identity.

Physical violence requires a playful attitude, as Eastman emphasized in his analysis of laughter. The act of violence should not cause genuine suffering in either the performer or the spectator. To elicit the audience's sympathy or to give the effect of real pain is to destroy the atmosphere for laughter. The comic possibilities of the situation are enhanced when the recipient of the violence deserves chastisement for his antisocial behavior. Thus a pompous politician or a sanctimonius puritan falling on the ice is much funnier than a kind old lady would be. Comic literature is filled with all kinds of fights, duels, beatings, spankings, combats, and tumbles. The pratfall, the black eye, the sore foot, and the custard pie in the face are standard gags.

Aristophanes shows his fondness for the use of physical devices over and over in his plays, although he was also capable of lifting the level of his material to social satire and to flights of delightful poetic fantasy. A typical use of low comedy in one of Aristophanes' plays occurs in *The Frogs*, which is, in part, a venture into literary criticism of the tragic works of Aeschylus and Euripides. In this particular scene, the god Dionysus betrays his cowardice when he and his servant, Xanthias, have made their way to Hades.

> *(The central door opens and the porter,* AEACUS *comes out with three other slaves to* DIONYSUS, *who, fearful of his reception, pretends he is* XANTHIAS.)
>
> AEACUS: Here, seize this dog-stealer and lead him
> forth to justice, quick.
> DIONYSUS: *(Imitating* XANTHIAS)
> Here's fun for somebody.

XANTHIAS: *(in a Heraclean attitude)*
Stop, zounds! Not one step more!

AEACUS: You want to fight?
Ho, Ditylas, Sceblyas, and Pardocas,
Forward! Oblige this person with some fighting!

DIONYSUS: *(while the Scythians gradually overpower* XANTHIAS*)*
How shocking to assault the constables—
And stealing other people's things!

AEACUS: Unnatural,
That's what I call it.

DIONYSUS: Quite a pain to see.

XANTHIAS: *(now overpowered and disarmed)*
Now, by Lord Zeus, if ever I've been here
Or stol'n from you the value of one hair
You may take and hang me on the nearest tree!
Now, listen; and I'll act quite fairly by you;
(suddenly indicating DIONYSUS*)*
Take this poor boy, and put him to the question!
And if you find me guilty, hang me straight.

AEACUS: What tortures do you allow?

XANTHIAS: Use all you like.
Tie him in the ladder, hang him by the feet,
Whip off his skin with bristle-whips and rack him;
You might well try some vinegar up his nose,
And bricks upon his chest, and so on. Only
No scourges made of leek or young shalott.

AEACUS: A most frank offer, most frank—If my treatment
Disables him, the value shall be paid.

XANTHIAS: Don't mention it. Remove him and begin.

AEACUS: Thank you, we'll do it here, that you may
Witness exactly what he says. *(To* DIONYSUS*)*
Put down your bundle,
and mind you tell the truth.

DIONYSUS: *(Who has hitherto been speechless with horror, now bursting out)*
I warn all present,
To torture me is an illegal act,
Being immortal! And whoever does so
Must take the consequences.

AEACUS: Why, who are you?

DIONYSUS: The immortal Dionysus, son of Zeus;
And this is my slave.

AEACUS: *(To* XANTHIAS*)*
You hear his protest?

XANTHIAS: Yes;
All the more reason, that, for whipping him;
If he's a real immortal he won't feel it.

DIONYSUS: Well, but you claim to be immortal too;
They ought to give you just the same as me.

XANTHIAS: That's fair enough. All right, whichever
Of us you first find crying, or the least bit
Minding your whip, you're free to say he's
No true god.

AEACUS: Sir, you behave like a true gentleman:
You come to justice of yourself!—Now then,
Strip, both.

XANTHIAS: How will you test us?

AEACUS: Easily;
You'll each take whack and whack about.

XANTHIAS: All right.

AEACUS: *(striking* XANTHIAS)
There.

XANTHIAS: *(controlling himself with an effort)*
Watch now, if you see me even wince.

AEACUS: But I've already hit you!

XANTHIAS: I think not.

AEACUS: Upon my word, it looks as if I hadn't,
Well, now I'll go and whack the other.
(strikes DIONYSUS)

DIONYSUS: *(also controlling himself)* When?

AEACUS: I've done it.

DIONYSUS: *(with an air of indifference)*
Odd, it didn't make me sneeze!

AEACUS: It is odd!—Well, I'll try the first again.
(He crosses to XANTHIAS.)

XANTHIAS: All right. Be quick. *(The blow falls)*
Whe-ew

AEACUS: Ah, why "whe-ew"?
It didn't hurt you?

XANTHIAS: *(recovering himself)*
No; I just was thinking
When my Diomean Feast would next be due.[1]

This scene, in addition to employing the mechanism of physical violence, also makes use of another very well-worn comic device—mistaken identity, which lends itself especially well to low comedy because it provides an easy means for complicated misunderstandings. Plautus utilized this familiar pattern when he wrote the *Menaechmi,* the story of the reunion of long-lost twins. When Shakespeare reworked this same story for his *Comedy of Errors,* he further complicated the plot by adding a set of twin servants, which multiplied the opportunities for mistaken identity. In Goldsmith's *She Stoops to Conquer,* Tony Lumpkin purposely causes mistaken identity by telling Marlow and Hastings that his home is

1. Aristophanes, *The Frogs,* trans. Gilbert Murray, in *The Complete Greek Drama,* ed. Whitney J. Oates and Eugene O'Neill, Jr. (New York: Random House, 1938).

an inn. The two visitors subsequently treat their host as the landlord and his daughter as a maid.

As a variation of the mistaken identity device, playwrights frequently have made use of disguises which have resulted in mixups and deceptions. In *The Wasps,* Aristophanes created an amusing scene in which Philocleon attempts to escape from his house by a series of outlandish efforts, the most ingenious being his disguise as smoke coming out of the chimney. In English comedy, frequent use was made of "breeches" parts in which young women disguised themselves as men, which led to all manner of involvements such as Viola's fearful duel with Aguecheek in *Twelfth Night. Charley's Aunt,* one of the most popular of modern farces, is based on a situation in which a young Oxford undergraduate passes himself off as an elderly aunt from South America. Molière in *Scapin* devised a scene in which the rogue hid his master, Geronte, in a bag to conceal him from imaginary danger, but once he has the old man secure, he proceeds to give him a beating, meanwhile pretending to be his enemy.

character

Farce usually deals with simple stock characters, often from ordinary walks of life. The romantic aspects of the story are often carried by pasteboard figures who have a talent for bumbling into awkward situations. The main burden of the comedy is in the hands of two kinds of characters—crafty manipulators who keep the action going, and awkward, unlearned or unsuspecting characters who are the targets of laughter. The manipulators are often tricky servants or parasites who live by their wits; those preyed upon are rustics, foreigners, foolish old men, hypocrites and poseurs of all kinds. Low comedians may be a part of a farce or they may be introduced into other kinds of plays such as in melodrama for comic relief. In English late eighteenth- and early nineteenth-century comedy, low, farcical characters were injected into the plays in such roles as farmers, sailors and Irishmen. Their ludicrous antics met with popular favor, and frequently they ran away with the show.

The speech and behavior of farcical characters is simplified as they race through the contrived mechanism of the plot. They do not think—they scheme, manipulate and act, often in devious ways, but toward clearly defined objectives. Because farce involves so much acting out of situations, the actor is given exceptional opportunities to develop a full pattern of behavior. The playwright's original sketchy design may be filled out and enhanced by the lively performance and personality of an imaginative comedian, so that the character becomes a memorable one in the theater. Roles which are especially susceptible to such enrichment are Tony Lumpkin in *She Stoops to Conquer,* Falstaff in *The Merry Wives of Windsor,* Lady Bracknell in *The Importance of Being Earnest,* and Sganarelle in *The Doctor in Spite of Himself.* In characterization especially, farce depends on the doing.

thought

The writer of farce does not have a message. His aim is to divert the audience's attention by providing a pattern of comic behavior. He manipulates character and situation to serve his comic purpose. At the end of the play, questions are answered, misunderstandings cleared up, the tangled threads of the story unraveled.

Because of its gay disrepect for conventional behavior, farce is sometimes criticized for its immorality, but farce is really amoral, unconcerned with ethical implications since the actions of the characters are removed from life and exist only in the theater by tacit agreement with the audience. Eric Bentley considers that farce performs a valuable function as a safety valve in releasing the pent-up frustrations imposed on man by civilization.[2] In this respect, farce may serve a Freudian purpose in that it gratifies repressed tendencies.

Certainly in farce, there is often implicit criticism of society and its mores—for example, the attack on pretentiousness and hypocrisy in Molière, Labiche, and Feydeau, but this is a by-product of their plays, not the essential reason for their existence. Farce exists primarily as a means of entertainment.

diction

Diction in farce is undistinguished by any literary pretensions. Only in rare instances has a playwright like Oscar Wilde combined the framework of farce and the repartee of social comedy, because wit depends on an intellectual frame of reference. A critical ear is incompatible with farce. The linguistic devices of low comedy are puns, repetitions, "tag lines," wisecracks, insults, vulgarisms, and deformed language. Although the language of farce is commonplace, it requires a special talent. The writer of farce must write dialogue that sharply distinguishes each character. The actor's speech must accompany or thrust the action forward, rather than impede it. Laugh lines demand a feeling for the flavor and cadence of language, and the ability to make dialogue crackle and snap. The playwright must have an excellent sense of theater so as to pace his dialogue, build for laughs, make effective use of repetition, and realize

2. Eric Bentley, *Let's Get a Divorce!* (New York: Hill and Wang, 1958).

the comic possibilities in the juxtaposition of words and phrases—the incongruities of human speech. Writing effective farcical dialogue may seem an easy task to the reader; actually it is an exacting and rather rare skill.

Two of the most successful writers of recent farce were George Kaufman and Moss Hart whose *The Man Who Came to Dinner* provides a successful example of farcical dialogue that makes use of the American penchant for the wisecrack and insult.

Sheridan Whiteside, a celebrated critic and raconteur, is visiting in a midwestern town when he falls on the ice. He decides to take advantage of the situation by feigning an injury and spending two weeks in the home of the Stanleys in Mesalia, Ohio. Seated in a wheelchair, he is pushed into the living room where he encounters the Stanleys and two of their friends who have come to admire the celebrity.

There is a hush as the wheelchair rolls into the room. Welcoming smiles break over every face. The chair comes to a halt; MR. WHITESIDE *looks slowly around, into each and every beaming face. His fingers drum for a moment on the arm of the chair. He looks slowly around once more. And then he speaks.*

WHITESIDE: *(quietly to* MAGGIE). I may vomit.

MRS. STANLEY: *(with a nervous little laugh).* Good morning, Mr. Whiteside. I'm Mrs. Ernest Stanley—remember? And this is Mr. Stanley.

STANLEY: How do you do, Mr. Whiteside? I hope that you are better.

WHITESIDE: Thank you. I am suing you for a hundred and fifty thousand dollars.

STANLEY: How's that? What?

WHITESIDE: I said I am suing you for a hundred and fifty thousand dollars.

MRS. STANLEY: You mean—because you fell on our steps, Mr. Whiteside?

WHITESIDE: Samuel J. Liebowitz will explain it to you in court. . . . Who are those two harpies standing there like the kiss of death?

(MRS. MCCUTCHEON, *with a little gasp, drops the calf's foot jelly. It smashes on the floor).*

MRS. MCCUTCHEON: Oh, dear! My calf's-foot jelly.

WHITESIDE: Made from your own foot, I have no doubt. And now, Mrs. Stanley, I have a few small matters to take up with you. Since this corner druggist at my elbow tells me that I shall be confined in this mouldy mortuary for at least another ten days, due entirely to your stupidity and negligence, I shall have to carry on my activities as best I can. I shall require the exclusive use of this room, as well as that drafty sewer which you call the library. I want no one to come in or out while I am in this room.

STANLEY: What do you mean, sir?

MRS. STANLEY: *(stunned)* But we have to go up the stairs to get to our rooms, Mr. Whiteside.

WHITESIDE: Isn't there a back staircase?

MRS. STANLEY: Why—yes.

WHITESIDE: Then use that. I shall also require a room for my secretary, Miss Cutler. I shall have a great many incoming and outgoing calls, so please do not use the telephone. I sleep until noon and require quiet through the house until that hour. There will be five for lunch today. Where is the cook?

STANLEY: Mr. Whiteside, if I may interrupt for a moment—

WHITESIDE: You may not, sir. . . . Will you take your clammy hand off my chair? *(This last to the nurse)* . . . And now will you all leave quietly or must I ask Miss Cutler to pass among you with a baseball bat?[3]

spectacle

Farce makes considerable appeal to the eye so that the scenery and properties are frequently essential for business and movement. A case in point is Peter Shaffer's *Black Comedy* in which the audience is asked to accept the convention that most of the action takes place in the dark, with the resultant mix-ups exploiting the comic possibilities of a staircase, lamp cords, furniture, and doors. In some plays the locale is an important aspect of the comic situation, such as in *The Front Page, Arsenic and Old Lace, Three Men on a Horse, Barefoot in the Park, You Can't Take It with You,* and, of course, the bedrooms of many French farces. The setting should provide the actor with the opportunity for vigorous and rapid movement. Since disguises, concealments, discoveries, and ridiculous costumes are standard farcical fare, this element is emphasized in the physical surroundings. Film comedians of the silent days were noted for their pantomimic ability. No one excelled Charlie Chaplin in his fertile imagination for comic business. Here, for example, is Gilbert Seldes' description of a sequence from one of Chaplin's early short comedies, *The Pawnshop,* which reveals what the actor may contribute to the performance:

> Charlie enters the pawnshop; it is evident that he is late. He compares his watch with the calendar pad hanging on the wall, and hastily begins to make up for lost time by entering the back room and going busily to work. He takes a duster out of a valise and meticulously dusts his walking-stick. Then proceeding to other objects, he fills the room with clouds of dust, and when he begins to dust the electric fan, looking at something else, the feathers are blown all over the room. He turns and sees the plucked butt of the duster—and carefully puts it away for tomorrow.

3. Moss Hart and George S. Kaufman, *The Man Who Came to Dinner* (New York: Random House, 1939).

With the other assistant he takes a ladder and a bucket of water and goes out to polish the three balls and the shop sign. After some horseplay he rises to the top of the ladder and reaches over to polish the sign; the ladder sways, teeters, with Charlie on top of it. A policeman down the street looks aghast, and sways sympathetically with the ladder. Yet struggling to keep his balance, Charlie is intent on his work, and every time the ladder brings him near the sign he dabs frantically at it until he falls.

A quarrel with his fellow-worker follows. The man is caught between the rungs of the ladder, his arms imprisoned. Charlie calls a boy over to hold the other end of the ladder and begins a boxing match. Although his adversary is incapable of moving his arms, Charlie sidesteps, feints, and guards, leaping nimbly away from imaginary blows. The policeman interferes and both assistants run into the shop. By a toss of a coin Charlie is compelled to go back to fetch the bucket. He tiptoes behind the policeman, snatches the bucket, and with a wide swing and a swirling motion evades the policeman and returns. He is then caught by the boss in another fight and is discharged.

He makes a tragic appeal to be reinstated. He says he has eleven children, so high, and so high, and so high—until the fourth one is about a foot taller than himself. The boss relents only as Charlie's stricken figure is at the door. As he is pardoned, Charlie leaps upon the old boss, twining his legs around his abdomen; he is thrown off and surreptitiously kisses the old man's hand. He goes into the kitchen to help the daughter and passes dishes through the clothes wringer to dry them—passes a cup twice, as it seems not to be dry the first time. Then his hands. The jealous assistant provokes a fight; Charlie has a handful of dough and is about to throw it when the boss appears. With the same motion Charlie flings the dough into the wringer, passes it through as a pie crust, seizes a pie plate, trims the crust over it, and goes out to work.

At the pawnshop counter pass a variety of human beings. Charlie is taken in by a sob-story about a wedding ring; he tries to test the genuineness of goldfish by dropping acid on them. Sent to the back room, he takes his lunch out of the safe, gets into another fight, in which he is almost beating the rival to death when the girl enters. Charlie falls whimpering to the floor and is made much of. He returns to the counter and the episode of the clock begins.

A sinister figure enters, offering a clock in pawn. Charlie looks at it; then takes an auscultator and listens to its heart-beat; then taps it over crossed fingers for its pulmonary action; then raps it with a little hammer to see the quality, as with porcelain; then snaps his thumb on the bell. He takes an auger and bores a hole in it; then a can-opener, and when he has pried the lid off he smells the contents and with a disparaging gesture makes the owner smell them, too. He then does dentistry on it, with forceps; then plumbing. Finally he screws a jeweler's magnifying glass into his eye and hammers what is left in the clock, shakes out the contents, measures the mainspring from the tip of his nose to arm's length, like cloth, squirts oil on the debris to keep it quiet, and, lifting the man's hat from his head, sweeps the whole mess into it and returns it with a sad shake of the head.

A pearl-buyer has meanwhile come in and Charlie retraces his steps to the back room (carefully stepping over the buyer's hat) and begins to sweep. His broom becomes entangled with a piece of tape, which fights back and gets longer and longer. Suddenly Charlie begins to tight-rope upon it, balancing with the broom, and making a quick turn, coming forward for applause. A final quarrel with the other assistant ensues. As they are swarming around the legs of the kitchen table, the boss comes in and Charlie flees, leaps into a trunk, and is hidden. As the others enter the room, the pearl-buyer, who has stolen all the valuables, holds them up with a revolver. Charlie leaps from the trunk, fells the robber, and embraces the lovely maiden for a fade-out.[4]

exercises

1. What are the appeals of farce?
2. What are the ingredients of a successful farce?
3. Contrast the characters in farce with those of high comedy.
4. Devise examples of farcial business built around a stage property such as a telephone, a bottle, a tire, a bunch of keys, etc.
5. Put the pieces of business together to make a short film sequence of action.
6. Using the scene from *The Frogs,* prepare the pantomimic action suitable for a film.
7. Mark the potential places for laughs in the scene from *The Man Who Came to Dinner* and explain the bases for them.
8. Describe three farcical actions or pieces of business used in a film or television show.
9. Create a comic scene based on mismatching.
10. Describe the atmosphere necessary for farce. How is it created?
11. Discuss the visual aspects of farce.
12. How is language treated farcically?

suggested reading

Henri Bergson, *Laughter,* trans. Cloudesley Brereton and Fred Rothwell, 1917.
Eric Bentley, *Let's Get a Divorce and Other Plays,* 1958.
———, *The Life of the Drama,* 1964.

4. Gilbert Seldes, *An Hour with the Movies* (New York: Harper & Row, 1924).

V. C. Clinton-Baddeley, *The Burlesque Tradition in the English Theatre After 1660,* 1952.
Marvin Felheim, *Comedy, Plays, Theory and Criticism,* 1962.
Paul Lauter, *Theories of Comedy,* 1964.

play list

Anton Chekhov, *The Brute; The Wedding*
Oliver Goldsmith, *She Stoops to Conquer*
Georges Feydeau, *Keep an Eye on Amélie*
George Kaufman and Moss Hart, *You Can't Take It with You*
Eugène Labiche, *Pots of Money*
Molière, *The Doctor in Spite of Himself*
Peter Shaffer, *Black Comedy*
William Shakespeare, *The Taming of the Shrew*
Neil Simon, *The Odd Couple*

realism and its derivatives

In the previous four chapters we have been considering *types* or *forms* of drama. Now we turn our attention to dramatic *modes*—realism and two of its derivatives, naturalism and expressionism. Type or form refers to a particular kind of dramatic composition, just as in painting we speak of a still life or a portrait painting, and in music we talk about a sonata or a symphony. By mode we mean the temper or spirit that affects the creator's point of view. The mode reflects the cultural climate in which a work of art was created. The classicism of fifth-century B.C. Greece grew out of the ideal of the golden mean and the emphasis on reason, so that classicism is characterized by beauty of form, proportion, balance, symmetry, and control. The good life was rooted in the words spoken by the chorus at the end of *Antigone:* "To be happy it is first of all necessary to be wise, and always remember to give the gods their due." When the neoclassicists in Renaissance Italy and France sought to create their own society of enlightenment celebrating the age of reason, they attempted to transplant the Greek ideas, with mixed results. In drama strict application of misinterpretations of Aristotle made it exceedingly difficult to write a playable work and resulted in a rigid theatrical style that emphasized form and rhetoric. It was an elevated drama in its use of verse,

highborn characters, and themes of love, honor, and loyalty testing the will of exemplary individuals.

In the eighteenth and nineteenth centuries the romantic movement made its impression on the theater and while it provided few actable plays for our present stage, it was an important transitional step between neoclassicism and realism. The spirit that animated romanticism was the concept of the "natural man" whose actions were governed by his heart. Its major representatives in Germany were Schiller and Goethe; in France Victor Hugo led a revolt with the manifesto that appeared as the preface to his *Cromwell* (1827). The rebellion found focus when Hugo's *Hernani* was given a tumultuous reception at the Comédie Française signaling the overthrow of neoclassicism.

The romanticists in the theater rejected the suppression of emotion and they discarded the rigid form of the old classics. They insisted on freedom for a wide scope of action celebrating man as a child of nature, and mixing beauty with the grotesque, the lowly with the elevated, the humble with the sublime. Their protagonists were picaresque figures—rebels and outcasts, men of action with uncomplicated motivations. The plays sought to express the sense of wonder and mystery of life; the action often led to the picturesque, the remote, and the exotic. In their language playwrights attempted to use an elevated verse, a colorful rhetoric that would imaginatively express their natural exuberance.

While romanticism was significant for clearing the stage of the austere rigidity of the past, its built-in tendency for excess made it susceptible to such abuses as too much straining for effect, too much superficiality in character, emotion, and situation, and in its basic function of theater as escape, too little contact with the real world and the facts of life. Nevertheless, the spirit of romanticism is an appealing one; it easily made its way into popular melodrama. Today not only do we find echoes of romanticism in motion pictures and television, musical comedies and opera, but nearly all of us wistfully compare our present regimented, mechanized, crowded world with the dream of the natural man.

As the intellectual climate of the nineteenth century was profoundly changed by science and technology, a new kind of drama was required: this was realism. In general, we may say that modern dramatic literature has centered around the form of *drame* and the mode of realism. Although in the last few years it has been under attack, realism has been surprisingly persistent and durable. Since most of our serious plays of the last century follow this mode, and since the current rebellion is antirealistic, we need to understand the background and rationale of this mode. In evaluating realism it is important to keep in mind the kind of artificial drama it was rebelling against, and the new thought the realist was seeking to express. Those who led the way were serious men, genuinely dedicated to presenting the truth. Their dramatic practice, like that of all playwrights, was to seek the most effective means for touching the minds and hearts of their audiences.

To set down a clear-cut definition of realism is a precarious task since realism varies with the attitudes of writers, critics, and literary historians. Furthermore, the writer has very little interest in creating a work that will neatly fit into a pigeonhole. The problem of definition is further complicated by the fact that the term realism has been used to refer both to a literary technique and a literary theory. In spite of the divergent meanings, there is fairly common agreement that realism relies on sense impressions; that it deals with the here and now; that it is "concerned essentially with detail"; that it is a "copying of actual facts"; that it is a "deliberate choice of the commonplace"; that it is a "factual interpretation of life"; that it is, in short, "truth." Since man expresses himself in art forms, which by their very nature are conventionalized and artificial, complete reality is impossible in art. The term "illusion of reality" is in itself an anachronism. What the realistic dramatist and actor strive to achieve is to "suggest actuality," and to give "the impression of truth" by employing symbols that communicate the effect of reality to an audience.

Any method of communication must necessarily rely on a set of symbols that have mutual acceptance and meaning to the artist and the person for whom the work is intended. The function of the artist is to create symbols and organize them in such a fashion as to elicit a desired, appropriate response. In the theater, the playwright uses all aspects of production as symbols—characters, setting, dialogue, light, sound, movement, and properties, which are arranged into a unified projection of the play, which is itself a symbol. The realist uses symbols that have a direct and immediate reference to life.

Symbols are dynamic. They vary as the artist responds to the environment and influences that press in upon him. Thus, every work of art is an expression not only of the individual who created it, but also of the social forces that shaped the artist and his attitudes toward life. A Raphael Madonna, a Bach chorale, a Louis Sullivan skyscraper, a Restoration comedy are more than works of individual men; they are also social documents of the age that produced them. The dynamic nature of symbolic expression is due not only to the artist's personality, but also to the philosophic outlook he shares with his contemporaries. A society which has a philosophic outlook in which reality is considered to have an existence and validity independent of the psychic processes does not demand of its artists the representation of actuality of objects and actions. Conversely, when a society becomes concerned primarily with the physical and material aspects of living based on sense knowledge, then the artist looks to real life for his means of expression. Throughout the history of Western civilization, there has been an ebb and flow of philosophic thought, now emphasizing a metaphysical view of life, now stressing materialism. In those periods when a materialistic attitude prevails, expression in the theater employs the techniques of realism. A complete aesthetic theory of realism could not evolve until the intellectual revolution of the nineteenth century, when the advance of science, materialism, and industrialism made such a theory not only possible, but inevitable.

the realistic movement

From the change in speculative thought arising from the works of such men as Darwin, Freud, and Marx, three implications are of particular significance to drama and the theater. The first of these was the dynamic notion of change. In place of the older, static concept of a perfect creation a few thousand years ago, the scientist presented the idea that all life is in a constant process of alteration, and, as a creature of nature, man too is subject to change.

A second implication was that man is a "biochemical entity." Said the biologist: there seems to be nothing about human life or behavior that is not susceptible to explanation according to naturalistic laws and principles. Man is a product of a callous nature, rather than a child of special providence whose life is subject to divine intervention and revelation. Man acts mechanistically. His physiology is as important as his intellect in determining his conduct. Man is merely the leading member of the simian group, and for the time being, the dominant species of the animal kingdom on this planet.

A third implication of the new thought was that man is subject to scientific study. He is a case study, capable of being examined and investigated.

These changes in speculative thought were variously interpreted. At one extreme, Zola and his fellow naturalists saw in the teachings of science license to emphasize the sordid and mechanistic aspects of life to the exclusion of all else. Their thinking was shadowed by a somber view of life which threw a blighting chill of determinism on all human conduct. At the opposite extreme, realists of the Spencer-Fiske persuasion saw in science a buoyantly optimistic assurance of the ultimate perfectability of mankind. They extended the doctrine of evolution to include the entire universe finding the promise of one glorious purpose—the elevation of mankind. Clarence Darrow reveals this interpretation in his article "Realism in Literature and Art" (*Arena*, IX, 1893):

> Realism worships at the shrine of nature. It does not say that there may not be spheres in which beings higher than man can live or that some time an eye may not rest upon a fairer sunset than was ever born behind the clouds and sea; but it knows that through the countless ages nature

65 Scene from a romanticized production of *Romeo and Juliet* at the Deutsches Theater, Berlin, 1886.

66 Realistic scenery in a scène from Hauptmann's *Teamster Henschel.* Note the box set.

67 Simplified realism in a modern staging of Ibsen's *A Doll's House,* designed by Harald Martin, Det Nye Theater, Oslo.

68 Realistic stage setting by Ernst Stern for Rice's *Street Scene*, 1930. The environment is stressed as a conditioning force.

69 (opposite) Another example of simplified realism by Harald Martin for a production of Ibsen's *Ghosts*, Det Nye Theater, Oslo.

has slowly fitted the brain and eye of man to the earth on which we live and the objects which we see, and the perfectly earthly eye must harmonize with the perfect earthly scene. To say that realism is coarse and vulgar is to declare against nature and her work.

In between the optimistic realist and the pessimistic naturalist was a variety of interpretations, but all found common agreement in stressing the importance of the individual and the significance of the environment as a formative influence on behavior. In addition, most realists were conscious of the humanitarian implications of the new way of looking at life. The artist plays a part in the elevation of mankind by insisting on the necessity of a congenial social atmosphere. The realist deals with the ugly and untrue because they are forces inimical to personal fulfillment. This point of view did not cause the realist to become a professed propagandist; his desire to be objective ruled against this. Nevertheless, humanitarian concern colors the selection of material, the delineation and motivation of character, and the nature of the dramatic conflicts.

The realistic movement had its origin in French fiction. Balzac, Flaubert, and the brothers Goncourt created conspicuous examples of the new attitude at work. The nature of that realism and its guiding principles is summed up in these words of Bernard Weinberg:

> Realism stating its case in "la bataille realiste," states it in approximately these terms: Romanticism and classicism, striving for an ideal beauty and seeking it mainly in the historical subjects, arrives only at affectation and falseness. Realism, on the contrary, aims to attain truth. Now truth is attainable only by the observation (scientific and impersonal) of reality—and hence of contemporary life—and by the unadulterated representation of that reality in the work of art. Therefore, in his observations, the artist must be sincere, unprejudiced, encyclopedic. Whatever is real, whatever exists is a proper subject for art; this means that the beautiful and ugly, the physical and spiritual, are susceptible of artistic treatment; it does not imply that the artist refrains from choosing his subject and his detail, for choice is fundamental in art. The principal object of imitation is always man; description of the material world, construction of plot, are thus subsidiary and contributory to character portrayal. In setting down his observations, the artist must of course arrange and dispose his materials; but he avoids all possible falsification of them by practicing the utmost simplicity of style and form. The product of this method is moral in the highest sense—truth being the highest morality—and is eminently adapted to the needs of a materialistic, "realistic" society.[1]

In French drama, the theory of realism was rooted in the teachings of Diderot, who in the eighteenth century called for "middle-class tragedy."

1. Bernard Weinberg, *French Realism: The Critical Reaction, 1830-1870* (New York: Oxford University Press, 1937).

In the early nineteenth century when Pixerécourt popularized romantic melodrama, he required realistic scenery employing practical steps, bridges, and boats for the exciting action of his bourgeois plays. When Scribe came to the theater, his technical dexterity in manipulating plots and his portrayal of types found in contemporary society gave to his plays an air of superficial probability. His skill as a craftsman resulted in the writing of what became known as "well-made plays," whose techniques were so popular in the theater that his structural pattern was widely imitated. Scribe was followed by Augier, an enormously successful playwright whose impartiality of treatment, careful depiction of background through the minute observation of objects and incidents, and competence in characterization took drama a step nearer to realism. Dumas *fils* continued the advance by his concern with the decadence of the social scene in such plays as *Le Demi-Monde* (1855) and *La Question d'argent* (1857). His treatment of men and women who were not heroic, but weak, sensuous, and selfish added a new role to the theater. Elsewhere in Europe, the intellectual revolution taking place found expression in the new playwrights—Henrik Ibsen, Leo Tolstoi, Anton Chekhov, August Strindberg, and Gerhart Hauptmann. These men were interested in telling the truth about the common man in everyday circumstances, but because their dramas were so outspoken and their subject matter was so bold, they found it difficult to get a hearing until the Independent Theater movement, a group of subscription theaters, was organized for the specific purpose of opening the doors of the theater to the new drama. Under the leadership of André Antoine in Paris, Otto Brahm in Berlin, Constantin Stanislavski in Moscow, and John Grein in London, this movement broke the shackles of tradition and introduced a new exuberant spirit into the drama, linking the stage once more with literature and life. Ibsen's *Ghosts* was an especially important play because of its sensational impact wherever it was produced. In America, in the last decade of the nineteenth century, James A. Herne and a number of disciples of the new realism in fiction attempted to introduce the new spirit into the drama through a production of Herne's *Margaret Fleming*, and the sponsorship of performances of the continental playwrights, but the audiences were not hospitable to the shocking *drame.*

In addition to the development of realism as literary theory during the latter part of the nineteenth century, there was also considerable change taking place in the techniques of writing and producing farces and melodramas which made up most of the popular stage fare. Characters of humble origin became more and more prominent; local color was exploited; native speech and costuming was more accurately reproduced; and the stage scenery and effects became increasingly substantial and convincing. Although much of the plot material and character motivation was patently artificial, realism made its influence felt, especially in the external aspects of production, even in those plays which were written primarily for entertainment.

The ultimate result of the revolution which took place in the late nineteenth-century theater was to win the twentieth century over to realism. While realism as a complete aesthetic theory soon lost its impetus, the techniques and attitudes of the realist have nevertheless continued to dominate our modern stage, even in the face of a great deal of experimentation with new forms, and despite a rather general dissatisfaction with its restrictive outlook.

observation and objectivity

Having received his inspiration from the scientist, the realist turned to him for his techniques, attempting to follow the basic concepts drawn from the scientific method. The first of these was dependence on observation. If the artist is to select symbols which will approximate a one-to-one relationship between symbol and referent, it is imperative that the object be known as completely as possible. The realist, therefore, came to rely on meticulous and precise observation, analysis and recording of specific details. Minutiae that previous writers passed by were accumulated a bit at a time to build up character or locale in much the same manner that Seurat used to apply his paint in tiny spots of broken color. And like Courbet and Manet, who took their easels out of their studio to paint commonplace subject matter from direct observation, rather than saints and miracles from their inspiration and imagination, the realistic writer looked hard at life at first hand and jotted down in his notebook the texture of his response. The realist was devoted to the sanctity of facts and the deduction of truth based on the evidence of collected data. It was his mission to see, hear, and report everything. Such an emphasis on observation affected not only the realist's choice of subject matter, but also his method of handling it. He must allow the plot to develop where an honest treatment of his characters takes it; he must depict the environment and its atmosphere with scrupulous fidelity; he must concern himself with people rather than plot; he must employ emotion without artificiality or sentimentalism; he must be faithful to the facts as he observed them.

A second technique of the realist was to maintain an attitude of objectivity toward his work, just as the scientist conducts his experiments, examines his data, and draws impersonal conclusions. As the realist avoids idealism and romanticism, he is equally opposed to cynicism and pessimism. As an impartial observer he attempts to escape personal bias and reports accurately on life as it is.

With this general background in mind of a literary theory stemming

70 Scene from *The Investigation* by Peter Weiss, directed by Erwin Piscator at the Freie Volksbühne, Berlin, 1965. Documentary realism from the records of the Auschwitz extermination camp.

71 Another play of documentary realism, *In the Matter of J. Robert Oppenheimer* by Heinar Kipphardt.

72 Realistic staging in an arena theater of Ted Shine's *Morning, Noon and Night*, directed by Owen Dodson, designed by Richard Baschky, at the University of California, Santa Barbara.

from the intellectual revolution of the nineteenth century and noting especially the impact of science, let us now consider the application of realism to specific dramatic problems.

plot

The dramatic structure of the realist resembles classical drama in its unity of action, time, and place, and in its concentration on characters caught in moments of crisis. Thus the realist generally uses a late point of attack, employs a few incidents, and ordinarily deals with a small group of characters over a short space of time. The result of this dramaturgy is a gain in intensity and dramatic tension because the action is continuous and concentrated, free from the extraneous diversions of constantly changing locales and complicated plots and subplots. The writer of popular nineteenth-century melodrama dramatized simple people in a complicated plot based on a pattern of physical conflicts. The realist reversed this approach by showing complex characters in a simple plot involving psychological action. The result was realistic *drame.*

Realistic plays are not full of arbitrary climaxes, with built-up "big scenes" of violent action. Even in moments of great stress, the emotional expression is often deliberately restrained, underplayed, suggested rather than exploited. The playwright learned that the most telling moments of his plays might be the quiet closing of a door, the distant sound of an axe on a tree. There is an absence of sensational and "stagy" devices, but not an absence of emotional effect. There is more genuine horror in the last scene in *Ghosts* when Mrs. Alving holds the morphia powders in her hand staring at her deranged son, than there is in a wide screen filled with the slaughtered bodies of an Indian massacre filmed in Technicolor.

To secure the semblance of reality, the realist was obligated to make his work seem logical and plausible, with no clanking machinery or whirr of motors. He avoided all manner of contrivances that might destroy illusion. He did not interrupt the action to make explanations, preferring to integrate his exposition of antecedent action by gradual revelation throughout the course of the play.

The realist's method of handling plot was responsible for clearing away much of the manipulated and hopped-up trickery of popular drama. Plays became much more credible, closer to actual experience and the observed facts of life. Because he based his dramas on ideas, rather than on external action, and because he was concerned with character revelation, the realist achieved an intensity of effect. On the other hand, his method of working narrowed the scope of action, slowed down the pace, and sometimes became downright sedentary. Critics were quick to point out that in his attempt to condense the action and frame it in a solid mold, amid a welter of concrete details, the realist sacrificed his chance to stimulate the imagination, and to give free play to his fancy. He had trapped himself in the stuffy atmosphere of a middle-class living room. As realism has developed in the past half century, the validity of this criticism has been acknowledged, and the contemporary playwright increasingly seeks ways to break through the confining walls to find a more poetic, a more theatrical realism.

character

The realist's interest in characterization was centered in problems of motivation. He discarded the stock silhouette figures of the popular theater so obviously manipulated by the playwright to suit the needs of the plot—figures which reacted from conscious intent based on contemporary morality. Such flimsy characterization did not jibe with the realist's concept of behavior rooted in the pressures of environment, the dynamics of childhood, and the interaction of desires and inhibitions. The new dramatist was primarily concerned with the analysis and interpretation of character in the light of these forces which conditioned him. As Taine, the nineteenth-century French critic and historian, had observed:

> Whether phenomena are physical or moral does not matter; they can always be traced back to causes. There are causes for ambition, for courage, or for truthfulness as there are for muscular contraction and for bodily temperature. Vice and virtue are products just as are vitriol and sugar. . . . Let us then seek out the simpler data of moral qualities as scientists those of physical properties.

The realist's attempt to achieve objectivity and his reliance on observation led him to bring into the theater an entirely new gallery of characters who were delineated in a new way. In the past, playwrights had used people of the lower classes—servants, domestic figures, and tradesmen; in the hands of skillful performers, some of these types created the effect of life-sized portraits, but they were only superficially real, and they often played minor or comic roles. Now the humble, the downtrodden, and the ordinary people took a central position on stage. They were revealed as complex individuals with conflicting psychological drives, products of heredity and environment. The playwright dramatized these people at critical moments of their lives, not those of violent physical action so much as inner crises, thus penetrating the surface and giving insight into their desires, aspirations, and frustrations. The realist seemed especially concerned with presenting women on the stage, and created such memorable feminine characters as Strindberg's Laura and

Julie, Chekhov's Madame Ranevsky and Nina, Shaw's Candida and Pygmalion, and Ibsen's Nora, Hedda, Rebecca West, and Mrs. Alving.

As the result of the realist's emphasis on observation, the new dramatist carefully detailed the external aspects of character, noting and describing costume, speech, and manners so that the actor found numerous clues for his performance.

In placing contemporary man in the spotlight on the stage, the dramatists limited the possibilities of achieving the elevation and magnitude of classic tragedy with its heroic figures. Furthermore, the deterministic concept of character motivation based on environmental conditioning ruled out the tragic hero with his free will and spiritual orientation. The protagonist of realism was a man of little stature, who was sometimes shown as the victim of circumstances, incapable of taking action against the forces which pressed against him.

The naturalists, as we shall see later in the chapter, carried the mechanistic and bestial aspects of man to an extreme in their overemphasis of the sordid and the bizarre. The realist found it possible to show both sides of men and dealt with many characters who had redeeming qualities—characters who were close to the norm in behavior and outlook.

The realists made significant contributions to drama in the integrity of their characterization, their concern with sound psychological motivation, their cumulative technique of character revelation, and their treatment of protagonists drawn from the common walks of life.

thought

As we have suggested earlier, realism was an outgrowth of the intellectual revolution of the nineteenth century; the emphasis on science and materialism was reflected in the new drama.

Since the change in speculative thinking depicted man as a superior animal, rather than a child of God, his behavior was conditioned by the physical forces about him. Hence, the new playwright took an interest in these forces and showed how man's conduct was determined not by his free will but rather by his environment. The scope of drama was lowered from the idealism and heroic stature of the romanticist and classicist, but it was broadened to include subject matter that preceding generations had ignored or disdained. The realist dealt boldly with new themes, many of them growing out of his awakened interest in the social sciences—economic conflicts, sex, domestic difficulties, social strife, and the interrelationships of men. Emulating the ways of science, the playwright attempted to record life objectively, so he pulled no punches, honored no taboos, found no material too commonplace or sordid for his probing. He became absorbed in the facts of man's existence here and now—commonplace facts about contemporary commonplace people. His observations of life caused him to discard everything that smacked of the theatrical, the artificial, the contrived, the sentimental. Like the late nineteenth-century painters who went out of the studio to draw directly from life, the dramatist recorded what he saw, rather than what he imagined or wished to see.

The result was to open the doors of the theater to the dramatization of the day-to-day struggles of ordinary life. In insisting on the right to select his dramatic materials from all walks of life, the realist brought about a franker, freer stage. The theatre audience sometimes found itself challenged to think as it was confronted with bold new themes. Dramatic literature had found a connection with the intellectual life of the time. Melodrama became *drame*.

diction

The realist's interest in accurate observation and reporting prompted him to capture an exact transcription of speech from life. Since he centered his attention on the common man in everyday circumstances, the playwright's dialogue frequently was ungrammatical, fragmentary, and disturbingly frank. To make the dialogue as lifelike as possible, the realist abandoned the theatrical devices of asides, soliloquies, unmotivated "purple passages," and the inflated bombast of "paper speeches." Even in scenes of strong emotional climax, the dramatist avoided rhetorical display, having learned the eloquence of a broken phrase, a small gesture, and silence. Stage dialogue became strictly utilitarian, serving to advance the plot or delineate character, rather than to call attention to itself. In attempting to record environment accurately, the playwright used dialects and provincialisms to enhance the local color.

As Bernard Shaw pointed out, another benefit that resulted from realism was the opportunity to introduce discussion into drama. The new dramatists were concerned with ideas and they took pains to stimulate the audience's thinking about their ideas by giving them expression on stage. Ibsen's and Shaw's characters not only act, they think—and they discuss their thoughts. Their dialogue becomes action—an investigation, an adventure, a verbal tug-of-war.

Critics of realism lamented that the speech of the new drama drove poetry out of the theater. It is true that the playwright turned his ear in another direction, and sacrificed the use of poetic speech—particularly the richness of imagery—but it is also true that much of the embellished dialogue of nineteenth-century romantic writers of melodrama was poor stuff—sentimental, pretentious, vapid, an unkempt garden of luxuriant

73 Naturalistic setting for Gorki's *The Lower Depths,* first produced at the Moscow Art Theater, 1902.

74 A Berlin production of *The Lower Depths*, 1903.

and overgrown clichés. Moreover, in the hands of skillful playwrights, realistic speech had a clarity and intensity that went directly to the heart of the matter. Hamlin Garland found much to admire in Ibsen's dialogue:

> How true and unconventional his style. We hardly realize how false and stilted current stage conversation is, till we hear the real word spoken there. His words come to us at times like the thrusts of the naked fist. They shake the hearer with their weight of real passion. In one sense it is astoundingly direct, and then again it is subtly indirect—as in life.

The realist's point of view toward diction was clearly expressed in a letter Ibsen wrote to Edmund Gosse, explaining why he did not use verse in writing *Emperor and Galilean:*

> You are of the opinion that the drama ought to have been written in verse, and that it would have gained by this. Here I must differ with you. The play is, as you will have observed, conceived in the most realistic style: the illusion I wished to produce is that of reality. I wished to produce the impression on the reader that what he was reading was something that really happened. If I had employed verse, I should have counteracted my own intention and prevented the accomplishment of the task I had set myself. The many ordinary insignificant characters whom I have intentionally introduced into the play would have become indistinct and indistinguishable from one another, if I had allowed all of them to speak in one and the same rhythmical measure. We are no longer living in the days of Shakespeare. . . . Speaking generally, the style must conform to the degree of ideality which pervades the representation. My new drama is no tragedy in the ancient acceptation; what I desired to depict was human beings, and therefore I would not let them talk "the language of the gods."

spectacle

Although realistic scenery had been employed in the theater in the past, its appeal was based on novelty and picturesqueness. The realist had quite a different purpose. He had learned from the scientist that environment conditions man's behavior, so it became important to show the environment in order to understand the man. Thus, realistic scenery is not a mere accompaniment of the action; it is a causal force of the action. It shapes and molds the characters and is an essential part of the symbolic configuration. In such plays as *Dead End, Street Scene,* and *Beyond the Horizon,* the setting is a major source of character motivation, with its sociological implication that to improve the man, it is necessary to improve his circumstances.

The realist's observation of actuality and his concern with the commonplace prompted him to locate the action in a setting crammed with the domestic details of everyday life. He filled the stage and action of his plays with properties, but in the hands of the genuine realist these were not mere clutter for verisimilitude; they were selected because of their organic and symbolic relationship to the characters, such as Hedda's pistols, Nora's macaroons, and Oswald's pipe. The use of such props illustrated the notion of the significant trifle. Incidentally, the props were an enormous help to the actors in achieving naturalness in performance.

Just as the realist rejected the cardboard cut-out stock figures of the past, likewise he discarded the "painty" two dimensional wing and groove, and backdrop setting. The box set (with three continuous walls, often capped with a ceiling), which had been introduced earlier in the nineteenth century, now became a standard requirement for realistic drama. Practical doors and windows, appropriate furniture, and genuine props were added to further the illusion of actuality. The environment became real. The actor was now surrounded by scenery, and played *within* a locale rather than in front of it. As a logical accompaniment of the new scenery came the convention of the "fourth wall"—a tacit agreement with the audience that the opening framed by the proscenium arch was the fourth wall of the set, thus giving the illusion of a solid room instead of a platform. The fourth wall defined the downstage limit of the acting area and confined the actor to the setting; he pretended not to see or communicate with the audience. Present-day realistic playwrights are no longer hemmed in by such conventions since, as we shall see in chapter 12, the stage and scenery are now very flexible and free.

While realism was until recently the predominant mode of drama, it had, and still has, the seeds of revolt within itself. Later we will deal at length with modern experiments, but now we will consider two offshoots of realism in the past—naturalism and expressionism.

naturalism

The term "naturalism," often used interchangeably with realism, is historically an independent movement that began in France in the 1870s under the messianic leadership of Émile Zola. Like the realist, the naturalist responded to the influence of science—especially to the concept of the environmental conditioning of contemporary man—and reacted against the popular theatrical fare of romantic melodrama. It was Zola who wrote the first naturalistic play and bombarded the senses of his contemporaries as he clamored for a dramatic method that would reflect the method of science:

> I am waiting for them to rid us of fictitious characters, of conventional symbols of vice and virtue, which possess no value as human data. I am waiting for the surroundings to determine the characters, and for

> the characters to act according to the logic of the facts. . . . I am waiting until there is no more jugglery of any kind, no more strokes of the magical wand, changing in one minute persons and things. I am waiting, finally, until this evolution takes place on the stage; until they return the source of science to the study of nature, to the anatomy of man, to the painting of life in an exact reproduction, more original and powerful than anyone has so far dared to place upon the boards.[2]

Zola's play *Thérèse Raquin* (1873) dramatizes the story of Thérèse and her lover, who drown her unwanted husband but are unable to live down their crime under the accusing eyes of the dumb and paralyzed mother of the victim. Zola's play was not a popular success, but his example led to similar attempts by others. Becque, in *The Vultures* (1882), pictured the destruction of a family and its fortune as the result of the preying activities of the dead man's business associates. Hauptmann, in *Before Sunrise* (1889), gave Berlin's independent stage, the Freie Bühne, a graphic view of the degradation of a Silesian coal-mining family suddenly grown rich, in a story of misery and death. His *Weavers* (1892) uses a rioting mob as the protagonist in a struggle between capital and labor. Tolstoi, in *The Power of Darkness* (1886), tells a grim story of illicit love, drunkenness, and murder, although he tempers the gloom with spiritual overtones. Strindberg's *Miss Julie* (1888) is a story of lust and suicide. Shaw, who wrote two plays in the naturalistic style, *Widower's Houses* (1892) and *Mrs. Warren's Profession* (1898), indicated his motivation for writing as he did: "I felt the need for mentioning the forbidden subjects, not only because of their own importance, but for the sake of destroying taboo by giving it the most violent shocks."

The naturalists differed from the realists by concentrating on the squalid side of life and giving their plays the effect of a "tranche de vie" (slice of life) free from contrived situations, climaxes, and curtains. They introduced a new collection of characters to the stage—the dregs of society, the wayward and twisted victims of the lower depths. Their characters were bedeviled by doubts and frustrations, torn by inner conflicts, ridden by passions. As Strindberg said, "They are conglomerates made up of past and present stages of civilization, scraps of humanity, torn-off pieces of Sunday clothing turned into rags—all patched together as is the human soul itself." The naturalist attempted to translate into concrete images what he had gained from the changing thought. The hard shell that protected the traditional views of love, authority, duty, honor, and morality was shattered when the playwright probed beneath the surfaces of life to investigate the innermost desires and passion of the individual in his relations with his mate, his employer, and his family.

2. Émile Zola, *The Experimental Novel* (New York: Cassell, 1893).

The naturalist's dialogue had a new texture and frankness as it reflected the speech of the lowborn and humble. And his themes had hitherto been considered too controversial or salacious for the theatergoing public. Although the new boldness aroused shocked protest in many places, the naturalists performed an important service in ridding the stage of bombast and sentimentality. As they attempted to reflect authenticity in diction, they also made painstaking efforts to show the locale of their action as accurately as possible, to emphasize their point that a man's physical surroundings mold his character. This objective led to an excess of clutter and an obsession with the solidity and authenticity of material objects, which at its extreme led Antoine at the Théâtre Libre to hang sides of beef on the stage.

As a literary style, naturalism gave way to the more moderate realism, which found ways of relieving the steady diet of misery, crime and disintegration, but the naturalist did succeed in bringing to the stage new characters and themes with honesty and forthrightness. Although naturalism as a movement lost its impetus, echoes of its quality are seen in the present theater in such plays as Kenneth H. Brown's *The Brig*, an attack on the inhumane conditions in a Marine Corps prison; in LeRoi Jones's plays of racial discrimination, *The Dutchman* and *The Toilet;* in two plays of drug addiction, *The Concept* and Jack Gelber's *The Connection.* The spirit of the naturalist is seen too in John Osborne's *Look Back in Anger,* the plays of Arnold Wesker, and in many other recent plays, such as Peter Weiss's *Marat/Sade,* on which Artaud's "theatre of cruelty" has left its mark.

expressionism

Another outgrowth of realism was expressionism. Actually the expressionist was a superrealist insisting that actuality is within. Beneath the social façade, there is a vast jungle where dwell man's secrets and often unconscious desires, aspirations, conflicts, frustrations, and hallucinations. It is this strange and confusing subjective reality that the expressionist wished to explore.

The Swedish playwright Strindberg was the first to state the expressionist's approach to drama: "Anything may happen; everything is possible and probable. Time and space do not exist. On an insignificant background of reality, imagination designs and embroiders novel patterns; a medley of memories, experiences, free fantasies, absurdities, and improvisations." A drama, he said, may have the "disconnected but seemingly logical form of a dream." He demonstrated his theory in two remarkable plays, *The Dream Play* and *The Ghost Sonata.* For a time, Strindberg was an isolated innovator, but from 1912 to 1925 expressionism became an important theatrical style, especially in Germany for those who knew the traumatic experiences of World War I and its aftermath.

The expressionist rejected the ordered structure of the realist since he wished to center his attention on specific instances without being obliged to provide a chain of causes and effects. He presented the essential action—the high points of an experience—without being bogged down by small talk or the machinery of plotting. The critical moments of a man's career were shown in a jagged series of explosive scenes. In Rice's *The Adding Machine,* Mr. Zero's crime and punishment were shown in seven fragmentary scenes; O'Neill's *The Hairy Ape* dramatized the important steps in Yank's quest for status; Kaiser's *From Morn to Midnight* was a disconnected series of events that showed a bank clerk's theft, spending orgy, and death; in Toller's *Transfiguration* a kaleidoscope of dream pictures illustrated the horrors of war. Arthur Miller in *Death of a Salesman* effectively used expressionistic scenes combined with realistic ones to define Willy Loman's mental state. The expressionist flung open the windows of the mind and allowed the spectator to look in on the private, disordered, associative processes of his character. He rejected the carefully shaped, logically organized structure of the realist and used a fragmentary system of actions because it created the effect he desired—a view of the chaotic inner reality.

Characters in expressionistic plays are often depersonalized. They are not individuals but types who are given such names as the Gentleman in Black, the Billionaire, the Young Woman in Taffeta, Mr. Zero, the Blues and the Yellows. They are not psychologically complex except perhaps for the protagonist through whose eyes all of the action may be seen. To reveal the inner state of the character, playwrights revived the technique of the soliloquy so that the character could externalize his private thoughts. In witnessing the distortion that characterized the protagonist's subjective point of view, the spectator was often confused by bewildering symbols and actions, especially when the distortion was that of an abnormal psychic condition. Character itself was often handled symbolically and with great freedom as Strindberg indicates in *The Dream Play:* "The characters split, double, multiply, evaporate, solidify, diffuse, clarify. But one consciousness reigns above them all—that of the dreamer; it knows no secrets, no incongruities, no scruples, no law." Sometimes, the protagonist is the voice of the author, as in Toller's *Transfiguration* in which the hero, Friedrich, is the playwright protesting against militarism and embittered nationalism. Friedrich is something of an individual with a specific background, but he is also an abstract symbol of man appearing in many guises as a soldier, professor, sculptor, judge, priest, and laborer.

In general, expressionists have had an axe to grind. Their plays have been linked to social causes, as for example in Germany where the frus-

75 Dartmouth College's production of Strindberg's *The Ghost Sonata,* directed by Rod Alexander.

76 Stage setting by Emil Pirchan for Georg Kaiser's *Gas* at the Schiller Theater, Berlin, 1928.

KAISER: VON MORGENSBIS MITTERNACHT CESAR KLEIN

77 (opposite, top) Expressionistic staging of Ernst Toller's *Transfiguration*, designed by Robert Neppach.

78 (opposite, bottom) Stage design by Cesar Klein for Georg Kaiser's *From Morn to Midnight*, Berlin, 1923.

79 Setting for Alexander Tairov's production of O'Neill's *The Hairy Ape*, Kamerny Theater, Moscow.

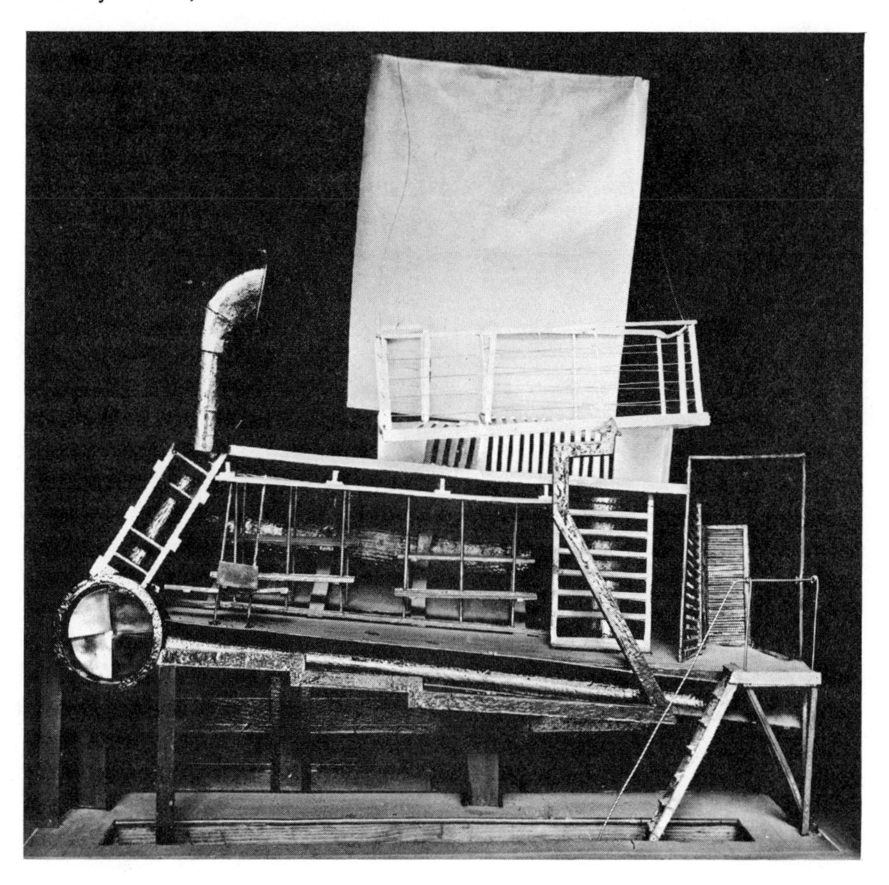

80 Setting by Lee Simonson for Elmer Rice's *The Adding Machine,* produced at the Theatre Guild, New York, 1923.

81 *Beggar on Horseback,* an expressionistic satire by Kaufman and Connelly. Produced by The Repertory Company of Lincoln Center.

trations and yearnings of a people tormented by guilt and despair found in expressionism not merely a theatrical style, but also a desperate and agonized plea for some kind of salvation. In Kaiser's *Coral,* the Billionaire's son revolts against the injustice of capitalism: "We are rich, and these others who stifle in torment and misery are men like us." Again in Kaiser's *From Morn to Midnight,* the author makes a direct attack on materialism: "Not with all the money from all the banks of the world can one buy anything of value. . . . Money is the crowning deceit of all."

American expressionists worked over familiar social themes in a much milder vein. O'Neill's *The Hairy Ape* is a criticism of our materialistic society and of human disorientation. His *The Emperor Jones* dramatizes man's inability to escape from his primitive past; Rice's *The Adding Machine* is a merciless satire on the plight of the little man trapped in a mechanistic world; and Kaufman and Connelly's *Beggar on Horseback* lampoons philistinism in America. But the expressionists were not so notable for their advanced thinking as for their theatrical ability to give new shape and expression to familiar ideas.

One of these ways of expression was a theatrical treatment of language to create effects and atmosphere as well as to advance thought. An interesting device was the use of short rhythmic bursts of staccato speech with a sharply marked tempo. The effect was to remove the speaker one step away from reality, reinforcing the offbeat atmosphere and the dehumanized characterization. A typical example occurs in Kaiser's *Gas,* part one:

> *(The door to left is flung open. A* WORKMAN*—naked—stained by the explosion totters in.)*
>
> WORKMAN: Report from Shed Eight—Central—white cat burst—red eyes torn open—yellow mouth gaping—humps up crackling back—grows round—snaps away girders—lifts up roof—bursts—sparks! sparks! *(Sitting down in the middle of the floor and striking about him.)* Chase away the cat—Shoo! Shoo!—smash her jaws—Shoo! Shoo! bury her eyes—they flame—hammer down her back—hammer it down—thousands of fists! It's swelling, swelling—growing fat—fatter—Gas out of every crack—the tube![3]

Rice, in *The Adding Machine,* uses telegraphic speech to lampoon the inanities of social conversation. Toller, in *Masses and Man,* likewise uses fragmentary dialogue to show the characters of the bankers in the stock exchange. Kaufman and Connelly in *Beggar on Horseback* satirize the mechanized business world in this passage:

3. Georg Kaiser, *Gas, I* (Cologne: Verlag Kiepenheuer & Witsch, 1918).

(Four business men, all with hats and newspapers, and all looking just alike, enter one at a time and step into an imaginary elevator.)

CADY: Good morning! Made it in twenty-eight minutes this morning!

FIRST BUSINESS MAN: Good morning! I got the eight-six this morning!

SECOND BUSINESS MAN: Good morning! I missed the seven forty-three.

THIRD BUSINESS MAN: Good morning! I always make the nine-two.

FOURTH BUSINESS MAN: Good morning! I thought you were on the eight-sixteen.

As mentioned earlier, the expressionists revived the soliloquy as a means of communication, with a single speech sometimes making up an entire scene, as in two instances in *The Adding Machine.* The expressionists' free use of language found new and interesting ways of using speech in the theater that anticipated most of the "innovations" of the absurdists and the present workers in the "open theater."

An expressionistic play expanded the possibilities of theatricalism, by which we mean an approach to drama that rejects the pretense of copying actuality, and instead, exploits the medium for itself. The purpose of dramatic production was to create theater—which was precisely what the expressionists did, often in their speech as we have just seen, in their episodic plots, and particularly in their use of spectacle. The realist stressed the appearance of actuality in setting to convince the spectators he was seeing real life; the expressionist used fragmentary, distorted images, skeletal settings and odd lighting effects because he was revealing a disordered world. In so doing, he acknowledged the limitations of the stage and created in a directly theatrical way. The phantasmagoria of weird landscapes, of dreams where images and symbols are projected in baffling and exaggerated shapes, colors, and patterns, made expressionism a designer's holiday. For example, in Kokoschka's fantastic play, *Hiob,* a parrot suddenly explodes and rises in the shape of a rosy cloud to heaven; in Kaiser's *From Morn to Midnight,* a tree struck by lightning becomes a human skeleton; and in Strindberg's *A Dream Play,* eerie landscapes appear, merge, and alter in the disconnected fragments of a nightmare.

The following excerpt from O'Neill's *The Hairy Ape* is an example of the distorted atmosphere of expressionism. Yank, an ignorant stoker emerging from the fireman's forecastle of a ship, finds himself among the social set on Fifth Avenue, New York, in an environment where he is completely alien:

(The crowd from church enter from the right, sauntering slowly and affectedly, their heads held stiffly up, looking neither to the right nor left, talking in toneless, simpering voices. The women are rouged, calcimated, dyed, overdressed to the nth degree. The men are in Prince Alberts, high hats, spats, canes, etc. A procession of

gaudy marionettes, yet with something of the relentless horror of Frankensteins in their detached, mechanical unawareness.)

VOICES: Dear Doctor Caiaphas! He is so sincere!

What was the sermon? I dozed off.

About the radicals, my dear—and the false doctrines that are being preached.

We must organize a hundred per cent American bazaar.

And let everyone contribute one one-hundredth per cent of their income tax.

What an original idea!

We can devote the proceeds to rehabilitating the veil of the temple.

But that has been done many times.

(YANK *after vainly trying to get the attention of the Easter Paraders)*

(He turns in a rage on the men, bumping viciously into them but not jarring them the least bit. Rather it is he who recoils after each collision. He keeps growling.) Git off de oith! G'wan, yuh bum! Look where yuh're goin', can't yuh? Git outa here! Fight, why don't yuh? Put up yer mits! Don't be a dog! Fight or I'll knock yuh dead!

(But without seeming to see him, they all answer with mechanical affected politeness: I beg your pardon. Then at a cry from one of the women, they all scurry to the furrier's window.)

THE WOMAN: *(ecstatically with a gasp of delight)* Monkey fur! *(The whole crowd of men and women chorus after her in the same tone of affected delight)* Monkey fur!

YANK: *(with a jerk of his head back on his shoulders, as if he had received a punch full in the face—raging).* I see yuh, all in white! I see yuh, yuh white-faced tart, yuh! Hairy ape, huh? I'll hairy ape yuh!

(He bends down and grips at the street curbing as if to pluck it out and hurl it. Foiled in this, snarling with passion, he leaps to the lamppost on the corner and tries to pull it up for a club. Just at that moment a bus is heard rumbling up. A fat, high-hatted, spatted gentleman runs out from the side street. He calls out plaintively: Bus! Bus! Stop there! and runs full tilt into the bending, straining YANK, *who is bowled off his balance.)*

YANK: *(seeing a fight—with a roar of joy as he springs to his feet).* At last! Bus, huh? I'll bust yuh!

(He lets drive a terrific swing, his fist landing full on the fat gentleman's face. But the gentleman stands unmoved as if nothing had happened.)

GENTLEMAN: I beg your pardon. *(Then irritably)* You have made me lose my bus.

(He claps his hands and begins to scream: Officer! Officer! Many police whistles shrill out on the instant and a whole platoon of policemen

> *rush in on* YANK *from all sides. He tries to fight, but is clubbed to the pavement and fallen upon. The crowd at the window have not moved or noticed this disturbance. The clanging gong of the patrol wagon approaches with a clamoring din.)*[4]

The expressionists' bold theatricalism demonstrated new and effective uses of the medium, it cleared the stage of the rigid three walls, and replaced the clutter with a few imaginative fragments, picked out by light on a relatively bare stage, which gave the actor the appropriate psychological setting for his performance. The creative influence of the expressionists was apparent in ballet, musical comedies, motion pictures, and in the simpler settings of realistic plays. Every experimental venture in the twentieth century is in debt to the expressionists for their conception of theater.

Naturalism and expressionism are passé and the revolt against realism is now going on. Actually, a revolt has gone on within the mode itself so that present-day realism bears little resemblance to Ibsen's. Our increased technical skills and facilities, the use of light, film, and sound, the arena and thrust stages give the playwright a previously unknown freedom. Moreover, today's audience, in its willingness to participate imaginatively in all kinds of new theatrical practices, has encouraged more creative and flexible playwriting and production.

The case against realism is couched in such terms as "narrow," "commonplace," "superficial," "contrived," "passive," and "illusionary." It is criticized as being a device for avoiding life rather than facing it—a process of hypnosis and delusion, deficient in spirit. In its selection of character and incident it is said to be too artificial. In its mechanically organized plots with their neat endings, it is charged with being too narrowly confined to a few unimportant people partitioned off from the real world, too much involved with psychological case studies rather than with the larger, more significant issues of society. It is said to make a fetish of external appearance and factual data, and to be theatrically pedestrian and trivial in its restricted setting, its limited vocabulary, plot situations, and style of performance.

In response to this criticism, those who support realism and its derivatives point out that historically it accomplished its initial objective of ridding the theater of much that was meretricious and false. Realistic playwrights returned the theater to a serious purpose and dealt with its fundamental theme—the dignity and integrity of the individual, and the vital interests of the common man. In their emphasis on the conditioning power of heredity and environment, the realists made the public aware for the first time of an important concept of human behavior. They

4. Eugene O'Neill, *The Hairy Ape* (New York: Random House, 1922).

created a respect for the objective observation of facts but they went beyond them to a concern with man's spiritual destiny in a changed and perplexing world. For example, some observers have criticized Ibsen's *Ghosts* because the ending is "bleak," without hope or elevation. This is precisely the point that Ibsen was making, that in the new world which was evolving, man was cut off from his spiritual heritage and that he was indeed alone. Ibsen's point has been well worked over since by the absurdists and Brecht—writers who despise realism.

The realist replaced inflated and artificial rhetoric with new means of communication in speech, action, and setting that encouraged maximum communication. The best of them were concerned with the problems that engage our foremost experimentalists today—self-realization and freedom from bourgeois conventionality.

In their efforts to imitate men's action, the realists turned the theater in a new direction with their emphasis on the careful observation of human behavior. They sought to give pleasure through learning by means of their fresh perceptions of contemporary man and his world.

exercises

1. Describe in detail a setting appropriate for a naturalistic play.
2. Using a familiar fable, story, or parable, treat the material expressionistically.
3. What are the characteristics of expressionistic painting?
4. Write a transcript of realistic dialogue.
5. Write a dream sequence suitable for the stage or film.
6. Contrast the treatment of character in realism, naturalism, and expressionism.
7. Create or find examples of visual material showing the distortion of reality.
8. Write a short biography of a naturalistic character.
9. Evaluate the importance of the visual aspects of naturalism and expressionism.
10. How significant is the element of thought in realism?
11. Since all forms of drama are conventionalized, how does the realist attempt to create the illusion of reality?
12. Watch a film or television show in an attempt to evaluate its reality. How was reality achieved or missed?
13. Find pictures that illustrate the difference in viewpoint between the realist, naturalist, and expressionist.
14. Write a soliloquy for an expressionistic character.
15. Discuss the differences in dramatic structure in realism, expressionism, and naturalism.

16. How do you account for the popular appeal of realism? What are its drawbacks?
17. What are the limitations of expressionism and naturalism?

suggested reading

Eric Bentley, *The Life of the Drama*, 1964.
———, *The Playwright as Thinker*, 1946.
Travis Bogard and William I. Oliver, *Modern Drama: Essays in Criticism*, 1965.
Robert Brustein, *The Theatre in Revolt*, 1962.
Barrett H. Clark, *A Study of the Modern Drama*, 1938.
Toby Cole, ed., *Playwrights on Playwriting*, 1960.
Robert W. Corrigan and James L. Rosenberg, *The Context and Craft of Drama*, 1964.
John Gassner, *Form and Idea in Modern Theatre*, 1956.
Anna Irene Miller, *The Independent Theatre in Europe, 1887 to the Present*, 1927.
Daniel Seltzer, *The Modern Theatre*, 1967.
Walter A. Sokel, *The Writer in Extremis: Expressionism in Twentieth-Century German Literature*, 1959.
Raymond Williams, *Drama from Ibsen to Brecht*, 1968.

play list (realism)

Edward Albee, *Who's Afraid of Virginia Woolf?*
Anton Chekhov, *The Cherry Orchard; The Sea Gull*
Friedrich Duerrenmatt, *The Physicists*
Max Frisch, *The Firebugs*
Frank D. Gilroy, *The Subject Was Roses*
Lorraine Hansberry, *Raisin in the Sun*
Henrik Ibsen, *Ghosts*
Heinar Kipphardt, *In the Matter of J. Robert Oppenheimer*
Arthur Miller, *The Price; A View from the Bridge*
Sean O'Casey, *Juno and the Paycock*
Eugene O'Neill, *Desire under the Elms*
Clifford Odets, *Awake and Sing; Golden Boy*
John Osborne, *Look Back in Anger*
Harold Pinter, *The Homecoming; The Caretaker*
Luigi Pirandello, *Six Characters in Search of an Author*
Jean-Paul Sartre, *No Exit*
George Bernard Shaw, *Heartbreak House*

August Strindberg, *The Father*
J. M. Synge, *The Playboy of the Western World*
Tennessee Williams, *The Glass Menagerie*

play list (naturalism)

Henri Becque, *The Vultures*
Jack Gelber, *The Connection*
Maxim Gorki, *The Lower Depths*
Gerhart Hauptmann, *The Weavers*
LeRoi Jones, *The Dutchman*
John Steinbeck, *Of Mice and Men*
August Strindberg, *Miss Julie*
Émile Zola, *Thérèse Raquin*

play list (expressionism)

Georg Kaiser, *From Morn to Midnight; Gas*
George S. Kaufman and Marc Connelly, *Beggar on Horseback*
Eugene O'Neill, *Emperor Jones; The Hairy Ape*
August Strindberg, *The Dream Play*
Ernst Toller, *Man and the Masses*

departures from realism

The twentieth century has seen a motley parade of rebels and visionaries marching to the beat of varied drummers. They follow an odd assortment of leaders or meander in broken ranks; some they follow are sometimes obscure, sometimes vulgar, but always defiant. There is a sparkle in their eye and a sense of urgency and zeal that cannot be denied, despite their incongruous appearance. They may not know for sure where they are going, but they are on the march—and it is a march of protest, a boisterous, vigorous, articulate protest. The world must change, and the theater with it. The linking of these two objectives is important, for the discontent is with the total human condition.

This uneasiness, which characterizes the temper of our society, had its roots in the revolutions in the science and technology of the nineteenth century. We have already seen how that disruption touched off a rebellion in theater under the label of realism and its derivatives as man tried to orient himself to a materialistic and mechanical world. But his quest for meaning and identity was subverted by the holocaust of the First World War. Man's faith in political institutions and the beneficence of scientific progress was shaken by the spectacle of toppling regimes, the barbarism of mechanized warfare, and the dehumanization of man.

chapter 9

Those closest to the flames were infected by a deep sense of frustration and cynicism, which broke out in the savage distortions of the expressionists and in the dadaist's brash assault on everything. The Great Depression, the Second World War, the uneasy peace under a dangling bomb, and the ruthless struggle for power turned cynicism and doubt into a general malaise instead of a localized infection confined to the defeated or the have-nots. The result has been a universal sense of concern, a gnawing doubt about the ability of man to match his ingenuity with his wisdom. And it is this concern that has put the marchers on the move.

Beginning with realism, as we have seen, some dramatists have raised questions about man's place in an increasingly perplexing and disordered universe, but the arts were not at the center of our culture. And theater, a social institution usually tied by its purse strings to the status quo, has often lagged behind the others in revolutionary fervor. Until recently, dissidents have had a difficult time in attracting sympathetic audiences with the ability to pay. The popular function of the commercial theater used to be to provide relaxation, not friction nor serious investigation of the serious problems of society. Some questions one did not ask in public. The audience might lend an ear to the voice of protest if it were as witty as Bernard Shaw's, or tolerate political didacticism if it were as theatrical as Brecht's, but the main course of the drama was not obstructed by militant dispute. As the outside world became more precarious, however, the protest grew louder, and the walls could no longer keep out the clamor. Indeed, because those within began to bring their doubts with them, the theater could no longer remain aloof. The rebels found their way into song, film, and the visual arts; they turned coffeehouses into theaters, found audiences on the sidewalks and in the streets, and staged their own brand of events wth such impressive numbers and raucous insistence that their message came through: the world must change and the theater with it. While no one seriously looks to the theater for social salvation, the backstage doors have swung hesitatingly open, and the murmur in the wings makes the audience restive and reluctantly open to the word.

The rebels protest both form and content in drama. They would relegate the traditional, carefully structured system of action to the scrap heap, for to them system and order are suspect. Human experience, they say, is not tidily organized into a beginning, middle, and end. Life comes at us in spurts—without clear causes or predictable effects. Man is not a rational, logical creature. The protesters find support for their view of man in such statements as Freud's description of the id: "a chaos, a cauldron of seething excitement with no organization and no unified will, only an impulsion to obtain satisfaction for the instinctual needs, in accordance with the pleasure principle." The form of art, the rebels insist, reflects the form of our lives—bewildering, confusing, illogical, incomprehensible.

As for the content of the drama, it must deal forthrightly with the larger issues of the human condition. It is not enough, the rebels said, to dwell on the petty squabbles of little lives or probe into the personality problems of insignificant individuals. The visionaries asked for a theater that would rise up against all powers and institutions that belittle and enslave man. Nor should the drama concern itself with the clichéd situations of humdrum existence. Man is an iceberg with vast inexplicable forces, pulls, and radiations beneath the surface of his visible world, and the arts should somehow make this manifest.

In spite of great diversity among those who reject the past, a common cluster of ideas informs their aesthetic base. Let us look at the visual arts, whose development anticipated the rebellion in the theater. Kurt Schwitters (1887–1948), one of the most prominent of the dadaists, developed his "Merz pictures"—collages made up of all kinds of found objects fastened together—as an attack on traditional bourgeois art. He explained his purpose in these words: "Art is a primordial concept, exalted as the godhead, inexplicable as life, indefinable and without purpose. . . . The medium is unimportant. I take any material whatsoever if the picture demands it. When I adjust materials of different kinds to one another, I have taken a step in advance of mere oil painting, for in addition to playing off color against color, line against line, form against form, etc., I play off material against material."[1]

Another group of rebels were the surrealists who, like the dadaists, took the point of view that "man must escape from the control of reason," and that the artist should "surrender to the dark forces of the unconscious." These men were interested in exploring the world of dreams and the imagination. They improvised games of "automatic writing and drawing"—creations entirely free from rational control, that are made up of strange and distorted images. André Breton, the chief spokesman, said that the surrealist "took pleasure in reuniting the sewing machine and the umbrella on the dissecting table."

The works of art growing out of dadaism and surrealism are characterized by incongruous combinations of objects and figures, simultaneous action, fragmentation, and the distorted and seemingly irrational atmosphere of a dream. These characteristics of visual art objects are similar to those of much of the avant-garde drama, for they are rooted in the investigation of the inner life of man.

1. Kurt Schwitters, quoted in Robert Motherwell, *The Dada Painters and Poets* (New York: Wittenborn, Schultz, 1951).

Let us make this resemblance clear with a specific instance from the theater. Peter Brook, one of the most creative and articulate directors in the contemporary theater, makes this statement about dramatic content:

> What's the difference between a poor play and a good one? I think there's a very simple way of comparing them. A play in performance is a series of impressions; little dabs, one after another, fragments of information or feeling in a sequence which stir the audience's perceptions. A good play sends many such messages, often several at a time, often crowding, jostling, overlapping one another. The intelligence, the feelings, the memory, the imagination are all stirred. In a poor play, the impressions are well spaced out, they lope along in single file, and in the gaps the heart can sleep while the mind wanders to the day's annoyances and thoughts of dinner.[2]

In preparation for a production of Peter Weiss's *Marat/Sade* by the Royal Shakespeare Theatre in London, Peter Brook set up a "theater of cruelty" following some of the teachings of the theater rebel, Artaud. *Marat/Sade* takes place in a madhouse where the inmates find psychological release through the reenactment of their crimes. In his experimental workshop, Brook worked with his actors on concentration, simultaneous playing, improvisations, "transformations" (going from one character or situation to another without transitions), and forms of nonverbal expression.

The performance of *Marat/Sade* was a weird mixture of characters and situations objectifying the inner states of the inmates. Many of the audience were confused and baffled by the apparent lack of focus or clarity of purpose—the same reaction expressed by those who first saw the works of Schwitters and the surrealists. And Brook's evaluation of the production bears a striking resemblance to their statements when he says:

> From our practical experience I can report that the force of the performance is directly related to the imaginative richness of the material: the imaginative richness is the consequence of the amount of levels that are working simultaneously: this simultaneity is the direct result of Weiss' daring combination of so many contradictory techniques.[3]

Some of those who wrote for and worked in the theater sought meaning and purpose by turning back to elemental sources, and their

2. Peter Brook, "Introduction to *Marat/Sade*" by Peter Weiss, (New York: Atheneum, 1965). From the introduction by Peter Brook to the play, *The Persecution and Assassination of Jean-Paul Marat as Performed by the Inmates of the Asylum of Charenton Under the Direction of the Marquis de Sade*, by Peter Weiss. Copyright © 1965 by John Calder Ltd. Reprinted by permission of Atheneum Publishers.
3. *Ibid.*

82 Georges Braque's *The Table*, 1928. A nonrepresentational arrangement of objects seen from several points of view at once.

83 Joan Miro's *Person Throwing a Stone at a Bird,* 1926.
The painter captures the seemingly irrational atmosphere of a dream.

84 Kurt Schwitters' *Merz: Santa Claus*, 1922. A collage of papers and cloth.

85 Pablo Picasso's *Guernica*, 1937. A powerful combination of objects and figures, simultaneous action and fragmentation that projects the distorted quality of a nightmare.

creative efforts showed echoes of the past in myth and ritual. Their thinking went like this: We should look for new perceptions in symbols, metaphors, and indirect expression. We should be open to the workings of mystery and magic, to the deep inexplicable forces within nature and ourselves. We need to see character as more than external appearance or the product of its present environment. We should be responsive to the meanings beneath and beyond mere words—to be aware of rhythms, images, and forces that make all nature one. Out of this cluster of ideas came the vision of theater echoing in its purpose those of ancient rites and myths.

Those who follow this line of thought propose that we return to our ancient heritage to rediscover metaphysical values that are not expressed in direct statements, but symbolically through metaphor to reveal archetypal ideas which Philip Wheelwright describes as "a set of depth-meanings of perduring significance within a widely shared perspective, and transcending the limits of what can be said via ordinary literal speech."[4]

Carl G. Jung, who devoted his career to an investigation of man's relation to his unconscious, identified the relevance of this symbolic heritage to contemporary man in these words:

> Modern man does not understand how much his "rationalism" (which has destroyed his capacity to respond to numinous symbols and ideas) has put him at the mercy of the psychic "underworld." He has freed himself from superstition (or so he believes), but in the process he has lost his spiritual values to a positively dangerous degree. His moral and spiritual tradition has disintegrated and he is now paying the price for this breakup in world-wide disorientation and dissociation.[5]

antonin artaud

One of the most provocative and colorful figures among the twentieth century's avant-garde who called for a return to primitive rituals was Antonin Artaud (1896–1948). A tormented iconoclast, he sought a "theater of cruelty" whose purpose and methods would find its roots in ancient rites and the nonverbal ceremonies of the Orient. From 1927 to 1929 he experimented in his Theatre Alfred Jarry, named in honor of another innovator who wrote *Ubu Roi* in 1896, and is sometimes credited as the first of the absurdists because of his mockery of traditional values and conventional drama. Artaud's importance is not for his practical

4. Philip Wheelwright, *The Burning Fountain* (Bloomington: Indiana University Press, 1954).

5. Carl G. Jung, *Man and His Symbols* (Garden City, N.Y.: Doubleday, 1964).

work in the theater, but for his astonishingly prolific imagination. His book *The Theater and Its Double* (1938) advances many ideas that are the basis for the contemporary revolt in the theater.

Artaud's criticism springs basically from his dissatisfaction with the shape of the world about him. He says: "I believe that our present social system is iniquitous and should be destroyed."[6] And again: "There are too many signs that everything that used to sustain our lives no longer does so, that we are all mad, desperate and sick."[7] The existing theater outrages Artaud because it fails to deal seriously with man's social and moral systems. The theater has lost its feeling for seriousness and laughter. It has "broken away from the spirit of profound anarchy which is the root of all poetry." He calls for a rejection of the idolatry of fixed masterpieces which are reserved for the self-styled elite and are not understood or appealing to the public. He rages against the falsehood and illusion of popular distractions that serve as an outlet for our worst instincts. These descriptive and narrative distractions provide stories that satisfy only peeping toms—a theater to decorate our leisure with intimate scenes from the lives of a few puppets. He repudiates well-made plots, which serve only to exploit the psychological aspects of human interest. He was enraged to see the theater offering stories about money, social careerism, the pangs of love, and sugar-coated sexuality—stories that fail to touch the public interest; stories that leave no scars.

Artaud was not merely an anarchist determined on a course of destruction; he was rather a true revolutionary dedicated to change. While his criticism of the modern theater is scathing, he is even more vehement when it comes to suggesting a cure. Extraordinarily creative about all aspects of the stage, technical as well as theoretical, he envisions a radically different kind of drama and production techniques to implement it. While he was never able to realize his ideas in his own Theatre Arthur Jarry very thoroughly, the audacity and sweep of his imagination can scarcely be ignored by anyone involved in the contemporary theater.

The emphasis in his thinking was to create a theater that "stages events, not men," that deals with the metaphysical concerns of ancient rites—"an exorcism to make our demons flow." The theater must give us "crime, love, war, or madness, if it wants to cover its necessity." It must deal with "atrocious crimes" and "superhuman devotions" as the ancient myths do. The notion of cruelty stems from the mystical, magical forces of a "theater in which violent physical images crush and hypnotize the sensibility of the spectator seized by the theater as by a whirlwind of higher forces." His intention was to free the repressed unconscious

6. Antonin Artaud, *The Theater and Its Double*, trans. Mary C. Richards (New York: Grove Press, 1958).
7. *Ibid.*

in dramatic performance which resembles a plague because "it is the revelation, the bringing forth, the exteriorization of a depth of the latent cruelty by means of which all perverse possibilities of the mind . . . are localized."

The violence and cruelty to which he makes constant reference are not included for their own sake but as a part of the process of purification which "causes the mask to fall, reveals the lie, the slackness, baseness, and hypocrisy of our world. . . ." The theater is a means of ridding society of its institutionalized violence. For after experiencing the cruelty that he envisions in the theater, Artaud says, "I defy the spectator to give himself up once outside the theater to ideas of war, riot and blatant murder."

Such a concept of the function of the theater reminds us, of course, of Freud's approach to psychoanalysis through the release of neurotic symptoms. Artaud's perspective also bears a striking resemblance to Aristotle's view of catharsis—the purgation of emotions, as we have seen in tragedy. In his *Politics*, speaking of the effect of music, Aristotle describes the so-called homeopathic theory of catharsis, which seems analogous to Artaud's purpose:

> In listening to the performances of others we may admit the modes of action and passion also. For feelings such as pity and fear, or, again, enthusiasm, exist very strongly in some souls, and have more or less influence over all. Some persons fall into a religious frenzy, whom we see as the result of the sacred melodies—when they have used the melodies that excite the soul to mystic frenzy—restored as though they have found healing and purgation. Those who are influenced by pity and fear, and every emotional nature, must have a like experience . . . and all are in a manner purged and their souls lightened and delighted.[8]

The effect described by Aristotle is apparently close to the experience that Artaud sought in his theater—incidentally, an experience not without parallels in the rock festivals of our day.

Artaud conceives of theater as total spectacle that must have the "ceremonial quality of a religious rite." Made up of violent and concentrated action "pushed beyond all limits," it is addressed to the senses and to the theatricality of the unconscious.

The physical theater should be a single unit that combines the acting area with the auditorium and thus insures maximum communication. He proposed an architectural arrangement in which the spectators would be surrounded by the action. Experiments would be made with lighting and color to evoke "luminous vibration." Instead of a conventional set-

8. Aristotle, *Politics*, trans. Leon Goldman, cited in Aristotle's *Poetics*, trans. Leon Goldman, commentary by O. B. Hardison, Jr. (Englewood Cliffs, N.J.: Prentice-Hall, 1968).

ting, space would be used on all possible levels with overlapping images and movements—a combination of hieroglyphic characters, ten-foot-high manikins, masks, "metaphysics of speech," gesture, and objects of strange shapes and sizes.

Artaud rebelled against the conventional use of language in the theater. To understand his attack, one must remember his background; for the French, more than any other people, have placed a high value on polished diction, and the tradition of their theater is rich in rhetoric. Artaud found the language of the theater "dead and fixed in forms that no longer respond to the needs of the time." He objected to the "tyranny of the word" and the dictatorship of the writer. Actually, his rebellion was against the conventionalized nature and form of drama, and in his call for a new theatricalism, language was his first target. He wanted to get away from mere words addressed to the mind. He proposed to use language in a "new, exceptional and unaccustomed fashion." He wanted to replace the utilitarian spoken word with an active language "beyond customary feelings and words," to create a "subterranean current of impressions, correspondences and analogies." Communication in his theater was not merely actors making speeches, but the stage was to be a place filled with its own language to include sounds used for their "vibratory quality," onomatopoeia, cries, and intonations. He wanted words to have about the same importance "as they have in dreams." Indeed, Artaud urged an extension of theatricalism so that everything that occupied the stage would create an effect on the senses, even to the point of physical shock.

Too much criticism of Artaud has been directed at his vivid rhetoric rather than at the spirit of his ideas. He is not a pessimistic, destructive sensationalist. At the core, his views are serious, humane, and positive. He invites us to take the theater seriously, to cut through the sham and hypocrisy of society, to face ourselves honestly, and to trap our deep, latent powers that will enable us to take a "superior and heroic attitude." The process involves the cruel practice of exposing society and *one's self* with complete honesty. Here is the voice of one who sees ahead and links future to past:

> Either we will be capable of returning by present-day means to this superior idea of poetry and poetry-through-theater which underlies the myths told by the great ancient tragedians, capable once more of entertaining a religious idea of the theater (without meditation, useless contemplation, and vague dreams), capable of attaining awareness and a possession of certain dominant forces, of certain notions that control all others, and (since ideas, when they are effective, carry their energy with them) capable of recovering within ourselves those energies which ultimately create order and increase the value of life, or else we might as well abandon ourselves now, without protest, and recognize that we are

no longer good for anything but disorder, famine, blood, war and epidemics.[9]

jean genêt

A direct spiritual descendant of Artaud is another Frenchman, Jean Genêt (b. 1910), who conceives of the theater in terms of symbol and ritual. Just as the existentialists found it necessary to reorient themselves philosophically to a shattered world by creating their individual sets of values, likewise Genêt shaped his own existential view of the world from his strange, tormented childhood and early adult life. An illegitimate child, an unwanted orphan, he found out at age ten that he had no connection with the world, and from that discovery he developed his own inverted hierarchy of values. "I rejected a world which rejected me." Since he had no identity and no status he turned to a life of crime and homosexuality. He attempted to find his life by losing it. While serving a prison sentence, he began to write and showed so much artistic promise that some leading French intellectuals secured his release. In his plays *The Balcony, The Blacks, The Maids,* and *The Screens,* he has gained recognition as one of the most provocative playwrights of our day, and in his works some of Artaud's ideas of a theater of cruelty have been most successfully realized.

Out of his personal anguish, he visualized dramatic works of myth and ceremony but in a world of reversed values. Instead of climbing the heights and seeking salvation, man finds his spiritual identity by plunging into the depths of darkness and evil. The soul is redeemed only by death, and only the criminal with the dedication of a saint can attain grace. Murder is the highest crime, and the act of betrayal is a sacrament.

A metaphor that Genêt finds appropriate to his purpose is a series of mirrors, some of them placed at odd angles, some that invert or distort the image, and some of which, like Alice's looking glass, allow us to see through into an oddly perverted wonderland. His metaphor suits his purpose well, for Genêt is concerned with the varied facets and layers of reality: the discrepancy between the genuine and the illusionary, and the loss or disguise of identity through assumed appearances and roles. In his plays, the spectator is often bewildered by the dazzling surfaces and the strange perspectives so that he is not sure if he is seeing an actual character in a genuine event, or a pretender in a masquerade.

In a brothel, disguised as a sacristy, Genêt's *The Balcony* presents a many-layered structure of actions to explore his favorite themes—the quest for status, power, and identity. Madame Irma's establshment offers erotic revels for the gratification of inhibited desires and longings for

9. Artaud, *Theater and Its Double.*

status. The gas man, for example, assumes the role of a bishop hearing the confessions of a prostitute who has assumed the role of a penitent. Two other customers enact the status of a general staging his own heroic death, and an attorney general trying the case of a criminal. In the world outside the brothel, a rebellion results in the assassination of the reigning queen and her leaders. Irma successfully masquerades as the queen, and her three customers have the opportunity to test their status. They are accepted as genuine, but the process destroys their treasured illusions. Irma's lover, the chief of police, plays the role of National Hero and longs for the recognition that only imitation gives; when he is finally flattered by impersonation, the chief can go to his tomb where he will be reflected endlessly in a series of mirrors. As the plays ends, Irma turns out the lights and tells the audience to go home "where everything will be even falser than here."

The Blacks shows a troupe of black performers (the playwright refuses to allow a performance by white actors) reenacting the ritual killing of a white woman before a court of Negroes wearing white masks and assuming the role of authority. In the end they become victims of a ceremonial killing by the criminals. We learn that the rite onstage is a cover for the actual trial, conviction, and shooting of a Negro traitor, which the whites are not permitted to see. At the end the audience realizes the rift between the two races so that no real communion can take place—only pretense.

Like Artaud, Genêt admired primitive rituals and the Oriental theater. He was enamored of the masks, the rich use of spectacle, and the communal act of participation in an event of primary significance enacted in mystery and symbols. He saw the playwright's purpose fulfilled as, in Artaud's phrase, "a master of sacred ceremonies." Ritual provided the opportunity for gaining status by assuming roles and participating in significant acts. In Genêt, these become reflections of the dark areas of the unconscious where primitive rites and sado-masochistic fantasies hold their strange spell—a many-faceted view through the myths of cruelty whose cathartic powers of liberation celebrate a collective ecstasy.

Despite his skill in inventing fascinating visual and verbal images and his serious concern with ceremonial action, Genêt's ritualized drama may not elicit the emotional fervor that Artaud envisioned. He is likely to keep our attention so engaged in identifying the realities behind the illusions, the actual identities behind the masks, that we are not free to respond emotionally. The alienation is cerebral despite his vivid sense of the theatrical. In addition, Genêt's reversed hierarchy of values and actions tends to repel rather than invite participation. His system of action, based on reflections, reminds us that we are not looking directly at reality. We understand the nature of his protest, but we are unable to find our identity in his quest to lose his own.

jerzy grotowski

One of the most vital forces in the contemporary theater is the Polish Laboratory Theater and its moving spirit, Jerzy Grotowski (b. 1933), whose seriousness of purpose and ability to create dramatic experiences with the authenticity of myth link him with Artaud and Genêt. His mark has been made not on the basis of his contribution to drama but to performance, for he and his actors have made an enormous impression through their talent and dedication. He achieves an intensity and excitement by a nearly literal return to the concept of theater as "bare boards and a passion," for in his "poor theater" he discards the usual paraphernalia of scenery, properties, lighting effects, music, and even the stage itself. The playing area may be among the spectators who are located in a variety of places in a hall or theater. His performances are aimed at a special kind of audience, small in number, who come to a production for a serious experience. Grotowski says, "We are concerned with the spectator who has genuine spiritual needs and who really wishes, through confrontation with the performance, to analyze himself." The seriousness of his purpose, as demanding as that of Artaud, is to attain a "secular holiness." And like Artaud, his theater is primarily performance-oriented but centered exclusively in the actor rather than in theatrical objects and effects. His performances suggests the evocative power of myth and religious rites, but without specific referents. The effect comes through the force of the emotion rather than in literal terms. Grotowski's productions possess an aspect of cruelty in the overwhelming agony and suffering through which the characters receive release.

Two of his best-known works, *The Constant Prince* and *Apocalypsis cum Figuris,* convey the quality of an authentic ritual without explicit identification. *The Constant Prince* is a free adaptation of Calderón's seventeenth-century Spanish play in which five characters act out the hypocrisy and corruption of the world and cause the humiliation, anguish, and death of the Prince in an emotionally charged atmosphere that suggests the crucifixion. The *Apocalypsis cum Figuris* is a work assembled out of the experiments of the actors and directors in which the verbal aspects are improvised in rehearsal as needed. When the production takes shape, quotations are substituted from well-known sources: Dostoyevski, the Book of Job, the New Testament, T. S. Eliot, and the Song of Solomon. Although the Bible is often a verbal source and the characters are named after biblical characters, the work does not make a precise religious statement, but the impact of the production is described as an explanation of the sources of myth—a fusion of religion and drama. The effect that Grotowski's theater achieves is chiefly the result of the shattering quality of the acting. His performers are remarkably trained in all aspects of their craft—speech, mime, and gesture—but in addition they convey the impression of a monastic zeal as if the body were the outward manifestation of the secrets of the soul.

Grotowski's conception of theater is a return to the mainstream from which it came, as he indicates:

> I am tempted by elementary and archaic religious and national taboos. Fascinated and tremulous, I feel the need to collide with these values, I want to blaspheme, to free my impulses and provoke a confrontation between personal experience and epochal experience and prejudice. This element of our productions has been variously called "collision with the roots," "the dialectics of Mockery and apotheosis" or even "religion expressed through blasphemy; love speaking through hate."[10]

bertolt brecht

Bertolt Brecht (1898–1956), a German dramatist, is one of the most influential and provocative figures of the twentieth-century theater. Although he is not concerned with the inner life of man as the other rebels have been, Brecht links himself wit the changing theater through his rejection of traditional forms and effects of drama and their restricted view of man in favor of a kaleidoscopic presentation of man, the political and social animal. He was a resourceful innovator who advanced and defended his theories vigorously, but his real importance lies in the plays that he wrote and the productions given of them at The Berliner Ensemble, one of the most remarkable acting companies of our time. Brecht was a rebellious spirit who mixed his theatricalism with political propaganda, who explored this "ugly, brutal, dangerous" man in the seamy side of his existence with incredible verve and gusto. He was a brilliant inventor and a notorious borrower, whose proclivity for criticism of man and all his institutions naturally included as overthrow of the conventional theater and led him to create his own imaginative "epic theater."

Traditionally, the epic form was sharply separated from drama, the latter being characterized by compact action that could be presented by living performers, and the epic, because of its freedom of time, place, and action, being confined to the written word. But Brecht looked on these two forms as no longer irreconcilable because technical advances enabled the modern theater to exploit the narrative through projections, films, lighting, and machinery for changing scenery more rapidly. Furthermore, Brecht felt that the most important human experiences were no longer personal stories of individuals but, rather, significant social events and the forces that caused them. Brecht called efforts to realize

10. Jerzy Grotowski, "Towards a Poor Theatre," *The Tulane Drama Review*, 12, 3 (Spring, 1967).

this kind of concern "epic theater." Borrowing freely from the Oriental tradition, his theater became *presentational,* that is, it communicated directly with the audience, rather than *representational,* with the pretense of actuality occurring behind a fourth wall. Using all kinds of visual aids, the narrator talks directly to the audience and the actors are frankly performers showing the audience the action, rather than trying to create the impression that they are genuine characters who are personally involved in the outcome. Brecht's purpose was to make his audiences think, rather than feel. Hence, his attempt to "distance" the spectator, to which he applied the term *Verfremdungseffekt* ("alienation effect") from the German verb *verfremdungen* ("to make strange").

Since he was dealing with social content rather than emotions, Brecht sometimes described his stage as a "tribunal," in which he wanted "to teach the spectators to reach a verdict." The analogy is an apt one. As in a trial, instead of presenting a tightly-knit plot, the stage is used to present evidence piece by piece, to introduce witnesses with conflicting testimony who are interrupted and cross-questioned. They testify by giving facts or relating events, rather than by impersonating. Evidence is presented in a variety of exhibits—weapons, drawings or photographs of where the action occurred, documents, letters, tape recordings, slides, models, and films. The intention is to put the event itself on trial.

To achieve his desired "cool" effect, Brecht wished to avoid the practices of the illusionistic theater that aims consciously at arousing strong emotional identification with the personal fate of the hero. His directions for staging are resolutely anti-illusionistic. When the audience enters the theater, stage hands may be working on the set, which is not concealed from them by a closed curtain. Lights are mounted on stands or pipes in full view of the audience. The scenery is fragmentary, just enough to locate the action, and the actors do not confine themselves within it, but break through the fourth wall. When Mother Courage goes on a journey pulling her wagon, she walks on a large turntable—an obvious piece of stage machinery. As for the acting, Brecht was contemptuous of the Stanislavski method of character and impersonation. He intended that actors in the epic theater should not impersonate their roles, but that they should demonstrate the action as if they stood outside their parts.

What about the plot structure of the epic theater? A comparison with film editing may help us here. Sergei Eisenstein, the great Russian filmmaker, advanced a theory of "montage" in which he pointed out the aesthetic importance of the relation of one image to another. The elementary formula for editing is to join images together in an orderly sequence. Eisenstein had a running controversy with Pudovkin, another celebrated Russian filmmaking pioneer. The latter felt that cutting should be a *linkage* showing a natural relationship of image to image. But Eisenstein insisted—and modern filmmakers are following his example—that there were enormous aesthetic and psychological potentials in the juxtaposition of *unrelated* images, or images out of sequence, or in contrast to one another, or overlapping, or simultaneous, as we see them in collages. The effect of breaking the normal sequence, of deliberate dissonance of aesthetic friction that Eisenstein called *collision,* offers the filmcutter exciting aesthetic possibilities.

To a certain extent, Brecht realized this potential in designing the shape of his action because his plots often startled and shocked the audiences, thus counteracting the tendency toward illusion. He made use of this practice by deliberately breaking the mood of a scene, by interrupting action with music, by playing irony against sentiment, comedy against seriousness, and by the constant use of inversion and reversal.

As a young man coming out of a bitter experience in the military as a medical orderly, and acutely aware of the social and economic calamities of postwar Germany, Brecht wrote savagely out of his view that "the meanest thing alive, and the weakest is man." His early plays are filled with depravity and crime and illustrate his cynical theme that virtue brings no reward; indeed, ethical behavior is really a sign of stupidity. He looked at all men with suspicion, for the poor are as cruel as the rich. As for justice—it is a delusion.

After he accepted Marxism, he came to believe that the evils of the world could be cured by revolution, and to that premise he devoted a number of his *Lehrstücke,* or learning pieces. In 1928 Brecht, along with Kurt Weill who wrote the music, staged his most commercially successful work, *The Threepenny Opera.* Brecht borrowed the plot of John Gay's *The Beggar's Opera,* a fashionable London hit of 1728. But where the original had been a lighthearted lampoon of the aristocracy, Brecht's play was a scathing satire of the bourgeoisie. He created a vivid collection of depraved characters, thieves, swindlers, prostitutes, and crooks who infest a human jungle—a jungle whose code is summed up in the pawnbroker Peachum's words: "What keeps a man alive—he lives on others by grinding, sweating, defeating, beating, cheating, eating some other man." But Brecht relieved the sting of the characters and situation through his considerable gifts as an entertainer, which he was never quite able to suppress despite his political purpose. He was fond of slapstick, vaudeville, sporting events, clowns, and beer-hall entertainers, and his theatricalism stems in part from the direct and earthy quality of these kinds of performers and performances.

Brecht's mature years are notable for his three "parables," which constitute his major contribution: *The Good Woman of Setzuan, Mother Courage and Her Children,* and *The Caucasian Chalk Circle.*

The good woman of Setzuan is a compassionate young prostitute, who is rewarded for her hospitality to three wandering gods when they set her up in a shop. Because she has no talent for money-making, others exploit her generous nature and bring her misery. In desperation, she assumes the role of a heartless, male cousin. Only under the disguise of ruthlessness and avarice can she provide for herself and her unborn child. At the end, she is left unable to reconcile herself to the evil ways of the world. She says to the gods: "Something must be wrong in your world. Why is there reward for wickedness and why do the good receive such hard punishment?" The gods whom she has befriended give no answer.

Mother Courage, which Brecht wrote just before the outbreak of World War II, is a bitter attack on militarism as an aspect of capitalism. To Brecht, heroism invariably comes from human error and brutality. His attention is not centered on the military action, which is narrated with legends and slogans, but on Mother Courage, a camp peddler in Germany during the Thirty Years War (1618–1648). She is a scheming, salty character who will use any means to serve her purpose. And her purpose is to survive by buying and selling life's necessaries and to protect her children from harm amid the shifting fortunes of princes and their marauding bands of soldiers. Her wagon symbolizes her view that war is "just the same as trading," and "you must get in with people. If you scratch my back, I'll scratch yours. Don't stick your neck out." It is while she is involved in bargaining that each of her children die. In a magnificently theatrical scene, Courage's good-hearted, mute daughter Kattrin climbs up on a rooftop and drums a tattoo to warn the villagers of the invading soldiers, until she is shot down. Like Miller's Willy Loman, Courage's absorption with profits causes her destruction, but she must go on—and at the end having learned nothing but with her spirit apparently unquenched, she finds it possible to go on dragging her load of misery behind her.

In his last work, *The Caucasian Chalk Circle,* written in 1944–45, Brecht's tone mellowed and the political message was incidental. The story concerns a young girl, Grusha, who saves the despotic governor's infant son during a rebellion. She makes her escape with the child, submits to a marriage of convenience, and is brought ultimately to trial; thanks to an eccentric judge she is allowed to keep the child because she has demonstrated true motherly spirit.

The "epic" qualities of the play are seen in the prologue and epilogue that frame the main story, the sharp break between Grusha's adventures and the trial scene, the extension of the social environment to include the military uprising and the comic marriage, and in the use of song and dance.

As we look at Brecht's plays, we are struck by the contradiction between his theory and practice. He speaks of scientific objectivity when one of the sources of his power is the towering indignation that gives his work such force and texture. His didactic purpose is deadly serious, but his lyrical gifts, his flair for the comic, and his talent for showmanship burst through the seams of his intent. He repudiates realism and the Stanislavski method of acting because it is based on emotional involvement, and Brecht speaks of his wish to keep the audience "cool" and estranged. Ironically, his plays offer some of the most irresistible acting roles in the theater which, time and time again in performance, arouse the emotions of their audiences profoundly. This contradiction brings us back to the playwright's problem of relating action and its effect.

Let us examine two widely quoted statements of Brechtian theory and attempt to square them with his practice.

In the chart below, Brecht makes a comparison between the traditional stage and his own:

The Dramatic Theater	*The Epic Theater*
the stage embodies a sequence of events	the stage narrates the sequence
involves the spectator in an action and	makes him an observer but
uses up his energy, his will to action	awakes his energy
plot	narrative
implicates the spectator in a stage situation	turns the spectator into an observer, but
wears down his capacity for action	arouses his capacity for action
provides him with sensations	forces him to take decisions
experience	picture of the world
the spectator is involved in something	he is made to face something
suggestion	argument
instinctive feelings are preserved	brought to the point of recognition
the spectator is in the thick of it, shares the experience	the spectator stands outside, studies
the human being is taken for granted	the human being is the object of the inquiry
he is unalterable	he is alterable and able to alter
eyes on the finish	eyes on the course
one scene makes another	each scene for itself
growth	montage
linear development	in curves
evolutionary determinism	jumps
man as a fixed point	man as a process
thought determines being	social being determines thought
feeling	reason[11]

11. Bertolt Brecht, *Brecht on Theatre*, trans. John Willett (London: Methuen, 1964).

A second important statement, which Brecht included in "Little Organum" in 1948 after his plays were written, reads:

> Since the public is not invited to throw itself into the fable as though into a river, in order to let itself be tossed indeterminately back and forth, the individual events must be tied together in such a way that the knots are strikingly noticeable; the events must not follow upon one another imperceptibly, but rather one must be able to pass judgment in the midst of them. . . . The parts of the fable, therefore, are to be carefully set off against one another by giving them their own structure, that of a play within a play.[12]

Brecht is describing here his technique of alienating the audience by breaking up the structure into separate events in order that the spectator can "pass judgment in the midst of them"; the knots must be "strikingly noticeable." What is the basis for this theory of structured action? To encourage the spectator to think rather than to feel. But action has a way of speaking stronger than words.

In his major works Brecht selected basic formulas for *stimulating feeling* by using the standardized patterns of melodrama and romanticism. In *The Threepenny Opera* he employed a dashing rebel with a price on his head, the enemy of a corrupt social system—a clichéd romantic hero. Brecht was able to accomplish his effect despite his central action by making Mack the Knife a corrupt character in a corrupt world. The atmosphere is mordant, not heroic. There is little humanity and no genuine suffering—and through inverted justice Mack is freed and rewarded at the end. In *Arturo Ui* Brecht again uses a romantic central action—the rise of a little man—but again his hero's evil ways and kinship to Hitler keep us at an unnatural distance. The actions accomplish the intended effects.

In Brecht's three parables, *The Good Woman of Setzuan*, *Mother Courage*, and *The Caucasian Chalk Circle*, the action follows the most surefire melodramatic device of all: women in distress try valiantly to protect their children against overwhelming forces of evil. In spite of Brecht's avowed purpose of interrupting the sequence to avoid empathic response, an audience has a way of holding on to the emotional momentum, just as an exciting football game on television holds the audience in suspense through the interruptions by commercials and the opening and closing of refrigerator doors. Despite the "noticeable knots" and Brecht's theory of keeping each event separate, his practice suggests that step by step his structure in these three parables intensifies the emotional response. We do care about the outcome. In a tribunal, the evidence and

12. Bertolt Brecht, "Little Organum for the Theater," trans. Beatrice Gottlieb, *Accent*, 11 (1951).

testimony form a structure leading to a verdict that completes the action and arouses suspense. If you put a woman on stage, even a sharp-tongued, grasping one, show her attachment and devotion to her children, place them in jeopardy, and give the audience concrete signs of suffering, the effect is to gain audience sympathy. This engagement is especially true if the dramatist creates generous, well-intentioned characters like Shen Te, Grusha, and Kattrin. Dramatize an action showing a woman trying to save a child by crossing an abyss over a rickety bridge pursued by brutal soldiers, and the audience will root for her. Show a mother the bullet-riddled body of her child and force her to conceal her agony for fear of losing her own life, and the audience will be stirred.

Brecht was aware of the emotional consequences of the actions he placed on stage, and he took great pains to divert the normal response in another direction. Furthermore, the plays are not melodramas because at the end reward and punishment are not parceled out according to individual merits. Even in the case of Grusha, the ending is not personal but social. Nor is there an orderly world of good and evil. By showing with abrasive humor the futility of heroism and virtue, Brecht combats sentiment for justice. Instead of conceding to the audience's eagerness for wish fulfillment, he tramples on it. His frankly theatrical way of showing an action is intended to dilute the emotional content. In performance, however, what counts more than the degree of realism is the audience's *willingness to believe.* And an audience is quite capable of believing in actions in all kinds of styles, including the "epic."

Brecht is a very significant force in the contemporary theater not only because of his theories of a new kind of theater, but because of the imaginativeness of his productions and plays. He gave the experimental theater of this century what it needed most—a first-rate playwright. He broke the mold and made it work. He gave us a fresh insight into the uses of drama, enlarged its scope, and gave it a new direction.

the absurdists

The opening of Samuel Beckett's *Waiting for Godot* in 1953 focused the spotlight of attention on a new dramatist and subsequently a new theatrical movement known as "the theater of the absurd." When the curtain opened the first night, the audience saw two bedraggled bums, Estragon and Vladimir, waiting in a deserted place for a mysterious Godot. His identity is not clear and their relationship to him is never made explicit. A master driving a heavily burdened slave appears briefly, and later a boy enters to inform the tramps that Godot will not arrive tonight. The play ends as it began with the two waiting. While they wait, they talk, and their conversation explores such themes as death and sal-

86 Scene from the Royal Shakespeare Company production of Peter Weiss's *Marat/Sade*, a theatrical collage of characters and actions.
Photo © Max Waldman, 1970.

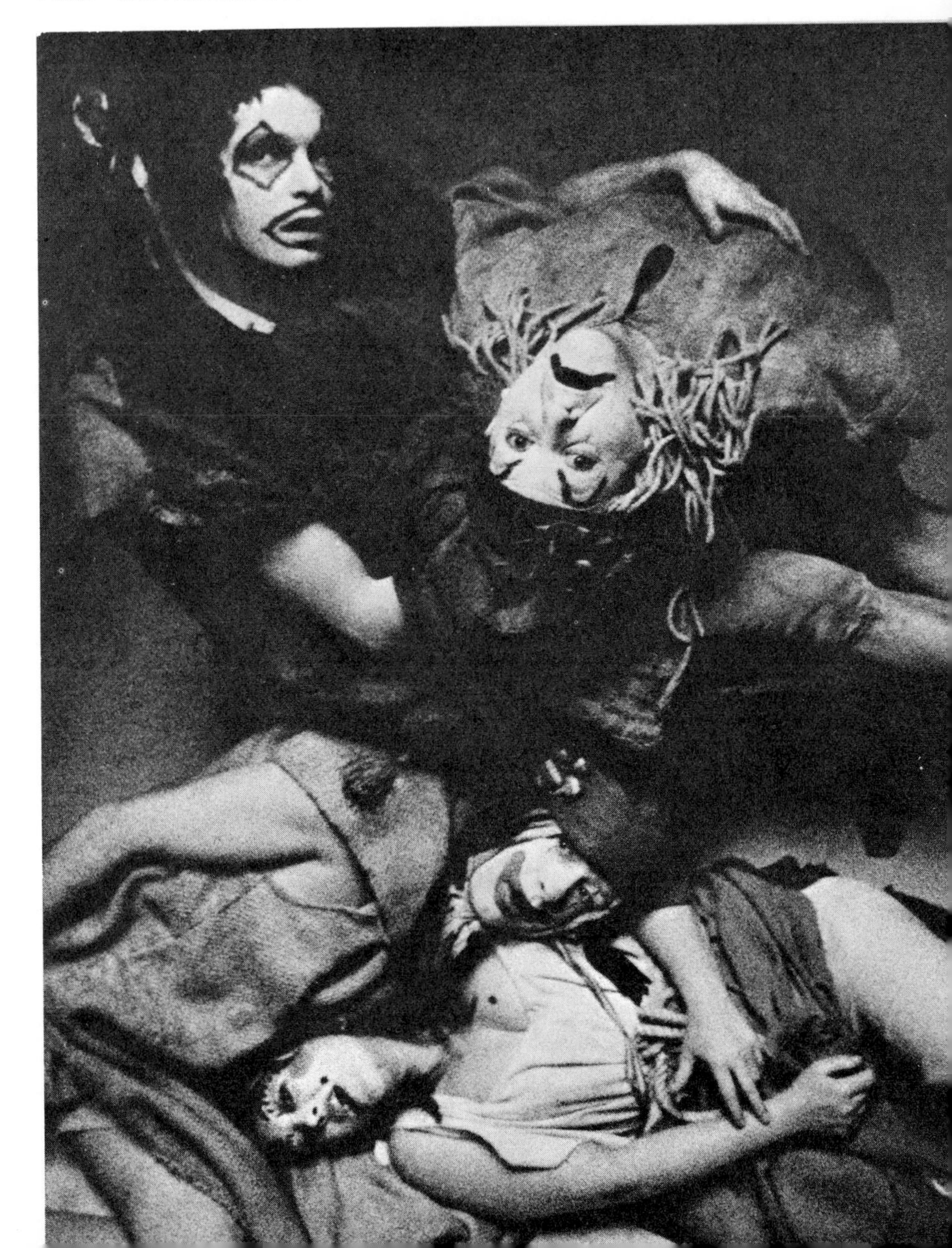

87 Scene from Genêt's *The Balcony* as produced at the Circle in the Square Theater, New York.

89 Kattrin sounding the alarm on the rooftop in Brecht's *Mother Courage,* performed by the Berliner Ensemble.

88 (opposite) Grotowski's production of *The Constant Prince* at the Polish Laboratory Theater. Drama returns to ritual.

90 Scene from the premiere production of Beckett's *Waiting for Godot,* at the Théâtre de Babylone, Paris, 1953.

91 (opposite) *Waiting for Godot,* directed by Frederick Thon at the University of California, Santa Barbara.

92 *Waiting for Godot* at the Munich Kammerspiele. Directed by Fritz Kortner.

93 *Waiting for Godot* at the Octagon Theatre, Perth, Western Australia. Directed by Michael Addison.

vation, the need for affection, the perplexed state of man, their personal biological problems, and the recurrent motif—waiting for Godot. The dialogue is interlocked with a wealth of seriocomic business, and the lines as well as the action provide an effective vehicle for the performers.

The audience greeted the play with mixed reactions. Some found it bewildering and dull; others, provocative and fascinating. In any case, the play made a remarkable impression throughout the theater world, and *Waiting for Godot* became the prime example of absurdist theater. In addition to Beckett, the most prominent absurdists are Eugène Ionesco, Arthur Adamov, the English Harold Pinter, and the American Edward Albee. These absurdists are not neatly compartmentalized and each of them works in a variety of ways. What brings them together is the absurdist point of view, foreshadowed by Camus in his celebrated statement in *The Myth of Sisyphus:*

> A world that can be explained by reasoning, however faulty, is a familiar world. But in a universe that is suddenly deprived of illusions and of light, man feels a stranger. His in an irremediable exile, because he is deprived of memories of a lost homeland as much as he lacks the hope of a promised land to come. This divorce between man and his life, the actor and his setting, truly constitutes the feeling of Absurdity.[13]

Earlier writers had foreshadowed the movement in several ways. Pirandello in his juxtaposition of the serious and the comic, his concern with illusion and reality, and the difficulties of human communication, was an important forerunner. Kafka's stories and novels, and particularly Barrault's production of *The Trial* in 1947 with its nightmarish treatment of weird and puzzling actions, set an interesting example. And in the forthright theatricalism of the expressionists and Brecht, the absurdists found encouragement to strike out along new lines.

Another dramatist who was spiritually related to the absurdists was Alfred Jarry whose *Ubu Roi* caused a sensation when it was first produced in Paris in 1896 because of its blatant presentation of human grossness and sensuality.

Jarry's intentions were clear: "When the curtain rose, I wanted the stage to be before the audience like a mirror . . . in which the vicious one would see himself with the horns of a bull and the body of a dragon, according to the exaggeration of his vices; and it is not surprising that the public was stupefied at the sight of its ignoble reflection which had not yet been completely presented to it."[14]

Jarry's play dramatizes the career of King Ubu whose wife, like Lady Macbeth, drives him to murder the King of Poland in order to gain

13. Albert Camus, *The Myth of Sisyphus* (New York: Knopf, 1955).

14. Alfred Jarry, cited in Leonard Cabell Pronko, *Avant-Garde: The Experimental Theater in France* (Berkeley: University of California Press, 1962).

the crown for himself. His evil ways force him to hide in a cave where he is haunted by the spectres of his victims. The content of the play is not as important as Jarry's prophetic view of the world and his way of handling theatrical materials. The sacrilegious spirit of his attack, the naive directness of his characters and their speech, his sense of raillery—these are seeds that found root later on.

Jarry used the theater in a new way in order to produce a new effect. This was precisely the case with the absurdists who viewed the conventional drama with contempt. They wanted to put it to new uses. In order to understand their point of view, we must take into account the fact that those who led the movement and gave it stature shared a similar experience: Beckett (born in Ireland), Ionesco (born in Rumania), and Adamov (born in Russia) all lived in Paris during World War II. At first hand they witnessed the military defeat of France, and suffered through the occupation by the German forces. The defeat meant the destruction of the political and social fabric and the ruin of civilian morale, and the occupation resulted in an agonizing sense of frustration in the face of overwhelming power. The existentialists—Sartre, Anouilh, and Camus—responded to this experience by using conventional literary forms to probe into such philosophic questions as the role of man in the universe and the effect of materialism on the human spirit. Their answers suggested that man was utterly alone and that he must create his own world, his own set of values. The absurdists, who lived through the same era, asked the same questions but did not arrive at the same answers. They generalized from their experience. They felt that there were no answers—life was absurd. And it was this attitude that they put into action in the theater. They were dramatizing a simple but terrifying idea: Man is lost.

Waiting for Godot begins with Estragon's line: "Nothing to be done." And the play ends:

> VLADIMIR: Well, shall we go?
> ESTRAGON: Yes, let's go.
>
> *They do not move. Curtain.*

Harold Clurman calls our attention to a parallel passage in Pinter's *The Birthday Party:*

> STANLEY: How would you like to go away with me?
> LULU: Where?
> STANLEY: Nowhere. Still we could go.
> LULU: But where would we go?
> STANLEY: Nowhere. There's nowhere to go. So we could just go. It wouldn't matter.

LULU: We might as well stay here.
STANLEY: No. It's no good here.
LULU: Well, where else is there?
STANLEY: Nowhere.

Man doesn't go because there is no purpose to his going. As Camus said, man has no homeland to return to and no promised land before him. He has lost his identity in a dehumanized world; he has lost his perspective in a world without God or a fixed scale of values, and he has lost his reason for going because there is really no place where he can make a meaningful connection. From bitter experience he is wary of hollow ideas and men. He is trapped in the frustrations of an enigmatic universe.

Let us recall the man in Beckett's *Act Without Words, I*. Here is a character struggling at first toward a variety of objectives that are always tantalizingly out of his grasp, no matter how hard he tries to reach them, or how high he climbs. He is at the mercy of some mocking fate. There is no sense to going on. He cannot even take his own life. He submits. Notice the contrast with *Antigone* in which we see sharply defined individuals with reasons for their choices and with the freedom to choose. The absurdists' world offers no such options, and so they dramatize actions to illustrate their theme—man is lost in an absurd world. Here are some of their typical situations:

A mild-mannered professor tutors a bright, confident girl student for her "total doctorate." At first the characters seem involved in a normal situation of question and answer but a metamorphosis sets in. The professor's latent aggressiveness breaks out and the student, now nearly incoherent, is stabbed to death. She is the fortieth victim of the day. The corpse is removed and a new student arrives to being the process over again. (Ionesco: *The Lesson*)

An elderly couple on a lonely island await the arrival of distinguished guests to hear the orator's important message. As the invisible guests arrive, the couple greet them and fill the stage with chairs. When the orator comes, the couple throw themselves out the window and his message is gibberish. (Ionesco: *The Chairs*)

Two professional killers hide in a basement kitchen waiting for their next job, but their hideaway is discovered. Footsteps are heard overhead, a note appears under the door, and the dumbwaiter begins to move bearing messages demanding more and more food. Finally a message comes that one man is to assassinate his partner. (Pinter: *The Dumbwaiter*)

A lonely, guilt-ridden pianist seeks sanctuary in a seaside rooming house. It is revealed that in the past he has offended someone with considerable power. Two sinister strangers appear and the fear-wracked Stanley realizes they are after him. A mock birthday party staged in his honor turns out to be a grotesque ritual when Stanley goes beserk. At the end the two men take the crushed Stanley away in a long black car. (Pinter: *The Birthday Party*)

A family replaces an adopted child with a handsome physical specimen of American manhood, who turns out to be hollow inside. (Albee: *The American Dream*)

In such plays as these, the playwright abandons the notion of depicting psychologically complex characters. They are more apt to resemble puppets or marionettes because they are not personally responsible for their actions. They have been set in motion by an outside force. They cannot act rationally because there is no longer such a thing as logical behavior. They have no means for creating a complete identity, and since communication is virtually impossible, they are not able to relate to one another with understanding and affection.

In a world devoid of meaning, language loses its value. Ionesco wrote his first play, *The Bald Soprano*, as the result of his efforts to learn a foreign language by memorizing standardized phrases. The play parodies the spoken word by exposing its banal vacuity. Here is its opening:

Scene: A middle class English interior, with English armchairs. Mr. Smith, an Englishman seated in his English armchair and wearing English slippers, is smoking his English pipe and reading an English newspaper, near an English fire. He is wearing English spectacles and a small gray English mustache. Beside him, in another English armchair, Mrs. Smith, an Englishwoman, is darning some English socks. A long moment of English silence. The English clock strikes seventeen English strokes.

MRS. SMITH: There it's nine o'clock. We've drunk the soup and eaten the fish and chips and the English salad. The children have drunk English water. We've eaten well this evening. That's because we live in the suburbs of London and because our name is Smith. *(Mr. Smith reads and clicks his tongue.)*

MRS. SMITH: Potatoes are very good fried in fat, the salad oil was not rancid. The oil from the grocer at the corner is better quality than the oil from the grocer across the street. It is even better than the oil from the grocer at the bottom of the street. However, I prefer not to tell them that their oil is bad.

(Mr. Smith continues to read, clicks his tongue.)

MRS. SMITH: However, the oil from the grocer at the corner is still the best.[15]

15. Eugène Ionesco, *The Bald Soprano*, from *Four Plays by Eugène Ionesco*, trans. Donald M. Allen (New York: Grove Press, 1958).

Ionesco has a special flair for satirizing language in his use of gibberish, nonsense words, and broken speech. On the other hand, Beckett and Pinter have a gift for the use of common language that in its diction and rhythm has almost the evocative power of poetry in its ability to suggest meanings beneath the surface. Albee has a good ear for the flavor of the American idiom plus an aptitude for parodying our colloquial speech. The dialogue in an absurdist's play is open to many interpretations and is remarkable for what it leaves to the imagination.

In an attempt to produce their desired effects, the absurdists have created their own arsenal of weapons: the use of shock effects by inverting behavior, by contemptuous mockery of sacrosanct ideas and institutions, by their candor and sometimes their bold frankness. Their comedy, often used ironically, crops out in unexpected places. They present the bizarre, the grotesque, and the unusual. They startle and astonish the audience by their wild flights of fancy and their sometimes incredible inventions. They keep an audience off-balance by concealing their hands, making sudden shifts in direction. They bewilder the spectator and then lead him to a startling discovery. They use the theatrical tricks of the circus clown, the slapstick comedian, and the music-hall entertainer, as this comic routine from *Waiting for Godot* indicates:

> *Lucky has left his hat behind. Vladimir finds it.*
> VLADIMIR: Must have been a very fine hat. (*He puts it on his head. Estragon puts on Vladimir's hat in place of his own which he hands to Vladimir. Vladimir takes Estragon's hat. Estragon adjusts Vladimir's hat on his head. Vladimir puts on Estragon's hat in place of Lucky's which he hands to Estragon. Estragon takes Lucky's hat. Vladimir adjusts Estragon's hat on his head. Estragon puts on Lucky's hat in place of Vladimir's which he hands to Vladimir. Vladimir takes his hat. Estragon adjusts Lucky's hat on his head. Vladimir puts on his hat in place of Estragon's which he hands to Estragon. Estragon takes his hat. Vladimir adjusts his hat on his head. Estragon puts his hat in place of Lucky's which he hands to Vladimir. Vladimir takes Lucky's hat. Estragon adjusts his hat on his head. Vladimir puts on Lucky's hat in place of his own which he hands to Estragon. Estragon takes Vladimir's hat. Vladimir adjusts Lucky's hat on his head. Estragon hands Vladimir's hat back to Vladimir who takes it and hands it back to Estragon who takes it and hands it back to Vladimir who takes it and throws it down.*)
> How does it fit?
> ESTRAGON: How would I know?
> VLADIMIR: No, but how do I look in it?
> (*He turns his head coquettishly to and fro, minces like a mannequin.*)
> ESTRAGON: Hideous.
> VLADIMIR: Yes, but not more so than usual?

ESTRAGON: Neither more nor less.

VLADIMIR: Then I can keep it. Mine irked me. *(Pause.)* How shall I say? *(Pause.)* It itched me.[16]

The absurdist, antitheater in his approach to plot, makes no pretense of interesting the audience in story or character. Martin Esslin, a foremost authority on the absurdists, has pointed out that one of the distinctions between their drama and that of more conventional writers is that in the latter the action moves toward a clearly defined objective. Spectators, he says, look for the answers to such questions as: "Will Hamlet revenge the murder of his father?" "Will Nora leave her husband?" (Surely an oversimplification since most people who go to see Shakespeare or Ibsen are not primarily prompted by curiosity regarding the outcome.) In the absurdist theater, says Esslin, the spectator is interested not so much in "what is going to happen *next*" as he is in "what is *happening*." This is an interesting observation, but many examples give a quite different impression. In such plays as *The Chairs, The Leader, The Lesson, Waiting for Godot, The American Dream, Homecoming, The Birthday Party,* and *Rhinoceros,* the play does move forward; it does raise the question of what will happen next. The difference in the outcome from the traditional play is that the ending does not answer the questions raised, or else the ending is contrary to the expectations of the characters or the audience. The great leader has no head, the orator can only babble, the gorgeous young man is a hollow shell, the intellectual is really a barbarian, and Godot never comes. The playwright gives you a set of figures to add up, but your total is zero. An absurd play is characterized by an absurd ending because that is how the playwright feels about the world. In some plays he doesn't give us an answer at all, but brings the action back to the beginning of the circle, which is another way of saying that life is absurd because there are no answers.

Esslin's point is well taken: the absurdist does not offer you a neatly organized, carefully selected set of signs, nor does he lead you by the hand so that you will know where you are all the time. You may get lost and return to your starting place. You may be the victim of a sudden ambush or a strange trap; you will be baffled by directional signs pointing every which way, or straight down. You may find yourself in a completely foreign place among strangers speaking in unknown tongues, behaving in odd ways. But the playwright has a map of the territory and he knows what he is about, although his method may baffle you. He may ask you to look at the stars, and then pour a bucket of water over your head; he may invite you to climb a tree to find your way, and then chop it down from under you. But there is method in his seeming madness:

16. Samuel Beckett, *Waiting for Godot* (New York: Grove Press, 1954).

94 The London Royal Court Theatre production of Alfred Jarry's *Ubu Roi*.

95 (opposite) Scene from Ionesco's *The Leader* at the Buffalo Festival of the Arts Today, 1965.

96 A modern staging of Euripides' *The Bacchae* at Yale University.

97 Scene from Sam Shepard's *Operation Sidewinder*, a satire on our technological society combining Hopi Indian rites, a Volkswagen, and a computer in the form of a computer snake. The Repertory Theater of Lincoln Center.

98 *The Serpent* by Jean-Claude van Itallie in an arena staging at the University of California, Berkeley. Directed by Douglas Johnson.

the action determines the effect. The absurdist offers you an absurd experience because he wants you to be vividly aware that the world is absurd.

If the absurdist rejects a carefully organized chain of action, has no interest in story values, makes little effort to reveal the psychological aspects of characters, is uninterested in emotional involvement, refrains from specific identification of locale or character, what effects do his works achieve as theater?

Some spectators are bewildered and irritated because the action in an absurdist play seems nonsensical. Others enjoy it as a kind of intellectual game by trying to piece together the bits of experience offered to them. Their critical faculties are involved, and they enjoy the learning process of seeking a fresh perception imaginatively presented. They may delight in the playwright's skill of execution or in that of the performers. At a more profound level, the theatergoer becomes acutely aware of the universality suggested by the specific stimulus of the play, and from his awareness may come a strong sense of personal involvement in the playwright's statement. In this case, the action on stage begets action in the audience—but it is *intellectual* action as man confronts an irrational universe. Step by step the dramatist has created a structure of action which heightens intellectual tension that may have emotional consequences. The thrust may be not so much forward as it is downward. Ionesco himself describes the process as "through an increasingly intense and revealing series of emotional states." Ionesco puts it this way:

> Theater is for me the outward projection onto the stage of an inner world; it is in my dreams, in my anxieties, in my obscure desires, in my internal contradictions that I, for one, reserve for myself the right of finding my dramatic subject matter. As I am not alone in the world, as each of us, in the depth of his being, is at the same time part and parcel of all others, my dreams, my desires, my anxieties, my obsessions do not belong to me alone. They form part of an ancestral heritage, a very ancient storehouse, which is a portion of the common property of all mankind. It is this, which, transcending their outward diversity, reunites all human beings and constitutes our profound common patrimony, the universal language. . . .[17]

It is a cutting process—or perhaps more accurately, a probing one, a penetration, rather than a thin slice off the top layer. The absurdist does not invite you to pleasant escape into a make-believe world; instead he tears away the facade and says this irrational absurd world is your world. Where do you go from here?

17. Eugène Ionesco, "Impromptu de l'alma," *Théâtre II* (London: Calder and Boyars, 1958).

In this sense the action in an absurdist play is cumulative, a process of intensification that raises questions of importance so compelling that we carry them away with us from the theater.

open theater

As we have seen, much of the recent protest in theater is against the old forms—particularly the structured story line, the psychological aspects of individual characters, and the importance of dialogue. The result is a search for new forms, for new uses of theater. In some instances "classics" are ransacked for basic situations; the original dialogue is replaced by the contemporary idiom, eliminated altogether, or improvised by the actors. In other instances, the plot becomes a loose amalgam of situations that grow out of games, improvisations, and acting exercises as variations on a central theme. In still others, the theater is rejected entirely except for performers in action with objects and music for the pleasure of the creative act itself.

These efforts have come from outside the professional theater, from coffee-house and off-off-Broadway theaters or from actors' and dancers' workshops. Ellen Stewart's *La Mama Repertory* and Joseph Cino's *Coffee Cino* have provided an enormous outpouring of theatrical energy—more than four hundred new plays by some two hundred playwrights who have been given the opportunity to see their work in production. From them have come a number of promising new dramatists—among them Jean-Claude van Itallie, Megan Terry, and Sam Shepard—who have given the stage a new sense of freedom through their use of mixed-media games, their experiments with ensemble play, and their fresh handling of action and language. Working directly with actors, their approach to a theater piece is to build it from the inside out. Beginning with a theme, usually one dealing with some social problem, the company devises exercises, games, and improvisations. A writer or director works with the group, gradually sorting out the most effective and appropriate lines and situations until a complete working sequence evolves. The director and writer then give shape and discipline to the structure; the play emerges, is rehearsed, and performed. By its nature it is not fixed, with a well-made plot; rather it is a series of sketches and characters illustrating a theme—a collage of disparate items with no formal structure, no formal transitions, and no clear-cut delineation of character. Examples of such plays are Megan Terry's *Keep Tightly Closed*, the New York Open Theater's *Terminal*, van Itallie's *America Hurrah* and *The Serpent: A Ceremony*, and Grotowski's *Apocalypsis cum Figuris*.

A specific example is Megan Terry's *Viet Rock*, which grew out of Joseph Chaikin's Open Theater Workshop. Working with the general theme of a protest against the Vietnam War, the actors began by gathering factual material from the mass media or personal experiences. Miss Terry describes their purpose:

> We acted out personal stories and tried to get at the roots of our drives toward anger and aggression. To deal with the bewilderment, shame and confusion created by this war, we felt we had to explore our negative feelings, drives and fantasies. We also explored loss, grief and regret. We tried to get at the essence of violence.[18]

The workshop members explored their own sense of aggression, their fantasies and negative feelings, and put them in concrete actions and language, the visual images being considered more important than words. A permissive atmosphere encouraged as much freedom and individual creation as possible. Out of the experiments Megan Terry formed a play that was then directed by two directors and produced as a kaleidoscopic protest of the war. A summary of the opening scenes suggests the form.

The action begins as the male actors become babies lying on the floor being cared for by the females. An attitude of contentment is disrupted by the sudden appearance of a sergeant who calls the men to attention. They leap to their feet and form a line for their induction physical examinations, which are being conducted by the women who now serve as impersonal doctors and nurses. Two women draw to one side of the stage and assume the roles of mothers of the inductees. The next sequence is at boot camp with the men going through a drill, while now the women are futile protesters on the outside. Three of the protesters pour gasoline on themselves in simulated self-immolation. The recruits and the sergeant discuss the patriotic duties of a citizen. The group forms a plane and flies to Asia where they bail out; as each floats toward the earth, he speaks his thoughts. The sequence continues, developining various facets of the war in a series of broken scenes but unified by a central theme.

happenings

Outside the theater, another experiment has produced such actions as these:

A man stands before a canvas and paints a message which reads "I love what I am doing." As he nears the end of the sentence he paints more and more rapidly, finishes the message, drinks one jar of paint,

18. Megan Terry, "Introduction to *Viet Rock*," *The Tulane Drama Review*, 11, 1, (Fall, 1966).

pours two other jars over his head, and dives through the canvas. (Dine: *The Smiling Workman*)

A man on a driftwood-filled beach plants a stick in the sand and invites his companions to join him in building shelters for their own use. At first individuals build separate structures but gradually they are joined until at the end of three hours a communal village is formed. (Halprin: *Driftwood*)

At a lonesome county dump, men build a wooden tower while women form a nest with saplings and string. The men roll an old wrecked car into the dump and smear it with strawberry jam. The women screech, go to the car, and lick the jam. The men destroy the nest in a terrible din of shouts, whistles, and pounding on metal. They demolish the car with sledge hammers, set fire to it, and watch it burn. (Kaprow: *Household*)

These are typical examples of "happenings." What is the intended effect of such actions? It is perhaps easier to indicate what it is not. The creators of happenings ("environments," "activities," "mixed means," etc.) reject the conventional theater and most of its practices, including language, plot, realism, psychological identification, characterization, and form.

Their aim is "perceptional enhancement." The intended effect of the action is to expand the consciousness, to extend our perceptions beyond the ordinary level of rational thinking. In our "mind-blowing," psychedelic world we have become acutely aware of the rich lode of our inner experiences. As Marshall McLuhan says, "Once more reality is concerned as being *within* one, and the search of truth has become an inward trip." In a new kind of theatrical experience the makers of happenings wish to break through the established patterns of controlled language and action to a new experience of intuitive perception and heightened sensitivity not tied to formal themes or meanings. Old forms are rejected because they are fixed and confining. New sensory responses are sought in actions that are open and spontaneous. The evaluation of a happening is based on how well its creator animates the space and time he allots for himself, and the desired effect on the spectator is, as Allen Kaprow says, that "one becomes more attentive."

Michael Kirby defines happenings quite opaquely as "a purposefully composed form of theater in which diverse elements, including non-matrixed performing, are organized in a compartmented structure."[19] By "non-matrixed performing" Kirby means without specific referents of time, place, and character—in other words, a rejection of "the plot line and clichés of dramatic technique." By "compartmented" structure he means that elements of the production are simultaneous or disconnected.

The happening is still in a state of flux as those who work with it

19. Michael Kirby, *Happenings* (New York: Dutton, 1965).

99 Scene from *The Atonement,* one of Ann Halprin's "myths," performed as an improvised happening.

100 Guerilla theater as a strike weapon in El Teatro Campesino's production.

constantly explore new possibilities. Its undefined form is susceptible to infinite change and varied individual practices. Each work follows the conception of an individual creator who devises the basic activities, selects the space, sets the duration of the event, and chooses the participants and properties. The creator may find his inspiration by observation, by chance (such as rolling dice), by devising variations on a theme, a place, or a property, or, as Kaprow does, by random consultation of the yellow pages of a telephone book. Performances may be given in theaters, although the different atmosphere to be found in lofts, public buildings, halls, and natural environments is often preferred. The performers avoid characterization and seldom relate to one another. They merely make the creator's inventions visible in performing their assignments so that their manner is functional rather than creative and often seems primitive and amateur. Their tasks tend to fall into such patterns as wrapping, dressing and undressing, carrying, building, destroying, pouring, stuffing, inflating, and pounding.

Since the form began with painters and sculptors it is natural for the happening to rely heavily on visual stimuli. The environment is created or augmented by arrangements that are often selected for their symbolic as well as functional value, such as various devices for making tunnels, walls, compartments, piles, and buildings. Familiar and everyday materials and objects are often used—plastic, cloth, paper, junk metal, and rags—which often suggest assemblages that have escaped from their frames. Because of their background as easel painters and sculptors working with visual materials in static forms, the makers of happenings are probably most successful in their appeal to the eye rather than in their ability to handle significant or connected action. In their frequent use of untrained performers they also lose potential values in the quality of movement and the dynamic use of space which the skilled actor and dancer can give. Again, as visual artists, they distrust the spoken word, so their events restrict the use of dialogue and fill the void with music, sound, and noise.

Another break with the theater of the past is that traditionally dramatic production is a fusion of various elements directed toward a center of interest, while happenings often seek "no favored focus" in the use of film, music, light, tape recordings, and dance and action. These elements may compete with one another in a simultaneous barrage on the senses—a collage in action. From the confusion that results the audience is challenged to perceive some order or meaning for itself. Like so many other innovations in the arts, happenings emphasize the creative process rather than the final product and technical skill yields to intuitive perception in an effort to link the form to primitive, preverbal communal rites but without the latter's symbolic function or meaning. In the new theater, events do not exist for the sake of content, but for themselves.

The act is its own excuse for being. Happenings employ various media to create a form of action that appeals to the total sensorium in a laudable effort to enhance our perceptions.

An experimenter who has been identified with happenings but who is closer to the mainstream of the theater because of her experience and ability in handling movement is Ann Halprin, director of the Dancers' Workshop in San Francisco. Furthermore, she brings to her work an unusual discipline and clarity of purpose. Her aim is "to release people's buried creativity by answering their basic needs through ritual"—"mutually creating art." She frequently works with untrained performers because of her interest in "a theater where everything is experienced for the first time." The participants are briefed in advance and then invited to join in such activities as improvising dances, finding one's way by touch, exploring a maze, constructing an environment, and storytelling by candlelight. The rituals center about such basic ideas as aggression, bewilderment, sensualtiy, conflict, sexuality, and confrontation.

A specific example of a Halprin myth is *Carry*. Drums play as two lines of participants are seated on high platforms and face one another. After a time, volunteers are requested to carry someone through the passage between them. One man carries a girl to the accompaniment of the drum and the lights, which follows the rhythm of the action. Other couples volunteer; then combinations are tried—two carry one, five carry two. The carrying takes a variety of forms, exploring archetypal situations, such as a mother carrying her child in her womb; a priest being carried to a sacred place; a groom carrying his bride across a threshold, mourners carrying a body to the grave. As the carrying continues, it takes on the quality of Bacchanalian revelry, and in the end everyone participates in the carrying process.

Such events seem more promising than the usual happening; for they are created, to some extent, and directed by a disciplined dancer during performance, by a person who is skilled in movement and has the ability to handle a group of people, both trained and untrained, so that the imaginations of the performers are liberated.

theater of protest

Still another part of the parade is a form of theatrical activity that has remained in the streets. Throughout history, comedians have used invectives and satire to delight the masses, often to offend those in authority with ridicule and irreverence. The so-called guerilla theater is a modern instance that uses performance techniques as political propaganda, sometimes for enlightening the proletariat as in Russia in the 1920s, sometimes for attacking those in power as in Germany during the early 1930s. Its format emphasizes a simple idea by means of short skits with dialogue, mime, and music and is suited to performance in public places with almost no equipment. During the Depression in this country, Marxist propagandists followed this agit-prop pattern of theater.

More recently specific companies of performers have appeared, each with its own message and style of production. El Teatro Campesino in California is a performance group that used comedy and music effectively to promote the United Farm Workers strike. The Bread and Puppet Theater of New York works through pageants, parades, and workshops to make a serious plea for compassion and understanding. Meanwhile, in developing their own kinds of demonstration to attack their adversaries —generally some aspect of the establishment—a variety of protest groups, especially among the young, have extended the uses of theater in new ways and skillfully exploited the visual potentials of dramatic action.

The changing world clearly requires a changing theater and so the parade goes on, its final destination unknown. The faces and voices we have identified demand that the theater produce new effects—a consciousness of the frightening circumstances of man's physical and social world, an expansion of his powers of perception, and a sensitivity to his latent resources within. At some point the new will link with the old to create systems of action and structures of feeling that will reflect and reveal man's quest for the renewal of his spirit and the expansion of his mind.

exercises

1. Make a collage.
2. Using the absurdist's point of view, find or create the appropriate visual atmosphere of absurdism.
3. Collect a dozen unrelated pictures and arrange them in some kind of order so as to achieve a specific effect.
4. Write an American version of a domestic scene based on the model of *The Bald Soprano*.
5. Use a familiar incident or situation as the basis for an improvised scene. Act it out as children. As adults.
6. Prepare the initial action for a group to perform as an experiment in "open theater."
7. Perform a happening using a very simple action such as building a structure or rearranging objects.
8. Write an example of dialogue based on Pinter.
9. Using Brecht's chart on "epic theater" as a model, make a chart showing a comparison of film and drama.

10. Describe the uses of drama and the theater as a means of social protest.
11. Write an analysis of the dadaist movement with particular emphasis on its attitudes.
12. What are the advantages of structured patterns in the arts? What are the disadvantages?
13. Experiment with dramatic situations in which you attempt to communicate by nonverbal means.
14. What does drama gain and lose by its dependence on written language?
15. Using Freud's view of man, describe the difficulties of communication.
16. Experiment with "automatic" writing and drawing. Evaluate the results.
17. To what extent do the arts depend on technique?
18. Evaluate Jung's view of contemporary man's difficulties.
19. Discuss the role of symbols in art.
20. Evaluate Artaud's concept of the theater and its function.
21. Describe Genêt's world view.
22. What are the characteristics of Grotowski's "poor theater"?
23. What is Brecht's contribution to the modern theater?
24. What changes does Brecht suggest for the theater?
25. Rewrite the opening scene of *Hamlet* or *Antigone* as a Brechtian play.
26. Write a brief outline for an absurdist play. Write out in full the denouement.
27. Rehearse and perform the hat business from *Waiting for Godot*.
28. What are the limitations of absurdism?
29. Experiment with improvisation using theater games. Explore the possibilities of a specific theme such as survival, hostility, communication, isolation.
30. Improvise a dramatic situation in which there are several actions going on simultaneously. Evaluate the results.
31. What are the potentials of a happening?

suggested reading

Antonin Artaud, *The Theatre and Its Double*, 1958.
Eric Bentley, *The Playwright as Thinker*, 1946.
Robert W. Corrigan, ed., *Theatre in the Twentieth Century*, 1963.
Peter Demetz, ed., *Brecht: A Collection of Critical Essays*, 1962.
Bernard F. Dukore and Daniel C. Gerould, eds. *Avant-Garde Drama: Major Plays and Documents Post World War I*, 1969.
Martin Esslin, *The Theatre of the Absurd*, 1961.
———, *Brecht: The Man and His Work*, 1960.
Wallace Fowlie, *Dionysus in Paris*, 1960.
David Grossvogel, *The Self-Conscious Stage in Modern French Drama*, 1958.
Jerzy Grotowski, *Towards a Poor Theatre*, 1969.
Richard Kostelanetz, *The Theatre of Mixed Means*, 1968.
Charles Marowitz and Simon Trussler, eds., *Theatre at Work*, 1968.

Marshall McLuhan, *Understanding Media*, 1964.
José Ortega y Gasset, *Dehumanization of Art*, 1948.
Leonard C. Pronko, *Avant-Garde: The Experimental Theatre in France*, 1962.
James Roose-Evans, *The Experimental Theatre*, 1970.
Richard Schechner, *Public Domain*, 1969.
Robert J. Schroeder, *The New Underground Theatre*, 1968.
Kenneth Tynan, *Curtains*, 1961.
Walter Wager, *The Playwrights Speak*, 1968.
Gerald Weales, *American Drama Since World War II*, 1962.
———, *The Jumping-Off Place: American Drama of the 1960's*, 1969.
George Wellwarth, *The Theatre of Protest and Paradox*, 1967.

play list

Edward Albee, *The American Dream*
Antonin Artaud, *The Spurt of Blood*
Guillaume Apollinaire, *The Breasts of Tiresias*
Samuel Beckett, *Endgame; Happy Days*
Bertolt Brecht, *The Caucasian Chalk Circle; The Good Woman of Setzuan; Arturo Ui*
Jean Genêt, *The Blacks; The Balcony; The Maids*
Michel de Ghelderode, *Pantagleize*
Eugène Ionesco, *The Killer; Rhinoceros*
Alfred Jarry, *Ubu Roi*
Bernard Kopit, *Oh Dad, Poor Dad, Mamma's Hung You in the Closet and I'm Feelin' So Sad*
Harold Pinter, *The Birthday Party*
Megan Terry, *Keep Tightly Closed; Viet Rock*
Peter Weiss, *Marat/Sade*

the director

When Aeschylus staged his earliest extant Greek tragedy, *The Suppliants* (c. 492 B.C.), he must have learned that producing a play is a complex and tricky business. Like directors who followed him, he had scores of problems to solve and decisions to make. Roles had to be assigned, costumes designed and constructed, entrances and exits marked out, and rehearsals conducted until the play was ready for presentation before the discriminating Athenian audience.

Even a cursory glance at *The Suppliants* indicates the need for painstaking planning and rehearsal. The play tells the story of the fifty daughters of Danaus who seek sanctuary at Argos from the pursuing sons of Aegyptus. At the climax of the play the Herald and his attendants attempt to carry off the maidens by force, but they are rescued by the king, who refuses to release them.

Perhaps the most difficult task that Aeschylus faced in producing his play was training the chorus of fifty maidens, who recite and chant more than six hundred lines of poetry, sometimes combining words with dance, and sometimes engaging in vigorous action when they cling to the altar in terror, pleading for asylum. In addition to the careful preparation of speech and choreography of the chorus, it was necessary to provide them with appropriate costumes—striking Egyptian robes, dark masks, and linen veils fastened to their heads with gold bands. In the action of the other performers, two entrances required special care. In the first, the

king and his retinue make a dramatic entrance, probably using horses and chariots. The second complicated entrance occurs when the Herald and his coterie appear and threaten to tear the suppliant maidens away from the altar. Although this play has a simple plot, its implicit demands for the movement of a large group of performers must have required arduous rehearsal. We may be sure that Aeschylus was grateful for his military experience when he prepared *The Suppliants* for performance.

Throughout the history of the theater, the manifold tasks of play production have been handled in a variety of ways. The assigned archons and Greek playwrights were in charge of the presentation of tragedies. In the medieval cycle plays, with their fragmentized episodes, many of them requiring realistic staging, an enormous amount of organization was necessary, much of which was parceled out to various participating groups. In the Elizabethan theater, with its permanent professional companies of actors and playwrights, the theater manager selected the plays and assigned the casts. Undoubtedly, the playwrights took considerable interest in seeing that their works were performed as they intended them to be. And just as Hamlet found it expedient to advise the players about their style of acting in the play-within-the-play, it requires little stretch of the imagination to believe that Shakespeare made a similar effort in the performance of his dramas at the Globe. Molière, in the seventeenth-century French theater, labored for twelve years with his troupe in the provinces, polishing and perfecting the performance of his plays before returning to Paris. That Molière not only set an example for his company but took care to improve the quality of his productions is suggested by his wry comment that "actors are strange creatures to drive."

In the eighteenth and nineteenth centuries, such stars as David Garrick and William Macready attempted to make play production less haphazard, but in general, many of the responsibilities of organization were delegated to underlings, or ignored altogether. Often, plays were patched together with "typed" characters assigned to roles with little or no genuine rehearsal, and almost no concern for ensemble acting. Stock sets were refurbished on a makeshift basis and little attention was paid to lighting. Costuming was mostly a matter of individual taste, and apparently no one worried about the resulting incongruities. There were, of course, a few notable exceptions to these practices. Charles Kean staged remarkable productions of Shakespeare in the 1850s, for which special scenery was designed and painted with accurate geological and botanical detail. In his production of *A Midsummer Night's Dream* in 1856, Kean was praised for the harmony of effect that resulted from music, scenery, and choreography especially created for the occasion. A decade later, the Bancrofts introduced rehearsal reforms which were in the direction of greater unity.

the modern director appears

The Duke of Saxe-Meiningen in Germany performed an invaluable service for the theater through his exemplary staging of Shakespeare and Schiller, in which he emphasized ensemble acting and the use of appropriate scenery and costume. The tour of the Duke's troupe through the major cities of Europe (1874–1890), inspired theater workers elsewhere to emulate his synthesis of production.

With the appearance of realism and naturalism in the latter part of the nineteenth century, actors and directors became increasingly concerned with unifying all elements of the performance. The new plays demanded a new approach to staging. André Antoine led the way with his Théâtre Libre in Paris; Otto Brahm followed his example in the Freie Bühne in Berlin; and Constantin Stanislavski worked along similar lines at the Moscow Art Theatre.

In addition to the independent theater pioneers, two visionaries championed the concept of unity in play production in a series of notable stage designs, as well as in their writings. These men were Gordon Craig and Adolphe Appia, whose contributions are discussed in chapter 12. At this juncture in our discussion of directing, the point needs to be made that there were several forces at work in the late nineteenth-century theater which lead to the guiding principle that all aspects of play production should grow from a central interpretation. The corollary of this idea was that in order to secure such unity, there must be a single creative intelligence responsible for designing the whole production, namely, the director. This idea is widely accepted in the contemporary theater, and a number of men have assumed this dominating role, notably Max Reinhardt, Alexander Tairov, Stanislavski, Vsevolod Meierhold, Leopold Jessner, Tyrone Guthrie and Erwin Piscator.

Directors work under varied rehearsal conditions depending on the type of theater they serve. A Broadway director may find it necessary to throw a play together in three weeks; in Russia, some plays have taken two years of rehearsal. Meierhold, after two months of rehearsal, had not settled on any one of the three characters for a one-act play. Max Reinhardt preplanned his performances to the last detail so that the rehearsal period was one of teaching the actors what he wished them to do; Arthur Hopkins simply turned his actors loose with occasional stimulation and encouragement, his idea of direction being to "put on a play without anyone realizing how it was done." Some directors find that the law of diminishing returns sets in for rehearsals lasting longer than three hours; David Belasco was known to rehearse for twenty hours at a stretch. Meierhold gave his actors every piece of business and read every line for them; Bertolt Brecht sat and waited for his actors to show him the meaning of his own plays, and Eugene Vakhtangov conducted round-table discussions with his casts, trying to arrive at a common interpretation. Directors even vary in their concept of the actor's function. Huntley Carter reported: "Stanislavski told the actor he must forget that he is on the stage. Tairov told the actor he must remember nothing else. Meierhold told him he must remember that he is one of the audience."

the function of the director

As the unifying force in the production of a play, the director has a number of specific assignments. From the time that the script is placed in his hands until the curtain rises on opening night, it is the director who initiates and controls all aspects of the presentation of the play. He analyzes the script, auditions actors, casts the roles, sets the basic floor plan for the sets, supervises the design of costumes, scenery and lighting, instructs the cast in the meaning of the play, and conducts rehearsals during which he blocks out the action, assists the actor with his interpretation of his character and the reading of his lines, and finally polishes, times, and unifies the play into a cohesive whole. Everything about the interpretation and performance of the play is his business.

The director's function may be indicated by quoting representative statements by four outstanding men of the theater. John Mason Brown said that the "director is a critic in action." Tyrone Guthrie, well known for his highly personalized productions, said: "The director, then, is partly an artist presiding over a group of other artists, excitable, unruly, childlike and intermittently 'inspired.' He is also the foreman of a factory, the abbot of a monastery, and a superintendent of an analytic laboratory. It will do no harm, if in addition to other weapons, he arms himself with the patience of a good nurse, together with the voice and vocabulary of an old-time sergeant-major." Vsevolod Meierhold, a Russian director noted for his theatricality, describes his purpose in these terms: "A director builds a bridge from the spectator to the actor. Following the dictates of the author, and introducing on the stage friends, enemies, or lovers, the director with movements and postures must present a certain image which will aid the spectator not only to hear the words, but to guess the inner, concealed feelings." The eminent French director Louis Jouvet described his task in these words: "He must organize that area where the active players on the stage and the passive players in the auditorium meet each other, where the spectators penetrate and identify themselves with the action on stage."

the director as an interpreter

As we have indicated in our previous discussion, the function of the director as the interpreter of the play is a contemporary concept. When such playwrights as Aeschylus, Shakespeare, and Molière, experienced theater men, worked directly with the actors, the shape and meaning of the performance was undoubtedly determined by the writer. But where the dramatists were not trained in the ways of the theater, or not available (some of them being dead), the individual actor was left to his own devices, which usually meant in the case of a star that he was concerned only with presenting himself in a favorable light, regardless of his colleagues, except as they affected his performance. With the coming of contemporary drama, the director assumed the responsibility for integrating the production, and his most important influence was that of interpretation.

The director begins by working with the script. He must have a complete understanding of the play. This goes far beyond a mere acquaintance with the story line or even an intimate knowledge of the play's structure. Drama shows men in action—men making choices, reaching for objectives, withdrawing, attacking, or resisting. And all of this action is about something. There is a residue of meaning beneath the surface of the physical action. The play is a commentary on the characters' attitude toward life. *Death of a Salesman* is more than a story about a tired old man; it is also an attempt to reexamine the values that many contemporary men live by. *Juno and the Paycock* is not only the story of a brave woman and her incorrigible husband; it is also an attack on the ignorance and narrowness of the slum-dwellers of Dublin. *A Streetcar Named Desire* is not merely a case study of the deterioration of a weak woman; it is a disturbing picture of sensitivity being ground under by brutality. The director must search for the core or spine of the action, the larger implications and significance of the externals of the plot. His first task, then, is to gain insight into the play which the dramatist has created.

Now let us consider some specific examples of directors at work on the interpretation of a play.

Norris Houghton in *Moscow Rehearsals,* a fascinating account of his visit to Russia in the 1930s, describes Meierhold's approach to directing a play. He read it through a single time, trying to grasp the meaning of the author, noting his first impression of the script. When he produced a play, Meierhold often changed the text to suit the interpretation he gained from his first reading. Once Meierhold determined the motivating idea, he visualized a tentative plan for the scenery and lighting. He came to the first rehearsal without any notes or promptbook, but apparently with his head swarming with ideas, which he released spontaneously as he worked with the actors on their interpretation of the lines and their invention of movement and business. A staff of eight to twelve assistants recorded in detail every aspect of each rehearsal, so that by the time the play reached production there was a vast accumulation of material about the play and its performance.

Norris Houghton describes Meierhold's interpretation of Chekhov's *The Proposal,* which he gave to the actors at the first rehearsal: "Two things are essential for a play's production, as I have often told you," Meierhold begins.

> First, we must find the thought of the author; then we must reveal that thought in a theatrical form. This form I call a *jeu de théâtre* and around it I shall build the performance. Molière was a master of *jeu de théâtre:* a central idea and the use of incidents, comments, mockery, jokes—anything to put it over. In this production I am going to use the technique of the traditional vaudeville as the *jeu.* Let me explain what it is to be. In these three plays of Chekhov I have found that there are thirty-eight times when characters either faint, say they are going to faint, turn pale, clutch their hearts, or call for a glass of water; so I am going to take this idea of fainting and use it as a sort of leit-motif for the performance. Everything will contribute to this *jeu.*[1]

After this introduction Meierhold read the script to the cast and dismissed the rehearsal.

The noted German director Max Reinhardt, famous for his theatricalism, like Meierhold, dictated every detail of the production. However, he did not depend on the inspiration of the moment. Reinhardt's presentations were the results of months of careful preparation during which time he developed a complete annotated account of the play. The purpose of his rehearsals was to teach his interpretation line by line to the actor. R. Ben-Ari, who worked with Reinhardt, describes his methods in this fashion:

> Reinhardt comes to work with his secretaries and his assistant directors all laden with books. They are volumes with interpretations and explanations, with various data, drawings and symbols relating to the production —the evidence of colossal artistic and technical work which was done in preparing the manuscript for the stage. In these books the working out of every scene, every phrase, is recorded exactly and in detail—precisely when this or that player, when this or that group has to move to another part of the stage; how many musical intervals they have before they move; how much space they have to move in; the exact moment when the light is to go on. All this put together gives birth to the Reinhardt production. Reinhardt, himself a wonderful actor, influences his actors in such a way that they are compelled to do everything that he shows them. Reinhardt's personality dominates one to such an extent that one must copy all his intonations, all his emphases. These are wonderful in themselves, and of the deepest and most convincing sort, but they come to life through Reinhardt and not through the actor.[2]

1. Norris Houghton, *Moscow Rehearsals* (New York: Harcourt, Brace and World, 1936).

2. R. Ben-Ari, "Four Directors and the Actor," *Theatre Workshop* (Jan.–March, 1937).

Just as Reinhardt felt free to mold the actor into a preconceived image, he also assumed the power to interpret the play as he wished, with the result that in some of his productions, the original play was merely a point of departure, which he embellished and enlarged upon, like a musician improvising on a theme.

Although not as extreme in his domination of the interpretation as Meierhold and Reinhardt, Tyrone Guthrie, a celebrated contemporary English director, takes a good deal of latitude in his ingenious interpretations of Shakespeare, moving around freely in time and space. Guthrie does not preplan his productions, although his preliminary study of the play leads him to an underlying mood. Once in a rehearsal, he shapes the play to his preconception, usually through persuasion rather than outright dictatorship.

Two American directors who owe a good deal to Stanislavski in their method of approach to the directing of plays are Harold Clurman and Elia Kazan. Both of these men make a careful study of the script in advance, searching for a basic interpretation, their interest centering on the psychological backgrounds of the characters in the play. As they analyze the play, Clurman and Kazan make notes to guide their thinking during rehearsals. These personal notes are interesting for revealing the ways in which these directors arrive at their interpretations.

Here are a few sample notes from Clurman when he was preparing for a production of *The Member of the Wedding:*

> *The main action of the play:* to get "connected."
>
> It all happens in a hot summer atmosphere, the world is "dead"—the people suspended. Everything is slightly strange, not altogether real.
>
> A mighty loneliness emanates from this play. It is as if all the characters were separated from the world—as if the people were only a mirage in a vaporous space making wraiths of the people.
>
> More decisive than any of these notes is my line by line "breakdown" of the script, which indicates the aim of each scene and what particular actions and adjustment (mood) moment by moment the actor must carry out and convey. These actions—what the character wants to do and why—together with any physical action (or "stage business") which might result from the character's purpose are duly noted by the director, or, in most cases in my own work, they may be left to the actor's nature and imagination—under the director's guidance—to accomplish.[3]

These sample notes record Kazan's interpretation of the stage production of *A Streetcar Named Desire:*

> *Theme*—this is a message from the dark interior. This little twisted, pathetic, confused bit of light and culture puts out a cry. It is snuffed

3. Toby Cole and Helen Krich Chinoy, *Directing the Play* (Indianapolis: Bobbs-Merrill, 1953).

> out by the crude forces of violence, insensibility and vulgarity which exists in our South—and this cry is in the play.
>
> *Style*—one reason a "style," a stylized production is necessary is a subjective factor—Blanche's memories, inner life, emotions are a real factor. We cannot understand her behavior unless we see the effect of her past on her present behavior.
>
> This play is a poetic tragedy. We are shown the final dissolution of a person of worth, who once had a great potential, and who, even as she goes down, has worth exceeding that of the "healthy," coarse-grained figures who kill her.[4]

To keep his interpretation of each scene clearly before him, Kazan broke the play down into its component parts and placed a label on each scene:

> *Scene 1:* Blanche comes to the last place at the end of the line.
> *Scene 2:* Blanche tries to make a place for herself.
> *Scene 3:* Blanche breaks them apart, but when they come together, Blanche is more alone than ever. (etc.)[5]

Just as they searched for the core ideas of the plays as the basis for their interpretations of the total meaning, similarly Clurman and Kazan probed for the "spines" of action that determined the character's behavior.

These are some of the notations Clurman made about the character of Frankie in *The Member of the Wedding:*

> Her main action—*to get out of herself.* Getting out of herself means *growth.* . . . She has "growing pains": she is both tortured and happy through them. . . . The juices of life are pouring through her. She is a fragile container of this strange elixir.
>
> Growth twists and turns her—as it does us—gives us new shapes. Frankie twists and turns. The play is the lyric drama of Frankie's growth. At the end of the play, she runs or twirls out—"to go around the world." She has achieved her aim—imaginatively. She is ready "to get out of herself."[6]

He continues detailing her chief qualities, each one suggesting clues to her actions and behavior on stage.

Kazan made similar notations, but he is even more explicit; his comments on the character of Blanche alone run more than five pages. These notes are extremely significant in revealing the way in which a director studies the play and the characters' motivations before he brings

4. *Ibid.*
5. *Ibid.*
6. *Ibid.*

the play to life on stage. These are a few of Kazan's observations about Blanche:

> Blanche is a social type, an emblem of a dying civilization, making its last curlicued and romantic exit. All her behavior patterns are those of the dying civilization she represents. In other words her behavior is *social*. Therefore find the social modes! This is the source of the play's stylization and the production's style and color. Likewise Stanley's behavior is *social* too. It is the basic animal cynicism of today. "Get what's coming to you! Don't waste a day! Eat, drink, get yours!" This is the basis of his stylization, of the choice of his props. All props should be stylized: they should have a color, shape and weight that spell: style.
>
> *Her problem has to do with her tradition.* Her notion of what a woman should be. She is stuck with this "ideal." It is her ego. Unless she lives by it, she cannot live; in fact her whole life has been for nothing. Even the Alan Gray incident as she now tells it and believes it to have been, is a necessary piece of romanticism. Essentially, in outline, she tells what happened, but it also serves the demands of her notion of herself, to make her *special* and different, out of the tradition of the romantic ladies of the past: Swinburne, Wm. Morris, Pre-Raphaelites, etc. This way it serves as an excuse for a great deal of her behavior.
>
> Because this image of herself cannot be accomplished in reality, certainly not in the South of our day and time, it is her effort and practice *to accomplish it in fantasy.* Everything that she does in *reality* too is discolored by this necessity, this compulsion to be *special.* So, in fact, *reality becomes fantasy too.* She makes it so!
>
> *An effort to phrase Blanche's spine:* to find *protection,* to find something to hold onto, some strength in whose protection she can live, like a sucker shark or a parasite. The tradition of *woman* (or all women) can only live through the strength of someone else. Blanche is entirely dependent. Finally the doctor![7]

Kazan and Clurman work from a close analysis of the text, probing into the psychological roots of the action. Tyrone Guthrie seems to work in an entirely different manner. In preparing a play he says:

> . . . I should like to discuss what to me is the most interesting part of the job, the blending of intuition with technique. If I may elaborate those terms, by intuition, I mean the expression of a creative idea that comes straight from the subconscious, that is not arrived at by a process of ratiocination at all. It is my experience that all the best ideas in art just arrive, and it is absolutely no good concentrating on them hoping for the best. The great thing is to relax and just trust that the Holy Ghost will arrive and the idea will appear.[8]

7. *Ibid.*

8. Tyrone Guthrie, "An Audience of One" in Toby Cole and Helen Krich Chinoy, eds., *Directors on Directing* (Indianapolis: Bobbs-Merrill, 1953).

He goes on to say that inspiration must be backed up by a very "cast-iron technique."

Directors not only vary in their methods of working with the actor on his interpretation, they also vary in their approach to the script itself. A play exists on many levels at the same time, and the director's interpretation may, therefore, stem from many sources. Craig based his interpretation on color, Reinhardt on spectacle, Stanislavski on characterization. A director may find justification for his analysis in the imagery of the poetry, in significant symbols, or in the atmosphere of the locale. He may find inspiration for his point of view in music, movement, scenery, speech, theme, or social milieu. Whatever the approach, the director is the ultimate interpreter of the play.

the director as a craftsman

The director begins as an interpreter of the play. Secondly, he is a skilled craftsman capable of revealing the full meaning of the play to an audience in tangible theatrical terms.

Although this text is not a manual of play production, nor is it our intent to discuss in detail every phase of the director's function, it may be helpful in understanding his contribution to the presentation if we indicate the use of at least one of his tools—stage movement.

A play in the theater is dynamic. It is in a continual process of ebb and flow, action and reaction, adjustment and readjustment. Through its characters, changes take place: the frustrated boy finally gets the girl; a woman comes to understand herself through suffering; a hero falls from a high place to catastrophe; the downtrodden little man achieves status.

When Aristotle described the playwright's approach to writing a play, he suggested that his first step was to frame the central action. The director follows a similar process by searching first for the *main action* of the play, sometimes referred to by theater people as the "spine," or the "superobjective." In Clurman's analysis of *The Member of the Wedding,* he found that the main action was to get "connected." Franco Zefferelli in speaking of a production of *Hamlet* saw the hero as "living in a hard world—with no elasticity about it—a closed world, with high walls, no windows, lots of storms. Like a prisoner in a tower." Peter Brook found his approach to *Romeo and Juliet* in a single line: "These hot days is the mad blood stirring." Thus, the director works his way through the play, line by line and scene by scene, finding the most effective means of forming the action. Sometimes the director envisions almost all the action and gives it to the cast. Other directors set a general framework and then encourage the actor to work creatively within it. Joan

Littlewood, the colorful English director, approaches the play through the actor as she did in Behan's *The Quare Fellow*, through improvisation to capture the feel of the play before tackling the script. The play is laid in a Dublin prison, so she had her cast begin by simulating aspects of prison life such as the dull marches in the "yard," and the bleak confinement of cell living.

The director concentrates a good deal of his attention on blocking out movement, inventing business, and grouping his characters. The playwright may provide directions for such essential plot actions as entrances and exits, duels, love scenes, death scenes, etc., and the context of the lines may provide clues for movement. For instance, it is clear in act 1, scene 1 of *Hamlet* that Horatio joins the soldiers in their vigil, that the ghost enters, and that the three watchers attempt unsuccessfully to restrain him. But the director must go far beyond his bare framework of action to devise movement and groupings which will bring out the full dramatic content of the scene. The director is concerned not only with *what* happens; he is also interested in *how* an action is performed. How does the ghost make his appearance? How does Horatio's expression of fear differ from that of the soldiers? How does Horatio attempt to stay the ghost?

Since a play is dynamic, the attention of the audience must be shifted constantly from one character to another. Unlike the motion-picture director who can concentrate the camera on a specific person or object at will, eliminating from the screen all extraneous matter, the stage director must find other means to evoke and sustain a steady flow of attention. One of his most important means for this purpose is the use of movement. For example, the opening scene of *Hamlet* is a rather simple one since it is short, relatively uncomplicated and requires only five characters; yet the movement and grouping need careful planning (see pages 64–73). The director's primary consideration probably will be to establish the audience's acceptance of the ghost. Most likely it will be kept remote from the audience, played in dim light and deep shadow, and perhaps elevated in position. The actor must be able to move freely and without noise so that his entrances and exits create the illusion of an apparition in space. The attempts of Horatio and the soldiers to strike at the ghost must not destroy the feeling of majesty and dignity of the dead king. In the grouping of the three watchers, Horatio must be given the dominant position since the others look to him for counsel. Moreover, he carries the burden of the dialogue and has several long speeches, so that he must be placed in an advantageous position to project his lines to the audience.

The director uses his blocking to create the appropriate emotional climate for the action. As we have seen with the openings of *Antigone* and *Hamlet* the director may have to search the dialogue for clues. On the other hand, many modern dramatists provide very specific directions. As an example, John Osborne's *Look Back in Anger* which started the "new wave" of British drama, begins with a detailed description of a flat in a Victorian house followed by these stage directions:

> *At rise of curtain:* Jimmy and Cliff are seated in the two armchairs R and L, respectively. All that we can see of either of them is two pairs of legs, sprawled way out beyond the newspapers which hide the rest of them from sight. They are both reading. Beside them, and between them, is a jungle of newspapers and weeklies. When we do eventually see them, we find that Jimmy is a tall, thin young man about twenty-five, wearing a very worn tweed jacket and flannels. Clouds of smoke fill the room from the pipe he is smoking. He is a disconcerting mixture of sincerity and cheerful malice, of tenderness and freebooting cruelty; restless, importunate, full of pride, a combination which alienates the sensitive and insensitive alike. Blistering honesty, or apparent honesty, like his, makes few friends. To many he may seem sensitive to the point of vulgarity. To others, he is simply a loudmouth. To be as vehement as he is, is to be almost non-committal. Cliff is the same age, short, dark, big-boned, wearing a pullover and gray, new, but very creased trousers. He is easy and relaxed, almost to lethargy, with the rather sad, natural intelligence of the self-taught. If Jimmy alienates love, Cliff seems to exact it—demonstrations of it, at least, even from the cautious. He is a soothing, natural counterpoint to Jimmy. Standing L, below the food cupboard, is Alison. She is leaning over an ironing board. Beside her is a pile of clothes. Hers is the most elusive personality to catch in the uneasy polyphony of these three people. She is tuned in a different key, a key of well-bred malaise that is often drowned in the robust orchestration of the other two. Hanging over the grubby, but expensive, skirt she is wearing, is a cherry red shirt of Jimmy's, but she manages somehow to look quite elegant in it. She is roughly the same age as the men. Somehow, their combined physical oddity makes her beauty more striking than it really is. She is tall, slim, dark. The bones of her face are long and delicate. There is a surprising reservation about her eyes, which are so large and deep they should make equivocation impossible. The room is still, smoke-filled. The only sound is the occasional thud of Alison's iron on the board. It is one of those chilly spring evenings, all cloud and shadows. Presently, Jimmy throws his paper down.[9]

Few playwrights give such detailed assistance to the director and actor in establishing mood. Usually the director, with the assistance of the actor, must rely on his own ingenuity to create atmosphere. Sometimes a director will invent an entirely new scene in order to provide the appropriate mood for his interpretation. An example of this reveals Stanislavski's ability to devise movement and business. Gorchakov, a

9. John Osborne, *Look Back in Anger* (Chicago: The Dramatic Publishing Co., 1959).

101 Sketch by the Duke of Saxe-Meiningen for a production of *Julius Caesar*. Note the careful blocking for the entire ensemble.

102 Pictorial realism in the staging of Charles Kean's production of *Henry VIII* at the Princess Theatre, London, 1855. This production ran for 100 performances and established the long-run policy.

103 (opposite) A spectacular scene from Reinhardt's lavish production of *The Miracle*, Dortmund, 1927.

104 (opposite) Scene from Vakhtangov's staging of *Turandot*, Moscow, 1922. This production was famous for its forthright theatricalism.

105 Erwin Piscator's "epic" staging of *The Good Soldier Schweik*, Berlin, 1927. All elements of the theater were combined in this production.

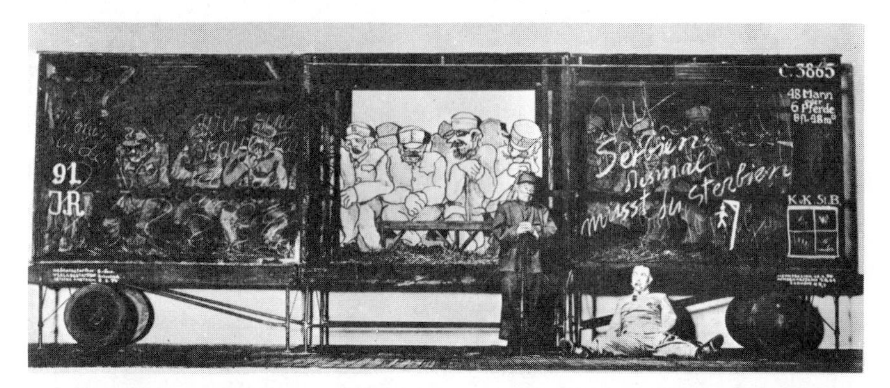

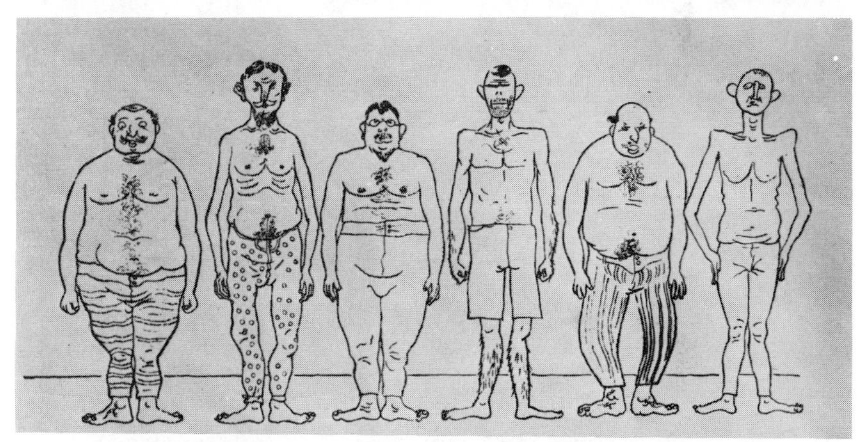

106 (opposite) Meierhold's celebrated production of Gogol's *The Inspector General,* Moscow, 1926.

107 Scene from Brecht's *The Life of Galileo,* at the Berliner Ensemble.

108 Bertolt Brecht directing *Mother Courage* at the Munich Kammerspiele, 1950.

visiting director at the Moscow Art Theatre, was directing a student production of *The Sisters Gerard.* After witnessing a rehearsal, Stanislavski gave Gorchakov the following suggestions:

> My advice to you is not to present the first scene of the play as it is written. Don't begin with the revolt. You rob yourself of a much better moment for it later in the play—in the prison. My advice is to create an alarming mood in the first scene. We remember from history of the period that there was scarcely any bread in Paris. And because of that just before the revolution, bread was hidden from the people. Naturally there were groups of people who always tried to be near the bakery in case bread was brought in or taken out. In your direction of the first scene you have a long line tell each other about their misfortunes. I find this scene too static and too obvious. There is nothing in your scene that arouses the audience's imagination.
>
> Here is how I advise you to do the scene. Divide your bread line into two groups. The actors who are in these groups should live with all the thoughts and relationships that I assume you worked out with them. Spread your groups in different places on the square. Within each group there will be a conversation. Within some there will be arguments about certain questions. Establish the movement of people from one group to another and the motives for their changing places. For this kind of grouping you can use certain spots, such as the fountain, cafe, tables, the arch, the pillars, and the statue. Five or six people should come in as the scene begins; some people should leave and then return. All this has to be done without any excitement, rather slowly. The basic physical problem is waiting; perhaps they will bring the bread. The inner action is preparation for the great events and discussion of the situation in the city and of the debate in the National Assembly. Once in awhile, in one or another of the groups, someone bursts out with a loud sentence. Choose several phrases, serious and meaningful. Don't let your people declaim, and whatever people say in the group should come as the result of the discussion or arguments they are having. Let them speak mostly with their eyes. The object of their attention should be the bakery, the baker who appears at the window, the policeman walking on the streets, those who do not agree with the majority opinion that things are wrong in Paris.[10]

Stanislavski went on from this general outline to detail the movement of the individuals in the scene. Although this lengthy invention is rather exceptional for a stage director to add to a play, the description above is an illuminating example of how Stanislavski's specific movement and business stemmed from a basic physical problem and the "inner action" which serves as the spine for the scene as a whole.

10. Nikolai M. Gorchakov, *Stanislavsky Directs,* trans. Miriam Goldina (New York: Funk & Wagnalls, 1958).

the director at work

The director blocks the action of the play to indicate character relationships. Congenial people draw together; enemies keep their distance until there is a showdown when they are brought face to face in open conflict. The director shows the moment-by-moment psychological interrelationships of his characters by graphic representation. Performers must be given opportunities to act out their emotions, to give pictorial evidence of the psychological climate of the social environment. A dominating figure may be given an elevated position, face front, emphasized by a bright light, a striking costume, visual focus, movement; a subservient character may grovel on the floor, in dim light, in a drab costume, closed in from the audience. The director composes a series of constantly changing pictures that present the emotional states of the characters. He is concerned with all aspects of movement—its extent, speed, shape, direction, length, the position of the mover, his manner of moving, and the relationship of his action to the furniture, scenery, and other characters.

The first scene in *Hamlet* suggests that Bernardo, Marcellus, and Horatio are closely allied; they are friendly men sharing a common objective. The cold night and the atmosphere of foreboding draws them together. The ghost enters and they recoil in fear from the dreadful sight. Horatio recovers himself, bravely assumes command, and advances on the ghost pursuing him until he disappears in the darkness. Then the watchers are joined together again trying to find answers to the questions which the appearance of the ghost has raised. This opening scene with its homogeneity of grouping makes an interesting contrast to the one which follows in which Claudius and Gertrude are holding court. They make overtures to soothe the troubled and alienated Hamlet, but he spurns their efforts and isolates himself from the King and Queen and those who seek royal favors.

Another function of the director closely allied to the blocking of movement is that of inventing and assisting the actor in creating "stage business," by which we mean the detailed actions of the individual characters, such as using a cane, opening a letter, pouring tea, smoking a pipe, etc. Stage business is similar to movement in its uses. In general, it is the director's and actor's way of giving life and verisimilitude to the acting of a play. Again, like movement, business may be inherent in the playwright's script, such as Hedda burning Lövberg's manuscript, Juliet drinking the potion, and Captain Boyle cooking his "sassige." However, much of the business that is not essential to the plot but is necessary for enriching the performance is imposed on the presentation by the inventiveness of the director and actor. This is especially true in comedy where one of the marks of the skilled performer is his ingenuity in creating original business. (The example of Charlie Chaplin's performance cited on pages 147–149 is a case in point.)

An extreme example of a director who dictated the business down to the last detail is described by Houghton in his account of Meierhold's rehearsals of Chekhov's *The Proposal:*

> The next rehearsal I attended was devoted to setting "business." The stage was crowded. The center part of it was set for the action. Meierhold sat at one table at the edge of it; his assistants sat at two other tables; the usual crowd of onlookers filled the wings and footlights. The actors took their places for the opening scene. "Let us begin!" said Meierhold. The first two speeches were read. Meierhold was at once on his feet.
>
> "As you say 'Ivan Vassilyevich!' the second time, clap your hands—so," he directed. "And you, Ivan, turn your head slightly to the left . . . just a little further . . . There! And at the same time, distend your neck. Watch me do it. . . . That's it. Now let us try it again. . . . That was better. Only your handclap, Stephan Stepanovich, must be more affectionate. Place your wrists directly opposite each other as you clap, instead of side by side. That will make a smoother, more sliding clap. . . ."[11]

At a later rehearsal, Houghton comments on Meierhold's amazing, seemingly spontaneous flow of ideas. His invention of a piece of comic business is especially interesting:

> Meierhold had been inventing a dozen pieces of business to point his *jeu,* the fainting–water-drinking motif. Ivan Vassilyevich had done as much with the glass and carafe of water as he could. Finally as the rehearsal drew near its close, Meierhold rose suddenly. "Watch me and do likewise," he ordered. Then he read the line: "If it were not for these terrible agonizing palpitations, Madam, if it were not for the throbbing in my temples—" He paused, looked about him wild-eyed, seized the carafe, held it in his outstretched hand a moment, then lifted it and emptied its entire contents over his head! With his hair and nose streaming water, he finishes the line: "I should speak to you very differently!"[12]

A final example of a director at work shows the detailed care of a theater craftsman as he translates his interpretation of the play into concrete images.

The following example records Stanislavski's preparation for a projected performance of *Othello* at the Moscow Art Theatre in 1929. This excerpt shows Stanislavski's way of interpreting the first few lines of the scene in act 3 when Othello, his suspicions aroused, comes to Desdemona's bedchamber. The first line is spoken by Emilia, Desdemona's nurse.

11. Houghton, *Moscow Rehearsals.*
12. *Ibid.*

EMILIA: Look, where he comes.

(In the last pause Emilia hears steps below. She rushes to the stairs, sees Othello coming and then hurries to Desdemona so as not to be compelled to call out. Her movement shows alarm and excitement.)

Emilia thinks differently from Desdemona. She did not like Othello's behavior during the day. It does not seem the way to spend one's time during the first days of one's marriage.

Hearing that he is coming and thinking of last night's wonders, Desdemona wants to meet him suitably. She runs to the mirror to touch up her hair.

Emilia waits respectfully at the stairs to disappear at the first opportune moment and not to disturb the husband and wife.

DESDEMONA: I will not leave him now till Cassio
Be call'd to him.

She speaks these words while smartening herself up. Her hair done, she runs to the banisters to meet Othello.

(*Enter* OTHELLO)

Pause. Othello's entry should be delayed to underline its significance. He enters trying to seem cheerful and cordial at all costs and not make Desdemona see how he feels inside.

How is 't with you, my lord?

She speaks, leaning over the banisters. Thus their meeting takes place as follows: flirting lightly, Desdemona at the banisters looking at him questioningly and trying to find out how he is, while Othello stops on the stairs, having had not time to come up yet. Their heads are on a level.

OTHELLO: Well, my good lady. O, hardness to dissemble! (*Aside*)

He tries to sound cheerful. Desdemona suddenly puts her arms around him over the banisters, leaving his head uncovered. His face is turned to the audience, she is showing the back of her head.

How do you, Desdemona?

Desdemona stops dead still in the embrace. He starts at it. The embrace is intolerable, but he restrains himself. One can see by his arms how he would like to, but he cannot make himself, put them around her. His face shows suffering. The embrace over, however, he will try again to seem, if not gay, at least calm.

By the way—it would be better were the actor to make it his task to be cheerful; should he not succeed in being sincere about it, even better: this failure will accentuate the artificiality which Othello requires at the moment.

Pause. This scene of meeting and embrace must be played right through to the end; do not be afraid of prolonging the pause.[13]

directors in the new theater

The directors we have been discussing were mostly concerned with traditional drama and conventional practices. What of the director involved in the new forms of theater?

As we have seen, Brecht in his "epic theater" was attempting to find a new way of writing and producing plays. His situation was unique in that he was a playwright, and a theorist, and a producer. He was able to demonstrate his theories with his own plays at the Berliner Ensemble—and his effects were revolutionary.

When Brecht worked with the actors on the production of his own plays, he constantly struggled against the old tendencies of empathic identification. One of his favorite ways of explaining to his casts the quality of epic playing was to cite the example of a witness describing a traffic accident he had seen. The acting was "not to cast a spell over anyone, but to repeat something which had already occurred"; that is, "the incident *has* taken place, the repetition *is* taking place."

In the notes which he prepared for the production of *Mother Courage,* Brecht describes the business in detail for each of the characters involved. For example, in Kattrin's drumming scene he provided a complete scenario of action for the soldiers, peasants, and Kattrin, including the kind of actions and the attitudes of the participants.

Kattrin's action must "steer free of heroic cliché," Brecht said, and the scene must avoid "wild excitement." In order to counteract the temptation toward emotional involvement he suggested that the soldiers should appear apathetic, Kattrin's drumming should be interrupted, and the peasants' dialogue be spoken as though secondhand. For example, one peasant says, "The watchman will give us warning." Brecht was attempting to avoid the immediate impression of "unique, actual horror" in order to give the effect of repeated misfortune. "Fear must show through the ceremony in this scene." But despite these efforts to achieve objectivity Brecht had to admit: "Spectators may identify themselves with Dumb Kattrin in this scene; they may project their personality into this creature; and may happily feel that such forces are present in them, too."

At the end of the play when Mother Courage, completely alone in an unfriendly universe, drags her wagon into the gathering darkness,

13. Konstantin Sergeevich Alekseev, *Stanislavsky Produces Othello,* trans. Helen Nowak (London: Bles, 1948).

Brecht intended the audience to see her as an object lesson of one whose life and energies have been wasted in the traffic of war of which she is a willing part. But the solitary image was so loaded that the premiere in Zurich created a strong empathic response of compassion. Brecht is reported to have rewritten the part in an effort to make Courage less sympathetic.

Despite the fact that he was never able to reconcile his theories completely with the effects his plays created in the theater, Brecht gave the modern director a new and provocative way of using the actors and the stage.

Jerzy Grotowski's creative work as director of the Polish Laboratory Theater is unique since its orientation is spiritual rather than theatrical, and he serves not merely as a stage director but as a secular priest providing a means of individual self-development directed toward "a search for the truth about himself and his mission in life." His actors undergo a demanding discipline and a rigorous program of training which has made their performances before small, selective audiences an impressive exploration of the uses of theater. The heavy demands on the actor and the limited availability of Grotowski's theater to the public restrict his influence and few will attain his degree of commitment, but he has given us an authentic example of the dramatic potential of ritual and myth.

Peter Brook is a contemporary director who, although schooled in the traditional theater, is acutely aware of the drawbacks of what he calls the "deadly theater." He is responsive to and challenged by the new forces at work on the stage, and by word and example he points the way to the future. His approach is geared to answer his own question: "The whole problem of the theater today is just this: how can we make plays dense in experience?" As a partial answer, he seeks a theater which has the same freedom and "density" as that of Shakespeare. He says:

> Shakespeare seems better in performance than anyone else because he gives us more, moment for moment, for our money. This is due to his genius, but also to his technique. The possibilities of free verse on an open stage enabled him to cut the inessential detail and the irrelevant realistic action: in their place he could cram sounds and ideas, thoughts and images which make each instant into a stunning mobile.[14]

In his controversial production of Weiss's *Marat/Sade,* Brook fashioned a "total theater" out of a welter of sensory stimuli that resulted in the "density" he was talking about and that links him to Artaud. His production offered an emotional impact that recalls primitive ritual in its use of incantation, ensemble miming, discordant music and the force of

14. Peter Brook, Introduction to Peter Weiss's *Marat/Sade* (New York: Atheneum, 1965).

the acting, which seemed to be on several levels at once. The action of the play is set in a madhouse where the inmates act out their crimes, giving the director unique opportunities for theatricality and macabre business, such as the mass guillotining to the accompaniment of raucous sound effects and the pouring of red paint down the drains, as some of the inmates jump into a cavity so that only their heads show next to the guillotine.

Although Weiss's play is intrinsically not a great work of art, Brook found much to admire about it in terms of its theatrical richness.

> . . . It is above all in the jangle produced by the clash of styles. Everything is put in its place by its neighbour—the serious by the comic, the noble by the popular, the literary by the crude, the intellectual by the physical: the abstraction is vivified by the stage image, the violence illuminated by the cool flow of thought. The strands of meaning of the play pass to and fro through its structure and the result is a very complex form: as in Genêt, it is a hall of mirrors or a corridor of echoes—and one must keep looking front and back all the time to reach the author's sense.[15]

Preliminary to the production of *Marat/Sade* Peter Brook and Charles Marowitz set up an experimental acting workshop affiliated with the Royal Shakespeare Company. Its purpose was to experiment with new kinds of acting—not the Stanislavski approach with its search for inner authenticity, but toward Artaud's vision of shaping the image of communication from a sequence of movements and gestures. The actors experimented with such exercises as one actor beginning to improvise a pantomime, a second actor recognizing the action and joining in with a related piece of business. A variation of this exercise was for the second, third, and subsequent actors to avoid relationships to preserve their own isolation. Other experiments involved disconnected incidents played as separate fragments without logical character or developmental relationships. The actors were stimulated to respond to change, to play games and scenes in which their attention would be on the subtext, to merge actions with disparate moods and rhythms. It is apparent from the nature of these exercises that Brook was seeking the "density" of experiences he was speaking of earlier, and at least a partial realization of a theater of cruelty. It should also be clear that Brook's acknowledged admiration for Brecht's alienation concept was at work in the striking theatricality, the discontinuity, and the specific locale and characters distanced by the larger view.

Some critics of the new theater have resented the director's power over the interpretation of a play, but with our present experimental and

15. *Ibid.*

chaotic theater it would appear that the director will have even more of a free hand in the future. The innovations now going on will probably mean less fidelity to the original concept of the playwright and more attempts at varied forms of theatricality—ritual, "total theater," "open theater," "epic theater," and even "anti-theater." For the new director, the script is likely to become less a guide to a known territory than an adventure in an unknown land.

As the new forms of theater emerge it becomes increasingly important for the director to work with an established group of actors with time and freedom to experiment or to take artistic risks. The creative theater demands workshops, laboratories, and extended rehearsals in which the participants are encouraged to investigate and explore fresh ways of working and responding. As we have seen, the most exciting and original ventures have come from just such dedicated groups, working with inspiring leaders like Brecht, Brook, and Grotowski.

exercises

1. Trace the evolution of the modern director.
2. What are the functions of the director?
3. Watch a play, film, or television show concentrating on the grouping of characters. What principles of design are applied? Describe some of the most effective moments of the production and evaluate the direction.
4. Study a short play. Make a ground plan and block the action.
5. Collect pictures which include the grouping of several characters and discuss the composition.
6. Using six people, arrange them to illustrate hostility, grief, alienation, defeat, rebellion, etc.
7. Using six people, devise stage business to establish a specific locale or atmosphere.
8. Using your classmates as performers, create the atmosphere and action of a ritual without the use of words.
9. Direct a short scene played representationally, then presentationally.
10. Using your classmates as actors, block the opening scenes of *Hamlet* and *Antigone*.
11. Read a short play. Analyze its structure. What is the dramatic function of each scene? State the "spine." Analyze the characters.
12. Assuming that you are to direct a cast of inexperienced actors who will perform a short play, write out your remarks to your cast for your first meeting with them.

suggested reading

Konstantin Sergeevich Alekseev, *Stanislavsky Produces Othello,* trans. Helen Nowak, 1948.
Peter Brook, *The Empty Room,* 1968.
Toby Cole and Helen Krich Chinoy, eds., *Directing the Play,* 1953.
Alexander Dean, *Fundamentals of Play Directing,* 1941.
Norris Houghton, *Moscow Rehearsals,* 1936.
Michel Saint-Denis, *Theatre: The Rediscovery of Style,* 1960.
Oliver M. Sayler, ed., *Max Reinhardt and His Theatre,* 1924.
Samuel Selden, *First Principles of Play Production,* 1937.
Constantin Stanislavski, *The Sea Gull Produced by Stanislavsky,* ed. S. D. Balukhaty, trans. David Magarshack, 1952.

the actor

the actor's contribution

The life force of the theater is the living actor playing before an audience. Our mechanical age may find ways to record his voice and movement on film and ship his likeness from here to there in a small can, and his image may be projected in an enormous colored enlargement on a wide screen in an immense drive-in lot, or his range of action may be reduced to a 21-inch frame within our living room, but genuine theater begins and ends with the actor's living presence. His creation and interpretation give the theater its special quality. More than the stage settings or the director's skill in organization, sometimes more than the drama itself, it is the actor who gives to the theater its reason for existence. It is his histrionic sensibility that induces the audience to live imaginatively in the characters and drama before them. It is the actor who ignites the spark and fans the flame that warms and illuminates the audience.

As we have seen earlier, the impulse to imitate, to impersonate, to act, is a very old one in the race and a very early one in our own lives. Because of the peculiarly subjective and intimate nature of acting, the creative processes of the actor are difficult to define and describe. Since acting is a private creation, the actor may work through intuition and the unconscious, by means which he himself does not fully comprehend. Actors, like other artists, vary widely in their methods of approach.

Some actors insist that the performer must have complete emotional identification with the character he is playing; others are equally adamant that acting is a matter of technique. Interestingly enough, exponents of both extremes can cite brilliant examples of actors in defense of their position.

Not only does the actor's approach to his role vary with the individual, but he is a prisoner of his times, and especially of the kind of drama in which he appears. Although a modern actor like Laurence Olivier may play in many styles of drama from Sophocles to Shakespeare to Wilde, an Elizabethan actor like Richard Burbage was obliged to play according to the style of his own period. And no one approach serves all actors in all styles. An Athenian actor in the fifth century B.C. might be called upon to play several roles (some of them feminine) in a relatively short play, speaking verse before an outdoor audience of thousands. Compare the Greek actor's task with that of a performer in Japanese Noh drama who plays in an intimate theater seating several hundred people at the most. He performs in an elaborate costume, speaking the archaic language of the old aristocracy, chanting, singing, and dancing within an eighteen-foot-square stage, his every sound and gesture based on tradition, striving to give a performance worthy of his ancestors who played the same role six or seven generations before him. Consider the difference in demands placed on a contemporary actor as he moves from the stage to the screen. In a hit show on Broadway, his chief problem may be how to keep his performance as spontaneous and credible on the 300th night as it was on the first. The same actor working in motion pictures may satisfy the director if he can give a series of satisfactory performances of a few seconds' duration in two to six takes over a period of weeks. There is no one approach which can be universally applied to all acting roles from Oedipus to Willy Loman, Scapin to Cyrano, Lady Macbeth to Candida, Mrs. Malaprop to Lady Bracknell. There is no one acting style suitable for the naturalism of Gorki, the stylized Kabuki drama of Japan, the neoclassicism of Racine, the romantic comedy of Shakespeare, the sophisticated comedy of Congreve, the expressionism of Strindberg, and the epic style of Brecht. The actor's task varies with the conditions under which he works, and there is no rigid formula which can be applied in all cases.

the actor creates and interprets

The actor serves a dual function: he creates and he interprets. He does not simply reproduce a faithful copy from life. He selects, heightens, expands. Moreover, his creation is endowed with the stamp of his own personality. The actor creates a complete entity—not a static portrait which hangs in a fixed frame and position on the wall. His creation is fleeting, evanescent, constantly changing and adjusting, forming a flow of images which communicates the character's essence to the audience. The actor creates his role with expressive movement and vocal interpretation; he makes clear his relationship to the other characters on stage, who are frequently entangled in a complex web of emotional involvements. The symbols by which he projects the dramatist's meaning must be dynamic and interesting.

The actor is also an interpretative artist who stands between the original idea and its final effect. He works with emotional characters and situations, which must make the audience believe in the action and respond to it.

As an interpreter of the dramatist's creation, the actor works within circumscribed limits to develop the values of the play. When he works in a new play, he joins with the director in an exhaustive and sometimes painful process of investigating the play and his own powers. The rehearsal process is an exploration of the unknown. Somehow he must find the core of meaning and then the potential within himself to embody the meaning in the concrete images that the theater requires. This is a process of groping, of trial and error, of self-examination, and finally, hopefully, of maturation. The actor of integrity is faithful to his sources. He does not, as many actors have done, use the script as a point of departure to free-wheel in outer space. The play remains his constant frame of reference. Under the guidance of the director, he is related to the other characters who make up the whole. He is as much a reactor as he is an actor. He does not break the back of the play to display his own ego. He is not merely an exhibitionist who, like a basketball player, puts on a one-man fancy shooting-and-dribbling show. He passes the ball to his teammates; he supports, feeds, assists, and unites with the others in a total effort toward a common goal.

requisites of the actor

The first requisite concerns the actor's physical equipment. With the wide variety of roles available in drama, an actor may be almost any size and shape, but whatever his physical endowments, he must have his body under as precise control as the violinist has over his fingers and instrument. The actor should move and gesture easily and in a variety of ways to fit the demands of different kinds of characters and plays. He should look and feel as at ease in tights or a toga as he does in slacks. He should be as comfortable playing on a bare stage picked out in a cone of light as he is in a modern living room with chairs, cocktails, and cigarettes. He must have a feeling of movement that is expressive and meaningful, not only in his overt gestures but in a constant stream of subtle, nearly hidden images that reveal his full character and motivation to the audience. His movement must not be mere posturing: the first law of stage deportment is that every movement should have a meaning and purpose. The actor should be imaginative in the invention of business by which he enriches the character, indicates the mood, creates atmosphere, or reveals emotions. He should be able to handle his props and costume not only in authentic ways, but in reinforcement of the meanings of his lines and character through their use. Stanislavski, who is generally thought of in terms of character motivation, was thoroughly insistent on the actor's training of his body so that he possessed a supple and expressive instrument. In a class session with his students he demonstrated his skill with a fan in order to convince them of the need for gaining control over the "language of objects." Gorchakov, a visiting director in Moscow, describes Stanislavski's demonstration in these words:

> Then he showed us how one should talk with a fan. The fan quivered in his hand like the wings of a wounded bird, revealing his excitement. Stanislavsky's figure, face, and half-closed eyes were seemingly calm. Only the movement of his hand and a slight trembling of the closed fan showed his inner excitement. Then the fan opened with a sharp impulsive movement, flying up and hiding his face for an instant, and just as suddenly it lowered and closed. We understood that in this brief moment the face hidden by the fan had time to give vent to feeling and time for a deep sigh or a short laugh. And it was possible that the hand lightly brushed away a tear with the aid of the fan. Then the fan, with scarcely a noticeable movement, ordered someone supposedly nearby to come closer and sit next to him. The fan stopped trembling. It opened calmly and began to sway softly in his hand as though listening attentively to the person sitting next to him. Then the fan smiled and even laughed. "We swore to him later that that's exactly what we heard." The fan closed again for a second and lightly struck the hand of the person next to him as though saying, "Oh, you are mean!"—and then suddenly covered the blushing face. Now his eyes entered the conversation. First they sparkled under the lace-edged fan; then they looked over the fan and half hid behind it.[1]

A second requisite of the actor is a voice that is easily understood, free from tension and unpleasantness. He must be able to read a variety of materials from the verse of Romeo and Orestes to the grunt-and-groan dialogue of *The Hairy Ape*. He must understand and be able to communicate the full intellectual and emotional content of each line of dialogue as it relates to his character and to the play as a whole. He must be able to sustain and make effective a long narrative passage or solil-

1. Nikolai M. Gorchakov, *Stanislavsky Directs*, trans. Miriam Goldina (New York: Funk & Wagnalls, 1958).

oquy, or engage in the rapid repartee of smart comedy with such precise timing that he maintains the pace, without stepping on the laughs. He must read his lines in context with other players creating the appropriate action and reaction, and setting the exact mood and emotion of the moment.

Finally, the actor must possess a quality difficult to define, which the great French actor Talma referred to as an "excess of sensibility." He meant by this a vivid imagination and an acute awareness which is indicated by the actor's insight into the role, an understanding of what the play and the character are all about, and in performance, a keen sense of his effect on the audience and the other members of the cast. One of the deadliest defects of an actor is the inability to assess the effect of his performance, especially in comedy when in striving too hard to "milk" laughs, the insensitive actor unconsciously destroys himself. The actor's sensibility enables him to perceive the response he is receiving and gives him the means of projecting the playwright's full meaning in a performance that is highly personal and unique, yet one that is fitting and compelling, merging smoothly into the total effect of the production.

Beyond these three attributes, many people would suggest that the actor needs to possess a spark, a magnetism, a personality that projects out into the audience and woos and wins it. Many of our popular stars, especially in motion pictures, may have this as their sole talent.

evolution of modern acting

Up until modern times, the actor learned his trade mostly by observation and experience. In the past, the stagestruck youth watched the stars in action, became an apprentice, and worked his way up from a spear-carrier to a speaking part, assimilating what he could by his contact with the veterans. The beginner might be taken under the wing of an experienced actor or a sympathetic manager and be given pointers about acting, but in general, the newcomer was left pretty much to his own inspiration, imagination, and powers of observation. A number of published works appeared from time to time on elocution, oratory, rhetoric, and stage deportment, chiefly emphasizing oral interpretation and the use of the voice, and there were occasional attempts to define characteristic emotional states and to relate them to specific postures, gestures, vocal qualities, and facial expressions, but these were entirely subjective and mechanical. The great teacher was the theater itself, where through trial and error, the actor groped for his interpretation and perfected his technique for achieving effects. Those who struck the public's fancy at their first attempt in the major theater centers were fortunate. Others, like Molière and Mrs. Siddons, two of the greatest performers of all time, met with initial failure and had to spend years in the outlying provincial theaters, mastering their craft before making their triumphant returns to Paris and London.

In the latter half of the nineteenth century, as a part of the scientific revolution in which nearly everything was examined, classified and catalogued, a Frenchman, Delsarte, devised an elaborate system of acting based on purely mechanical techniques. He found in man a trinity consisting of the torso, the "vital zone"; the head, the "intellectual zone"; and the face, the "moral zone." Each zone and every part of the mechanism was in turn divided into trinities, each producing its own specific expression. The student of Delsarte learned to act by memorizing and utilizing the appropriate gestures, vocal qualities and inflections. For example, in order to depict fear, the actor followed this description:

> When violent and sudden, terror opens very wide the mouth, shortens the nose, draws down the eyebrows, gives the countenance an air of wildness, covers it with deadly paleness, draws back the eyebrows parallel with the sides, lifts up the open hands—with the fingers spread to the height of the breast, at some distance before it, so as to shield it from some dreadful object. One foot is drawn behind the other putting the body in posture for flight. The heart beats violently, the breath is quick and short and the whole body is thrown into a general tremor.

This artificial and external school of acting was opposed to another approach based on the inner life of the character being portrayed. In part this resulted from the contemporary interest in psychology, but the strongest impulse came from the new drama of realism and naturalism, in which the playwright took his cue for his methods and his point of view from the scientist, attempting to record with strict fidelity the observed facts of man's existence even though they showed him in commonplace or sordid surroundings. Because the new science taught that man was conditioned by his environment, the naturalistic playwright depicted the physical surroundings in accurate detail as a causal force in his characters' motivation and behavior.

In 1877, Henri Becque, responding to the new influence, wrote a naturalistic play called *The Vultures,* a somber study of what happens to domestic life when the forces of the economic jungle are unleashed to prey on helpless and unsuspecting victims. In 1882, the Comédie Française was persuaded to give the play a production, but unfortunately, it was played in the traditional style of acting in which the performers declaimed with exaggerated gestures and inflections, rising from their chairs for their speeches and directing much of their dialogue to the audience, thus destroying the atmosphere of Becque's play. It was not until 1887, when Antoine gave *The Vultures* a sympathetic and effective performance at the Théâtre Libre, that the full impact of the drama was

109 *Actresses Dressing in a Barn,* an engraving by William Hogarth, 1738, showing the vicissitudes of performers on the road.

110 Edmund Kean, a celebrated nineteenth-century English actor, in *Hamlet.*

111 Edwin Forrest, one of America's most popular nineteenth-century actors, in *Macbeth*.

112 The opening scene of *King Lear*, Royal Shakespeare Theatre, 1968.

113 Meierhold developed a system of acting called biomechanics, a style requiring actors trained in gymnastics and ballet.

114 Acting is reacting. Scene from Sean O'Casey's *Purple Dust* at the Berliner Ensemble.

realized. Antoine recognized the need for a new way of acting in the new plays as he indicated in a letter to the French critic, Sarcey:

> The fact is that this new drama required interpreters who are new or renewed. Plays founded on observation should not be played in the same way as stock plays are played or as fanciful comedies are produced. To understand these modern people one must leave behind all old conventions; a realistic drama must be played realistically. . . . The characters in *La Parisienne* or *Grandmère* are people like us, living not in spacious halls with the dimensions of cathedrals, but in rooms like our own, by their fireplaces, under the lamp, around the table, and not as in the old repertory, close to the prompter's box. They have voices like ours, their language is that of everyday life, with its contradictions, its familiar tricks of speech, and not the rhetoric and lofty style of our classics.

Antoine demonstrated his ideas in performances in which he and other members of his casts attempted to secure complete absorption in their roles, using such unconventional stage behavior as turning their backs on the audiences and speaking in a conversational manner with the fragmentary gestures of real life.

Antoine's ideas took root and a revolution occurred in the theater, driving out the old inflated bombastic acting with its pyrotechnic displays of the stars. The ground was ready for the modern style of acting, but it was not a one-sided victory. While the old exhibitionist school of acting had its faults in its overflow of sentiment and wallowing emotionalism, it was also true that the traditional actor could make verse sing, and he knew how to win and hold an audience in the palm of his hand. The virtues that Antoine brought to modern acting were a style that was simple, restrained, and uncluttered with mannerisms and posturing. But in relinquishing the old traditions, the contemporary actor lost much of his unique flair and flavor when he donned his blank mask. John Mason Brown aptly referred to the new style as the "transom school of acting" in which there are "teacup comedians and gas-jet tragedians."

The new playwrights who wrote in a naturalistic or realistic manner introduced a new type of character to the theater audience. The protagonists were no longer picaresque heroes, romantic adventurers, or highbrow ladies and gentlemen in evening clothes. They might be the outcasts of society—drunkards, criminals, the insane—the victims of their environments or of their passions. Many of these characters were psychologically complex, as the primary purpose of the new dramatists might be the revelation of conflicting desires that resulted in aberrant conduct. Strindberg indicates the complex motivation of his protagonist in *Miss Julie:*

> And what will offend simple brains is that my action cannot be traced back to a single motive, that the viewpoint is not always the same. An

event in real life—and this discovery is quite recent—springs generally from a whole series of more or less deep-lying motives, but of these the spectator chooses as a rule the one his reason can master most easily. A suicide is committed. Bad business, says the merchant. Unrequited love, say the ladies. Sickness says the invalid. Crushed hopes say the ship-wrecked. Now it may be that the motive lay in all or none of these directions.[2]

the stanislavski method of acting

With the demands of this new kind of characterization, it was inevitable, as Antoine insisted, that new methods of acting should be devised. The most famous and most important innovator was Constantin Stanislavski, who not only wrote at length about his method of acting but also demonstrated his ideas through his teaching, his directing, and his own acting. The great Russian actor-director worked out his system at the Moscow Art Theatre, of which he was one of the founders. As the result of years of experience in the theater, and of his self-analysis and the observation of others, he formulated his method of acting during the first decade of the twentieth century. His ideas were made known in his three books, *My Life in Art*, *An Actor Prepares*, and *Building the Character*, and through his work with his students and actors, a number of whom became teachers, spreading his gospel throughout the theatrical world.

The Stanislavski "method" is not a beatnik style of acting for hopped-up performers who are off on an emotional jag. It is not based on sheer raw feeling without consideration of the techniques and skills of movement and speech. These common misconceptions about the method are the result of the notoriety of some of the actors who have misapplied, misunderstood, or distorted the basic tenets that Stanislavski formulated.

Stanislavski's purpose was to devise an objective, regularized technique by which the actor could gain control of his body and emotions for the appropriate interpretation of his character and the play. Instead of depending on haphazard inspiration, Stanislavski searched for a system with basic principles by which the actor could discipline his art. Much of his emphasis was in *preparing to act* by means of a conscious technique for causing inspiration as a conditioned response. His books are full of examples by which he sought the practical application of his techniques as he worked with students and actors.

The following explanation in Stanislavski's own words sums up his

2. August Strindberg, "Preface to *Miss Julie*," trans. Edith and Warner Oland, in *Plays of Strindberg*, vol. 1 (New York: Bruce Humphries, 1912).

thinking. He is explaining his method to Gorchakov, a director who was working with Stanislavski in Moscow.

> Now what are these basic principles of my method? First, my method gives no recipes for becoming a great actor or for playing a part. My method is the way to the actor's correct state of being on the stage. The correct state is the normal state of a human being in life. But it's very difficult for an actor to create this state on the stage. He must be physically free, must control his muscles, and must have limitless attention. He must be able to hear and see on the stage the same as he does in life. He must be able to communicate with his partner and to accept the given circumstances of the play completely.
>
> I suggest a series of exercises to develop these qualities. You must do these every day, just as a singer or pianist does his scales and arpeggios.
>
> My second principle concerns the correct state of being on stage. This calls for the correct actions in the progressive unfolding of the play: inner psychological actions and outer physical actions. I separate the actions in this manner intentionally. It makes it easier for us to understand each other during rehearsal. As a matter of fact, every physical action has an inner psychological action which gives rise to it. And in every psychological inner action there is always a physical action which expresses its psychic nature; the unity between these two is organic on the stage. It is defined by the theme of the play, its idea, its characters, and the given circumstances. In order to make it easier for himself, an actor must put *himself* into the given circumstances. You must say to yourself, "What would I do *if* all that happens to this character happened to me?" I believe this if (I call it jokingly the magic *if*) helps an actor to begin to *do* on the stage. After you have learned to act from yourself, define the differences between your behavior and that of the character. Find all the reasons and justifications for the character's actions, and then go on from there without thinking where your personal actions end and the character's begin. His actions and yours will fuse automatically, if you have done the preceding work as I suggested.
>
> The third principle of the method—the correct organic (inner plus outer)—will necessarily give rise to the correct feeling, especially if an actor finds a good basis for it. The sum of these three principles—correct state of being, actions and feelings—will give to your characters an organic life on the stage. This is the road which will bring you closest to what we call metamorphosis. Of course this takes for granted that you have understood the play correctly—its idea and its theme—and that you have analyzed the character accurately. And beyond all this, the actor must have a good appearance, clear and energetic diction, plastic movement, a sense of rhythm, temperament, taste and the infectious quality we often call charm.[3]

3. Gorchakov, *Stanislavsky Directs.*

In order to develop the ability to control the state of being, it is noteworthy that Stanislavski and other "methodists" prescribed a rigorous program of training, which, in addition to dance, fencing, movement, and voice and diction, included a series of exercises on the memory of emotions, concentration, observation, imagination, and improvisation. In addition considerable emphasis was given to the analysis of plays and characters, seeking out the basic meanings and objectives as the so-called spine of interpretation.

Too often the "method" actor in this country has displayed a tendency to exaggerate emotional identification, as if the only procedure the performer needed to follow was to feel the feeling, become the character, let the role possess him. This has given rise to the "sweat-shirt" school of acting, where the cardinal aim is to become so involved in the character that the actor tears a passion to tatters, and where the logical result would be that in playing *Othello* a new Desdemona would be needed each evening. (There is historical precedent for such complete emotional identification, for we are told that the Roman actor Aesop actually murdered a slave during an outburst of passion in a performance.)

Some of the blame for misunderstanding and misapplying the method must be credited to Stanislavski himself and to his followers. While he ostensibly devised an objective method for acting, some of his techniques for stimulating the inner life are clearly subjective, if not in the realm of the metaphysical. This is particularly true when the exponents of the method concern themselves with "radiation," "currents," and "imaginary centers." An example illustrates how the unwary might be led astray. This passage on the use of "radiations" comes from Michael Chekhov, who, before coming to America, worked for a number of years in the Russian theater, and who devised his own conception of the method which he describes in his book *To the Actor.*

> Imagine that within your chest there is a center from which flows the actual impulses for all your movements. Think of this imaginary center as a source of inner activity and *power* within your body. Send this power into your head, arms, hands, torso, legs and feet. Let the sensation of strength, harmony and well-being penetrate the whole body. See to it that neither your shoulders, elbows, wrists, hips nor knees stanch the flow of this energy from the imaginary center, but let it course freely.
>
> So long as the center remains in the middle of your chest (pretend it is a few inches deep), you will feel that you are still yourself and in full command, only more energetically and harmoniously so, with your body approaching an "Ideal" type. But as soon as you try to shift the center to some other place within or outside your body, you will feel that your whole psychological and physical attitude will change, just as it changes when you step into an imaginary body. You will notice that the

> center is able to draw and concentrate your whole being into one spot from which your activity emanates and radiates. If, to illustrate the point, you were to move the center from your chest to your head, you would become aware that the thought element has begun to play a charteristic part in your performance. . . .
>
> Try a few experiments for a while. Put a soft, warm, not too small center in the region of your abdomen and you may experience a psychology that is self-satisfied, earthy, a bit heavy and even humorous. Place a tiny, hard center on the tip of your nose and you will become curious, inquisitive, prying and even meddlesome. Move the center into one of your eyes and notice how quickly it seems that you have become sly, cunning and perhaps hypocritical. Imagine a big, heavy dull and sloppy center placed outside the seat of your pants and you have a cowardly, not too honest, droll character. A center located a few feet outside your eyes or forehead may invoke the sensation of a sharp, penetrating and even sagacious mind. A warm, hot and fiery center situated within your heart may awaken in you heroic, loving and courageous feelings.[4]

It is in such statements as these that the seeds of misunderstanding about the method have been sown.

While the central idea of the Stanislavski system is control, an admirable objective for any actor, it should be kept in mind that there are serious doubts about its effectiveness in all kinds of drama and all styles of production. The method may be ideal for working under conditions which permit long months of rehearsal and experimentation in which the actor strives for maximum identification with the character he is playing, but the method is quite inappropriate for the training of a Japanese Kabuki actor whose objective is to suggest the traditional movement and gesture of a puppet. Nor was the method applicable to Meierhold's "biodynamics," a kind of acting devised to meet the acrobatic and athletic requirements of mechanized platforms, ramps, and steps. Nor does it seem ideal for those kinds of comedy in which the actor avoids emotional involvement. Besides these limitations, method acting may be misinterpreted to the extent that the actor approaches every role as if it were a clinical case study in abnormal psychology.

The value of Stanislavski's ideas has been discussed widely. Most of the criticism of the method centers about its abuse. Too many disciples and performers have exaggerated feeling and inspiration and paid too little attention to the originator's insistence on the importance of technique. Those who emphasize technical training point out that the actor must have complete mastery of his voice and body so that he is free to move and speak in a way that is expressive, projectile, and appropriate. It is not enough for Romeo to feel like fighting a duel; he must know how to fence. In reading a comic line, it is not enough to

4. Michael Chekhov, *To the Actor* (New York: Harper, 1953).

think that the dialogue is funny; the delivery requires skillful timing. Generations of outstanding actors who gave brilliant performances in the theater long before Stanislavski testify to the fact that their acting was mostly a matter of cool and calculated technique or personal intuition. Every actor must find his own procedure. The value of the Stanislavski system is that it provides one way by which the actor may regularize his approach to his art.

An interesting and potentially profitable new way of approaching acting comes from Eric Berne's *Transactional Analysis in Psychotherapy*, in which he analyzes behavior in terms of three kinds of transactions: pastimes, games, and intimacy.[5] A pastime is an interrelationship in which the characters have no ulterior purpose, as in *Waiting for Godot*. Games involve two kinds of relationships—the social, or overt, level and the psychological, or concealed, level (such as a salesman entertaining a potential customer at dinner, with the dinner on the social level, and his wish to make a sale on the psychological level). Intimacy is a social transaction in which the person's motive is clear (such as a salesman making his pitch directly).

There are other aspects to transactions such as the three ego states of each individual—the Parent, the Adult, and the Child—and there are five levels of gain. Arthur Wagner discusses these in an informative article in which he relates Berne's theories to drama and to his own work with actors.[6] An interesting use of this method of analysis is in the first scene of *King Lear* in which Lear sets up the game of "benevolent father and loving children" by asking his three daughters, "Which of you shall we say doth love us most?" Goneril and Regan play the game by their flattering answers in order to gain the reward, but Cordelia refuses to copy her sisters and her answer causes the king to break out into a fit of childish rage.

As Wagner says, the approach is in the Stanislavski tradition but "Berne offers to the actor a way of looking at character and at interaction between characters which helps the actor to make selections that are more specific and immediate than the traditional Freudian methods of contemporary theater."

the actor's way of working

The special nature of the actor's way of working is described by Peter Brook in these words:

5. Eric Berne, *Transactional Analysis in Psychotherapy* (New York: Grove Press, 1961).

6. Arthur Wagner, "Transactional Analysis and Acting," *The Tulane Drama Review*, 11, 4 (Summer, 1967).

> Acting is in many ways so unique in its difficulties because the artist has to use the treacherous, changeable and mysterious material of himself as his medium. He is called upon to be completely involved while distanced—detached without detachment. He must be sincere, he must be insincere; he must practice how to be insincere with sincerity and how to lie truthfully.[7]

The way in which an actor approaches a new play and builds a character has been the subject of endless conjecture and controversy. Actors themselves freely acknowledge their inability to describe what actually happens to them in performance. The literature of the art of acting is filled with conflicting statements indicating that the process is too personal for clear-cut intellectual analysis. To quote Brook again:

> Outstanding actors like all real artists have some mysterious psychic chemistry, half conscious, yet three-quarters hidden, that they themselves may only define as "instinct," "hunch," "my voices," that enables them to develop their vision and their art.[8]

The actor places his faith in his feelings. This point is made again and again in a series of interviews that Lillian Ross conducted with outstanding stage and motion-picture performers for *The New Yorker*,[9] in which are found such representative statements as these:

> It's when you start to rehearse, with other people, that things begin to happen. What it is exactly I don't know, and even don't want to know. I'm all for mystery there. Most of what happens as you develop your part is unconscious. Most of it is underwater. (Kim Stanley)

> Once you set things you do and make them mean certain things, you then respond to the stimuli you yourself set up. Then you *feel*. (Maureen Stapleton)

> When I'm building a role, I start with a series of mental pictures and feel. (Hume Cronyn)

> Every actor has, as a gift from God, his own method. My particular method is to go first by the sense of taste. I actually have a physical taste for every part. Then I go to the other senses—hearing, seeing, touching. Thinking comes much later. (Vladimir Sokoloff)

In working on a new play, many actors testify to an initial period of trial and error before the image becomes clear. Geraldine Page, an

7. Peter Brook, *The Empty Space* (New York: Atheneum, 1969).
8. *Ibid.*
9. Lillian Ross, "Profiles: The Player," *The New Yorker*, October 21, 1961; October 28, 1961, and November 4, 1961. Reprinted by permission. Copyright © 1961 The New Yorker Magazine, Inc., October 28, 1961.

outstanding American actress, sees her role developing like a jigsaw puzzle, a small piece at a time. Henry Fonda says, "I baby up on a part. I get the feeling gradually."[10] Apparently many actors go through a similar experience until all at once "a bell rings," or "there is a spark," or "suddenly there is a click." Henry Fonda describes the phenomenon in this way: "I always know when it feels real to me. . . . When my emotion takes over in a part, it's like a seaplane taking off on the water. I feel as if I were soaring. If five times out of eight a week the emotions take over, you've got magic."[11]

Geraldine Page makes an interesting observation concerning character identification:

> When you take the character over and use the character, you wreck the fabric of the play, but you can be in control of the character without taking the character over. When the character uses *you,* that's when you're really cooking. You know you're in complete control, yet you get the feeling you didn't do it. You have the beautiful feeling that you can't ruin it. You feel as if you were tagging along on an exciting journey. You don't completely understand it, and you don't have to. You're just grateful and curious.[12]

This statement suggests the interesting dichotomy of the actor who, while assuming the role of another character, still remains in complete control of himself. Whether the actor's approach to his craft is emotional or sheerly technical, it must be recognized as a very personal and highly individualized process that defies complete definition or understanding. Nevertheless, there are certain general steps that may be followed.

Like the director, the actor's initial task in approaching a play is that of analysis. He searches for the core idea, the "spine." What does the play mean? What is the effect supposed to be on an audience? What is the desired emotional impact? What gives the play its dramatic tension? The actor, under the guidance and stimulation of the director, analyzes the play to establish its basic interpretation.

The actor may begin by examining the play's structure. Does it have the tightly knit, causal sequence of the Aristotelian tradition? Or is it fragmented in the style of the expressionists? Or does it have the wide sweep and disconnected incidents of a Brecht parable? What kind of effect is the central action supposed to have, and what is the contribution of each scene and character to that effect? The actor will want to know the style of the play and the production. By style is meant the manner of production, the quality of the actions and images. For example,

10. *Ibid.*, Oct. 28, 1961.
11. *Ibid.*, Oct. 28, 1961.
12. *Ibid.*, Nov. 4, 1961.

it is obvious from the opening lines of *Antigone* that the play is in classical style—the characters are elevated, their language dignified, their actions controlled. There is nothing trivial or folksy about the event. The visual style will support the tone of the play in scale, form, and color. Contrast the Greek play with the realism of *A Doll's House*—its ordinary characters, its highly personalized, domestic atmosphere, its seemingly frivolous, colloquial conversation. Its style suggests a homey interior, everyday dress, and acting and speaking that resembles actuality. The style of the particular production is determined by the director, who may elect to perform the play in a manner other than the original one as, for example, a cowboy version of *The Taming of the Shrew*, or a Molière comedy in the Italian commedia dell'arte style. The actor must realize the implications of the style in his manner of speech and action as well as in accepting the conventions of the theater. If the play is a period piece, will the acting style be an attempt at complete historical accuracy or will it simply be suggested—or parodied?

The analysis of the play should lead the actor to an understanding of the pervading atmosphere of the play. Does it suggest the hot, sensual quality of *A Streetcar Named Desire?* Is the mood one of menace as if some alien force were trying to break in as in many Pinter plays? Does the environment require the tempo and flavor of big-city corruption as in some of Brecht's works? The dominating atmosphere of the play provides the actor with clues to his interpretation and method of playing—the tempo, his use of props and business. From his study of the total play, the actor sees not only the relationship of his character to the action as a whole, as a part of a larger metaphor, but he also finds many sources of inspiration for the interpretation of the spirit and quality of the playwright's creation.

The actor not only analyzes the play as an individual but, working with the director and other actors in rehearsal, he explores interrelationships that expand his concept of the individual role. Through improvisations, games, transformations, and various exercises to stimulate his imagination, memory, and sensory responses, he increases his sensitivity to the full potential of the play and develops an awareness that enhances his ability to respond and to act.

After the actor has a clear comprehension of the play's structure, atmosphere, style and basic interpretation, he studies his individual character. He may begin by approaching the character from the outside, making an inventory of his age, occupation, appearance, manner of speaking and moving, physical condition, posture, movement, carriage, and dress. He may take his observations directly from life; if it is a period play, he will find it profitable to study historical pictures showing the costume, architecture, and manners of the time.

The actor will find four main sources of information about his character in the script. In modern drama, the playwright frequently provides a character description which will give him some of the details listed above. Some playwrights, like Shaw, provide very complete portraits down to the color of the eyes and shape of the nostrils. Other contemporary playwrights may simply give the actor the barest hint, such as "a waiter," "a young man of twenty-four," or "a tramp." In period plays, the dramatist usually gave no character description at all.

A second source of information comes from the lines the actor speaks. The playwright has usually taken great pains to write dialogue that represents and delineates the character. Lines, of course, are susceptible to a variety of interpretations and it is obvious that two different actors playing the same role may find marked differences in the reading of the dialogue. Indeed, the same actor may give a variety of interpretations of lines in different performances. The skillful playwright goes beyond the literal meaning of the words and uses dialogue as a means of revealing his characters as well as advancing the plot. The actor, therefore, must search his lines for their essential meaning, not only in reference to the immediate context, but also to the revelation of the total character.

A third clue in the actor's analysis of the role is the character's actions. Is he an active agent or is he acted upon? What change does he undergo during the course of the play? What emotions are aroused? What is his primary objective and how does he go about reaching it? How much of the inner man is revealed by what he does? To what extent does he understand his own motives? What choices and decisions does he make and how do they affect him? Do his actions make him a sympathetic character?

Finally, the actor learns a good deal about his role from the reaction of other characters to him—what they say and do. The actor must understand his dramatic purpose in the struggle, which is frequently revealed by the reaction of other characters to him. Shakespeare sometimes delineates his characters sharply in the lines of another character: "Yon Cassius hath a lean and hungry look." Coriolanus was captured in one sentence: "When he walks he moves like an engine, and the ground shrinks before his treading; he is able to pierce a corselet with his eyes, talks like a knell, and his hum is a battery." But it is mostly in the interaction of characters that the playwright indicates their motivations.

It is from this kind of preliminary analysis of the script that the actor determines the broad outlines of his role. Suppose he is cast in the part of Horatio in *Hamlet*. Let us glance at a single scene and consider the hints that Shakespeare has provided for playing the character (see pages 64–73).

Shakespeare provides no character description and no stage directions, but we may make many inferences about Horatio and his behavior.

115 Ryszard Cieslak in Grotowski's production of *The Constant Prince*. His actors seek to expose the spiritual processes of the performer. Photo © Max Waldman, 1970.

116 A modern experimental production of *Antigone* by the Freehold Theatre of London. The obvious theatricalism of the performance gives classical drama a fresh impact.

Marcellus helps to establish him with the line, "Thou art a scholar, Horatio." He is obviously a young man—an intellectual, a friend of Hamlet's. He is probably well dressed, wearing a doublet, tights, possibly a cloak or cape, and carrying a sword. He brings to this soldier's post an air of courtly polish by his aristocratic bearing. His voice and speech should be authoritative, refined, and flexible, with crisp commands to the ghost and fellows of the watch, and fully aware of the beauty of the poetic lines at the end of the scene. Physically, he is strong and vigorous.

Within a very few lines, Shakespeare provides considerable information about Horatio. His first speech, "A piece of him," shows a touch of good-natured humor despite the fact that he has been persuaded by the fearful soldiers to come out late at night in the bitter cold to see something he regards as a mere fantasy. "Tush, tush, 'twill not appear," shows his scholar's skepticism. But sixteen lines later, Horatio has seen the ghost, and is compelled to say, "It harrows me with fear and wonder," key lines of the scene. He "trembles and looks pale." Thus, Shakespeare in dramatizing Horatio's conversion from skepticism to belief has established the credibility of the ghost.

Despite his "fear and wonder," Horatio takes the initiative as he attempts to question the ghost. It disappears and Horatio says, " 'Tis strange," and he immediately seeks for the significance—not merely the personal one, but the larger meaning and any possible political implications. "This bodes some strange eruption to our state." Then Horatio explains to the soldiers the threatened conflict with Fortinbras. His feeling of foreboding as he recalls the fall of Julius Caesar is good preparation for the later action of the play as well as an indication of Horatio's scholarship and of his concern about the welfare of his country.

With the second appearance of the apparition, Horatio takes more vigorous action. "I'll cross it, though it blast me. Stay illusion!" Horatio's poetic passages at the end of the scene are a change of pace showing his sensitivity. Then he becomes a man of action again as he goes to tell Hamlet what he has seen.

During the few lines of this opening scene, Horatio's actions reveal his skepticism, his change to belief when he confronts the ghost, his attempt to force it to speak, and finally his determination to seek further for the solution to the mystery.

The soldiers' reactions to Horatio show that they respect him and look to him for assistance and assurance. They have confidence in him, asking Horatio to come with them and share their vigil in an attempt to solve the mystery.

Horatio has a number of dramatic functions in this first scene. He helps to establish the validity of the ghost, thus reinforcing the "fear and wonder" atmosphere. His exposition provides the framework of the political background of the play, and Horatio's action carries the progress of the plot forward as he goes to tell Hamlet about the strange apparition he has seen.

An actor playing Horatio would of course make a complete study of the play, searching for all the evidence he could find that would help him to create a fully realized character. He would work in conjunction with the director, who would see the part of Horatio in terms of the larger design of the entire production. During the rehearsal period, the actor would experiment with the reading of the lines, the movement and business, and the interaction with the other members of the cast until the character became a substantial person with a life of his own.

The art of acting is really the art of reacting. It is not alone through the recital of his lines that the play comes to life, but in the response of the actor to the words and actions of others, and his reaction to objects. A mere reading of Horatio's lines aloud gives an incomplete and flat version of this dramatic scene. Shakespeare cries out for movement: "How now, Horatio? You tremble and look pale." "I'll cross it, though it blast me. Stay illusion!" "Stop it, Marcellus." "Shall I strike at it with my partisan?" These lines are cues for action. This scene, with its interplay among the characters must be projected by living actors to realize the full content of Shakespeare's creation. This interaction among the characters and the emotional overtones that accompany and reinforce the lines—these constitute the theatrical elements the reader is liable to miss in his armchair. Memorable moments in the theater are often the result of the actor's particular and expressive way of reaction: Claudius's blanching as he sees the re-enactment of his crime, Lady Macbeth rubbing her guilty hands, Mrs. Alving's horror when Oswald asks for the sun—these are key moments only the actor can express.

As the theater changes in the twentieth century to meet the changing conditions of society, new approaches to acting continue to be found. Those who reject realism search for a new means of performance as well as writing. Brecht experimented with a direct theatricalism in his epic style and made entirely new demands upon the actor. Artaud redefined the theater in terms of ritual that has nothing to do with the ordinary social behavior of people engaged in small talk in a parlor. The absurdists use actors as symbols of the human condition, rather than as individual personalities, so that specific identity is inconsequential to them. And such innovations as the open theater, multimedia theater, and happenings use the actor as a part of the creative process and in performance their roles may be functional rather than interpretative. As for Grotowski and those who follow the concept of acting as ritual, their approach is a whole new concept of theater as a means of spiritual redemption. And so the present theater is characterized by a wide variety of experimentation in an attempt to find new perceptions and fresh experiences that are relevant today.

In our previous discussion of Brecht, we referred to the playwright's demands in the epic theater, particularly for alienation. The actor was no longer making a bid for sympathy, nor was he creating the illusion of a genuine character. The actor should not be a single, unalterable figure, but rather a constantly changing one who becomes clearer through the way in which he changes. Brecht wanted his actors to distance their performances in time by playing events as if they were historical, emphasizing their "pastness." The actor was not to give the illusion that he was going through an action, but that he was giving an account of it. In defining his approach Brecht used the word *zeigen*—to point to, to refer to, like a teacher using the blackboard.

His plays require a new approach to acting. His actors need a lightness, a quickness that make them flexible and changeable. They need the child's sense of play used by actors in the Chinese theater whose manner makes things strange and striking. The actor is required to develop his skill in the gestic area, that is, the area of the behavior of one person toward another in social relationships, and its influence on such things as the carriage of the body, vocal inflection, and the facial expression. Some basic "*gestus*" (gists or cores of the action) suggested by Brecht were: Richard III woos the victim's widow; God and the Devil wager over the soul of Faust; Wozzeck buys a knife to kill his wife.

Brecht's Berliner Ensemble earned a worldwide reputation for its excellent productions of his plays, but despite the actors' efforts at alienation, their live presence denied the attempt to keep the action in the historical past, and audiences were caught up emotionally by the great characters and the imaginative theatricality.

Grotowski's "poor theater" is an extraordinary example of the specialized use of theater as ritual. Working with a small group, the Polish Actor's Laboratory has required a monastic dedication from its "holy" actors that has enabled them to achieve an astonishing level of performance. Actually the participants are not so much performers as they are disciples exploring their spiritual resources through ritual. Their concern is not at all with character identification or plot development; they are engaged in an attempt to "liberate the body and the spirit" through a process of self-discovery.

While Grotowski's theater has aroused an enormous amount of interest and the acting of his company is universally admired, his narrow concept of theater and its rigorous demands on the actor suggest that this kind of venture will have few followers. But he has in his own way found an acting style close to the spirit of Artaud and he has revealed to actors and directors great new possibilites for expressiveness in movement, speech, and sound. And, with remarkable effectiveness, he has reduced the theater to its simplest terms.

Another new aspect of acting has grown out of the "open theater" concept, in which a group of actors create their own script through their experiments with exercises, games, transactions, and improvisations. Its final form may be shaped by a writer and a director, but in the main it is a group effort. Improvisation, long used as a rehearsal technique for opening up the imagination of the actor and freeing him from clichés and mannerisms, has now become the creative process itself. The problem with such a method is that the level of the dialogue, action, and thought is at the mercy of performers, who are not as likely to reach the same level of articulateness as a gifted playwright. The rejoinder to this observation is that such productions subordinate the importance of the verbal content to the cohesive, creative act of a company bringing many talents to the creative process instead of one. That there is a viable area of the dramatic expression in this kind of venture has been demonstrated by the New York Open Theater productions of *Viet Rock* and *Terminal.* Such a theater is also valuable in developing flexible and aware actors who can respond to one another and to their audiences.

Not only is the contemporary actor faced with a wide divergence of dramatic forms and styles, but the changing shape and place of the acting area also demands a great deal of flexibility. The proscenium-arch theater encouraged illusion within the form. The reintroduction of the thrust stage puts the actor in an entirely different relationship with his audience, so that he no longer plays within a protective shell but is exposed and out on a platform where he is forced to rely more on his own resources. Moreover, the shape of the thrust stage gives quite a different spatial feeling than that within the proscenium. The actor's action is apt to be more theatrical, while at the same time his proximity to the audience makes his playing seem more intimate. The actor faces a similar situation in the arena type of production except that he has almost no setting to support him and the size of the acting area and of the house lends even more intimacy, increasing the actor's need for concentration and the importance of his ability to suit his performance to the scale of the architecture. As new theaters develop there is a tendency to move the actor into new physical relationships with the audience by having the actors perform on all sides of the spectators or even within the audience space itself.

The American actor has for a long while suffered from the lack of a repertory system such as most foreign theaters use. Until recently, most new plays in this country were produced on Broadway by a company brought together for the specific play. Often the cast and production staff were strangers to one another, and the cast was restricted to a few weeks of intensive rehearsal. The objective was a hit to run for a year or two. In contrast to this, the system prevalent in Europe is a series of permanent repertory theaters with their own resident companies, production staffs and, very often, schools. Instead of working toward a single production, the company works toward a season of plays, with new and old plays offering a balanced diet. This system enables an actress like Maggie Smith to play one night in *The Beaux' Stratagem* and the next in Chekhov's *The Three Sisters,* while at the movie house down the street she may be seen in her Oscar-winning performance of *The Prime of Miss Jean Brodie.* In Shakespeare's time, an actor might play in as many as three dozen plays a year, getting up in a new play each week.

The advantages of the repertory system to the actor are obvious. He not only has some sense of security, but he also has the opportunity to develop his craft by playing in a wide range of parts and plays, he has the chance to explore and experiment, and he works with a company of people who form an artistic entity. Repertory companies are now appearing in major centers in this country, and they will be an enormous stimulus to our future actors.

exercises

1. How does empathy affect the playing and reception of a performance?
2. What are the requisites of a good actor?
3. To what extent should an actor become emotionally involved in his role?
4. Discuss the relationship of the actor's performance to theatrical conventions.
5. Describe the differences between acting on the stage and on film.
6. Describe the most memorable performance you have seen by an actor. Account for the effectiveness of the portrayal.
7. What was Antoine's contribution to modern acting?
8. Read the opening scenes of *Hamlet* and *The Doll's House.* What style of acting is required for each?
9. What are the limitations of the realistic style of acting?
10. Describe Stanislavski's contribution to the art of acting.
11. Describe Delsarte's approach to acting.
12. Study a one-act play. Make a complete description of one of the major roles, including the character's appearance, manner of speaking and moving, motivation, and social background. What function does the role serve in the play?
13. View a performance of a play, film, or television show, concentrating on a single performer. Was his performance credible? How effective was his stage business? Was his performance in harmony with the rest of the cast? How well did he listen and react?
14. Using the opening scenes from *Hamlet, Antigone* and *The Doll's House,* conduct tryouts in class for the roles. Justify the casting.
15. What new demands are made on the actor by departures from realism?

suggested reading

Richard Boleslavsky, *Acting: The First Six Lessons,* 1933.
Bertolt Brecht, "A New Technique of Acting," trans. Eric Bentley, *Theatre Arts,* 33, (Jan. 1949).
Michael Chekhov, *To the Actor: On the Technique of Acting,* 1953.
Toby Cole and Helen Krich Chinoy, eds., *Actors on Acting,* 1949.
George Funke and John E. Booth, eds., *Actors Talk About Acting,* 1961.
John Hodgson and Ernest Richards, *Improvisation: Discovery and Creativity in Drama,* 1966.
Charles McGaw, *Acting Is Believing,* 1955.
Sonia Moore, *The Stanislavski System,* 1968.
Viola Spolin, *Improvisation in the Theatre,* 1963.
Constantin Stanislavski, *An Actor Prepares,* trans. by E. R. Hapgood, 1936.
———, *Creating a Role,* trans. E. R. Hapgood, 1961.
Raymond Williams, *Drama in Performance,* 1968.
Garff Wilson, *A History of American Acting,* 1966.

stage design

You will recall that Aristotle placed the element of spectacle sixth and last, but this does not mean that the visual aspects of dramatic production are inconsequential. It is no mere anomaly of usage when we say we are going to *see* a play. In certain periods, theatrical performances have reversed Aristotle's order, exploiting scenery, costuming, and lighting as the chief means of audience appeal. At other times, it was the convention of the theater to use little or no specific graphic representation of locale. However, such stages were not lacking in spectacle. The permanent architectural features of the Greek, Elizabethan, and Noh theaters were enhanced in performance through the use of movement, dance, and elaborate costuming and properties, and the playhouses themselves delighted the eye, as we shall see in the chapter 13.

Our present interest in stage design is twofold: to sketch the pictorial tradition that has dominated the Western theater since the Renaissance, including a brief statement about modern experimentation, and to consider the scene designer's function and his methods of working.

the pictorial tradition

Our current convention of pictorial representation of the dramatic environment is only a few centuries old. Medieval drama with its mani-

fold stations was often staged with elaborate attention to realistic detail in order to secure the maximum amount of identification from the spectator, as Lee Simonson points out in his excellent book *The Stage Is Set.* But essentially our scenic tradition stems from the Renaissance innovation of the proscenium arch at the Farnese Theatre in Parma, Italy (1618). This theater exerted an enormous influence on playwriting and on all phases of production, especially stage design, and it continues to affect our practice today.

Two factors were especially influential in the kinds of sets that appeared in the new proscenium-arch theaters. First, the Italian painters were intrigued by the possibilities of design with linear perspective, by which they could produce the illusion of depth on a flat surface. This led to the construction and painting of scenery built of wood and canvas in direct imitation of architecture and natural pheomena. Verisimilitude and solidity were given to the settings by making those units nearest to the audience three-dimensional, and gradually reducing the space between set pieces until the upstage area was completely two-dimensional. As time went on, perspective settings became more and more elaborate, until they became astonishing mazes of corridors, fountains, pillars, and buildings so huge and spectacular that the actor was completely dwarfed on stage. The Bibiena family inaugurated the use of several vistas by running their perspective scenery at divergent angles, thus making possible overwhelming visual displays. The second factor influencing stage decoration was the custom of creating extravagant effects—floats and arches for court pageants and festivals. This taste for ostentatious display and the novelty of perspective scenery were combined in the theaters when designers swamped the stage not only with eye-filling scenery but also with all kinds of sensational mechanical stunts, such as great floating clouds and chariots, dazzling fountains, and enormous fires which were frighteningly lifelike. While at first the perspective set served as a neutral background for the production of many plays under royal and aristocratic patronage, the practice was to create specific scenery and effects for specific plays and occasions. Thus, the tradition of illusional picture settings was established—a tradition from which the theater has not escaped to this day.

As the public stage grew and professional companies were forced to make their own way financially, it was impossible for many theaters to afford the expense of extravagant scenery. Furthermore, the action of many plays demanded scenery that could be shifted rapidly. A mechanical system was developed consisting of backdrops and wingpieces on which were painted a variety of scenes. Wings were portable screens of wood and canvas which could be slid in and out of grooves at the sides of the stage. Rows of these wings, set parallel to the footlights, lined the acting area. Entrances and exits were made by simply walking between the wings. A series of backdrops, flown at the rear of the stage, completed the vista of the setting. Overhead, borders of canvas masked the flies from the spectator. Although these stock pieces were obviously two-dimensional, painted contrivances, they satisfied the audience's taste for reality. Not only were individual pieces of scenery standardized, but every theater owned a series of stock sets, such as an Italian garden, a prison, a mountain pass, a drawing room, a woodland glade, a kitchen, and a palace. These sets were used again and again as the various plays demanded. Occasionally, extra care and money were expended to design and construct scenery for specific productions, and this fact became a special point of publicity, such as for Charles Kean's staging of Shakespeare. But by and large, most drama in the eighteenth and nineteenth centuries was performed in stock sets of standardized units of wings and backdrops.

In the chapter on realism and naturalism we noted the nineteenth-century efforts to achieve appropriateness of environment not only as the visual background of the action but as a conditioning force on character. The naturalist went to great lengths to make his settings as credible as possible, but his excessive concern with imitating the surface aspects of life led to meaningless clutter as he attempted to implement the idea of the "significant trifle." The realist tempered the naturalist's approach with a degree of moderation and simplification. He performed a valuable service for the theater in clearing the stage of its flatness, its fake trim and unreal properties, it shoddy prettiness, and makeshift workmanship. Stage settings began to have a more substantial look, doors slammed, and windows could be opened and shut. The wings in the grooves were replaced by flats of canvas representing real walls which enclosed the acting area. Real properties were assembled, and the stage was filled with casual objects of daily living. The painted perspective tradition was wiped out, and there was a new sense of the material rightness of things. But most importantly, the idea was advanced and accepted that the scenery should serve as the specific and appropriate environment for the action of the play.

Realism was no sooner the accepted way of staging drama than it was challenged by the appearance of plays written in defiance of realistic practices, as in the works of Maeterlinck, Claudel, Yeats, and Hauptmann. But even more significant was the appearance of two pioneering spirits, endowed with poetic fervor and imagination, who led the way toward the new stagecraft.

gordon craig

Although Gordon Craig was trained in the English legitimate theater, his contribution does not lie in the practical aspects of scene painting and construction but rather in his point of view, which was that of a visionary who crusaded for an ideal art of the theater. He castigated the contemporary stage for its shabbiness, its exaggeration of realistic detail, and most of all for its lack of artistic purpose and direction. Craig conceived of the theater as an aesthetic unity in which all aspects of production would be harmonized. Toward this end, he called for a régisseur who would give this unified concept to the production of drama. Impatient with the actor, Craig even suggested replacing him with super-marionettes. His concept of design was based on the selection of a few simple, symbolic set pieces and properties, as his description of a designer illustrates:

> And remember he does not merely sit down and draw a pretty or historically accurate design, with enough doors and windows in picturesque places, but he first of all chooses certain colors which seem to him to be in harmony with the spirit of the play, rejecting other colors as out of tune. He then weaves into a pattern certain objects—an arch, a fountain, a balcony, a bed—using the chosen objects which are mentioned in the play, and which are necessary to be seen.[1]

Craig sought to replace imitation with suggestion, elaboration with simplicity. He insisted on the spiritual relationship between setting and action. He pointed out the emotional potentialities of figures moving in design, of shifting light and shadow, of the dramatic values of color. He emphasized that the theater was above all "a place for seeing." Craig illustrated his ideas with a series of provocative designs, and he sought to demonstrate his theories in production; sometimes these were doomed to failure because of impracticability, but sometimes they were brilliantly successful. Craig's contribution was not, however, in the utilitarian aspects of the theater; his real significance was in his dream, which he persuaded others to see by the compelling force of his enthusiasm and argument.

adolphe appia

The other pioneer of modern staging was the Swiss Adolphe Appia, who in 1899 published his seminal work, *Die Musik und die Inscenierung,* in which he called for reforms in the theater. Appia began with the actor, and insisted that the design must be in harmony with the living presence of the performer. When a forest was required on stage for example, it was not necessary to give an accurate representation, but to create the atmosphere of a man amidst the trees. The attention of the

1. Gordon Craig, *On the Art of the Theatre* (London: Heinemann, 1905).

audience should be focused on the character, not distracted by detailed branches and leaves. Painted stage settings are incompatible with the actor because of the contrast between his plasticity and the flatness of his scenic surroundings: "The human body does not seek to produce the illusion of reality *since it is in itself reality!* What it demands of the *décor* is simply to set in relief this reality. . . . We must free staging of everything that is in contradistinction with the actor's presence. . . . Scenic illusion is the living presence of the actor."

Appia suggested two tenets of good design: the lighting should emphasize the plasticity of the human form, rather than destroying it, and a plastic scene should give the actor's movements all of their value. Implicit in Appia's theories is the fundamental unity of all phases of production, with the major emphasis on the actor. Appia enforced his arguments by applying them to a series of designs for the production of Wagner's operas, fashioning uncluttered settings of simple forms in which skillful lighting created a remarkably appropriate and effective atmosphere. Appia's theories were well timed, since they coincided with the invention of the electric light, which gave theatrical production a marvelous dimension in design. Up until that time, stage lighting was an awkward and dangerous aspect of production, in which almost all effort went into merely getting enough light on the stage so that the audience could see. Now with electricity, lighting could be used for its evocative potential in creating and enhancing the mood of the play. Appia was the first to demonstrate this new force aesthetically.

The sparks kindled by Craig and Appia ignited and the "new stagecraft" made its appearance, based on the generally accepted point of view that scenery should augment and reinforce the atmosphere and meaning of the play, and that scenery should be utilitarian in providing the actor with a serviceable environment for his performance. This point of view is apparent from the following representative statements. John Gassner regards the function of the setting as a "psychological frame of reference"; Marc Blitzstein says that scenery "should be used to pull the play along its intended course," and Harold Clurman stresses its practicability: "A set is a utensil which cannot be judged until its worth is proved in practice by the whole course of the play's development on stage."

Robert Edmond Jones, a moving force in the progress of scene design in America, reflects his debt to Craig in his concept of the purpose of stage scenery:

> Stage-designing should be addressed to this eye of the mind. There is an outer eye that observes, and there is an inner eye that sees. . . . The designer must always be on guard against being too explicit. A good scene, I repeat, is not a picture. It is something seen, but it is something conveyed as well; a feeling, an evocation. Plato says somewhere: It is

> beauty I seek, not beautiful things. That is what I mean. A setting is not just a beautiful thing, a collection of beautiful things. It is a presence, a mood, a symphonic accompaniment to the drama, a great wind fanning the drama to flame. It echoes, it enhances, it animates. It is an expectancy, a foreboding, a tension. It says nothing, but it gives everything.[2]

meierhold and constructivism

Meierhold presents another example of a theatricalist at work. He was not primarily a designer, but an outstanding régisseur whose complete control of all phases of production had important and interesting effects on staging and design. Originally associated with Stanislavski, Meierhold's focus of attention was not on the actor but on the audience, and he used his considerable ingenuity to prod and stimulate it in a variety of ways. Some of his methods of capturing audience attention were extraordinary, as this passage indicates:

> A chair is shot up through the floor, beds actually fly, walls run . . . real automobiles and motorcycles run down the aisles, up over the orchestra rail and then among the populace upon the stage!
>
> There are no lights upon the stage. Two projectors, one from each side of the orchestra, next to the stage, throw light upon each actor in rotation as he plays, or upon the decorations, properties, etc., wherever the accent of the plot falls at that particular moment. . . . Movie captions, slogans . . . appear across the stage when they fit in with the action. As the act ends, the stage gets dark—finish. There is no curtain. . . . Sometimes, if the occasion warrants, an actor comes forward to where our footlights usually are, and shoots into the orchestra with a revolver, shouting "Entr'acte!"—"Intermission!"[3]

In his production of Gogol's *The Inspector General,* Meierhold used a semipermanent background of fifteen doors before which appeared a series of moveable platforms for individual scenes. One of them was a tall staircase with a trap door at the bottom for the spectacular exit of a character who stumbled and fell down the flight of steps. The floors of the platforms were tilted toward the audience so that the action seemed thrust out into the auditorium. This kind of staging exploited the dynamic possibilities of the setting as a machine for acting which had its roots in constructivism, originally an experimental movement among Russian sculptors but adapted for the stage by Meierhold. Inspired by the machine and reacting against the ostentatious decor of the decadent past,

2. Robert Edmond Jones, *The Dramatic Imagination* (New York: Duell, Sloan and Pearce, 1941).
3. Mordecai Gorelik, *New Theatres for Old* (New York: Samuel French, 1940).

117 Scene from Settle's *The Empress of Morocco*, at the Dorset Gardens Theatre, 1673. When the English adapted the continental style of theater, they exploited the pictorial effects made possible by the proscenium arch.

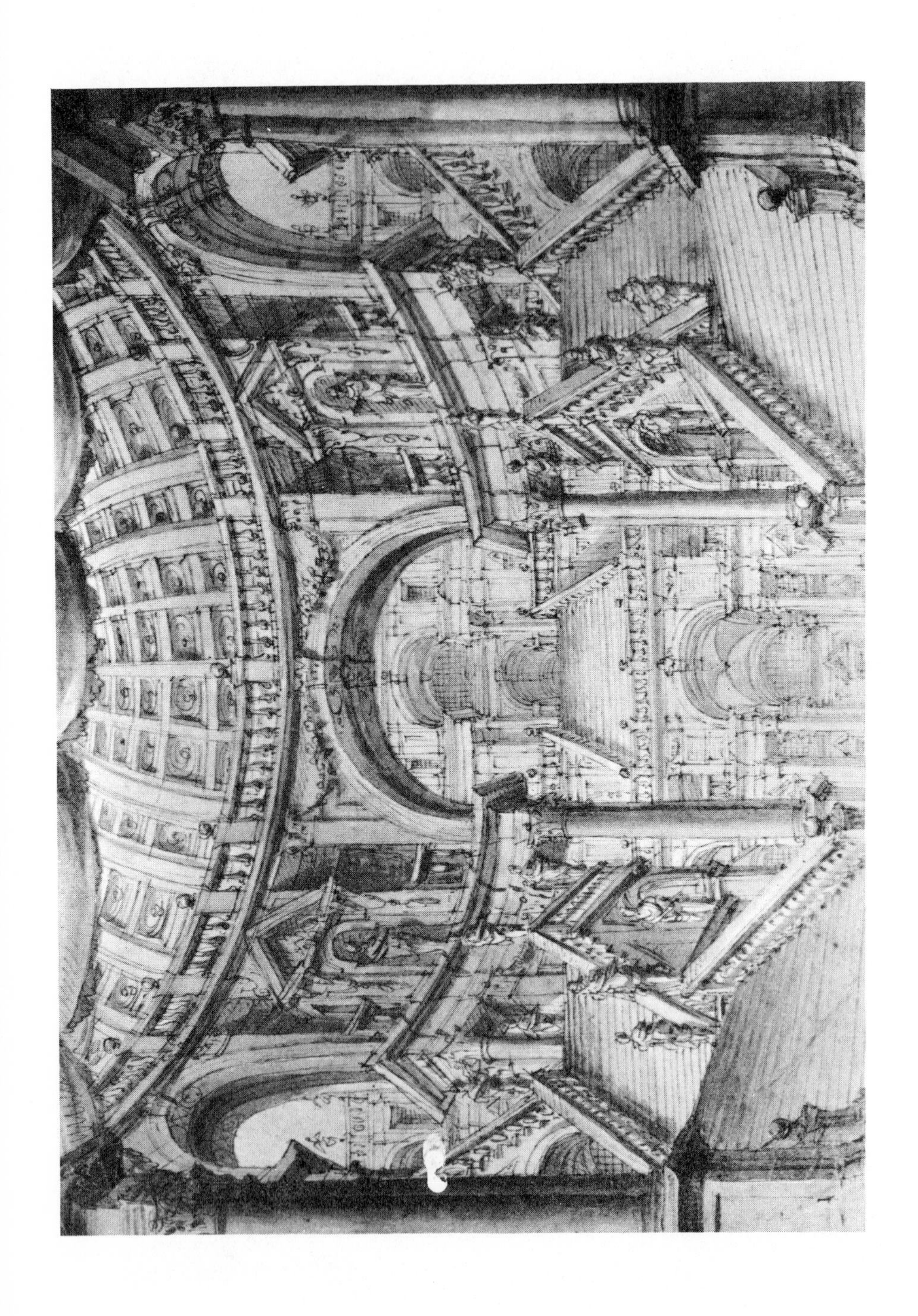

118 (opposite) Design for a stage set by F. G. da Bibiena (1657–1743). An example of the elaborate perspective staging that characterized much of the Renaissance theater.

119 Painted scenery using wings and backdrop for a production of Grillparzer's *Bruderzwist im Hause*, 1909.

120 A production of Dostoievski's *The Idiot* designed by Josef Svoboda for a production at the Old Vic Theatre, London, directed by Anthony Quayle, 1970. Note how the atmosphere of the locale has been established by projections rather than by painted set pieces.

121 Cutaway drawing of the National Theater, Munich, 1896, showing an electrically operated revolving stage used in conjunction with a sky cyclorama. Such mechanical devices simplified the use of rapid changes of scenery.

122 Drawing by Appia for a scene from Wagner's *Die Walküre, 1892.* Atmosphere is created by skillful use of light and the plastic quality of the setting.

123 Model of a constructivist set for *The Man Who Was Thursday,* directed by Alexander Tairov.

124 A constructivist set by L. Popowa for *Der Gewaltige Hahnrei,* 1922.

125 Model set for Meierhold's production of Ovstrovsky's *The Forest*, Moscow, 1924.

126 The actual set of *The Forest* in use. Note the possibilities for action and the variety of the playing areas.

the constructivist creates stage settings of skeletonized ramps, stairways, bridges, and similar structural forms. The spectator sees the bare bones of the setting against the brick stage-wall, unrelieved by any decorative or aesthetic intention. The constructivist stage is based entirely on its practicability as a tool for action. Its advantages are that it is frankly theatrical, it gives the performer extraordinary opportunities for movement and the use of space, and it is arranged for fluent and uninterrupted action.

epic theater

One of the most interesting efforts in experimental drama has been the epic theater that began in the 1920s as the result of the work of Erwin Piscator and Bertolt Brecht. The latter, in addition to being a director (and married to his leading actress, Helene Weigel, who is also a director), was also a playwright who put his theories into practice, even to inventing a new approach to acting. The epic theater-worker revolts against the tradition of Ibsenian realism. He is not concerned with the personal problems of a man and his wife in a home; epic drama calls for a larger arena of action showing the dynamics of social forces at work. Hence, the epic theater playwright and designer pay no attention to the unities; they demand instead a stage that will serve for many fragments of action, some of them occurring simultaneously. In 1928, Piscator's production of *The Good Soldier Schweik* offered a brilliant and stimulating example of the new style. A dramatization of a novel, the play concerns the life of a private soldier as he is ground down by the stupidity and brutality of war. His story is told in a kaleidoscopic arrangement of scenes, recitations, songs, and explanations. In addition to the usual facilities of the stage, Piscator used slides, posters, charts, maps, graphs, a treadmill for moving scenery and actors, and a motion-picture screen on which were projected cartoons, captions, and film sequences—all joined together in a welter of sights and sounds.

A descriptive excerpt from Gorelik indicates the nature of Piscator's production:

> "I'll do my duty for the Emperor to the end," adds Schweik. On the screen a Russian soldier is swimming in a pond. A bush rolls on with the Russian's uniform hanging on it. "A souvenir," thinks Schweik. He puts it on. A shot rings out, and a Hungarian patrol rushes on and seizes him in loud Hungarian tones. "What do you mean, prisoner?" Schweik demands. "I'm on your side. . . ." A shell bursts. Schweik falls. From the upper corner of the screen a procession of crosses starts toward the audience. As the crosses, growing nearer in perspective, reach the lower edge of the screen, a muslin drop, lowered downstage, catches them once more,

> bringing them still closer to the spectators. A rain of crosses falls upon this wry comedy as the lights begin to go up.[4]

Brecht's *The Private Life of the Master Race,* another epic drama, dramatizes the experiences of a German panzer crew moving across Europe from the early stages of the war until it is defeated by the Russians. The play is really a series of one-act plays depicting the effects of Nazism and warfare on the crew. The various threads are knit together by lyrical passages. The, play begins with this stage direction:

> A band plays a barbaric march. Out of the darkness appears a big signpost: TO POLAND and near it a Panzer truck. Its wheels are turning. On it sit twelve to sixteen soldiers, steel helmeted, their faces white as chalk, their guns between their knees. They could be puppets. The soldiers sing to the tune of the Horst Wessel Song.

There follows a series of scenes such as "The Betrayal," "The Jewish Wife," and "The Informer," dramatizing various phases of Nazi terrorism until the Panzer is bogged down in Russia. The sequences are bridged by voices out of the darkness and the roar of the armored car.

Other notable Brecht plays are *The Caucasian Chalk Circle* and *The Good Woman of Setzuan.* In America, epic theater techniques were used by the Federal Theatre in production of the Living Newspaper series during the 1930s. The epic style is a deliberate attempt to break with tradition, to move away from the struggles of a single individual and consider instead the dynamics of social change. Since Brecht was a man with a message, he utilized all of the resources of the stage as visual aids to get his ideas across. In his attack on the illusional theater, Brecht called for a new style of acting, one of "alienation" (*emfrendung*), which would emphasize his message and avoid emotional involvement in the story. The playwright avoided creating suspense and identification, because he wanted the audience to retain control of its critical faculties so that they were conscious of the idea.

It is apparent that epic theater is not merely a matter of design, but a complete concept of dramatic writing and production whose techniques make use of the theater and scenery in a new and often startling way.

the architectural stage

Still another revolt in the modern theater, but in quite a different direction, has been the rejection of scenery altogether. Recalling the

4. *Ibid.*

simple platform for acting of the Greeks, Elizabethans, and Noh drama, efforts have been made to devise a formal, unchanging "architectural" stage without a proscenium arch or any machinery of the theater except lighting. It is argued that such a stage provides a more functional and flexible place for the actors' performance. In dropping the pretense of picturing nature, it frees the spectator from visual distractions and the time lags between scenes, and focuses his attention on the play rather than on its surroundings. Moreover, the architectural stage offers exceptional freedom of movement, allowing the actor space in all directions rather than restricting him almost exclusively to lateral action as he is in the proscenium-arch theater.

Jacques Copeau's Théâtre du Vieux Colombier in France provided the most notable experiment in architectural staging. With a few portable screens and properties and skillful use of lighting, Copeau's theater proved to be remarkably effective for the production of a wide variety of plays. Other attempts have been made to use architectural stages, mostly for the production of Shakespeare, the best examples being at Stratford in Canada, the American Shakespearean Festival Theater in Connecticut, and the Guthrie Theater in Minneapolis.

the scene designer at work

The designer begins his work on a specific play by studying the script. He may want to record his initial impression of the play after a first reading, or he may prefer a thorough analysis of the script before he arrives at a central dramatic image. He searches the play for answers to numerous questions that occur to him: What is the mood of the play? What is germane to the play's meaning in its geographical location or historical period? What images continue throughout the play? How will the actor move? What are the most important scenes, and what areas will be used for them? Does the play have a unique flavor or style? The designer's preliminary study may give him answers to many questions that will stimulate his imagination and give his mind some problems to solve. During this early preparation, the designer is not primarily concerned with the practicalities of construction, painting, and shifting. At the moment he is after the feel and texture of the play.

The designer then meets with the director who helps him to find the answers to his questions. The director may have very specific ideas of the areas of the stage he wants to emphasize; he may have a definite color scheme in mind; he may even have a preliminary floor plan showing the arrangement of walls, entrances and exits, platforms, and stairways. Or his ideas may be nebulous, a general impression of his production without a clear-cut form. The designer mines the director for his ideas, looking for specific instructions on the practical aspects of the setting and for inspiration that will stimulate his imagination when he creates the visual image.

Ordinarily, the next step for the designer is to make sketches of the impressions that occur to him as he searches for the fundamental creative ideas growing out of the director's interpretation of the play. Gorelik produces numerous small sketches in which he strives to express the "poetic image of the scene." He pays no attention to the practicalities of the stage in these preliminary sketches. For example, in his designs for *Golden Boy*, Gorelik began with the concept of a prize ring, even though there was no scene using such a locale in the play, but this basic image influenced his design of each of the scenes. In his design for *Thunder Rock*, which the author set in the interior of a lighthouse, Gorelik's first impression was of an *exterior* view of a lighthouse against a stormy sky. Ultimately, he created the interior set, but his original concept persisted in the final design. Robert Edmond Jones apparently visualized his designs so clearly in his mind that he was able to set them down completely with little or no revision.

The creative scene designer is not merely concerned with reproducing a faithful copy of a piece of architecture. He is not an interior decorator, nor is he simply a skilled draftsman who follows the director's orders in his arrangement of set pieces on the stage. Like the actor, the designer is also an interpreter who makes his own unique contribution to the values of the play. Some directors give the designer a fairly free hand, since they find considerable inspiration in the designer's way of solving the visual problems of the scenic environment. At times, the designer has exerted such power that his work completely dominates the production. But in general, the designer keeps his work subservient to the total effect, attempting to reinforce the meaning of the play with his designs.

The manner in which the designer studies the script is interesting. For example, Gorelik looks for a basic motif:

> As we study the script, we try to penetrate closer and closer to the deepest significance of the play. For myself, I usually work from the climactic scenes onward. That is, I try to visualize the most poignant or striking scenes. I try to understand the dramatic progression in intensity, or the change in quality, from one scene to another. When I know that I have provided for these essential scenes, I make the other scenes fit it. The climactic moments are like the piers of a bridge, on which the cables are afterward spun. I try, also, to fasten upon a *central scenic motif* for each setting. Does the composition of the room revolve about a door? A table? A view from the window? A color? A texture? Just as the director must

127 Theatricalism in a stylized stage setting by Granovsky, Théâtre Juif d'Etat, Moscow, 1925.

128 Fragmentary setting for *The Caucasian Chalk Circle* at the Berliner Ensemble.

129 Sketch by Mordecai Gorelik for Robert Ardrey's *Thunder Rock.*

130 Stage design for *La Celestina* by Vicente Viudes, Teatro Eslava Madrid.

131 Scene from a "Living Newspaper" production of *One Third of a Nation*, 1938. Set design by Howard Bay.

132 (opposite) Jo Mielziner's set design for Maxwell Anderson's *Winterset*.

133 Stage design by Salvador Dali for *Don Juan Tenorio*, Teatro Maria Guerrero, Madrid.

(on following two pages):

134 Gordon Craig's design for *Macbeth*.

135 Orson Welles' Federal Theater production of *Macbeth* in a Haitian setting by Nat Katson, 1936.

136 Set design by Robert Edmund Jones for the banquet scene in *Macbeth*.

find a central action, so the designer must find a central scenic theme related to the action.[5]

An illuminating example of Gorelik's thinking is indicated in his approach to Chekhov's *The Three Sisters:*

It is the *dramatic metaphor,* probably, which sums up, for each setting, all the thoughts which the designer may have. Thus, the attic bedroom of the *Three Sisters* is not only an attic, not only a bedroom, not only a girl's room, not only a European room, not only a room of the period of 1901, not only a room belonging to the gentlefolk whom Chekhov wrote about. On top of all that, and including all that, it may be for the designer, the scene of a raging fever.[6]

Jo Mielziner, another prominent scenic artist, describes his way of working, bearing in mind particularly the actor's use of the stage:

I used to begin working on a play by creating a visual picture of the *mise-en-scène.* I have since given that up, and nowadays, after reading the play through once, I go over it again, seeking this time to visualize in my own mind the actors in the important situations of the drama. This may give me an idea for a significant piece of furniture, a quality of light or shadow, a color combination; it may not be an entire setting at all—just something that is associated with the dramatic significance of the moment, but which may become the clue to, or indeed the cornerstone of, the whole setting.[7]

Still another example shows how the designer Donald Oenslager seeks to capture the atmosphere of the play:

Hamlet dwells in a dual world, the everyday world of external events which is the life of the Court, and the haunted, brooding world of the imagination which is the inner world of an avenging Prince, who drifts down endless corridors of dark, fir-bordered streams. . . . It is the conflict of these two worlds that unbalances his mind and goads him on to indecisive action and helpless frustration.

The way he distorts the external world through the eyes of his own inner world of the imagination must determine the nature and appearance of the scenes. Just as he sees the events of the Court in the curving mirror of his own brooding conjectures, so the scenes which he inhabits must appear as indefinite embodiments of his own inner pre-occupations. The members of the Court must seem to be resolved into dewy shadows

5. Mordecai Gorelik, quoted in John Gassner, ed., *Producing the Play* (New York: Holt, Rinehart and Winston, 1953).

6. *Ibid.*

7. Jo Mielziner, "The Designer Sets the Stage," *Theatre Arts Anthology* (New York: Theatre Arts, 1950).

> of this "too, too solid flesh" and cloaked in veiled fragments of reality. . . . For all the Castle scenes bare, chalky walls are pierced with tall tragic doors—always three, whose depth beyond is as black as Hamlet's sable suit. They must be high, very high, to admit his anguish and his spirit. Only flashes of red, the red of blood, livens the scenes—washed over walls, or splotched on characters' clothing.[8]

The sketches the designer creates should suggest the appearance of the setting as it will actually appear to the audience. It should be in proportion, and it must be capable of being reproduced within the limitations of the stage and theatrical materials. The sketch should also indicate the color schemes, and it may give some sense of the lighting.

These preliminary sketches are a basis for communication between director and designer. Once there is common agreement on the basic designs, the designer prepares a model set, which is a scaled replica constructed in three dimensions. It is usually rather rough in form since it is not intended for display, but for making the director aware of the plasticity of the set, the spatial relationships of the various parts, which are very useful to him in visualizing and planning movement. The model is also helpful to the designer in his preparation of the lighting, and it is extremely useful in solving difficulties of constructing and shifting scenery.

The next step in design is the preparation of working drawings through which the sketch and model are translated into actual scenery by the carpenters and painters. The working drawings usually include a scaled and dimensioned floor plan, elevations of the walls, a hanging chart of flying pieces, and detail drawings of special set pieces and properties. Complete specifications are a part of the drawings. In the professional theater, the designer may make only the sketches and the model, turning the preparation of the working drawings over to a draftsman, and the construction over to professional scene-builders and painters. In the educational and community theater, the scene designer often works through all steps of the design from the preliminary sketches to the actual construction, painting, and mounting of the set. In the European theater, where a permanent staff and company are employed, it is customary to construct the scenery in the theater, some of which are astonishingly well equipped in contrast to most of our Broadway theaters. For example, Norris Houghton reported that the Moscow Art Theater stage was 62 feet deep with a 55-foot turntable, and 66 sets of lines. The technical staff of the theater numbered 260. In the American professional theater, where productions are usually based on a single play, the scenery is generally built at a scene studio and taken to the

8. Donald Oenslager, *Scenery Then and Now* (New York: Norton, 1936).

theater for production. The technical staff is a minimal one, organized for one particular play.

Perhaps one of the most interesting ways of showing designers at work is to consider their efforts on the same play. The following are descriptive passages of three designers' approaches to *Macbeth*. The first is a celebrated statement of Gordon Craig, which illustrates his intuitive and aesthetic feeling for design:

> Come now, we take *Macbeth*. We know the play well. In what kind of place is that play laid? How does it look, first of all to our mind's eye? Secondly to our eye?
>
> I see two things. I see a lofty and steep rock, and I see the moist cloud which envelops the head of this rock. That is to say, a place for fierce and warlike men to inhabit, a place for phantoms to nest in. Ultimately this moisture will destroy the men. Now then, you are quick in your question as to what actually to create for the eye. I answer as swiftly—place there a rock! Let it mount up high. Swiftly I tell you, convey the idea of a mist which hugs the head of this rock. Now, have I departed at all for one-eighth of an inch from the vision which I saw in the mind's eye?
>
> But you ask me what form this rock shall take and what color? What are the lines which are the lofty lines, and which are to be seen in any lofty cliff? Go to them, glance but a moment at them; now quickly set them down on your paper; *the lines and their directions*, never mind the cliff. Do not be afraid to let them go high; they cannot go high enough; and remember that on a sheet of paper which is but two inches square you can make a line which seems to tower miles in the air, and you can do the same on your stage, for it is all a matter of proportion and nothing to do with actuality.
>
> You ask about the colors? What are the colors that Shakespeare has indicated for us? Do not first look at Nature, but look in the play of the poet. Two; one for the rock, the man; one for the mist, the spirit.[9]

The second description is of the banquet scene as it appeared in Max Reinhardt's production of *Macbeth*, designed by Ernest Stern. Lewisohn's account of the production emphasizes the overall severity:

> Take the scene of the banquet in *Macbeth*. Every line is a straight line, every angle a right angle. All form is reduced to a barbaric severity. But the two rectangular windows in the background through which the cold Northern stars glitter are narrow and tall—so unimaginably tall that they seem to touch that sky of doom. The torches turn the rough brown of the primitive walls to a tarnished bronze. Only on the rude table lie splashes of menacing yellow. There is something barren and gigantic about the scene—a sinister quiet, a dull presage.[10]

9. Craig, *On the Art of the Theatre.*

10. Ludwig Lewisohn, *The Drama and the Stage* (New York: Harcourt, Brace, 1922).

Stark Young describes the designs of Robert Edmond Jones for a production that appeared in New York in 1921.

> This design for *Macbeth* was the most profoundly creative decor that I have ever seen in the theatre. There was a stage enclosed with a background of black, flat so that no light was caught to break the complete darkness of it. Drawings or photographs can give at least a suggestion, and only a suggestion of the gold frames, or sharp gold lines, or the forms like Gothic abstractions, or however we may define them, which standing alone, against the black, defined the scenes. Three great tragic masks were hung to the front, high above the action, and from them vast daggers of light poured down, crossed, pierced, flooded the action below, as in the witches' scene or the banquet. The banquet hall with its gold and light figures moving, and above all else Lady Macbeth's robe, in which a hidden combination of many shades, an unheard-of-intensity of red was discovered, defied any conveyance in words.[11]

Each of these designs is valid in its own right. We see the designer's efforts to evoke the appropriate atmosphere of the play, to intensify its emotional content through judicious use of line, color, lighting, and texture. Each represents the approach to the task of the designer when he assists in the interpretation of a play, illustrating the contemporary philosophy of scene design.

the designer in the new theater

The cleavage between various *isms* in our theater today is largely a matter of academic argument, and while there is little profit in trying to separate various styles and modes into confining compartments, it may be helpful to distinguish between two points of view toward theatrical production. On the one hand, there are those in the Aristotelian tradition who look upon drama as an imitation of life. This attitude, referred to as *representationalism* by Alexander Bakshy, endeavors to create the illusion of actuality. The characters and events on stage have, for the moment, the authenticity of real life. On the other hand, there is *presentationalism,* in which it is frankly admitted that the theater is make-believe and that the actors are only pretending. Although less familiar to Western audiences, presentational staging has a long tradition on the stage, notably in the Oriental theater where symbolic conventions are readily accepted. For example, two coolies carrying flags on which are painted wheels become a carriage; a stick becomes a horse when a rider mounts it; and a table may be a bridge, a bed, or a mountain top. Al-

11. Stark Young, in Ralph Pendleton, ed., *The Theatre of Robert Edmond Jones* (Middletown: Wesleyan University Press, 1958).

though in America our traditions and experience are mostly with representational procedures, in such plays as *Our Town* the atmosphere of a funeral was admirably created on a bare stage by a handful of people carrying wet, black umbrellas. Another example of presentational theatricalism was Vakhtangov's production of *Turandot* in Moscow in 1922:

> At the beginning of *Turandot* the actors appear before the front curtain, wearing their ordinary clothes, and tell the audience what they are going to see. The curtain rises and, to a waltz tune, they all dress up in the bits and pieces they find lying about on stage, converting rags to riches by their imaginative use of them. Stage-hands then come on, dressed in dark blue kimonos and caps and, to the accompaniment of the lilting waltz, set the stage. Scenery descends from the flies, counter-weighted with gaily-coloured sandbags; as these soar into the air, doors and windows, pillars and arches glide smoothly on. So the play begins.[12]

The stage designer explores the new theater in a variety of ways. He responds to the revolution and experimentation in the visual arts in increasing the areas of perception, in relating the external image to the unconscious, in the juxtaposition of disparate objects and experiences through the use of simultaneous viewing and the combination of media, and in showing the dynamic nature of creation through the use of mobile forms and kinetic objects. Again, taking his cue from contemporary painters and sculptors the designer has opened up a world of possibilities in new materials. As Saulo Benavente put it:

> I believe that contemporary dramatic art and its typical dramatists such as Brecht and Duerrenmatt are partly rooted in the world of plastics, anodized aluminum, steel tube scaffolding, gas-filled lamps, nylon, electronic controls and polyethylenes, not to mention still and motion picture projections and mobiles *à la* Calder. As, furthermore, I am convinced that the primordial condition of the existence of the theater is the contemporaneousness of its forms of expression, I do not think that the designer today can refuse to make use of new materials, new techniques and new methods to lend the imagination a true reality, conforming to the times in which we live.[13]

In new materials, the designer has found fresh sources of visual impact through color, texture, and their structural quality has given him a freedom unknown to those who worked with wood and canvas; the new materials are strong yet lightweight, flexible, easy to manipulate,

12. James Roose-Evans, *The Experimental Theatre* (New York: Universe Books, 1970).
13. René Hainaux, ed. *Stage Design Throughout the World Since 1950* (New York: International Theater Institute, 1964).

and ideally suited to the flow that is so much a part of the changing forms of drama.

One of the most creative designers is the Czechoslovakian Josef Svoboda, whose combination of aesthetic and technological talents has enabled him to provide stunning examples of the new uses of the stage. His view of the theater is to provide "a vivid sense of separate elements imaginatively combined to express new insights into reality." He considers that his purpose as a designer is not to provide substitutes for decor or delineation of locale, but to create new stage space. His designs exploit the theatrical possibilities of kinetic scenery and multiple images which can react to or against the live performer on stage.

For his production of *Hamlet* in Brussels (1965), director Ottomar Krejca based his interpretation on the idea that the ghost was a fiction of Hamlet—his alter ego—so that the play is concerned with this dual role. Svoboda's technical solution to the alter ego concept was to use a mirror whose reflections he could control to reveal not only the protagonist's state of mind but the disparity of his surrounding world as well. For a production of the Capek brothers' *The Insect Comedy* he used two mirrors, twenty-five feet square, which were placed at an angle so as to reflect the decorated area of the stage floor, which contained a turntable. No regular scenery was used and only the stage floor was lighted. Svoboda's set design for *Romeo and Juliet* at the National Theater in Prague (1963) was made up of architectural components that moved in a variety of ways—rising, sinking, sliding laterally or forward and back to accommodate the action.

It is particularly in the use of projections that Svoboda has made such interesting contributions, for he is at once an artist and an engineer. One of his devices, the *diapolyekran,* is a complex screen on which simultaneous and synchronous slides and films can be shown and so controlled as to exploit the interplay between the images. His Laterna Magika is a multiscreen device designed for use onstage with the live actor. It enables the director to work with a visual collage of background or supporting material in a new way—as director Jan Grossman put it, to show "the multiplicity and contrariety of the world in which we live." Svoboda describes the use of projections in his designs for Gorki's *The Last Ones:*

> We stacked things, people, scenes behind each other; for example, action around the wheelchair downstage, above that a girl in a tub being stroked by twigs, "in front" of her a boy being flogged on the screen; then suddenly, a drape covering part of the screen opens and we see a small, live orchestra playing a waltz, with pomp—an imagine of the regime. A space collage using a triptych principle, truly a dramatic poem—what I wanted to do. A clear spatial aesthetic is formed by the contrast of stage action, flat projection, and live orchestra behind the screen on which the images

137 Scene from Thornton Wilder's *Our Town*, 1938, a production that used presentational staging.

138 Thrust-stage production of Tennessee Williams' *Camino Real* at the Vivian Beaumont Theater, Lincoln Center. Note the relation of the actors to the audience.

139 Josef Svoboda's setting for M. Macourer's *Das Susannchenspiel* at the State Theater, Frankfurt. The scenery has become a collage.

140 Setting by Josef Svoboda for *Romeo and Juliet* at the National Theater, Prague, 1963. The various platforms were capable of moving in different directions, including up and down.

141 Josef Svoboda's design for a production of *Hamlet* in Brussels, 1965, directed by Ottomar Krejca.

142 (opposite) Scene from Brussels production of *Hamlet*, designed by Josef Svoboda, directed by Ottomar Krejca.

143 Josef Svoboda's design for *Hamlet*, 1959, showing the use of mirrored surfaces.

144 Setting by Josef Svoboda for Gorki's *The Last Ones*, Prague, 1966, showing the use of projected scenery in conjunction with live action.

145 (opposite, top) Another scene from *The Last Ones* illustrating Svoboda's integrated use of projections and stage action.

146 (opposite, bottom) L. Zimmermann's setting for Duerrenmatt's *The Meteor* at the Munich Kammerspiele, 1966. The scenery is virtually an assemblage.

147 Setting by Josef Svoboda for Duerrenmatt's *The Anabaptists* at the National Theater, Prague, directed by M. Machecek.

> are projected. It's all structured like music, and a law is present. Break it and a new one is set up. This is what attracts me—leitmotifs and repetitions, then sudden contrast; plus tempo indications. Themes disappear only to crop up again later.[14]

The stage designer of the future will be confronted with new concepts of theater that will reject not only the tradition of illusion but the old relationship of the actor to the audience and architecture as well. An example of the direction in which some of our production will be going is indicated in James Roose-Evans's description of Grotowski's production of *Acropolis:*

> The production is set on a large rectangular stage standing in the middle of the audience. The platform is piled high with scrap metal. A ragged violinist appears and summons the rest of the cast, who hobble on in sacks and wooden boots. The action takes the form of daydreams in the breaks between work. The seven actors attack the mound of rusting metal, hammering in unison, and fixing twisted pipes to struts over the audience's heads. The audience, however, is not involved. They represent the dead. . . . At the end of *Acropolis* there is an ecstatic procession following the image of the Saviour (a headless corpse) into a paradise which is also the extermination chamber.[15]

It is apparent that with the trend toward a theater that will eliminate the boundaries between auditorium and playing space, and with freer forms of dramatic writing, the designer will be more and more concerned with the total environment of the action, and that with new materials and facilities, the only limitation will be the sweep of his imagination.

exercises

1. Select a specific play to design. Collect pictures appropriate to the atmosphere you wish to create.
2. For the locale of the play, describe the minimal set pieces.
3. What does the stage designer contribute to the production?
4. Discuss the function of scenery as the environment of the action.
5. What are the characteristics of constructivism? The architectural stage?
6. What were the contributions of Craig and Appia?

14. Jarka Burian, "Josef Svoboda: Artist in an Age of Science," *Educational Theater Journal,* 22, 2 (May, 1970).
15. Roose-Evans, *Experimental Theater.*

7. Draw a ground plan for one of the stage settings illustrated in this book, showing entrances and furniture arrangement.
8. From the stage directions describing the setting of a modern play, make a ground plan.
9. What are the limitations of illusionistic scenery?
10. Describe the use of perspective scenery.
11. Describe the use of scenery in the epic theater.
12. Describe the process of designing the setting for a play.
13. What innovations are being used by the contemporary designer?

suggested reading

Verne Adix, *Theatre Scenecraft*, 1956.
Adolphe Appia, *The Work of Living Art*, 1961.
Irene Corey, *The Mask of Reality: An Approach to Design for Theatre*, 1969.
Edward Gordon Craig, *Scene*, 1923.
Walter R. Fuerst and Samuel J. Hume, *Twentieth-Century Stage Decoration*, 2 vols., 1928.
A. S. Gillette, *Stage Scenery*, 1959.
Mordecai Gorelik, *New Theatres for Old*, 1940.
René Hainaux, ed., *Stage Design Throughout the World Since 1935*, 1956.
———, *Stage Design Throughout the World Since 1950*, 1964.
Hubert C. Heffner, Samuel Selden, and Hunton D. Sellman, *Modern Theatre Practice*, 4th ed., 1959.
Robert Edmond Jones, *The Dramatic Imagination*, 1941.
———, *Drawings for the Theatre*, 1925.
Donald Oenslager, *Scenery Then and Now*, 1968.
W. Oren Parker and Harvey K. Smith, *Scene Design and Stage Lighting*, 1963.
Kenneth Rowell, *Stage Design*, 1968.
Lee Simonson, *The Stage Is Set*, 1932.
———, *The Art of Scenic Design*, 1950.
Richard Southern, *Changeable Scenery, Its Origin and Development in the British Theatre*, 1952.

theater architecture

The physical theater exerts a considerable influence on those who work in it. The form, organization, and size of the playhouse affect the conventions of staging, the style of production, and the structure of the drama. For example, the Kabuki and Noh drama theaters of Japan with their passageways to the stage capitalize on effective entrances and exits in a manner unknown in Western drama. The unlocalized platform of the Elizabethan stage, combined with the inner and upper alcoves, gave to Shakespeare and his contemporaries a stage of exceptional versatility for presenting a complicated and animated plot in a way unknown in our present theater, except in motion pictures. To understand the drama of any period, it is helpful to know something of the characteristics of the theater which housed it.

A theater building, like a play, is the result of an interaction of various forces. Architecture is not a mere matter of styles and forms; it has a life of its own. A building reflects the propensities of those who created and occupy it, and they in turn are influenced by the architecture which they have produced. Thus, the variety of theater structures reveals to us something about the cultures in which they were built as well as something about the drama and the audiences which they served.

The size of the auditorium and its relation to the playing area has had interesting and varying effects. Obviously in a large, cavernous auditorium seating several thousand spectators, many of them remote from

the performer, all aspects of production must be exaggerated in order to carry to the audience. Conversely, the intimate, conversational style of present-day realism with its restrained underplaying, its fragmentary speech and gestures, would be lost in the Theater of Dionysus. The compact theaters of Elizabethan and Restoration England enabled the playwright to use complex and subtle speech, and the proximity of the audience encouraged intercommunication between performer and spectator. But we must not be too arbitrary in insisting that the size of the theater will always have a specfic effect on the play and playing. Despite the size of the Greek theater, the oral tradition made it possible to exploit nuances of language, while in the intimate Noh drama playhouse, the performance is the essence of aloofness and restraint. In general, however, we can suggest that the larger the audience, the greater the need for increasing projection, which in turn works against the illusion of realism.

From the illustrations of different theaters, we can note the variation in the size and arrangement of the playing area and the space for the audience. While different solutions and conventions work for different kinds of dramas and audiences, there are certain basic requisites that obtain in all playhouses. The audience must be able to see and hear, and the actor must have an area where he can perform. The comfort and convenience of the audience should be considered so that the spectator is freed from distractions and discomfort. The playing area may be of various shapes, sizes, and arrangements as long as it provides the actor with a workable space for his performance. At times, his requirements may be reduced to "bare boards and a passion," although our contemporary taste is for some kind of visual reinforcement of the mood and locale.

At first, performances were adapted to a threshing floor adjoining a hillside, a temporary platform set in an inn-yard, or the altar and stations of the church. But as drama grew more mature and complex, other demands were placed upon the physical surroundings which finally resulted in the design and construction of specific structures for plays. In Greece, when the playwrights added a second and third actor, the resulting development of theater art made it necessary to add to the altar and orchestra, the theatron for the audience, and the stage-house (*skene*) for the actors. And as a corollary, once the theater achieved a satisfactory architectural form, it in turn affected the playwright's construction of his dramas. An improvised stage in a banquet-hall or inn-yard served well enough for early English plays, but with the full flowering of Elizabethan drama, a complete, permanent structure became essential, whose form and conventions influenced the playwrights. Thus, theater architecture is both a cause and an effect, a stimulus and a response.

The theater must be appropriate to the kind of drama performed in it. We have had to learn this lesson the hard way through trial and error, such as the efforts to produce Shakespeare in the pictorial tradition of the proscenium-arch theater, with the consequent disastrous loss in fluency so essential for Elizabethan drama. Likewise, the production of Greek tragedy in our modern playhouses frequently is awkward, not only because we have no satisfactory way of handling the chorus, but also because our acting style and our taste for illusion are at odds with the conventions of the Greek theater. As a consequence, more and more attention is being paid to the development of a theater structure sufficiently flexible to meet the demands of classic drama as well as the modern.

In order to get some notion of various arrangement of theater buildings, let us now briefly examine four representative playhouses, noting their physical characteristics, and the consequent effects on drama and performance.

the greek theater

By the latter half of the fifth century B.C., the Greek theater had evolved from a simple dancing circle to its familiar amphitheatrical structure. The circular *orchestra* some seventy-five to ninety feet in diameter repeated the form of the original threshing floor where improvisations took place around the altar of Dionysus. The altar or *thymele* remained in the center of the circle in the permanent theater. The spectators were seated on stone benches in the huge theatron, which was built on a hillside. In the Theater of Dionysus on the Acropolis, eighty tiers of seats were arranged in concentric circles about the orchestra, accommodating an audience of from fifteen to twenty thousand people. The front row of seats was reserved for priests, with the throne of the Priest of Dionysus occupying the center.

Across the back of the orchestra was the *skene* or scene building, originally a temporary structure used for changing costumes and storing properties. Later it became a permanent stone building which was used as a facade for temples, palaces, and houses. The skene was pierced by three doors which served as entrances. It is conjectured that immediately before the skene there was a platform called the *proskenion* or *logeion* where much of the action may have taken place in the later plays. Some scholars think that the platform was a low one, and that the actors performed in the orchestra, but it seems logical to assume that the proskenion must have been high enough to afford the audience a good view of the actors over the top of the chorus who occupied the orchestra. Undoubtedly, some of the action took place in the orchestra, especially in the early plays when the chorus was such an essential part of the plot. On either side of the proskenion, two wings projected, called *paraskenia.* These had doors which may have served as side entrances.

Two mechanical devices are of special interest in the Greek theater.

The *deus ex machina* or "god of the machine" was a cranelike device for raising and lowering a god into the scene. Another mechanical contrivance was the *eccyclema,* some sort of portable platform which could be moved out into the audience's view for an interior scene, and for exhibiting dead bodies as in such plays as *Agamemnon* and *Medea.*

While it is difficult accurately to assess the specific influences of the theater on drama and its production, since there is an interaction of all elements, nevertheless, certain general conclusions seem valid from the evidence at hand. The great size of the Greek theater and the long gap between actor and spectator made the drama rhetorical in nature. The actor was a maker of speeches, skilled in the art of recitation and declamation. The members of the chorus required training in movement and singing, but the individual actor was one who spoke. Greek tragedies did not abound in the vigorous action of Elizabethan plays or nineteenth-century melodrama. The clash of protagonist and antagonist in Greek drama was a scene of reasoned discourse. Violence was deliberately kept off stage. The tragic actor's medium of communication was words. Greek drama was performed out-of-doors in the daylight, which meant that once the chorus made its entrance into the orchestra, it was present throughout the remainder of the play. This led to the creation of the dramatic *entrance* (*parodus*) and *exit* (*exodus*) of the chorus, as well as the retention and elaboration of choric odes which served to link the episodes of the play. The daylight performances in a curtainless theater were probably responsible for the convention of keeping scenes of violence offstage, since disposition of corpses is often awkward in dramatic production. The fixed architectural facade of the skene and the continuous presence of the chorus may account for the general practice of employing unity of time and place.

The Greek playwright not only was influenced by the physical theater, but he also exerted pressure on it, the most notable instances being the addition of the second actor by Aeschylus and the third by Sophocles, thus enlarging the role of the actors and diminishing the use of the chorus. This transition is reflected architecturally by the evolution of the skene from a temporary hut to a permanent stone structure. Once this complete theater was constructed, it affected the dramaturgy of the playwrights whose dramas were written for this specific architectural design.

The mammoth dimensions of the Greek theater compelled the actor to solve the problems of projection. His style of performance was necessarily enlarged by broad gesture, clear speech, and the use of mask and costume to increase his size and expressiveness. Such exaggeration ruled out the illusion of realistic acting. This does not mean that the audience thought of the style as artificial; the actor's integrity and sense of conviction, and his ability to convey emotion and speak expressively, gave his performance validity despite its conventions. The performance of the

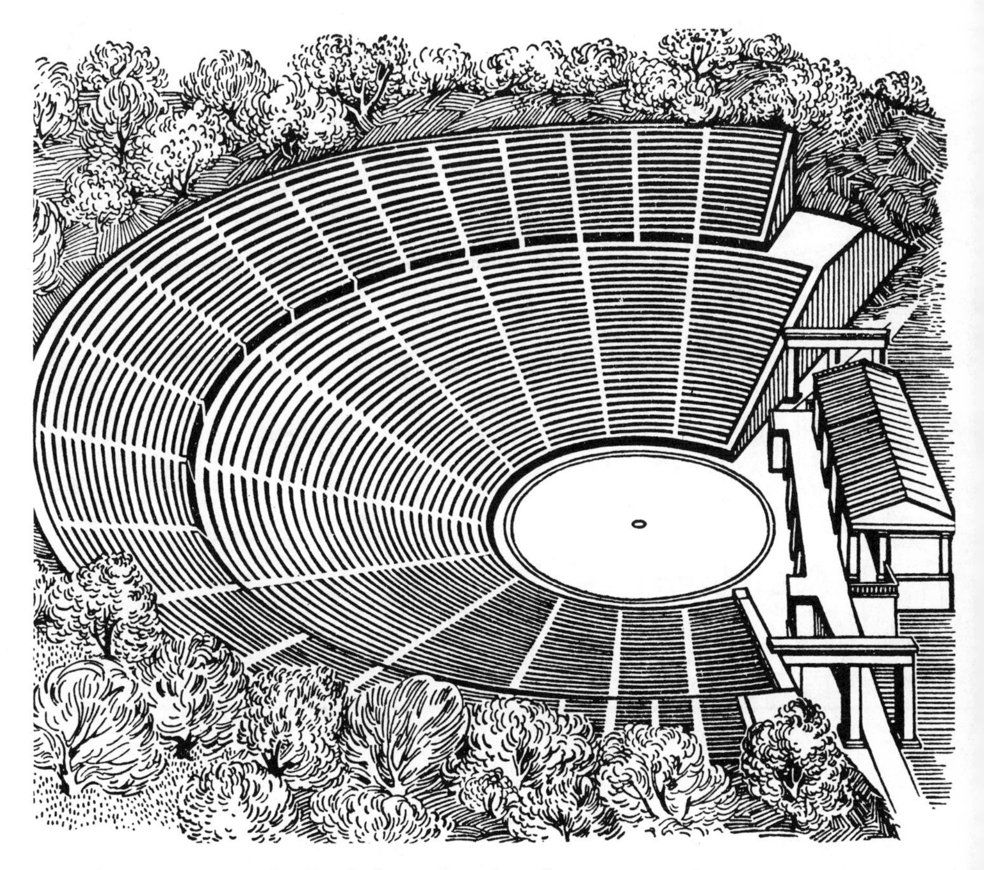

148 A reconstruction of a Greek theater based on the ruins at Epidaurus, which date from the fourth century B.C.

149 Traditional stage for Japanese Noh drama. On the right of the main playing area, an alcove for the chorus; at the rear, space for the musicians. At the left, the flower walk over which the actors make their entrances.

150 (opposite) A Kabuki theater in Tokyo, 1881. Note the entrances through the audience to the stage, which extends completely across the auditorium. The orchestra is behind the actors. The dark figure crouched upstage is an "invisible" property man.

新富座
大和や
梅林
中村や
丁子や
山田や
紀伊の国や
明治十四年六月二十日出版御届 画工兼出版人 新富町六丁目二番地 神山清七

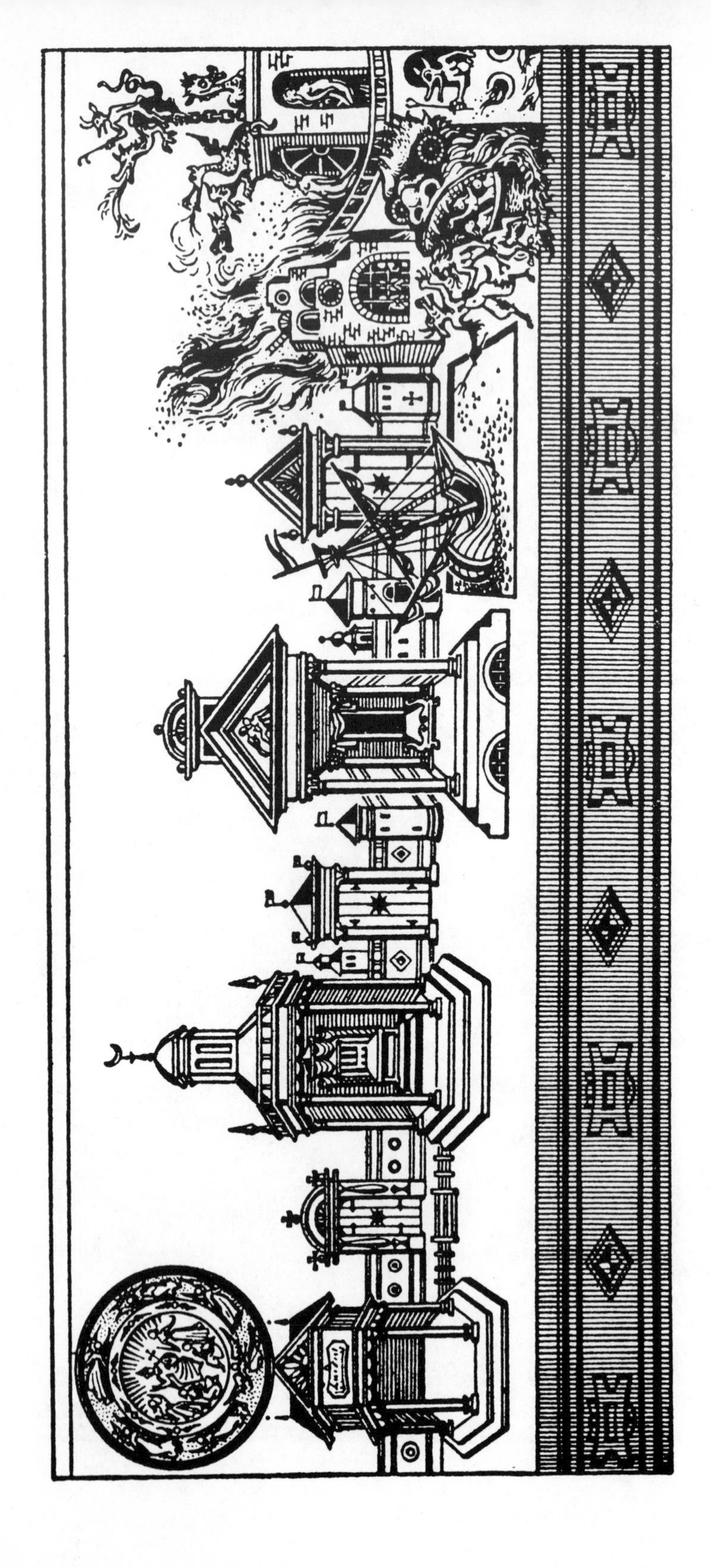

151 (opposite) A medieval mansion stage at Valenciennes, France, 1547. Note various "mansions" or stations with Heaven at one side and Hell-mouth at the other.

152 Dutch "pageants" showing the taste for ornate display that characterized the Renaissance theater.

153 A secular comedy performed on a temporary stage in sixteenth-century Germany as shown in a painting by Pieter Breughel.

chorus, retaining the circular movement of the original improvised dithyrambs performed on the threshing floor, was stylized in the use of dance and song. The length and positions of entrances and exits, and the huge orchestra placed great emphasis on the movement of the chorus and affected its direction and quality.

the medieval theater

Medieval drama was first performed in the church when dramatic episodes were used to augment such celebrations as those of Easter and Christmas. The faithful were shown scenes from the Bible—the Three Wise Men coming to the manger, the three Marys discovering the empty tomb. As the reenactment of the stories became more and more popular, various stations of the cathedral were utilized for each segment of the story, until in the thirteenth century drama became so expansive and secular that it was moved outside of the church, and laymen of the craft guilds took over the responsibility of dramatic production. Three elements of the improvised performances in the church were retained—the episodic structure of the plays, the representation of specific locales, and the convention of moving the action from station to station.

On the continent *stations* or *mansions* were used for *simultaneous staging*. That is to say, separate representational structures were built and painted for each specific locale utilized in the play. At Mons in 1501, *The Mystery of the Passion* employed sixty-seven mansions (stations) and required 48 days of rehearsal. In front of the stations, a common playing area called the *platea* or platform was used by the actor who made his entrances and exits through the appropriate structure. The stations might be arranged in a single line as they were at Valenciennes in 1547 on a stage 130 feet long, with Heaven at one end of the stage and Hell-mouth at the other. In between were a variety of other stations such as a Temple, the House of the High Priest, and a marketplace. An analogy might be made with the stock setting for a western movie, which consists of a block-long series of stations such as a saloon, a general store, the jail, another saloon, a livery stable, and a saloon. In the street in front of this facade, the actors move about from place to place according to the requirements of the plot. Another arrangement for simultaneous staging was locating the mansions around a central area such as a courtyard, in much the same fashion as separate booths are set up for circus side shows or carnivals. The audience occupied the center area and accompanied the action from one station to another.

Another solution for staging medieval drama was to bring the scene to the spectator by means of a wagon or *pageant stage*. The audience gathered at convenient places through the town, and the pageants appeared one at a time like floats in a parade. This method was particularly popular in England where over a hundred towns and villages used pageant stages for dramatic productions. The wagon was usually a two-story affair representing a specific place such as Noah's Ark or the Manger. The top level was open, but the lower level was enclosed by curtains for changing costumes, and for making entrances and exits. The main action of the plays, however, took place in the street around the wagon. As Thomas Woods Stevens, the eminent teacher and theater scholar, pointed out, the pageant stage anticipates the structure and conventions of the Elizabethan stage with its three acting areas—the upper and inner stages and the unlocalized platea.

The medieval drama sought maximum identification with the audience. As a part of the religious service, the clergy was concerned with impressing upon their flocks the message of salvation. Outside the church, laymen took naive pleasure in achieving realistic effects, particularly in harrowing scenes of torture, legerdemain, and spectacle. With considerable ingenuity and zeal they devised ways for showing miracles, depicting scenes of suffering and dying, and creating sensational effects with fireworks.

Medieval staging had several important consequences. The audience was in close proximity to the performer. There was no architectural separation, no spatial detachment. Furthermore, the introduction of comic material into serious drama and the use of lowly characters encouraged intercommunication and rapport between preformer and spectator. Other important effects were the establishment of a method and precedent for putting the essential action on stage. The playing area allowed for unrestricted freedom of movement, which meant that all of the action could be performed rather than be talked about. The physical characteristics of the medieval stage encouraged the use of episodic or loose-knit plot structure, the mixture of comic and serious material and characters, and stories filled with vigorous action.

The graphic representation of specific locale combined with the neutral playing area of the platea, had two interesting effects on subsequent dramatic development. In France, the pictorial tradition continued, but when drama went indoors again, the size of the theatre made it impossible to show more than a few mansions at one time. This, coupled with the misinterpretation of Aristotle by classical scholars in insisting on the unities, imposed a rigid structure on French playwriting which profoundly affected the future of their drama. In England, the reverse was true. The Elizabethan theater capitalized on the freedom of the platea as the main acting area, and virtually ignored the need for representational background. This flexible physical theater gave to Shakespeare and his contemporaries the opportunity to continue the medieval tradition of using a complicated plot, and putting much of the essential action of their stories on stage before the eyes of their audience.

the elizabethan theater

Scholars have traced the origin of the architectural features of the Elizabethan theater to many sources—the inn-yards, medieval and Renaissance art conventions, the Spanish and Dutch theaters, banquet halls, and the pageant stage. There is considerable conjecture and controversy over the exact features of the Elizabethan theater, which undoubtedly varied from one structure to another. We do have one specific contemporary source of information in the building contract for the Fortune Theater, which gives these exact dimensions: the exterior walls were 80 feet square, the stage 43 feet wide and 27½ feet deep. There were three balconies, 12, 11, and 9 feet high and about 12 feet wide. Note the size of the stage—an acting area more than double the size used for the production of most Broadway plays. A roofed canopy or *heavens,* supported by pillars from the platform, covered the rear of the stage.

The Elizabethan theater, which housed professional, residential companies, was usually a three-storied structure consisting of an inner courtyard surrounded by two or three galleries. The chief acting area was a large platform which projected into the courtyard. At the back of this stage were two alcoves used as supplementary acting areas. The remaining galleries were occupied by the audience. The *groundlings* stood in the pit before the platform. We may think of the Elizabethan theater as consisting of a large platea on which most of the action took place without any specific representation of locale other than that suggested by the dialogue of the play. The upper stage was used whenever an elevation was needed, such as in balcony scenes or perhaps for the action of a battle. The inner stage below was probably used for those scenes demanding a specific locale or an unwieldy property, and, no doubt, for the concealment of a dead body. These smaller areas were necessarily limited in use since they were rather small and the angle of vision for many of the spectators would have been very poor. In general practice, no graphic representation of specific locale was used or needed. Furthermore, the problem of sight lines made it impossible to back the actor with scenery since the audience sat or stood on three sides of the performers at various levels. The inference should not be made that the Elizabethan theater was crude or makeshift. On the contrary it was one of the most flexible theaters ever devised. As a means of presenting a story in action, it is only equalled by the motion picture. The Elizabethans were quite capable of making use of spectacle in court celebrations; their theater and its conventions was a matter of choice, not of necessity. It has been only during the last century that we have come to appreciate the merits of the Elizabethan theater which is eminently more suited to the production of Shakespeare's plays than our own modern proscenium-arch theater with its graphic tradition.

In the Elizabethan theater, scene followed scene without interruption, the action moving from one area or part of the stage to another as characters made their entrances and exits. Perhaps we may gain some idea of the use of the various parts of the stage by suggesting a conjectural use of the theater for act 1 of *Hamlet.*

Scene 1. "A platform before the castle." Upper stage, with characters entering from below.
Scene 2. "A room of state in the castle." Thrones for Claudius and Gertrude in inner stage. Court audience on platform. Close curtain at King's and Queen's exit to strike thrones.
Scene 3. "Polonius' house." Enter Laertes and Ophelia through curtain to platform to suggest interior. Play scene at left side of platform.
Scene 4. "The platform." Upper stage.
Scene 5. "Another part of the platform." Inner stage below for Hamlet and ghost. Ghost disappears through trap. When Marcellus and Horatio appear, use main platform for cellerage, etc.

The movement is kept continuous. Variety is achieved by the use of various places on the three acting areas, by the flow of action, and the colorful costuming. Where specific locale or atmosphere is needed, the playwright furnishes lines to create the effect. For example, note the atmosphere created by the first few lines of act 1, scene 1 of *Hamlet,* pages 64–73.

The Elizabethan theater was a fortunate architectural creation for the playwright in that it gave him an extremely flexible stage for acting out his story. Furthermore, the intimate quality of the playhouse made it possible for him to exploit the possibilities of the language to the full. Like the motion picture, the stage and its conventions enabled him to move freely in time and space, but without the cinema's compulsion for continuous movement. In Elizabethan drama, the action could pause for speech without violating the medium.

The Elizabethan actor had an excellent place for action and speech. The attention was focused on him, without competing scenery or mechanical intrusion. Moreover, he was thrust out among the spectators, enabling him to use rich and refined language, which was immediately expressive despite its complexity. The size and shape of the three acting areas also gave the actor excellent opportunities for varied movement in both size and direction. He had the dancer's freedom in the use of space. The architecture of the Elizabethan theater was a highly successful

154 Reconstruction by John Cranford Adams of the Globe, Shakespeare's theater, originally built in 1599. Note the large acting area projecting into the pit and the curtained alcoves above and below.

155 Semper-Tieck reconstruction of the Fortune Theatre from the original specifications. This was a rival house of the Globe.

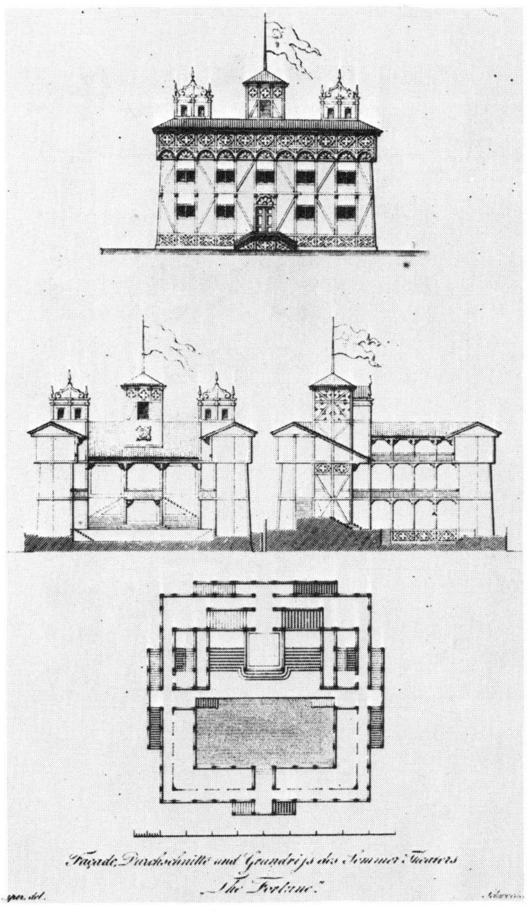

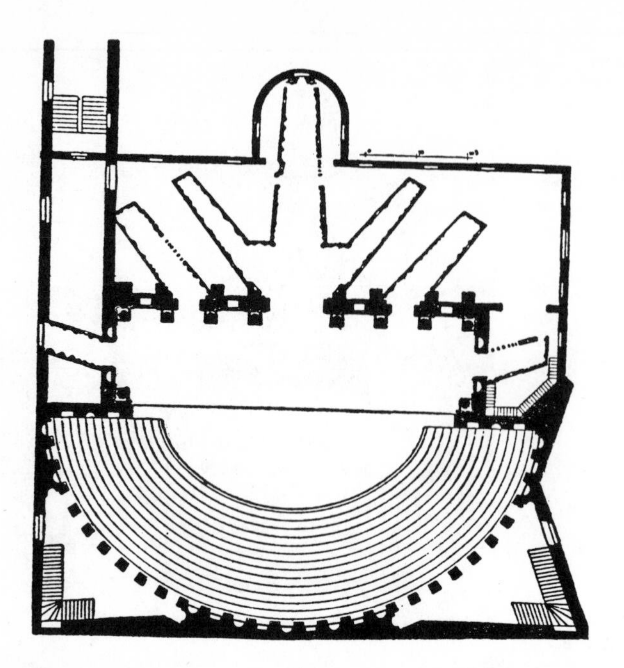

156 Ground plan of the Olympic Theater erected by Palladio in 1579 at Vicenza, Italy.

157 Olympic Theater interior. Note the perspective vistas.

158 Farnese Theater (1618–1619), Parma, Italy. A conventional court theater but with the stage framed by an arch, the prototype of the Renaissance proscenium-arch theater.

159 An eighteenth-century palace theater in rococo style at Schwetzingen, Germany, originally built in 1752 and reconstructed in 1937. Note the use of perspective vistas in the rows of wings and in the backdrop.

160 The eighteenth-century opera house at Bayreuth designed by Giuseppe Galli-Bibiena. Typical Renaissance taste for ornamentation and display.

161 Jacques Copeau's Théâtre du Vieux Colombier, 1924. An architectural stage showing the varied entrances and acting areas of a fixed formal stage.

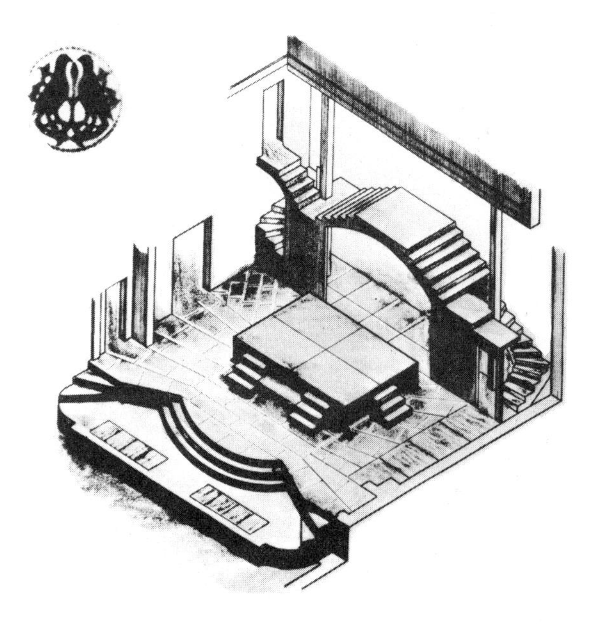

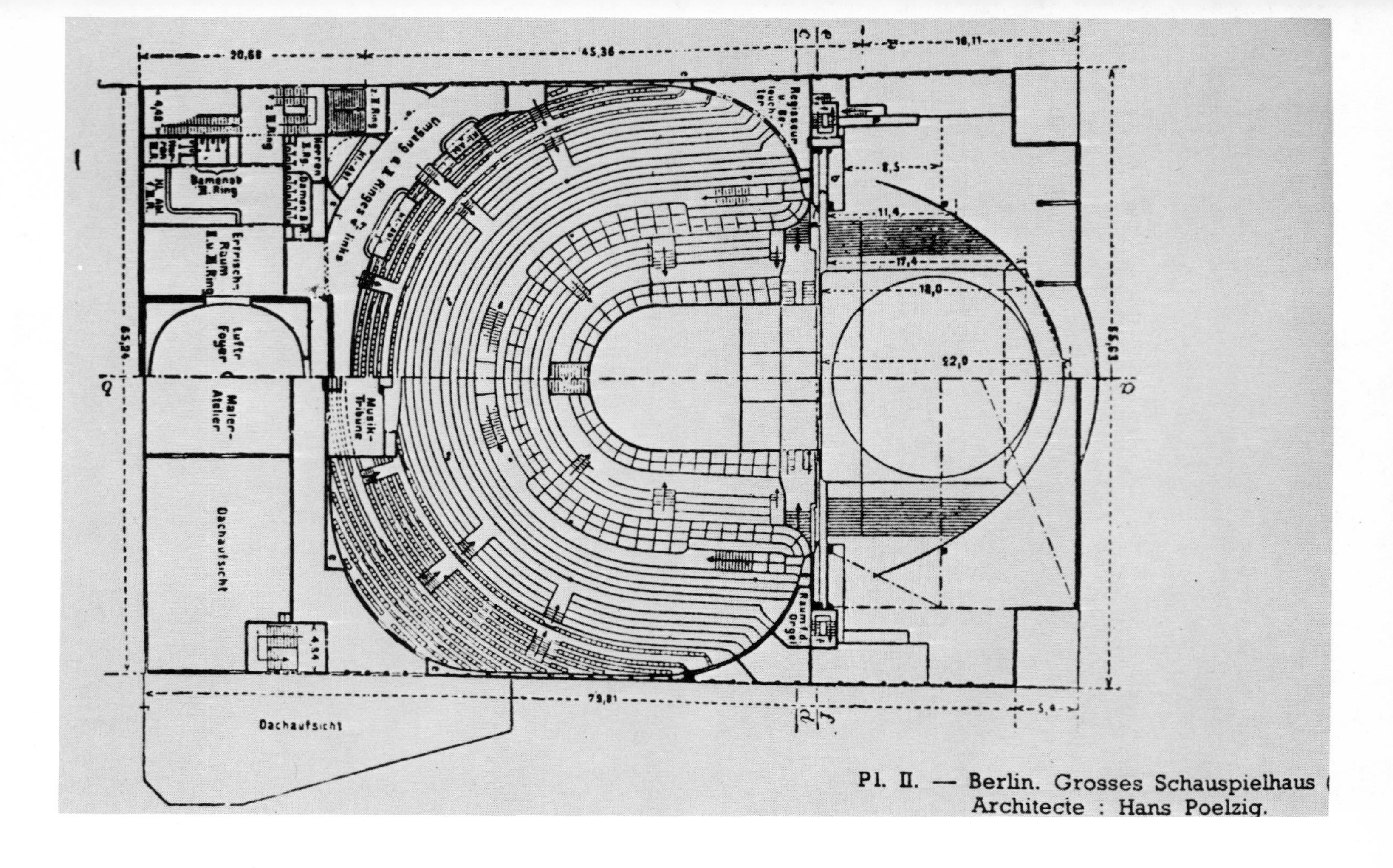

Pl. II. — Berlin. Grosses Schauspielhaus
Architecte : Hans Poelzig.

162 Plan of the Grosses Schauspielhaus in Berlin, "the theater of five thousand." Max Reinhardt exploited the possibilities of the large thrust stage.

163 Plan for a "total theater" by Walter Gropius, 1926. Notable for its varied arrangements for performers and audience relationships.

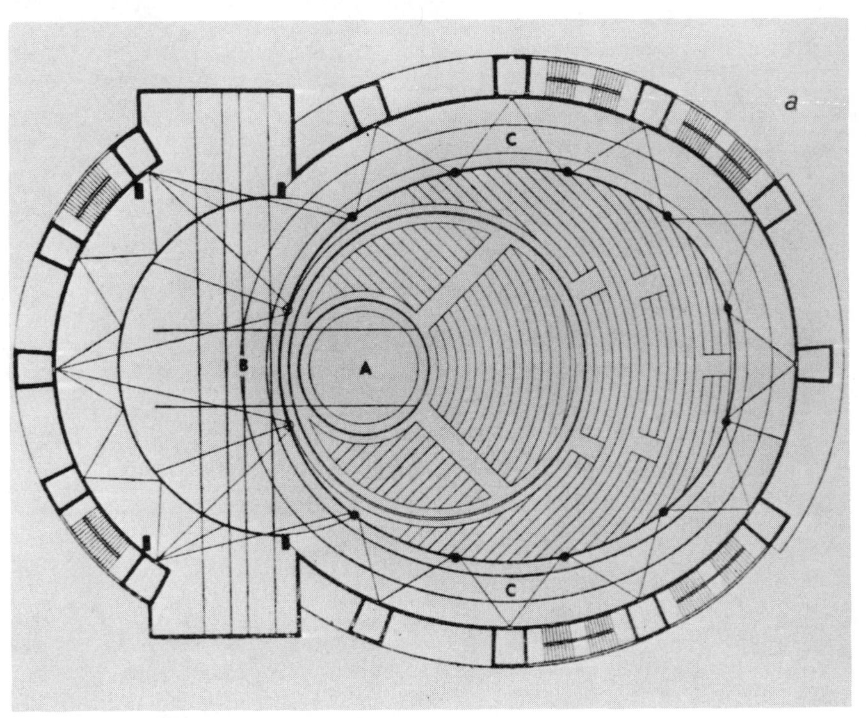

164 The thrust stage of the Shakespeare Festival Theatre at Stratford, Ontario, Canada.

165 Cross-section of the Shakespeare Festival Theatre, Stratford, Ontario, Canada.

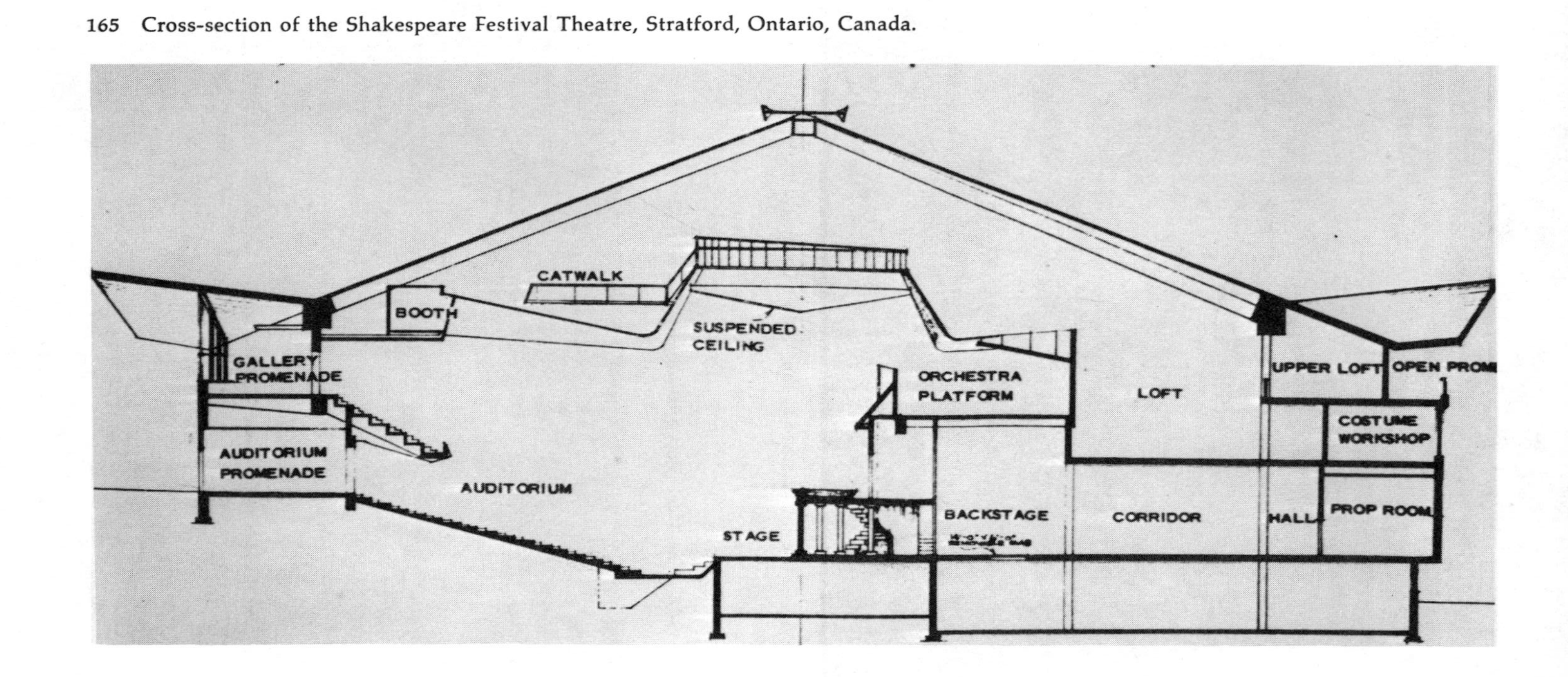

166 The thrust stage at the Tyrone Guthrie Theatre, Minneapolis.

167 The Mark Taper Forum, Los Angeles.

achievement in giving the playwright and actor a versatile and fluent stage.

the renaissance proscenium-arch theater

In the latter part of the fifteenth century, wealthy Italian noblemen became enamored of the drama with the result that a number of private theaters were designed. Architects were commissioned to adapt large halls, granaries, or other commodious buildings for dramatic productions which were given in connection with various social ceremonies. The general public did not attend these theaters except as occasional guests of a generous prince or duke. Drama was available to the lower classes in performances given by touring companies which played on improvised stages in public squares or market places. The association of the private theaters with aristocratic social events led to an emphasis on opulent decor which distinguishes the Italianate theater design.

Two important Renaissance theaters were constructed in "antique" style to satisfy the vogue of reviving things classical. The first was the Olympic Theater at Vicenza built by Palladio in 1579—a roofed-over replica of an ancient Roman theater with the notable addition of a stage facade backed by five entrances through which could be seen vistas of cityscapes in forced perspective. The second was the Farnese Theater at Parma, designed by Aleotti and erected in 1618. This became the first "modern" theater since the central opening of the stage was sufficiently wide so that the audience could see the action through the *proscenium arch.* As George Kernodle points out in his book *From Art to Theatre* the innovation of the framing arch grew out of the conventions of the visual arts. The proscenium arch wielded an enormous influence on dramatic production and composition from the Renaissance to the present.

Up until the Farnese Theater, the acting area was traditionally a platform before an ornamented facade. But with the introduction of the proscenium arch, the acting area was pushed back behind the opening, thus separating the actor from the audience psychologically as well as physically. The proscenium arch provided the Italian scene designer with an opportunity to experiment with linear perspective—an opportunity he was quick to exploit to an amazing degree.

In the early part of the seventeenth century, Italian opera achieved an enormous popularity, profoundly affecting architecture since many of the theaters erected on the continent for the next century and a half were intended for the production of elaborate musical spectacles. Since most of these were public structures, the auditoriums were large, usually accommodating from two to three thousand spectators. The auditorium assumed a narrow horseshoe shape so that spectators could see beyond the proscenium arch. Architects soon learned that tiers of galleries along the walls of the auditorium would enlarge the seating capacity. From three to seven galleries were built, supported by posts which separated the galleries into boxes. Up until this time in court celebrations, members of royalty occupied seats on the floor level directly in front of the stage, but several yards back. No one could sit in front of these seats for fear of obstructing the view. Now, in the new auditorium of the Renaissance, a royal box was placed in the center of the first gallery allowing a clear view of the stage, and making it possible to increase the capacity of the auditorium by adding seats to the floor level which was sloped to improve the angle of vision.

The stagehouse became gigantic in size and complex in organization when the scene designers and playwrights required increasingly spectacular sets and effects. For example, the Salle des Machines erected in Paris in 1660 had a stage 132 feet deep. Ingenious equipment was devised for producing all manner of sensational visual displays. Mechanical systems were worked out for changing scenery which consisted mostly of two-dimensional drops and wings which could be raised and lowered, or slid in and out very rapidly. Stock sets were constructed which were used again and again, although special occasions and productions called for new scenery.

By the end of the eighteenth century, Italian-style theaters extended all over the continent, and with the architecture, the practice was established of requiring changeable, pictorial scenery as the customary background for the performers.

The audience which was attracted to these public theaters was made up of the upper and middle classes. Their taste in theater fare was not so much for spoken drama as it was for opera, ballet, and spectacular exhibitions. Moreover, the play was not always the thing, since the theater was considered a social center. Boxes became private drawing rooms for gossip and entertainment, flirtation, and ostentatious show. In attempting to insure class, theater decor made extravagant use of ornamentation —the walls were covered with pseudo-baroque contortions of entablatures, wreaths, cornucopias, statues of nymphs and cupids, and fat rolls of swirling, gilded plaster, so that the total impreesion was one of a courtly love nest. An interesting parallel took place in America in the 1920s when the motion picture began to climb socially to the middle classes. Imposing "cathedrals of the silver screen" were constructed of such overwhelming design and dimensions that they became the dominant pieces of local architecture. An air of enchantment was produced through the use of soft lighting, luxurious carpeting, liveried attendants, mellow pipe-organ music, and rich surface decoration.

When the public theaters of the late eighteenth century became too crowded with irksome hoi polloi, there was a resurgence of smaller private theaters, more suitable for tasteful performances to be given to the genteel people of quality. However, the general characteristics of the European theater up through the nineteenth century followed the pattern of the Italian Renaissance opera house.

The general effect of the huge Renaissance theater was to encourage spectacle and music. The dramatist was compelled to create plays in which there was ample opportunity for lavish pageantry and show. Drama was forced to be grandiose in style. As a consequence of the size of the auditorium and of the competition of the scenery, the actor faced a difficult task in making himself seen and heard. Such a theater was not conducive to the development of spoken drama. It was smaller, private court theaters that gave the playwright a more congenial atmosphere in which to work.

From our brief description of four representative theaters it is clearly evident that the architecture imposes a strong formative pressure on the drama and its performance. Conversely, the physical theater reflects the needs and tastes of the dramatist, actor, and audience. Since this interaction is constantly at work, it is necessary to visualize a play in terms of the theater for which it was written.

modern theater architecture

Architects at the end of the nineteenth century were protesting against the infected atmosphere of traditionalism, and taking Louis Sullivan's statement that "form follows function" as a guiding premise, they began to experiment with new forms and new materials. But the theater planner found it difficult to escape from the established forms and styles. The forthright honesty of the new architecture clashed with the concept of the theater as a showplace, with its obligatory load of ostentatious decor.

As a result most theatrical architecture and production was dominated by the proscenium arch and its detachment of the spectator from the performer. The commercial theater in New York and London still has this handicap. Theaters are tied to box-office appeal; the buildings are crammed into parcels of expensive real estate with only the essentials for mounting a single play. Since the theater is rented on the basis of each individual production, it is economical to build the scenery elsewhere. There is little lobby or workshop space, and often there are no facilities for dining or exhibition.

In Europe where there is considerable state support of dramatic production as a cultural activity, theater buildings are often complete plants located in impressive and congenial surroundings. The theater may be augmented by restaurants, exhibition rooms, and generous lobbies and foyers. Since the repertory tradition with permanent residential companies is in force, facilities are provided for constructing and storing scenery, properties, and costumes, and there is ample space for the rehearsals necessary to keep a variety of productions ready for performance. Fortunately, this pattern is now being followed in this country in major cities and on many university campuses, giving the American theater an enormous new impetus.

Many of the changes made in theater architecture during the first part of the twentieth century were the result of the requirements of scene design and of the availability of electrical power. For generations, scenery consisted mostly of two-dimensional painted drops and wings, which could be readily shifted. A system of ropes and pulleys enabled stagehands to raise and lower the units, most of which were lightweight in construction because the emphasis was on illusionistic painting. But when scenery became three-dimensional and solid, some other means had to be devised for moving sets quickly, noiselessly, and economically. One of the solutions was to use a revolving stage which permitted several sets to be mounted at once on a turntable. During the first quarter of the century, many European theaters were equipped with revolving stages. Another solution was the elevator stage, which allowed an entire set to be moved very rapidly in or out of place. More recently, as scenery has become more suggestive and simplified, there has been a trend toward the use of wagon stages—portable platforms, large enough to mount sets. This method of shifting scenery requires a great deal of backstage space. In New York, where real estate prices are prohibitive, wing space for wagons is not often available, but in Europe and in many American communities, public land has been used for building large stagehouses suitable for this method of handling scenery.

Electric lighting and electronic control of illumination have made marked changes in theater construction. Most recent theaters have a wide variety of positions for mounting lighting instruments. There has also been considerable interest in experimenting with projected scenery. Good stage lighting has been one of the major gains in contemporary theater design.

Another trend in architecture has been to break through the proscenium arch. Sean O'Casey, the Irish playwright, put it this way: "Sculpture, architecture, literature, poetry and the domestic art are actively walking about in new ways, and the drama isn't going to stay quietly in her picture frame gazing coyly out at changing life about her, like a languid invalid woman looking pensively out of a window in the fourth wall."

Early innovations in removing the arch were Jacques Copeau's formal stage at the Vieux Colombier, Norman Bel Geddes's projects for

168 The thrust stage of the Festival Theatre, Chichester, England.

169 (opposite) Model of the new National Theatre, London.

170 The open stage of the new National Theatre, London.

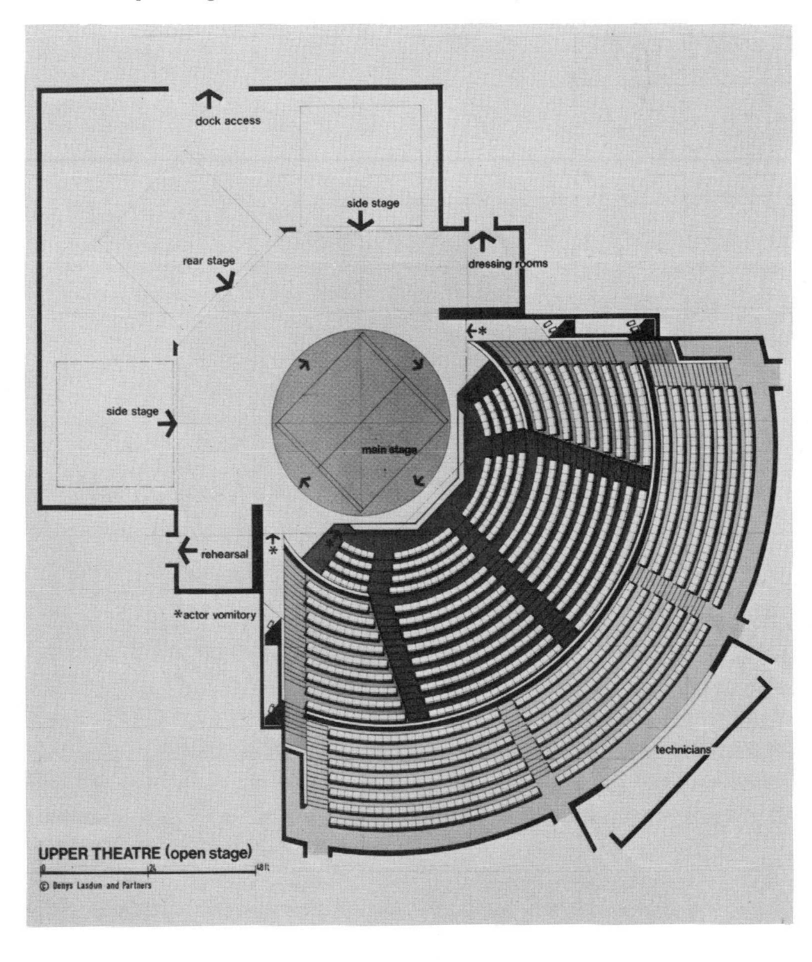

171 The National theater, Mannheim, Germany, during a production of Schiller's *The Robbers.* Note the acting area with the spectators on both sides.

172 The proscenium stage of the new National Theatre, London. Note the amount of stage space.

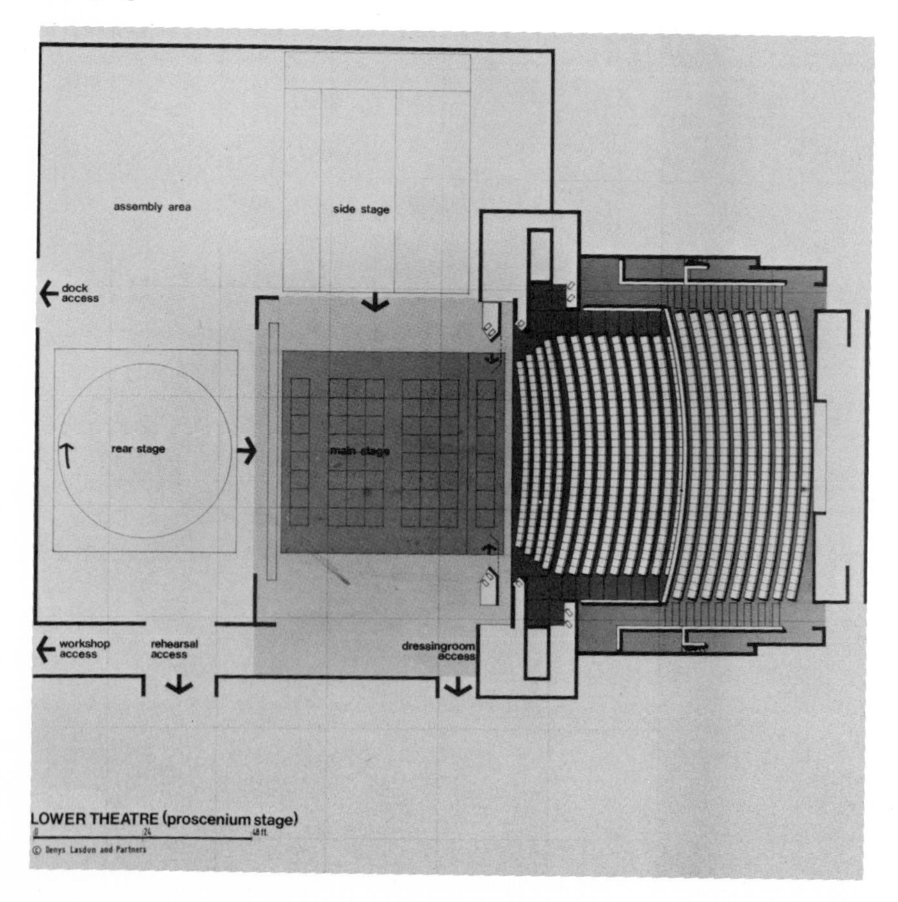

open stages, and Walter Gropius's design for a "total theater" in 1927. In this design the audience was to be made part of the scene through projections of films on the ceiling and on screens distributed through the audience. Furthermore, the circular front stage (occupying the same position as the orchestra in a Greek theater) and part of the orchestra seats were to be made mobile so that the circular front stage could be revolved a complete 180 degrees to the center of the audience, thus forming an arena. This would lead to the total elimination of aesthetic distance, imposing the play atmosphere on the audience. A complete identification of space is achieved and the words "audience" and "stage" become synonymous.

Designs for the new theater emphasize two concerns. First, there is a move toward a closer connection between spectator and performer, and second, there is a demand for freer, more flexible production. One way of securing a more intimate theater is to reintroduce the forestage or thrust stage, moving the playing area out in the auditorium. Notable examples of this design are the Shakespeare Festival Theater at Stratford, Ontario, the Tyrone Guthrie Theater in Minneapolis, and the Lincoln Center for the Performing Arts in New York City. Such thrust stages project into the seating area, which faces the actor from three sides. The stage is reached by entrances from the sides, the rear, above, and below, with the acting area admirably available to light sources. Because of the sight lines, scenery is suggestive and fragmentary and is located in the background so that the actor is no longer confined by canvas walls. In some instances attempts have been made to update old theaters by breaking through the existing proscenium arches with forestages, platforms, and ramps, but the results are less successful because of the fixed seating arrangements. The attempt to realize unity in performance will be achieved in some new experimental theaters in which separation dissolves completely into one large hall that has machinery to form many different kinds of playing-seating relationships.

Grotowski often alters the size and shape of his theater, sometimes mingling spectator and actor. Artaud, who as we have seen rejected everything about conventional drama, had some very specific ideas about a new kind of theatrical construction:

> The Stage—The Auditorium: We abolish the stage and the auditorium and replace them by a single site, without partition or barrier of any kind, which will become the theater of action. A direct communication will be reestablished between the spectator and the spectacle, between the actor and the spectator, from the fact that the spectator, placed in the middle of the action, is engulfed and physically affected by it. This envelopment results, in part, from the very configuration of the room itself.
>
> Thus, abandoning the architecture of present-day theaters, we shall

take some hangar or barn, which we shall have reconstructed according to processes which have culminated in the architecture of certain churches or holy places, and of certain temples in Tibet.

In the interior of this construction special proportions of height and depth will prevail. The hall will be enclosed by four walls, without any kind of ornament, and the public will be seated in the middle of the room, on the ground floor, on mobile chairs which will allow them to follow the spectacle which will take place all around them. In effect, the absence of a stage in the usual sense of the word will provide for the deployment of the action in the four corners of the room. Particular positions will be reserved for actors and action at the four cardinal points of the room. The scenes will be played in front of whitewashed, wall-backgrounds designed to absorb the light. In addition, galleries overhead will run around the periphery of the hall as in certain primitive paintings. These galleries will permit the actors, whenever the action makes it necessary, to be pursued from one point in the room to another, and the action to be deployed on all levels and in all perspectives of height and depth. A cry uttered at one end of the room can be transmitted from mouth to mouth with amplifications and successive modulations all the way to the other. The action will unfold, will extend its trajectory from level to level, point to point, paroxysms will suddenly burst forth, will flare up like fires in different spots. And to speak of the spectacle's character as true illusion or of the direct and immediate influence of the action on the spectator will not be hollow words. For this diffusion of action over an immense space will oblige the lighting of a scene and the varied lighting of a performance to fall upon the public as much as upon the actors—and to the several simultaneous actions or several phases of an identical action in which the characters, swarming over each other like bees, will endure all the onslaughts of the situations and the external assaults of the tempestuous elements, will correspond the physical means of lighting, of producing thunder or wind, whose repercussions the spectator will undergo.

However, a central position will be reserved which, without serving, properly speaking, as a stage, will permit the bulk of the action to be concentrated and brought to a climax whenever necessary.[1]

Artaud's view of architecture is worth quoting at length because many of his ideas are now being tried out. His view of the communal function of drama has found a response and theaters and performance halls are being planned that will provide for simultaneous playing in several areas at once, with the actors performing on all sides of the spectators and in their midst, and new uses of light and sound will be developed until the theater is no longer considered a building, but an example of kinetic sculpture.

1. Antonin Artaud, *The Theater and Its Double*, trans. Mary Caroline Richards (New York: Grove Press, 1958).

The impulse toward a freer, more flexible stage may lead to the rejection of illusionistic scenery in favor of the fashioning of a dramatic environment through the use of projected images and moveable units of platforms, stairways, ramps, and decorative forms which can be controlled electronically to make endless combinations.

What this all means, only time will tell, but we can hazard the guess that the real problems of the theater will not be solved by technical progress or architectural designs that join actor and spectator. Ultimately what keeps them apart or brings them together is the richness of their imaginations caught up in the action of the play.

exercises

1. How does the size of the theater affect play production?
2. Contrast the staging of plays in the Theater of Dionysus with that of the Globe.
3. What is the effect of the proscenium arch on dramatic structure?
4. What are the problems of producing an Elizabethan play in the modern theater? Of producing a Greek play?
5. Evaluate arena or center staging. What are its advantages and disadvantages? What kinds of plays would be most effective in an arena production?
6. Visit an auditorium or theater and evaluate its facilities for dramatic production.
7. What are the theatrical values of the thrust stage?
8. Following Artaud's suggestion, design a theater showing the areas for the actors and the audience.
9. Lay out a ground plan in which you convert a large room into an arena stage.
10. What are the trends of contemporary theater architecture?
11. How does the physical proximity of the actor to the spectator influence the production?
12. What are the difficulties of performing without a stage?

suggested reading

George Altman, Ralph Freud, Kenneth Macgowan, and William Melnitz, *Theatre Pictorial*, 1953.

Bernard Beckerman, *Shakespeare at the Globe, 1599-1609*, 1962.

Margaret Bieber, *The History of the Greek and Roman Theater*, 1961.

Oscar G. Brockett, *History of the Theatre*, 1968.

Harold Burris-Meyer and Edward C. Cole, *Theatres and Auditoriums,* 1949.
Bamber Cascoigne, *World Theatre: An Illustrated History,* 1968.
Barnard Hewitt, ed., *The Renaissance Stage,* 1958.
George Kernodle, *From Art to Theatre: Form and Convention in the Renaissance,* 1943.
Kenneth Macgowan and William Melnitz, *The Living Stage,* 1955.
James Hull Miller, *Small Auditoriums with Open Stages,* 1968.
Allardyce Nicoll, *The Development of the Theatre,* 5th ed., 1966.
———, *Masks, Mimes and Miracles,* 1931.

the audience

importance of the audience

The theater exists for the sake of the audience. It is for the spectator that the playhouse is erected, the drama written, the players rehearsed, the sets designed, and the performance given. It is the theatergoer's response that determines the fate of the play. As Giraudoux suggests, a new drama is like a piece of unfired pottery. Its true colors are not known until it has been exposed to the heat.

While the physical theater affects the way in which the playwright's play can be staged, it is the audience that dictates what kind of story he can tell. As Samuel Johnson observed:

> The drama's laws the patrons give,
> And we who live to please, must please to live.

Drama is a social and dynamic art that depends for its effect on the collaboration of playwright, performer, and spectator. Drama must be experienced as a group response to living actors. It is not like a painting, a poem, or a piece of architecture, which may be enjoyed in solitary contemplation and by gradual familiarity. The dramatic experience, like life itself, is evanescent, changing from moment to moment.

Most playwrights are like journalists who write for immediate con-

sumption; the obvious way of measuring a play's success is at the box-office. This in turn means that the playwright must write in such a way as to elicit a ready response from a sufficient number of patrons to pay the bills and ultimately show a profit. (In these days of astronomical costs for a Broadway production, this may mean playing to packed houses for at least four months.) In an effort to attract a large audience, the playwright feels the pressure to make his work as entertaining as possible, with the result that much of our drama offers little intellectual nourishment and slight meaning. The extreme effect of the compulsion to amuse a wide audience is seen in most of our motion pictures and television programs. Often, the appeals and techniques employed are obvious and hackneyed, the material is standardized into endlessly repeated formulas, and controversial and significant subjects are shunned. The writer constantly is obliged to keep foremost in his mind the need for showmanship that will attract everybody and offend no one. Gilbert Seldes, who has made a particular study of the audiences of our mass media, said:

> The concept of the audience as boobs is satisfying to hucksters and highbrows. It is not accurate, nor is it permanently acceptable to democrats. We might as well remember that the great frauds in medicine, the most appalling superstitions about witches, the wildest social and economic panaceas, and the foulest delusions about the nature of man were all accepted by the learned and well-bred long before they reached the "common people."[1]

Seldes goes on to make a plea to those concerned with mass media to raise their sights, and to present popular fare that will have a more meaningful content.

In the past generation we have developed an increasingly mature and discriminating following in the legitimate theater so that the contemporary playwright is able to appeal to a substantial audience by writing plays which have more than momentary interest. It should be remembered that many great masters of drama transcended the problems of audience appeal. Sophocles, Shakespeare, Molière, Sheridan, Lessing, Schiller, Jonson—these playwrights satisfied popular taste while creating outstanding landmarks of dramatic literature. But popularity itself is no criterion of lasting value because many plays of enormous commercial success are completely devoid of literary merit. Examples from the contemporary theater support this point. The list of long-run hits on Broadway shows thirty-four productions that have run over one thousand performances. Of these, eighteen were musicals, nine were farces, but not one serious, major playwright of any country is represented. This is

1. Gilbert Seldes, *The Public Arts* (New York: Simon and Schuster, 1956).

in sharp contrast to the long runs off-Broadway in which the top twenty plays include two Genêts, two Millers, and single works of Euripides, Brecht, Gelber, Pinter, Behan, Beckett, and Pirandello.

Many novelists who have aspired to be playwrights have failed in their attempts because they ignored, or did not grasp the importance of the necessity of winning an audience response. Only the writer who chooses to limit himself to a small and select hearing may neglect the needs of the theater audience. Writers whose convictions deviate too markedly from the norm, or whose symbols are too confusing, or who have too obvious an axe to grind, may succeed on the printed page, but they will not find the stage a hospitable haven for their plays. Pioneers of contemporary drama faced considerable difficulty in the initial public reaction to their plays as, for example, the cool or hostile receptions given to Chekhov's *The Sea Gull,* Ibsen's *Ghosts,* Hauptmann's *Before Sunrise,* Shaw's *Mrs. Warren's Profession,* and Herne's *Margaret Fleming.* The point needs to be made that there are many plays that can never hope to attract a popular audience because of their subject matter or their abstruse nature. Nevertheless, it is generally true that the dramatist must be aware of the needs of his audience so that he can engage them in a meaningful and interesting communion.

the nature of attention

To create a play and a performance that will evoke an appropriate response, it is essential for the playwright and the theater-worker to know something about the nature of attention. Attention comes in short spurts. Concentration requires constant renewal, because it is impossible for us to fix our attention on a single object and hold it there as we might a spotlight. Ordinarily, a theater audience comes with the expectation of giving its attention freely to the play, but if the drama is dull and the performance monotonous, if attention is not captured and sustained, the spectator makes his escape into a world of his own imagining.

There are two kinds of attention—voluntary and involuntary. Voluntary attention implies that the spectator looks and listens by an act of the will. He makes an effort to pay attention. Involuntary attention, on the other hand, requires no conscious effort; it results from responding to stimuli—we hear a scream in the night, a fascinating story, or our name spoken aloud by another. The theater-worker is interested in securing our involuntary attention. He employs such devices as bright lights and colors, movement, emotional stimulation, the use of space and elevations, sound, and visual focus. The director combats monotony by varying the groupings of his characters, by a change of pace, by making sure that actors do not imitate one another's pitch patterns, by inventing business and action—in a word, by every possible way of renewing attention. He aims to control and direct every instant of our attention throughout the course of the play. This is one of the director's most difficult tasks, since the play, by its very nature, is a stream of complex visual and auditory stimuli; attention constantly flits from one character to another and back again. The motion-picture director has far greater control of the spectator's attention because of his ability to focus the camera on one object, one person, one face at a time, eliminating all extraneous elements, and by the opportunity to edit a film after it has been shot and to order retakes if he thinks it desirable. But the stage director must find other means of achieving much the same effect.

A part of his problem in controlling attention is to avoid the distractions that plague a theatrical performance, such as late arrivals, program rustling, foot shuffling, coughs and wheezes, and the vicissitudes of production that may occur onstage—missed cues, a long wait, a poor costume, obvious make-up, scenery that shakes when the door is slammed, a crooked picture, light-reflecting surfaces. Some aspects of the production itself may destroy the audience's concentation, such as an unexpected novelty that arouses surprise and comment in the audience, scene shifts that take too long or involve too much noise, special spectacular effects, or an unexpected laugh. In a well-managed theater, every effort is made to focus and control the audience's interest so that their voluntary attention becomes involuntary as they become thoroughly engrossed in the action and the play.

the audience as a crowd

Although an audience comes together as individuals, the theater is a group effort. Through mutual stimulation in the release of emotions, the group may become a crowd. This has important psychological implications, because as individuals merge themselves into a crowd, marked changes take place. The individual loses his identity, becoming more susceptible to emotional appeals and more easily swayed than the single person in isolation. He relaxes his discrimination so that he becomes more gullible. The social psychologist Emory Bogardus states: "A heightened state of suggestibility is characteristic of a crowd. The preponderance of feelings over reason heightens suggestibility. The excitement that frequently prevails in a crowd throws persons off their guard. The force of numbers is overwhelming."

Thus, a theater audience loses some of its sense of personal responsibility. There is a temporary release from restraint with the result that, in a crowd, people may respond to stimuli that would leave them untouched as isolated individuals. For example, they may laugh in the theater at salacious humor they would consider vulgar in their own living-room. In the crowd situation, there is always the threat that the lowest common denominator will prevail. There is the pressure to conform, the contagion to join in. These psychological phenomena of audience behavior are at least a partial explanation of how the effectiveness of a play may be enhanced by a responsive audience, which willingly suspends its disbelief and succumbs to the emotions of the play.

types of audiences

Anyone experienced in theatrical production can testify to the fact that audiences vary from performance to performance. A Saturday night crowd will almost invariably outlaugh a Monday night one. A matinee audience with a preponderance of women shoppers reacts quite differently from one dominated by visiting businessmen. Audiences likewise differ from place to place. A performer meets a different reception in Las Vegas than he does in Boston. University campus theatergoers are in marked contrast to those in a community theater. A person may find his own response to a play varying according to the stimulation he receives from other spectators, the way he feels, the temperature of the auditorium, and the location of his seat. He will also notice that his reaction to a motion picture in a crowded theater is not the same as viewing a film in the seclusion of his own home.

Different kinds of plays attract different kinds of audiences. Compare an audience that attends an opera with that of a musical comedy, or note the difference between the spectators attending a farce and a tragedy. A striking example of audience variation may be seen in Japan where the archaic, restrained Noh drama is met with dignified, nearly reverent attention, while the popular Kabuki audience may give the performance a noisy and enthusiastic demonstration.

As a social institution, the theater has at times served as a tribunal, a propaganda agency, a house of the devil, a temple of worship, a meeting place for disreputable characters, a showcase for ostentatious display, and a place for intellectual stimulation. Its status and function has depended on the audience that patronized it. Consider, for example, three representative audiences.

the greek audience

The theater of Greece was a religious institution, which every free male attended as a public and sacred duty at the two main festivals in midwinter and early spring. The City of Dionysia, which offered competition in tragedies, was a profoundly serious occasion. The audience did not come to be amused or titillated. They came to share in the great searching problems of mankind—problems which elevated the human spirit through suffering.

The Athenian audience was a remarkable one because of their great zest for living and thinking. Art, literature, philosophy, and logic were not mere subjects of contemplation for them. They were active, inquiring men with an unquenchable thirst for learning. Their interests and tastes ranged widely, so that their infrequent dramatic productions could accommodate the tragic grandeur of Aeschylus and the comic irreverence of Aristophanes, whose uninhibited shafts of unsparing ridicule are a commentary on the amazing tolerance of Greek society.

The Greeks were a knowledgeable audience, steeped in their literary heritage, with keen ears for the rhythm and texture of language, and so thoroughly familiar with the plays of their time that they could identify specific passages of Euripidean and Aeschylean dialogue in Aristophanes' comedy, *The Frogs*. Such an audience invited dramas of great ideas and magnificent language. The religious base of the ritual challenged the playwrights to create elevated works involving profound and lofty content. The culture that produced the idea of the golden mean—moderation in all things—led to a drama that was clear and logically organized, free from the excesses of pathos and sentiment. Their search for truth in life resulted in drama that was unflinchingly and relentlessly honest in confronting evil, suffering, and catastrophe. Their intellectual tolerance and sense of balance enabled them to see the sense and nonsense of the Aristophanic satire that scathingly attacked the follies of the time. The Athenian of the fifth century B.C. was an astonishingly civilized man, and his level of culture is nowhere reflected so admirably as in the dramas that were created for his pleasure and edification.

the elizabethan audience

Like the Greeks, the Elizabethans had an enormous enthusiasm for life. Shakespeare's time was one of remarkable intellectual ferment, with great interest in language, literature, music, and politics. The Elizabethan looked on man as a creature of great potential. The spirit of the times was positive, dynamic, tumultuous.

The theater reflected the climate of the age. It was a professional theater to which more than thirty thousand customers a week flocked to see half a dozen competing companies in London offer the richest concentration of dramatic fare that the world has ever known. The theater

173 The audience participates in the action during the "Old Price" Riots at the Covent Garden Theatre, London, 1763. Note the deep apron stage and the proscenium doors and boxes.

174 (opposite, top) *Literary Controversy in the Gallery,* by Daumier.

175 (opposite, bottom) *A Colossal Success,* by Daumier.

176 *The Constant Prince* at the Polish Laboratory Theater, directed by Jerzy Grotowski, setting by Jerzy Gurawski. The playing area is surrounded by a fence over which the spectators view the performance.

177 View of the action for *Kordian,* text by Slowacki. The whole room suggests the interior of a mental hospital, with the spectators incorporated into this structure as patients.

178 Arrangement for Grotowski's production of A. Mickiewicz's *Forefather's Eve.* showing the spectators (in white) integrated into the action.

179 Integration of actors and audience in Brecht's *Baal*, directed by Georgij Paro, University of California, Santa Barbara.

180 The guerrilla theater takes a performance to the people.

appealed to the public's taste for pageantry and action, which elsewhere manifested itself in masques, processionals, and bear-baiting. The plays capitalized on the audience's interest in language, and the Elizabethan playwright enthusiastically followed the practice of medieval drama in putting as much vigorous and vivid action on stage as possible. Such a combination of words and action enlarged the appeal of drama so that all the motley audience could find something to suit their pleasure in the play. For the groundlings, there was exciting and violent action. For the discriminating, there was delight in the magnificent language and food for thought in the elevated ideas. The Elizabethan audience's interests and tastes covered a wide range, and for it the playwright wrote both serious and comic dramas, which were full-bodied, exuberant images of a turbulent and heady age.

the restoration audience

The Restoration audience offers a sharp contrast to the Elizabethan. When Charles II returned to the throne, the theater became the preoccupation of the court. The audience was made up of fashionable wits, fops, beaux, parasites, and women of easy virtue. So limited was the audience that only two theaters were active in London, despite the fact that the population had doubled since Elizabethan times. For twelve years one theater was sufficient to accommodate this narrow following.

The Restoration theatergoer did not take drama seriously. It was a plaything for fashionable people. Such patronage resulted in drama that was artificial and deliberately unconcerned with the stern realities of life. When the Restoration playwright attempted to write serious heroic dramas, the result was exaggerated and false pseudoclassic plays "full of sound and fury, signifying nothing." The special achievement of the period was high comedy, which dealt with the foibles of social conduct rather than ethics. Puritan morality was satirized. Comedies dealt with the complications of intrigue and defects of manners. Craftsmanship was careless, the content coarse, the atmosphere vulgar beneath a shiny surface, but the level of the playwrights' subject matter was rescued from oblivion by their brilliant use of language. They achieved a high polish in their repartee and their eloquence of style. The limited audience made it possible for the playwright to capitalize on personal invective and local and timely allusions. Thus, Restoration comedy is a particularly explicit example of the effect of an audience on the drama.

Perhaps these three historical examples are enough to make the point that people come to the theater for a variety of purposes, and that they constitute a vital force on the writing and production of plays.

the modern audience

Today's audience is a function of the status of the theater as a social institution. In Europe, professional dramatic production is widespread, since nearly every city has a permanent residential company which makes drama available on a continuous basis. These theaters, usually supported in part by the state, offer a repertory of both classical and new plays. Thus there is a permanent audience, sophisticated in the ways of the theater, which enables the producing group to work out a varied and continuous program of plays with some sense of security, not directly related to immediate box-office appeal.

In this country we have no permanent tradition of the theater, no national institution, and no American classical repertoire, but we have had a long background of professional production and theater attendance, especially before the coming of film. The development of television following World War II had a pronounced effect on both film and live theater. The film has been forced to seek for new ways to attract an audience. The availability of so much free entertainment came at a time of rising costs in production and higher ticket prices. One of the reactions to this was to expand the off-Broadway theater where costs could be cut and experiments made with new plays and different kinds of theater. By the mid-fifties nearly a hundred such theaters were in operation in out-of-the-way auditoriums, churches, and halls. But they soon became "farm clubs" for the main theaters, which picked off the most promising new talent and opened their doors to the experiments that had proved most appealing. The next development was the off-off-Broadway theater, which began in coffeehouses, cafes, and clubs and offered an opportunity for scores of new playwrights to show their works with minimal production facilities to audiences that had little or no contact with the main commercial attractions. From these experimental groups have come some of our freshest ideas and most promising talent: Jean-Claude van Itallie, Jack Gelber, Sam Shepard, Megan Terry, and Joseph Chaikin.

Meanwhile the regional theater has been a potent force with more than three dozen permanent companies, mostly repertory groups, in major cities like Los Angeles, Minneapolis, Houston, Washington, Dallas, and Seattle. They are not only developing their own audiences and corps of production talent, but occasionally staging new plays that find their way to Broadway. In addition, the college and university theaters, community and children's theaters are developing audiences for the future. Outside of the theater itself, performers are finding and creating their own audiences in such ventures as the Bread and Puppet Theater, guerilla theaters, and mime troupes performing in the streets, at shopping centers, rallies, parades and demonstrations, taking theater back to the people.

In recent times a good deal of thought has been directed toward the problem of building new theater audiences, especially among the young. Regional theaters have brought young audiences to their productions or taken them on tour to schools and colleges, and educational theaters at all levels are involving large numbers of students on both sides of the footlights. But thus far, the live theater has not connected with the young in the same way as music or the film. The door of the theater is wide open to new forms from that will include us all.

The rebellion in the theater is aimed at the audience. Through architecture, playwriting, and production the spectator is invited to join the action. Once upon a time he took a seat in the theater, settled back in the darkness, and drifted off to a make-believe world released from his mundane cares. Now he becomes an alert and sometimes active part of the theatrical environment. In such plays as *The Blacks* and *Marat/Sade* and some productions of Grotowski's Polish Laboratory, he assumes a role in the performance. Many playwrights now stipulate that some of their lines be addressed directly to the spectator, as in *The Great White Hope* and *We Bombed in New Haven.* In *The Connection,* members of the cast, in character, drifted through the audience asking for hand-outs during intermission. Ex-addicts in *The Concept* concluded the play by moving among the spectators and pleading with them, "Please love me." Audiences are sometimes invited to participate in the action, to dance, to come onstage, to ask questions, to argue, or to sit in silence after the final curtain. They are teased, touched, fondled, insulted, whispered to, and irritated. The new theater often attempts to break down the stereotyped actor-audience relationship through direct communication, physical participation, and various shock techniques. Experimental production seeks a new immediacy, intensity, and exuberance in an attempt to reach all levels of consciousness. New weapons have been added to the theatrical arsenal: uninhibited action, nudity, freedom of speech, dazzling effects with light and color, and overpowering music.

All current experiments in the theater are rooted in a single purpose —to widen the range of audience response. The rebellion is away from a narrow concept of drama as diversion and directed toward making theater a voice of protest, a means of enlightenment, a place of wonder, celebration, and release.

No one spent more effort analyzing and cultivating the appropriate response to his plays than Brecht. He contrasts the audience for conventional drama with the audience he sought for his theater:

> *The audience in the dramatic theater says:* Yes, I have felt that way too. —That's how I am.—That is only natural.—That will always be so.—

This person's suffering shocks me because he has no way out. This is great art: everything in it is self-evident.—I weep with the weeping, I laugh with the laughing.

The audience in the epic theater says: I wouldn't have thought that.—People shouldn't do things like that.—That's extremely odd, almost unbelievable.—This has to stop.—This person's suffering shocks me, because there might be a way out for him.—This is great art: nothing in it is self-evident.—I laugh over the weeping, and I weep over the laughing.[2]

Artaud, on the other hand, seeks the complete absorption of the audience:

It is a question then of making the theater, in the proper sense of the word, a function; something as localized and as precise as the circulation of the blood in the arteries or the apparently chaotic development of dream images in the brain, and this is to be accomplished through involvement, a genuine enslavement of the attention.[3]

Grotowski, like Artaud, seeks a special kind of involvement:

We do not cater to the man who goes to the theater to satisfy a social need for contact with culture: in other words, to have something to talk about to his friends and be able to say that he has seen this or that play and that it was interesting. We are concerned with the spectator who has genuine spiritual needs and who really wishes, through confrontation with the performance, to analyze himself . . . toward a search for the truth about himself and his mission in life.[4]

It is clear from these statements that no one kind of theater will meet the needs expressed by these leaders. They agree only on a seriousness of purpose in the uses of the theater to achieve their effects—which brings us back to Aristotle's observation that the effect is determined by the action presented.

Obviously we are in for a period of extended experimentation as efforts are made to find dramatic content that has meaning in our astonishing and often bewildering world. Whatever forms and functions the theater of the future assumes, we are fairly sure that somehow it must kindle a fire through imitations of men in action that will give us pleasure by sharpening our perceptions and enlarging our vision.

2. Bertolt Brecht, "Theater for Learning or Theater for Pleasure," trans. Edith Anderson, *Mainstream*, 11 (June, 1958).

3. Antonin Artaud, *The Theater and Its Double* (New York: Grove Press, 1958).

4. Jerzy Grotowski, quoted in *Time* (Oct. 29, 1969).

exercises

1. How does the audience affect play production?
2. Compare your reactions to a comedy on television and one in the theater.
3. Using the class as an audience, experiment with several kinds of stimuli simultaneously. Evaluate the effects.
4. Try several different ways of communicating information, such as speech, slides, and action. Which is the most effective?
5. Describe some techniques for controlling audience reaction.
6. Using the class as an audience, experiment with ways of creating the atmosphere for farce, tragedy, rebellion, etc.
7. After attending a play or film, make an analysis of the audience.
8. What limitations does the audience impose on play production?
9. Describe some means for holding the audience's attention.
10. What are the characteristics of a crowd?
11. What is the nature of attention?
12. Compare several kinds of audiences, such as those for serious music, a jazz concert, and a public lecture.
13. What are some ways of controlling an audience's response in the theater?

suggested reading

Herbert Blau, *The Impossible Theater: A Manifesto,* 1964.
J. M. Brown, *The Art of Playgoing,* 1936.
Stuart Hall and Paddy Whannel, *The Popular Arts,* 1964.
Barnard Hewitt, *Theatre, U.S.A., 1668–1957,* 1959.
H. L. Hollingworth, *The Psychology of the Audience,* 1935.
Marshall McLuhan, *Understanding Media,* 1964.
George Jean Nathan, *The World of George Jean Nathan,* 1952.
Allardyce Nicoll, *British Drama,* 1947.
Susan Sontag, *Against Interpretation,* 1965.

appendix the film

The motion picture is a form of art that has analogies to narrative literature, drama, and painting. Like fiction, film because of its remarkable flexibility has been used for narrative purposes. Since it generally uses characters in action who express themselves in dialogue, it has certain common ground with drama. And because it is a visual medium, film is allied to painting. But the motion picture has special qualities of its own that make it a distinct art form.

special qualities of film

Film differs from the written narrative in conveying all its impressions by images and sounds rather than in words on a page. Film differs from the stage in its freedom of action and its varied means of making perceptions. Since fiction and drama are conceived of initially in words, they have an inherent tendency to follow a logical sequence like the order of words in a sentence and the progression of ideas from paragraph to paragraph. Film, on the other hand, is created in terms of moving images, which in life are often apt to come to us in a random fashion or in odd clusters quite free from an inner logic. Film is similar to painting in that both are visual imitations, but painting in modern times has moved away from the representation of objective reality that the film by the very nature of its tools employs, faithfully recording what is set before the camera. While the painter may escape into a subjective world of his own imagination, the filmmaker often attempts to break away from photographed reality by distortion of images and sounds, by changing normal sizes, shapes, speeds, and rhythms, by imaginative points of view, and by creative arrangement of the flow of images. In any case, the artist's idea exists in his use of the medium itself and it can be perceived through an understanding of the potentials and limitations of that medium.

Let us consider some of the characteristics of the film by looking at the opening sequence of Laurence Olivier's motion picture script of *Henry V.*[1] Shakespeare's play, written in 1599, reflected the English spirit of the celebrated King whose career from prodigal prince to conqueror of France made him a legendary idol to the Elizabethans. It was appropriate then that Olivier should turn to this play as the vehicle for a patriotic gesture toward the end of World War II. The original play—nearly cinematic in its vigorous sweep of action and its strong narrative thread—must have taxed the facilities of Shakespeare's Globe to the utmost, and its epic quality made it particularly well suited for a film. (The abbreviations refer to the lengths of shots, the distance of the camera from the subject: L.S.—long shot; M.S.—medium shot; C.U.—close-up; M.L.S.—medium long shot.)

FADE IN: -- CENSOR TITLE.

FADE OUT:

FADE IN: -- EAGLE LION PRESENTS

BELLS

DISSOLVE TO:

A TWO CITIES FILM
In Technicolour

Made at D. & P. Studios

Recorded on
Western Electric
Mirrophonic
Sound system.

Colour Director Natalie Kalmus

Associate Joan Bridge.

FADE OUT.
BELLS STOP.

FADE IN.

To the Commandoes and Airborne Troops of
Great Britain.

The spirit of whose ancestors it has been humbly attempted to recapture in some ensuing scenes this film is dedicated.

FADE OUT.

1. The passages from Olivier's script below and on pages 307–308 are photo-reproduced from George P. Garrett, O. B. Hardison, Jr., and Jane R. Gelfman, eds., *Film Scripts One* (New York: Appleton-Century-Crofts, 1971).

FADE IN -- TITLE   MUSIC STARTS.

A LAURENCE OLIVIER PRODUCTION.

DISSOLVE TO:

TITLE 2.

A paper bill fluttering towards camera out of the sky. It hits the camera and reads: --

The Chronicle History of

KING HENRY THE FIFTH

with his battle fought at Agincourt in France

by

Will Shakespeare

will be played by

The Lord Chamberlain's Men

at the

GLOBE PLAYHOUSE

THIS DAY THE FIRST OF MAY 1600.

DISSOLVE TO:

L.S. Aerial View of London in 1600. CAMERA TRACKS BACK to reveal the City in extreme L.S. then TRACKS in to centre first the Bear Playhouse and then the Globe Playhouse. A flag is being hoisted up the Standard of this Playhouse.

C.S. The Globe Playhouse Flag unfurling and fluttering.

MUSIC STOPS.

M.C.S. Man in Globe Playhouse on small platform at foot of flagpole. He tightens the flag rope and makes it secure. He blows two fanfares. CAMERA TRACKS DOWN TO Orchestra Gallery below him.

ORCHESTRA STARTS TO PLAY.

CAMERA PANS LEFT to show people filling the top gallery of theatre. CAMERA continues panning round and down to the second gallery. A girl drops a handkerchief out of picture.

M.L.S. THE THIRD GALLERY. A man catches the handkerchief. CAMERA PANS LEFT to the ground floor entrance where the people are coming in. An orange Seller steps down into the theatre.

M.S. The Orange Girl walking into the Theatre offering her wares, CAMERA PANS LEFT with her and TRACKS SLOWLY BACK to reveal the auditorium in L.S. with the stage in background. A prompter gives a signal to the Orchestra to play a fanfare.

MUSIC STOPS.

M.L.S. Low angle shot the Orchestra Gallery. Man blows a FANFARE.

L.S. AUDITORIUM WITH STAGE IN B.G. A boy comes through the curtains on to the stage and holds a board up to the audience.

M.C.S. SIDE ANGLE OF THE BOY. He swings the board to camera on which is written --

The Chronicle History of
HENRY THE FIFTH
with his battle fought at Agin Court.

L. HIGH ANGLE SHOT FROM THE TOP GALLERY. Audience in f.g. The boy on the stage swings the board and exits through the curtains. Chorus enters and bows. Audience applauds.

CHORUS: O for a Muse of fire

M.C.S. Chorus.

That would ascend
The brightest heaven of invention:

He walks R. CAMERA PANS with him.

A kingdom for a stage, princes to act,
And monarchs to behold the swelling scene!

He walks L. CAMERA PANS with him.

Then should the warlike Harry, like himself,
Assume the port of Mars, and at his heels
Leash'd in like hounds, should famine, sword and fire,
Crouch for employment.

He walks R. to the centre of the stage CAMERA PANS with him.

But pardon, gentles all,
The flat unraised spirits, that hath dared,
On this unworthy scaffold to bring forth
So great an object.
Can this cockpit hold
The vasty fields of France? or may we cram
Within this wooden O the very casques
That did affright the air at Agincourt?

He walks to camera speaking directly to it in C.U.

On your imaginary forces work.

MUSIC STARTS.

CAMERA TRACKS BACK.

Suppose within the girdle of these walls
Are now confin'd two mighty monarchies
Whose high, upreared, and abutting fronts
The perilous narrow ocean parts asunder.
Piece out our imperfections with your thoughts;
Think, when we talk of horses, that you see them,
Printing their proud hoofs i' the receiving earth
For 'tis your thoughts that now must deck our kings,

CAMERA TRACKS BACK TO leave Chorus and Stage In M.L.S.

Carry them here and there; jumping o'er times;
Turning the accomplishment of many years
Into an hour-glass:

MUSIC STOPS

for the which supply
Admit me Chorus to this history:
Who, prologue-like, your humble patience pray,
Gently to hear, kindly to judge our play.

He bows and pulls the Stage Curtain aside.

The first thing that strikes us is the remarkable flexibility of film. Within this short opening we see a dozen different shots, ranging from a long shot of the city of London to a close-up of a handbill. We see the audience at all three levels of the building as well as in the orchestra. Seven individuals, a flag, a handkerchief, and a title board are singled out for attention. We also notice that film relies heavily on motion. Instead of seeing the action from a fixed point of view as a theatergoer did in Shakespeare's playhouse, the film spectator through the camera is constantly changing positions and angles, tracking and panning to pick out the relevant people and properties. Not only is the camera itself in constant motion in this opening scene, but it is photographing motion—the movements of the man at the flagpole, the orange seller, the prompter, the boy with the board, and so on. Film is a form of expression in visual images presented in motion.

Another observation we may make from the *Henry V* script is the enormous ability of film to provide information quickly and interestingly. Within a few seconds we know that we are in London in 1600, in the Globe Playhouse, just before the opening of Shakespeare's play. And the screen is alive with a variety of assorted images giving us a feeling of the period and the lively, expectant atmosphere in the theater just as the play is about to begin. Despite the fact that we see a varied collection of shots—long, medium, and close-up—from constantly shifting points of view, we have no difficulty in piecing these together in our heads to form a composite view. Film has the special ability to concentrate our attention on images in a telling way.

Another aspect of film, allied to the observations we have already made, is the expressive potential inherent in the editing process. After the film footage is shot, the editor has the task of selecting and assembling the images in the most effective way. He determines which images will be used, the order of their showing, the relationship between shots and their duration on the screen. In the opening of *Henry V*, notice how the images are arranged from the general view of the city to a view of the Globe, then the audience, then the individuals, and finally the speaker. The sequence of images is governed by the effect the director and editor wished to create in beginning the action and providing the appropriate atmosphere. Note, too, the connections the spectator makes for himself in "reading" the sequence of images. We see a girl drop a handkerchief in one shot, and in a following one we see a man catch it—and we tie the actions together mentally. Once the locale of the theater is established by long and medium shots, we associate individuals picked out in close shots with the theater even when we see them without the surroundings. Film has the ability to create in our minds its own sort of continuity.

As *Henry V* develops, another striking aspect of filmmaking is impressed upon us. We are aware of its great potential for moving the action from place to place in such varied locales as the French Palace, the stern of a ship, an inn, a battlefield, and a bivouac—all shown with convincing reality—a sharp contrast to the stage with its small platform and its billboards. Film's ability to place the action in authentic locales gives it a reality denied to the stage play. Moreover, film has great resources for showing kinds of action impossible in the theater, such as the magnificent battle scenes in *Henry V* with hundreds of men and horses and the remarkable shots of the archers.

The film of *Henry V* opens with vivid, dynamic action; Shakespeare's play begins as most plays do—with speech; the film is primarily addressed to the eye and the play primarily to the ear. Thus films and stage plays are two entirely different forms of the theater. Each has its own particular advantages and disadvantages that must be kept in mind when judging works in the two media. The fluency of the film makes it an ideal medium for narrative and educational material, while the stage excels in its ability to reveal character in compressed situations and to evoke a circular response between the performers and spectators because of their living communion in the theater.

the camera

The primary tool of the filmmaker is the camera. While it is sometimes compared to the eye, there are certain significant differences. We see with two eyes and the separation between them aids us in depth perception. Most films have been shot with a single lens, resulting in screen images that often appear flat; advancing and retreating movement is distorted and confusing. Many camera lenses have a fixed point of view so that they do not adjust instantaneously with the amazing mobility and subtlety of the human eye. Furthermore, the eye has an angle of vision of nearly 120 degrees, while most motion pictures are restricted to half that width. The most important distinction between the human eye and the camera is that of selectivity. What images will be recorded on film is a human judgment that must be made by the cameraman and the director. The camera has no powers of discrimination, it merely photographs what is set before it. But our eyes are responsive to our wills; we instantaneously select the images we choose to see. Nevertheless, the camera is a remarkably flexible instrument.

Sound film is made up of a series of photographic images on a film usually 35mm or 16mm wide. The images are photographed and projected at the rate of twenty-four per second. The retina of the human eye retains the image a fraction of a second after the picture has disappeared, thus causing a phenomenon called the "persistence of vision," by means of which the images are seemingly linked together in continuous motion. You may be interested to know that when you view a motion picture, you are actually sitting in complete darkness half the time. In the early motion pictures when there were fewer separate pictures per second, the result was a flicker effect: the images were not quite rapid enough to blend the film together. A standard reel of 35mm film is 1000 feet long; a standard reel of 16mm film is 400 feet long. A reel runs approximately ten minutes.

Individual pictures are called "frames"; one complete image is known as a "shot." A full-length film may be made up of hundreds of separate shots, each of which has been photographed separately. The editor combines them into the segments of the narrative called "sequences," which are longer units like chapters in a book. Shots may be of a few seconds' duration, such as those of several horror-stricken faces of individuals witnessing a terrible accident. Or some shots may be of considerable duration—a leisurely view of a canoe gliding across placid waters, approaching the camera. The length of the shot is appropriate to the effect desired. The process of motion picture-making is a cumulative one—of photographing and splicing fragmentary shots of people and objects in the most expressive way possible. A revealing example of this process is Pudovkin's description of an imaginary film sequence of a man cutting grain with a scythe. His outline of the hypothetical action illustrates the manner in which the cinema artist selects and composes his shots:

I tried in my mind's eye to shoot and construct the mowing of the grass approximately as follows:

1. A man stands bared to the waist. In his hands is a scythe. Pause. He swings the scythe. (The whole movement goes in normal speed.)

2. The sweep of the scythe continues. The man's back and shoulders. Slowly the muscles play and grow tense. (Recorded very fast with a "slow-motion" apparatus, so that the movement on the screen comes out unusually slow.)

3. The blade of the scythe slowly turning at the culmination of its sweep. A gleam of the sun flares up and dies out. (Shot in "slow motion.")

4. The blade flies downward. (Normal speed.)

5. The whole figure of the man brings back the scythe over the grass at normal speed. A sweep—back. A sweep—back. A sweep—back. A sweep . . . And at the moment when the blade of the scythe touches the grass—

6. —slowly (in "slow motion") the cut grass sways, topples, bending and scattering glittering drops.

7. Slowly the muscles of the back relax and the shoulders withdraw.

8. Again the grass slowly topples, lies flat.

9. The scythe-blade swiftly lifting from the earth.

10. Similarly swift, the man sweeping with the scythe. He mows, he sweeps.

11. At normal speed, a number of men mowing, sweeping their scythes in unison.

12. Slowly raising his scythe a man moves off through the dusk.

This is a very approximate sketch. After actual shooting, I edited it differently—more complexly, using shots taken at various speeds. Within each separate set-up were new, more finely graduated speeds. When I saw the result upon the screen I realized the idea was sound. The new rhythm, independent of the real, deriving from the combination of shots at a variety of speeds, yielded a deepened, one might say remarkably enriched, sense of the process portrayed upon the screen.[2]

Just as Pudovkin assembles a variety of shots to create the effect of a man mowing grass, note the same kind of construction in building one of the battle scenes in *Henry V*. The process is one of joining together a series of related or contrasting images in such a way as to create the effect of a great battle involving disparate elements. The process begins by establishing long shots of the locale, then the two armies, then to the specific groups and Henry.

2. V. I. Pudovkin, *Film Technique and Film Acting* (New York: Grove Press, 1960).

L.S. AERIAL VIEW OF THE BATTLEFIELD.

L.S. THE FRENCH ARMY.

FANFARE.

L.S. THE ENGLISH ARMY.

FANFARE.

M.S. Line of French Drummers.

L.S. French Crossbowmen moving up.

M.C.S. French drums.

L.S. French Cavalry moving up to battle position. The Constable signals with his sword and they turn left.

C.S. French Standards dip and move out of picture left.

M.S. Mire. The reflection and then the hoofs of French Cavalry cross the screen, CAMERA PANS LEFT with them.

FANFARE
DISSOLVE.

L.S. The French Cavalry in battle order at the walk.

M.S. A line of English Bowmen draw their bows.

M.C.S. Henry on his horse.

L.S. The French Cavalry break into a trot, then a canter then a gallop then a full tilt charge.

M.S. Line of English Archers with bows drawn.

M.C.S. Low angle shot of Henry with sword poised for signal to Archers. His glance changes from left to right.

L.S. The French Cavalry charging with English stakes in foreground.

M.C.S. Line of English Bowmen with bows drawn.

M.C.S. Henry -- he slashes down his sword.

MUSIC STOPS.

M.C.S. Line of English Archers -- they fire.

M.L.S. Line of English Archers -- they fire.

L.S. The French Cavalry with stake emplacements in foreground. Arrows sizzle through the air overhead and strike home. The French Cavalry rears.

MUSIC STARTS.

M.S. English Archers firing.

L.S. French Cavalry in confusion. Stakes in f.g.

M.S. French Cavalry in confusion.

M.S. French Cavalry in confusion.

M.S. French Cavalry in confusion.

M.C.S. French Charger rearing madly.

In addition to its ability to vary speeds, as we have seen in the *Henry V* filmscript, the camera is also flexible from the standpoint of mobility. In the early days of motion pictures, the camera was set up in front of the shooting area at a sufficient distance so that all of the action could be recorded. The scene was shot from a fixed point of view, with the result that the person seeing the movie occupied about the same position as a spectator seeing the action on stage. But it was soon discovered that a more effective way to tell a story was to use a variety of camera shots and movements. Today the camera is an amazingly mobile instrument which can pan horizontally and tilt vertically at a variety of speeds and angles. The camera can be mounted on a track, a boom, or a dolly; it can be raised, lowered, and swung out to the sides of a boom. It can be thrust forward, backward, or sideways. The variety of angles, positions, and movements is nearly endless. In the hands of a skillful cameraman it becomes an admirably fluid and expressive instrument.

The mobility of the camera enables the filmmaker to achieve not only a wide range of effects, but significant psychological statements as well. John Howard Lawson points out an interesting example in Olivier's motion picture of *Hamlet*. The film begins with a series of shots of the Castle at Elsinore and the platform above the sea, for the purpose of establishing a gloomy and fearful atmosphere. These are followed by the first scene of the play showing the appearance of the ghost before Horatio and the guards. As the scene ends, Marcellus uses a line that appears later in the play: "There is something rotten in the state of Denmark." As he looks toward the castle, the camera pans to the ramp leading to the building. A long camera movement follows, tracking through corridors and down staircases to the interior, crossing a courtyard before it centers on the window of the Queen's closet, through which is framed the Queen's bed. Thus, the camera not only bridges the action but is used to interpret the play by centering on a significant object.

We noted at the beginning of *Henry V* the terms *fade in* and *fade out*. Fading is a momentary darkening of the screen that interrupts the continuity, like darkening the lights in the theater or pulling the curtain to provide transitions. The fade in or out in a film is accomplished by

181 Confusion in the French ranks. The battle scene from Laurence Olivier's *Henry V* (1944).

182 A scene from *The Jazz Singer* (1927), the first motion picture to use sound.

183 The knight plays chess with Death in Ingmar Bergman's *The Seventh Seal* (1956).

184 The enormous popularity of *Love Story* (1970) showed that the American public still loves romance.

185 Nanook hurls a spear in *Nanook of the North* (1922), Robert Flaherty's documentary on the Eskimos. Flaherty is considered the creator of the documentary.

the gradual emergence or disappearance of an image on the darkened screen. Fading out and in is ordinarily used within the film to indicate that a sequence is finished and a new one is to begin—like the end of one chapter and the beginning of the next in a book.

After the title "A Laurence Olivier Production" appears another form of transition—the *dissolve.* This involves a gradual change from one scene to the next by superimposing the images so that continuity is not disturbed. Filmmakers often use the dissolve as the best way of indicating a short gap of time within a sequence.

The most frequently used transitional device is the *cut,* in which images succeed each other without interruption as, for example, the opening shots of *Henry V* showing the activity in the Globe theater. The abruptness of the cut is apt to convey a shock effect psychologically. The juxtaposition of the shots sets up an association in the mind of the audience which the skillful director exploits. Because of its directness, the cut is apt to be staccato, and it adds speed to the scene. Rapid cutting in a series of shots showing the villain struggling with the heroine, the hero striving to escape, and the marines on the way, for example, builds up excitement, while slow cutting with longer shots may be used for a solemn or dignified scene. The cut is the standard method of making a transition from one camera position to another, to show the similarity of two different objects, to show the reaction of characters to the action, and to develop parallel lines of simultaneous actions.

Within the action of the opening scene is a variety of shots—close, medium, and long. The long shot—"Aerial View of London in 1600"—and the following extreme long shot of the city are used to establish the general locale. Later on in the film, long shots of the battlefield and the French and English armies serve as an introduction to the warfare. A long shot is made by placing the camera at such a distance that the lens will include the complete area of action and as much of the environment as possible.

A medium shot is made by moving the camera close enough to the subject so that a center of interest is established; a particular person, group, or object is singled out, such as the man at the flagpole or the orange girl in the Globe theater, or the line of French drummers and the English bowmen drawing their bows in the battle sequence. The effect of the medium shot is to bring the spectator in toward the action so that he gets a greater sense of participation. A close shot places the camera even closer to the action and a close-up is used for even more intimacy and detail. In the Globe theater a close shot is used to show the playhouse flag unfurling and fluttering. In the battle scene, close-ups are shown of a horse neighing hysterically and of a dead boy. In between these shots are, of course, variations such as medium long shots, medium close shots, extreme long shots, and so on. Shots are the building blocks of filmmaking. By varying the length of each shot and the transitional devices, the director speeds up or slows down the action, gives his film its appropriate emotional content. By his selection of the order and relationship of the images he generates excitement, builds tension and suspense, and evokes a variety of emotional responses. In the work of a creative director you will see a variety of shots, a freshness of perception, an imagination that lifts his work above the level of the routine and mediocre.

The special characteristic of filmmaking is the influence of one shot on another. The shot may make its own statement but its importance to the filmmaker is what it means when it is joined to another. Kenneth Macgowan describes an experiment conducted by the Russian directors Kuleshov and Pudovkin in which they took short pieces of film showing a close-up of a man's face that Pudovkin says "did not express any feeling at all." He added separate shots of a bowl of soup, a dead woman in a casket, and a child playing with a funny toy bear.

> When we showed the three combinations to an audience which had not been let into the secret, the result was terrific. The public raved about the acting of the artist. They pointed out the heavy pensiveness of his mood over the forgotten soup, were touched and moved by the deep sorrow with which he looked on the dead woman, and admired the light, happy smile with which he surveyed the girl at play. But we knew that in all three cases the face was exactly the same.[3]

The motion picture, like painting, has the convention of a rectangular frame enclosing a two-dimensional surface. For many years the frame's proportion was four to three, but in recent years the wide screen has come into popular use, changing the shape of the frame to a wide band with three to four times more surface. Within the limitations of the frame, the cinematographer composes his pictures; his arrangement of his subjects is not based on a series of stills, however, but on a sequence of constantly changing images. The composition is dynamic and fluid. When you see your next motion picture, notice the use of angles and of diagonal lines to enhance the composition and direction of movement. In an excellent film you will also notice the skillful arrangement of shots and scenes in relation to one another so that there is a satisfying pattern of contrast and variety. The cameraman and director select the most effective way of expressing the content of a scene, excluding all that is extraneous and bringing out the psychological implications of the material. If the most effective shot requires a close-up of the actor's face, the camera moves in and eliminates the body. The background is made unobtrusive by removing it from the shot, concentrating light on the foreground or putting nonessential material out of focus.

3. Kenneth Macgowan, *Behind the Screen* (New York, Delacorte Press, 1965).

The director wishes to gain the maximum emotional impact from a scene. Can it be achieved most emphatically by a close-up of an actor's face, or several faces shown rapidly, or perhaps by his feet or hands, or a shot from the rear showing his entire figure? As an example of the director's imaginative use of his camera and editing, consider Eisenstein's classic sequence from *Potemkin,* one of the most notable and influential series of shots ever made. The following is Manvell's account of an excerpt from the sequence on the Odessa steps:

> The nurse and perambulator. Several shots show the nurse protecting the perambulator with her own body. The jackboots of the soldiers move down with almost mincing care, step by step. They fire. The nurse's mouth opens in pain. She clutches the buckle on her belt, and leans back against the perambulator. Cut from her hands slowly covered with the blood from her wounded stomach, to the wheels of the perambulator which her falling body gradually pushes down the steps; the action is prolonged for emphasis by cutting and recutting. Meanwhile the soldiers descend, keeping their neat line, firing precisely. The nurse's body is still launching the perambulator on its careering journey down the steps. Gradually shot by shot it is pushed away. Shot from overhead, from angles sideways, the perambulator goes down the steps, watched by the horrified elderly lady, until finally it topples over, throwing the child out. The climax approaches in a succession of shots mostly of variable duration from one to three seconds. All the elements: the crowd, the soldiers, the dead nurse, the perambulator, the bourgeois group are built together with rapid cutting.[4]

precursors of the film

Since the days of Leonardo da Vinci, various experiments prepared the way for the development of the motion picture. These experiments went in three directions: (1) the development of photography and the camera; (2) the illusion of movement through the manipulation of visual images; and (3) the projection of pictorial images on a flat surface, such as a wall. In the nineteenth century experimenters culminated their activities by producing several novelties that created pictoral images in motion, the most notable being the Edison Kinetoscope (1889), out of which evolved the motion picture camera and projector, preparing the way for the creation of films that could be shown to an audience. Pictures were photographed by the Kinetograph, the first genuine motion picture camera, which held fifty feet of film taken at sixteen images to the foot and forty-five frames to the second. These images were exposed to the viewer in a series of rapid flashes as he peered into the lens.

4. Roger Manvell, *Film* (Harmondsworth: Penguin Books, 1950).

At first such motion pictures were disreputable peep shows exhibited in penny arcades. In 1896 a projector was invented which made it possible to show the film to an enlarged audience, consisting mostly of the poorer classes whose tastes were satisfied by the novelty of movement. In 1902 the first movie house, the Electric Theater, was established in Los Angeles. The popularity of motion pictures was phenomenal, and soon movie theaters spread across the country.

The evolution and influence of the motion picture in the past three quarters of a century is amazing enough to challenge the film studio publicists' flair for hyperbole. Technical progress has changed the camera from a simple toy to a remarkably expressive instrument capable of genuine artistic achievement. Its potential has been expanded through the development of new lenses, improved film quality and developing techniques, and the addition of sound and color. The director and cameraman have learned to capitalize on the elements of graphic arts—line, color, form, and texture—with the additional aesthetic dimension of movement. Despite the limitations of overemphasis on box-office appeal and the vitiating and confusing practice of collaborative effort in film manufacture, motion pictures of artistic excellence have appeared, such as *Citizen Kane, High Noon, Grapes of Wrath,* and *The Treasure of Sierra Madre,* testifying to the aesthetic potentialities of the medium. And even the most routine of the formula pictures produced today is characterized by technical craftsmanship of a high order.

The economic growth of the motion picture industry was phenomenal. The novelty of the nickelodeon proved to be a remarkable public attraction. By 1908 there were eight to ten thousand nickelodeons in the United States, showing short films purchased from the more than one hundred motion picture exchanges which had suddenly mushroomed. With the development of the full-length feature as the standard product, permanent movie houses sprang up over the country. By 1916 there were more than twenty thousand such theaters. World War I gave American film production an enormous impetus since foreign production was virtually at a standstill. Within a short time American producers dominated the world market, and Hollywood emerged as the film capital of the world. Motion picture-making became big business with all its characteristics. Four major results can be seen in this development:

(1) The industry became highly organized for the process of manufacturing films, which meant mass-producing them according to proven formulas. The products became standardized romances, comedies, westerns, and "shockers," processed like canned goods with time-tested recipes calculated to satisfy the tastes of a wide public. If a particular film was especially popular, rival companies hastened to make imitations of it, and the originator promptly made sequels. Everything was done to exploit the widest popular appeal of story and performer.

(2) The star system became one of the most effective ways of standardizing the product and assuring a continuous market. Astronomical salaries were paid to matinee idols, glamorous lovers, and comedians, who repeated their performances in a series of films exploiting their particular talents and charms. Such stars as Charlie Chaplin, Douglas Fairbanks, and Mary Pickford became the American aristocracy. Their names on the marquees were the successful trademarks of the industry.

(3) As in other forms of big business, advertising became all-important to the film producer in selling his product. The big guns of publicity and advertising bombarded the American public with a relentless barrage of material emphasizing the personal attractiveness of the performers and the sensational and spectacular nature of the film stories.

(4) A final characteristic of big business taken over by the motion picture industry was the control of distribution. It was soon realized that there was a great deal of money to be made by taking charge of the exhibition of films. Chains of theaters spread across the country giving the owners control over both the manufacture and distribution of motion pictures. In 1928 alone, over $150,000,000 was spent in building new movie houses. Some of these "cinema cathedrals" were the dominant architectural landmarks of the community. The luxurious appointments of these new theaters helped to attract a new audience—the upper middle class, who had heretofore regarded films as popular fare for the undiscriminating masses. Another reason for new patronage was the development of sound in motion pictures. In 1927, when *The Jazz Singer* was first shown, our national film audience each week was 60,000,000. Within two years it had soared to 110,000,000 patrons a week.

the advent of sound

The advent of sound had several important influences. At first, filmmakers became preoccupied with the new element and movies became more static and more word-conscious. Hollywood turned to Broadway for plays, playwrights, and actors accustomed to working with the spoken drama. The result was a loss in cinematic quality as too much attention was given to the ear at the expense of the eye. The use of spoken dialogue meant that movies became more nationalized, since they lost the universality of stories told visually. On the other hand, the coming of sound enlarged the vocabulary of the screen so that characters could express themselves more completely. In comedy, the addition of bright dialogue introduced to the screen quite a different sort of fare than that restricted to pantomime. Acting in general became more natural, since speech gave the performer the ability to convey his thoughts and feelings in a more normal way.

The decade preceding World War II was beset with turmoil and pressures—at first from the severe economic disruption of the Depression, which cut heavily into the entertainment business, and then from the increasing tensions on the international scene that led to the outbreak of the war. Most motion pictures made in this interval were escape entertainment—lightweight comedies, romances, musicals, and gangster films. The latter, such as *Scarface* (1932), were very popular with their tough-talking characters shown in violent action in realistic big-city surroundings, but there was little thought back of the action. The symptoms of evil in politics, rackets, and crime were shown but there was little diagnosis of the causes. Nevertheless, occasional films of stature and honesty appeared, such as *I Am a Fugitive from a Chain Gang* (1932), *The Informer* (1935), *Grapes of Wrath* (1939), and *Citizen Kane* (1941). In the latter film, the young Orson Welles produced a highly original and widely influential example of the cinematic potential of the medium.

the postwar film

Following World War II, the motion picture audience declined as adults found other forms of recreation or turned to television. The courts removed control of theater chains from the major studios, thus opening up the possibilities for the distribution of a greater variety of films—foreign, experimental, and those appealing to a more discriminating audience. Independent producers went on location often to foreign locales to cut down on expenses as well as to exploit the attraction of new and exotic surroundings. The major studios, increasingly tied to television production, were slow to react to the changes taking place elsewhere, but as the products of the foreign filmmakers and independent producers began making inroads on the market, they too began to use the new cinematic techniques and to deal with fresh subject matter. Their new approach is evident in such films as *The Pawnbroker* (1965), *Bonnie and Clyde* (1967), *Petulia* (1968), *Midnight Cowboy* (1969), *Easy Rider* (1969), *The Landlord* (1970), and *McCabe and Mrs. Miller* (1971). The scathing satire and exuberance of the English *A Hard Day's Night* (1964) was reflected in the American comedies *Dr. Strangelove* (1964), *The Graduate* (1967) and *M*A*S*H* (1968).

The development of the film during the post-World War II era reminds us of the changes that took place when realism made its appearance in the theater in the late nineteenth-century theater. We remember that playwrights like Ibsen, Strindberg, Zola, and Becque revolted against frivolous melodrama and farcical popular fare and gave the stage a sense of carefully observed reality in their plays. The naturalist introduced to the Independent Theater a whole new range of characters—the downtrodden, the outcast, and the victims of society depicted with authentic detail in sordid surroundings. Expressionism, another derivative of realism, concerned itself with plays that captured the nightmarish internal life of disoriented characters. Now, with the impact of the war, independent filmmakers sought an uncompromising honesty that sharply contrasted with the standard Hollywood product.

Roberto Rossellini in *Open City* (1945) turned his camera on war-torn Rome and showed the barbarism of the conflict with utmost candor. Operating on a limited budget with minimal equipment, he often used nonprofessional actors in scenes showing the ravaged city. The force of such harsh reality was a startling contrast to the slick, glamorized American film. In the same neorealistic vein were Rossellini's *Paisan* (1946) and Vittorio De Sica's *Shoeshine* (1946) and *Bicycle Thief* (1949).

Another Italian director who has achieved international recognition through his highly original approach to the film is Federico Fellini. In 1954 Fellini scored a triumph with *La Strada,* a compelling and sympathetic story of a young girl who joins a traveling carnival troupe. His *La Dolce Vita* (1960) was notable for the fragmented quality of the narrative, creating a collage of sharply observed details. His *8½* (1963) shows the career of a director in an odd blend of the fantastic and the real. Other Fellini films are *Juliet of the Spirits* (1965) and *The Clowns* (1971).

Fellini, like other avant-garde filmmakers, experiments freely with cutting and color giving the viewer an unusual impact of sense impressions. His juxtaposition of disparate images negates the conventional logic of film continuity, substituting an incongruous and enigmatic atmosphere of symbols and metaphors without referents.

Two other internationally known directors are the Japanese Akira Kurosawa and the Indian Satyajit Ray. The latter's best-known works are his *Pather Panchali* (1954) and *Apu Sansar* (1959). Kurosawa's most notable pictures are *Rashomon* (1951), *The Seven Samurai* (1954), and *The Throne of Blood* (1957).

In Great Britain, John Osborne's play *Look Back in Anger* (1958) caused a shock wave in the theater that gave the stage a new spirit. His scathing view of contemporary life in England, his bitter denunciation of the establishment was a bright example for the "angry young men." This new spirit was quickly reflected in the film version of *Look Back in Anger* (1958), *Room at the Top* (1958), and *A Taste of Honey* (1962).

In France, the film became vigorously experimental. Just as the absurdists scorned the conventional theater in writing their antiplays, the avant-garde filmmakers rejected traditional cinematic practices and made no concessions to the wish-fulfillment desires of the audience; indeed, in some instances their films seem deliberately designed to confuse. The world they depict resembles Pinter's in its sense of terror lying just behind reality. The best known of these experimentalists are François Truffaut, Alain Resnais and Jean-Luc Godard. Truffaut's reputation was established by his semiautobiographical account of an adolescent boy, *The 400 Blows* (1959), notable for its absence of sentimentalism and its detached objectivity. Another child-centered film of his is *The Wild Child* (1970), which tells the story of the education of a barbarian boy who spent his childhood abandoned in a forest. Resnais, who began making documentary films, is best known for *Hiroshima Mon Amour* (1959) and *Last Year at Marienbad* (1961). These pictures recall Pirandello in their conflict between appearance and reality. The characters seem to have no roots, no family ties, no profession, often no specific locale, and no clear motivation for their actions.

Jean-Luc Godard's work is characterized by the dichotomy he expressed when he said: "I write essays in the form of novels or novels in the form of essays." His films are combinations of the romantic and the naturalistic, the personal and the social, movement and inaction, short takes and long tableaux, reality and abstraction. One of his controversial techniques is to employ long patches of dialogue in which the speaker may talk directly into the camera responding to an offscreen voice. Often he is not clear about the actions or motives of his characters. In *Made in the USA* (1966) he gives a confusing view of an assassination in which his methods are at odds with conventional cinematic practices. He deliberately omits such things as transitions, expository material, and insight into character. There are rapid, fragmentary shots along with long seemingly irrelevant conversations. His antinarrative techniques create an absurd and baffling world in which the viewer finds it difficult to locate himself, but the very ingenuity of his highly original mind makes Godard's work strikingly individual. Other examples of his enigmatic style are *Breathless* (1959), *Une Femme Est une Femme* (1964), and *Le Petit Soldat* (1960).

Ingmar Bergman, the Swedish filmmaker, has achieved a notable reputation because of his mastery of his medium and his uncompromisingly adult approach to his work. His carefully prepared scripts and his fine company of actors contribute greatly to the exceptional excellence of his work. Among Bergman's best-known films are *The Seventh Seal* (1956), *Wild Strawberries* (1957), *The Virgin Spring* (1959), and his trilogy *Through a Glass Darkly, Winter Light,* and *The Silence* (1960–1962). His first film in English, *The Touch* (1970), is simpler in form and simpler in its symbolism.

As new American talent became interested in the creative aspects of film, and as new technical advances made production easier, an underground or independent movement began. Many of the new filmmakers were avant-garde in that they scorned the Hollywood commercialized stereotypes and were interested in revolutionary ideas in techniques as well as subject matter. A new generation that by the age of twenty had already logged an estimated 15,000 hours of exposure to television, most of which was film, was oriented to a medium of flowing images. Heedless or critical of traditional cinematic techniques, they roamed everywhere shooting nearly anything that moved. As a result there is today an enormous interest in the film and an increasing number of experimenters, whose outpouring of energy has made them familiar with the potential of the medium. Free from the restraints of the commercial imperative, these new talents are bringing to the screen a verve and audacity that is hard to ignore.

film content

The early filmmakers soon learned that they had developed a medium suited to fantasy. The technical facilities of the camera—its mobility, its capacity for recording an infinite variety of subjects, its ability to leap around freely in time and space, its ease in distorting images, its ability to stop the action, slow it down, speed it up or reverse it—made the motion picture an intriguing vehicle for free flights of the imagination. In addition to the versatility of the camera, the imaginative expressiveness of the motion picture was enhanced by the ease with which individual images could be joined together. The pioneer, Georges Méliès, experimented with the new medium in a series of ingenious and zany films, among them *A Trip to the Moon* and *The Doctor's Secret,* which employed all manner of trickery. Characters were dismembered and reassembled, action was accelerated, slowed down and reversed, fantastic characters were flung into outer space. A decade later, the American producers of slapstick comedies recorded lunatic fantasies of furious and violent physical activity, which invariably culminated in a wild and weird chase at breakneck speed. Standard fantastic scenes showed dozens of Keystone cops racing through buildings in a flivver, up the sides of walls, across the water, ending up in a violent explosion that filled the air with steam and flying bodies. Another early development in fantasy were the animated cartoons depicting a never-never world of strange landscapes and comical, weird creatures in impossible antics. A serious attempt to realize the ultimate in fantastic expressiveness occurred in 1919, when Robert Wiene produced the expressionistic German film *The Cabinet of Dr. Caligari.* This nightmarish story, seen through the eyes of a madman, made motion picture-makers aware of film's potential for expressiveness through distortion. Because "seeing is believing," film has a unique ability to make the bizarre and the macabre seem authentic and the camera can make nearly anything seeable, from mechanical monsters to the landscapes of the moon. The producers of "spook" and horror movies have popularized the technical trickery of filmmaking, but there have been few attempts in serious motion pictures to dwell on fantasy, although there are such notable exceptions as the films of Cocteau, Bergman, and many of the Japanese. One area of the fantastic that has been exploited is the science-fiction film in which astonishing technical feats have been achieved, as in the recent *2001: A Space Odyssey* and *The Andromeda Strain*. While the film content of German expressionists was not widely imitated, they did leave considerable impact on the motion picture by establishing a realization of the effectiveness of organized patterns of dark and light, and they demonstrated the emotional force that could be achieved by the distortion of realistic form. Their technical ideas were quickly absorbed into the work of discerning directors, where their influence resulted in shots composed with unusual perspectives and exaggerated angular shapes.

Even a casual glance at the output of the film industry is enough to indicate that the general popular audience prefers motion pictures that give the illusion of reality. Although character and story may be glamorized and romanticized far beyond the bounds of credulity, the spectator expects and prefers that the images before him bear at least an external resemblance to life. Distortion and abstraction often bewilder and antagonize the viewer because he finds it difficult to fit them into his customary frame of reference. He wants to recognize what he sees. As Manvell observes:

> For realism means real people, honest, four-square, lovable, hateful, unambiguous people. Personality, character, individuality, unusual careers, go-getting, living, loving and dying, these are the staple interests of a realistic age. Along with it comes an interest in occupations, jobs, social backgrounds. Films not about high society are usually about people with a definite occupational background, gangsters, actresses, barmen, dancers, shop-keepers, policemen, taxi-drivers, engine-drivers, soldiers, sailors, airmen, schoolmarms, nurses, doctors, miners, bankers, racketeers, businessmen, detectives, inventors, musicians and writers. Though the story may not much concern their occupations, none the less it is good to know the girl marries a man with a job. However foolish, melodramatic, dull or thrilling the action may be, realism is the order of the day from an audience's point of view.[5]

After the novelty of such subjects as "Wash-Day Troubles," "Two Babies Pulling Each Other's Hair," and "View of the Surf at Dover" had worn off, the possibilities of film as a narrative medium began to be realized. In 1903, Edwin S. Porter produced *The Great Train Robbery*, in which he visualized his story in cinematic terms and conceived his film as the sum of its edited parts. The patterns of action and tension in this

5. *Ibid.*

early film are an integral part of the formula, since repeated endlessly, of physical combat, the chase, hairbreadth escapes, cliff-hanging suspense scenes—all calculated to arouse maximum excitement. Thus, the motion picture absorbed at once most of the characteristic content of popular nineteenth-century melodrama. Such pictures have immediate mass appeal, requiring no sophistication or insight to follow the stereotyped characters dashing through the antics of the prefabricated plots. Their emphasis is on narrative and spectacle, on a simple but courageous hero and a clearly defined, unmitigated villain. Character is not investigated, the minimal dialogue is pedestrian and utilitarian, and the thought is a repetition of conventional themes: murder will out, virtue is triumphant, love conquers all. The attitudes of the characters are not drawn from literature or life but come straight from their original source—dime-novels, "penny-dreadfuls," popular pulp "action" stories, and stage melodrama. The content is simple and superficial, filled with sentimentalism and black-and-white ethics in which the measure of a man is his skill with his gun or his fists. The solution to the problem of evil is a very simple one—eliminate the evildoer. Despite its obvious techniques and its lack of substance, the "action" picture continues to attract a popular audience, because it effectively uses the camera in presenting an exciting narrative in fluent action. Technical advances have provided color and a wide screen and have added to the visual effectiveness of the action motion picture even though its underlying superficial formula remains the same. Motion pictures in the melodramatic tradition are westerns, detective stories, most war pictures, and almost all adventure films. Attempts have been made to make such fare more mature in its appeal by making the characters more psychologically complex, by replacing the sentimental appeal with a tough, cynical view of life, and by exploiting new aspects of human behavior formerly banned by censorship. It was only natural that television should adopt the action formula as staple fare for attracting a wide audience.

A most pervasive element of the motion picture, especially in America, has been romance. Few pictures are made without it. Even in films which deal seriously with social problems, the moviemaker usually insists on injecting a love story, which most often becomes the pivot of the action. The love story is frequently based on the Cinderella theme, but it achieves a kind of surface realism by using familiar contemporary backgrounds. The historical romance is often visually impressive with its monumental settings, enormous and spectacular mob scenes, and pictorial beauty, but the material is still basically centered on a love story. Such technical triumphs are tributes to the art director's ingenuity rather than sincere explorations into significant content.

Romances provide characters with whom the audience can identify itself; the victory which rewards the hero's suffering and struggle brings a sensation of success and pleasure to the onlooker. The absence of any substance from so many of these films is compensated for by the exaggeration of personal attractiveness. Charm conquers all. Wish-fulfillment devices are used to draw a veil over life and character. Such pictures are artfully produced with a smooth presentation of the narrative, facile acting, handsome and credible backgrounds and costumes, and sensuous photography and music. But the emphasis is on the externals. Character and personality take second place to easy audience identification. Controversial material is gingerly sidestepped. The safe, the standardized, the tried-and-true dominates the screen.

With the relaxation of censorship, the romantic element was sometimes given a new twist with distorted characters and relationships, and a strong emphasis on sex and its aberrations. Or the romantic element was treated with a harsh cynicism. During the course of this trend the film *Love Story* (1970) appeared and its widely appealing simple story of two young people in love became an enormous box-office hit, reminding the industry that the romantic element was still a favorite one with the public.

In recent years, the new freedom from censorship and the demands of a more select audience to whom television fare and formula pictures have become anathema have encouraged filmmakers to deal with more significant content. A new generation expects the film to find new and compelling ways to appraise man and his world.

the documentary film

Although the motion picture became primarily a narrative medium for entertainment, there was an early and abiding interest in making nonfiction films. Motion pictures were made of far-off lands and native life, of semiabstract symphonic sketches of city life and machinery. Educational films were made for instructional purposes and institutional pictures were filmed for public relations. All these were given new impetus with the coming of sound and their use today is widespread.

An outstanding development of the nonfiction film was the production of documentaries in which the filmmakers interprets reality in a creative way. The most important early effort along such lines was Robert Flaherty's *Nanook of the North* (1922). To make this picture, Flaherty rejected the studio traditions, living and working with the natives before he filmed them. He recorded their struggle for survival at first hand; he knew their customs and observed their skills and craftsmanship before he shot an enormous quantity of footage which he painstakingly edited himself. Other examples of early documentaries are Cavalcanti's *Rien que les Heures* (1926) and Ruttman's *Berlin* (1927), both of which are symphonic treatments of city life. But the documentary movement did not really get under way until 1928, when a British governmental agency set up a film unit for the creation of industrial and social films under the direction of John Grierson. He wrote the following about documentaries:

> First principles. (1) We believe that the cinema's capacity for getting around, for observing and selecting from life itself, can be exploited in a new and vital art form. The studio films largely ignore this possibility of opening up the screen on the real world. They photograph acted stories against artificial backgrounds. Documentary would photograph the living scene and the living story. (2) We believe that the original (or native) actor, and the original (or native) scene, are better guides to a screen interpretation of the modern world. They give cinema a greater fund of material. They give it power over a million and one movements, and power over a million and one images. They give it power of interpretation over more complex and astonishing happenings in the real world than the studio mind can conjure up or the studio mechanic can re-create. (3) We believe that the materials and the stories thus taken from the raw can be finer (more real in a philosophic sense) than the acted article. Spontaneous gesture has a special value on the screen. Cinema has a sensational capacity for enhancing the movement which tradition has formed or time worn smooth. Its arbitrary rectangle specially reveals movement; it gives maximum pattern in space and time. Add to this that documentary can achieve an intimacy of knowledge and effect impossible to the shim-sham mechanics of the studio, and the lily-fingered interpretations of the metropolitan actor.[6]

Outstanding documentaries were made in Great Britain under the sponsorship of government agencies and industries, the chief filmmakers being Grierson, Basil Wright, Edgar Anstey, and Paul Rotha. The types of documentaries produced varied considerably according to personal points of view. Paul Rotha, for example, looked upon the documentary as more than an artistic or faithful recording of actuality; he had its potential for propaganda in mind:

> Real and creative thought must be about real things. Let cinema explore outside the limits of what we are told constitutes entertainment. Let cinema attempt the dramatisation of the living scene and the living theme, springing from the living present instead of from the synthetic fabrication of the studio. Let cinema attempt film interpretations of modern problems and events, of things as they really are today, and by so doing perform a definite function. Let cinema recognize the existence of real men and women, real things and real issues, and by so doing offer to State, Industry, Commerce, to public and private organizations of all

6. John Grierson, *Cinema Quarterly*, Edinburgh, Winter 1932.

> kinds, a method of communication and propaganda to project not just personal opinions but arguments for a world of common interest.[7]

In a single decade nearly three hundred British documentaries were made, among them such distinguished pictures as *Drifters* (1929), *Shipyard* (1935), and *Night Mail* (1936). Interest in making documentary films spread elsewhere. In America, Pare Lorentz made two outstanding documentaries, *The Plow That Broke the Plains* (1936) and *The River* (1938). *The March of Time* (1935) ushered in a new form of dynamic journalism, recording the world crisis in vivid terms. The Russians, who very early learned the effectiveness of the film as an instrument of education and propaganda, produced a number of remarkable films, such as Vertov's *The Eleventh Year* and *The Man with the Movie Camera.* A considerable number of documentaries were made in Holland and France, and a few notable isolated examples in Germany and Italy.

With the coming of World War II, the factual film was given an enormous impetus as hundreds of films were produced by and for governments as tools of instruction or propaganda, to be shown to the troops and in factories, schools, and movie houses. The short nonfiction film suddenly found a new popular audience. Since the war, the development of television has provided a new market for films, many of them essentially documentary in style.

Striking documentaries have been made about great works of art and the men who created them, among them *Van Gogh, Rubens, The Titan,* and *The Mystery of Picasso.* A recent widely popular documentary was *Woodstock,* in which the performers and the reaction to the performance of a "rock" festival were shown with considerable ingenuity. Following the lead of Rossellini, documentary makers have filmed and interpreted the atmosphere of great cities. Examples are *Terminus,* a film about Waterloo Station in London, and *In the Street,* a record of the streets of New York.

One of the effects of the documentary film has been to stress the importance of honesty in recording and interpreting actuality. The result has been that films are shot in the actual environment of the action, often using or simulating the techniques of film reporting such as insufficient or raw lighting and candid, unposed shots, fuzzy and of brief duration. Such simulation is used to give the viewers a sense of authenticity, as if the action were footage shot during an actual event. This documentary quality characterizes such films as *The Longest Day* (1962), about D-day and the invasion of France; *The Train* (1964), about an attempt of the Germans to capture the art treasures of France; *Is Paris Burning?* (1967), about the Nazi plan to destroy the city, and *The Last Battle* (1967), about the fall of Hitler.

7. Paul Rotha, *Documentary Film* (New York: Hastings House, 1964).

In addition to documentaries made with attention to cinematic and, often, aesthetic values, an incredible amount of footage has been shot in an effort to record the events of the world about us. Some of it has attained a remarkable level of expression in covering flights into space, adventures on the moon, riots, strikes, demonstrations, rescues, political campaigns and elections, assassinations, and important meetings and speeches. Never before has the eye of man seen so much so often.

exercises

1. Discuss the difference between motion and action as they apply to stage and film.
2. Using Pudovkin's example of a man mowing grass, make an outline showing the shots needed for changing a tire, buying a wig or a pair of shoes, or baby's first birthday cake.
3. Prepare a script for telling a joke visually.
4. Review a feature film, concentrating on the element of thought.
5. Watch a short film on television and describe the use of the camera from the point of view of movement and variety of shots.
6. Using the opening of *Henry V* as a guide, prepare a scenario for the opening of *Antigone* as a film.
7. Describe the differences between stage and film in handling exposition and dialogue.
8. What is the importance of "persistence of vision"?
9. How does mass production and distribution affect film content?
10. Outline the shooting sequence for a short documentary film.

suggested reading

Rudolf Arnheim, *Film as Art,* 1957.
Alan Howard Casty, *The Dramatic Art of Film,* 1970.
Sergei M. Eisenstein, *Film Form,* 1949.
George P. Garrett, O. B. Hardison, Jr., and Jane R. Gelfman, eds., *Film Scripts One, Film Scripts Two,* 1971.
John Grierson, *Grierson on Documentary,* 1970.
Lewis Jacobs, *The Rise of the American Film,* 1967.
Arthur Knight, *The Liveliest Art: A Panoramic History of the Movies,* 1957.
Ernest Lindgren, *The Art of the Film,* 3rd ed., 1968.
Kenneth Macgowan, *Behind the Screen,* 1965.
Roger Manvell, *Film,* 1950.
Parker Tyler, *Underground Film: A Critical History,* 1970.

glossary

(It is suggested that the reader also refer to the Index since many terms are given extended treatment in the text.)

acting area or "playing area" The part of the stage used for performance.

aesthetic distance The psychical detachment between a work of art and those who respond to it. Experimentalists are now trying to eliminate this area of separation.

alienation A technique used by Bertolt Brecht in his "epic dramas" to negate the emotional involvement of his audience in order to make an intellectual appeal to his political views.

antagonist The character of force in opposition to the protagonist or hero.

apron The stage area in front of the main curtain.

arena stage An arrangement for "central staging" of plays with the acting area in the middle of the room surrounded by the audience.

aside A dramatic convention in which the actor speaks his private thoughts aloud, unnoticed by other actors.

automatism A comic theory based on mechanical repetition. See Bergson in Index.

backing Stage scenery used to mask the openings so as to prevent the audience from seeing the offstage areas.

beat A basic unit for rehearsal.

blocking The director's organization of the stage movements of his cast.

bourgeois drama Pseudoserious plays involving middle-class society, with the general emphasis on pathos and morality.

business The individual actions of the characters in a play, for example, taking a drink, smoking a pipe, writing a letter.

catharsis The act of purging or cleansing, usually in connection with tragedy. Aristotle says that tragedy arouses fear and pity, and that these emotions are purged away and leave the audience in a state of purification.

chorus In Greek drama a group, varying in size from twelve to fifty, that recited lines in unison. As the first element to develop in Greek drama, it provided information and, in its most elaborate state, commentary on past actions and forebodings about future ones. With the invention of the second and third actors, the chorus became gradually less important. In later drama, the chorus was a single actor who communicated directly with the audience in giving them essential information.

classical drama Usually refers to the dramas of ancient Greece and Rome. See also **neoclassicism.**

climax The strongest point of emotional tension. Most plays have a series of climaxes cumulating in a major climax.

comedy Drama designed to entertain the audience, usually resulting in a happy ending.

comedy of humours Comedy of character based on a dominant trait such as greed or jealousy. Popularized by the Elizabethan playwright Ben Jonson.

comedy of manners Social comedy that satirized characters wittily in terms of their shortcomings as measured against a specific code of conduct. For example, *The School for Scandal.*

commedia dell'arte Improvised Italian comedy of the sixteenth, seventeenth, and eighteenth centuries put together out of stock roles in formula situations. Performed during this period by small companies of professional actors who were very popular all over Europe.

confidant(e) A minor character paired with a major one, who shares the latter's confidences, usually for expository purposes.

contamination The practice of combining plot materials from two or more plays to make a new one. Originally used to describe the practices of Plautus and Terence in reference to their borrowings from Greek comedy, the term was extended to the general practice of the Elizabethans in making new plays from old material.

conventions Common agreements between theater-worker and spectator concerning the manner of production, that is, certain "ground rules" that determine how the game is played. For example, the physical separation of actor and spectator.

crisis A time of decision; a turning point.

cyclorama Drapery or canvas usually hung in a half circle to mask the wings and backstage areas. It often represents the sky, or it may be a simple drapery.

denouement The resolution or unraveling of a plot so that an equilibrium is usually restored.

deus ex machina In the Greek theater, a "god from a machine." A mechanical device used for the intervention of some outside agent to resolve the plot. As a general term, it refers to the intervention of any outside force to bring about a desired end.

diction Aristotle's fourth element—the language of the play; the words that the actors speak.

discovery The revelation of important information about the characters, their motivations, feelings, and relationships. Discovery is often accompanied by recognition *(anagnorisis)* when a character learns the truth about himself.

downstage The area of the stage closest to the audience.

drame Any play that deals seriously with themes, characters, and ideas of the present day and is of keen interest to a middle-class audience.

empathy Literally, "feeling into." The imitative motor response of the spectator.

epic theater The nonillusionistic theater of Piscator and Brecht, dealing with broad themes, with loosely organized plots presented in a frankly theatrical style.

exposition Dramatic techniques for acquainting the audience with antecedent information and background material.

expressionism A style of drama in which an attempt is made to present "inner reality," the man beneath the skin. Often distorts the normal to present symbolic action in dreamlike sequences.

farce Low comedy, written for amusement, usually emphasizing physical action.

flat The most useful element of stage scenery, consisting of a wooden frame generally covered with muslin or canvas to represent walls.

flies The space above the stage out of sight of the audience, where scenery can be "flown."

foreshadowing Techniques for preparing the audience for the action that follows.

forestage In the modern theater, the area in front of the proscenium arch. In the Elizabethan theater, the forestage was a large projecting platform that was the main acting area.

fourth wall A convention of theatrical production that assumes the separation of performer and audience.

gridiron ("grid"). The open framework above the stage from which suspended scenery is hung.

guerilla theater The use of performance techniques for propaganda purposes presented in public places by means of simple skits, mime, music, and parades.

happening A performance intended to provide perceptional enhancement through the use of varied aspects of the theater, music, and the visual arts, presented as a spontaneous, nonformal event often involving total participation and emphasizing sensory response.

high comedy A general term referring to the kind of comedy that evokes thoughtful laughter through its concern with character, ideas, and dialogue.

histrionic sensibility The spectator's ability to perceive and discriminate actions and visual symbols, just as in music the trained ear discriminates sounds.

imagery Communication by means of concrete and particular meanings through the use of language devices such as metaphors, similes, and clusters of related words.

improvisation Spontaneous invention by the performers of actions, dialogue, and characters usually around a basic idea, situation, or theme. Although widely used for actors' rehearsal and training, it is now employed in happenings and other experimental forms of theater.

incongruity A comic theory based on the use of contrast.

irony A discrepancy between what a character plans or anticipates and what actually occurs.

linear plot One that follows a carefully articulated sequence of action generally organized in chronological order.

magnitude The elevation that Aristotle says should characterize tragedy. May refer to character, thought, diction, and spectacle.

melodrama Pseudoserious drama that is played at the game level and exploits exciting action.

method acting Stanislavski attempted to devise a systematic approach that enabled the actor to gain more control over himself and his performance. Involves control of the voice and body, the "correct state of being" on stage, and inner psychological response as the basis for outer physical actions.

mise-en-scène All of the visual aspects of the staged production.

mixed media performances Experiments that may involve a combination of the arts and technical equipment such as tapes, slides, and films.

motivation Logical justification, or the giving of plausible reasons, for the behavior of the characters in a play.

myth Archetypal stories that suggest widespread cultural beliefs, events, and feelings.

naturalism An exaggerated form of realism that emphasizes a sordid and deterministic view of life. First appeared in France in the late nineteenth century as a response to the scientific revolution.

neoclassicism An attempt in the sixteenth, seventeenth, and eighteenth centuries to "regularize" dramatic techniques by following scrupulously what were thought to be the practices of the ancients, e.g., adherence to the "unities," use of a chorus, preservation of "decorum" in language and action, avoiding acts of violence on stage, and use of only royal or noble characters.

objective A dramatic character's goal.

open stage Sometimes referred to in connection with attempts to break away from the proscenium-arch theater so as to play as close as possible to the audience. Also refers to experimental productions freed from the strictures of a prepared script.

pathos The "suffering" aspect of drama, especially that quality which evokes pity.

pity and fear The emotions aroused and purged in tragedy. Pity goes beyond pathos to include compassion and shared grief; fear goes beyond fright to include awe and wonder.

plot The structure of the incidents; the formative agent of drama; dramatic composition.

point of attack The moment in a play when a precipitating force sets the mechanism in motion and disrupts the equilibrium; the first complication.

presentational staging Production that is frankly theatrical, free from the illusion of reality. The performer confronts the audience directly.

probability An attempt by the playwright to establish credibility or, as Aristotle says, to make the action of a play seem "necessary and probable."

properties ("props") Includes objects used by the actors in the production of a play, such as letters, weapons, food.

proscenium arch The architectural frame through which the spectator views the stage.

protagonist The chief character in a play.
purgation See **catharsis.**
realism Drama that attempts to establish authenticity through the use of the observed facts of daily existence.
recognition See **discovery.**
representational staging Production that imitates experience, that seeks to create the illusion of reality.
ritual Social customs, events, and ceremonies whose repeated actions are directed toward specific goals.
romanticism In contrast with classical drama, romantic drama concerns itself with adventurous, emotionally loaded characters in remote and exotic circumstances.
reversal An Aristotelian critical term *(peripety)* referring to a sudden change in the fortunes of the protagonist.
scenario The skeletal outline of the plot.
skene Originally a small hut at the back of the orchestra in the Greek theater, which later became the stage-house.
"slice of life" Describes a play that attempts to give the impression of unorganized actuality, without an apparent beginning, middle or end. Used principally in naturalistic drama.
soliloquy A "solo" speech of a single character.
spectacle The visual aspects of a produced play.
stage left or right Left or right side of the stage from the actor's point of view as he faces the audience.
stylization Theatrical production that usually emphasizes the visual aspects and the manner of performing.
subtext Interaction beneath the surface of the spoken language of a play.
surrealism A literary movement that began in France in the 1920s, exploiting the irrational and unconscious with particular emphasis on dreams.
sympathetic magic Primitive ceremonies that men used in an attempt to enlist the help of gods by enacting their desired objectives.
theatricalism The direct use of all aspects of the theater to exploit the play as a staged work.
theme The general subject of the playwright's concern; his interpretation of the meaning of his action.
thought Aristotle's third element. The reasoning aspect of drama—the argument, the theme, the meaning.
tragic flaw An Aristotelian concept of an "error in judgment," a frailty in an otherwise good and prominent man that leads to his downfall.
tragic hero The central figure in a tragedy. Aristotle described him as a prominent man "not pre-eminently virtuous and just, whose misfortune is brought upon him not by vice and depravity but by some error of judgment."
transactions An approach to action through the "games theory" of Eric Berne that analyzes behavior in terms of the social, or overt level and the psychological, or concealed level.
unity of action All parts of the play are essential and organic, free from subplots or extraneous diversions.
unity of place All of the action occurs in one locale.

unity of time The action of a play takes place, as Aristotle suggested, "within the single revolution of the sun." The play covers a short span of time.

upstage The acting area farthest from the audience.

"well-made play" Dramatic technique perfected by the French playwright Scribe, in which all aspects of plot are carefully worked out in a logical cause-and-effect relationship.

wings The area offstage of the acting area.

(Acknowledgments continued from page iv.)

58: from *The Great White Hope* by Howard Sackler. Copyright © 1968 by Howard Sackler, pp. 102-103. Used by permission of the publisher, The Dial Press.
60: from *The Birthday Party.* Copyright © 1959 by Harold Pinter, pp. 87-88. Reprinted by permission of Grove Press, Inc.
85–86: Jean Anouilh, *Antigone.* Trans. by Lewis Galantière. New York, Samuel French, 1946, pp. 34-35.. Reprinted with permission of Dr. Jan van Loewen, London.
113-14: from Georges Feydeau, *Keep an Eye on Amélie.* London, 1958, pp. 2-3. English version by Brainerd Duffield, Feydeau Estate, 1958. By permission of Dr. Jan van Loewen.
141–43: Aristophanes, *The Frogs,* trans. by Gilbert Murray, in *The Complete Greek Drama,* ed. Whitney J. Oates and Eugene O'Neill, Jr., Random House, copyright © 1938, pp. 945-946. Reprinted by permission of the publishers.
146–47: Moss Hart and George S. Kaufman, *The Man Who Came to Dinner,* copyright 1939 by Random House. Reprinted by permission of the publishers.
147–49: from pp. 361-364 in *The Seven Lively Arts* by Gilbert Seldes. Copyright 1924 by Harper & Row, Publishers, Inc.; renewed, 1952, by Gilbert Seldes. Reprinted by permission of the publishers.
168–70: Eugene O'Neill, *The Hairy Ape,* Scene V. Copyright 1922 by Random House. Reprinted by permission of the publishers.
196: Eugène Ionesco, *The Bald Soprano,* from *Four Plays by Eugène Ionesco,* trans. by Donald M. Allen. Copyright © 1958 by Grove Press, Inc. Published by Grove Press, Inc.
197–98: Samuel Beckett, *Waiting for Godot.* Copyright © 1954 by Grove Press, Inc. Published by Grove Press, Inc.
220: reprinted by permission of S. G. Phillips, Inc. from *Look Back In Anger* by John Osborne. Copyright © 1957 by S. G. Phillips, Inc., pp. 9-10.
221: from *Stanislavsky Directs* by Nikolai M. Gorchakov, trans. by Miriam Goldina, copyright 1954 by Funk & Wagnalls. Reprinted by permission of the publisher.
224–25: K. S. Alekseev, *Stanislavsky Produces Othello,* trans. by Helen Nowak. Reprinted by permission of Geoffrey Bles, Ltd., London, 1948.
243: from *The Empty Space* by Peter Brook. Copyright © 1968 by Peter Brook. Reprinted by permission of Atheneum Publishers.
258, 259–60: Mordecai Gorelik, *New Theatres for Old.* Copyright, 1940, 1962, by Mordecai Gorelik. Reprinted by special arrangement with Samuel French, Inc.
283: Antonin Artaud, *The Theater and Its Double.* Copyright © 1958 by Grove Press. Translated by Mary Caroline Richards, pp. 96-97. Reprinted by permission of the publisher.
300–303, 307–308: film script for Shakespeare's *Henry V* (1944) by courtesy of The Rank Organisation.

PHOTOGRAPHS

2: Hal Bergsohn from painting in the collection of Walter G. Silva   3: Hal Bergsohn   4: Hal Bergsohn, from Wilhelm Kraiker, *Die Malerei der Griechen* (Stuttgart: Kohlhammer, 1958)   5: Donald McKague   6: D. A. Harissiadis   7: courtesy Professor Wendell Cole   8: Hal Bergsohn, courtesy Trustees of the British Museum   9: Hainer Hill, courtesy Berliner Ensemble   10: Vera Tenschert, courtesy Berliner Ensemble   11: Vera Tenschert, courtesy

Berliner Ensemble 12: Photo: D. A. Harissiadis 13: Percy Paukschta, courtesy of the Berliner Ensemble 14: courtesy Theatermuseum, Munich 15: Ilse Buhs 16: courtesy Theatermuseum, Munich 17: Jaromír Svoboda 19: Vandamm, New York Public Library, Astor, Lenox and Tilden Foundations 21: Angus McBean 22: Vera Tenschert, courtesy Berliner Ensemble 23: Percy Paukschta, courtesy Berliner Ensemble 24: Vandamm, New York Public Library, Astor, Lenox and Tilden Foundations

25: courtesy Mark Taper Forum 26: courtesy Theatermuseum, Munich 27: courtesy Victoria and Albert Museum 29: by permission of the Royal Shakespeare Theatre 30: courtesy Theatermuseum, Munich 31: Jaromír Svoboda 32: Bob Clayton 33: courtesy Stratford Shakespearean Festival Stratford, Ontario, Canada 35: Jaromír Svoboda 36: courtesy Victoria and Albert Museum 37: courtesy Theatermuseum, Munich 34: Hildegard Steinmetz 38: courtesy Ed Hearn 40: courtesy Theatermuseum, Munich 41: Hildegard Steinmetz 42: from *The London Stage* (London: Sherwood and Jones, n.d.) 43: courtesy Victoria and Albert Museum 44, 45: from *The London Stage* 46: courtesy Paul List Verlag; from *Daumier und das Theater*, ed. Hans Rothe (Leipzig, 1925) 47, 48: courtesy Victoria and Albert Museum 49: courtesy Trustees of the British Museum

50: T. F. Holte, by kind permission of the Royal Shakespeare Theatre 51: George Ballis, courtesy Teatro Campesino 52: Ilse Buhs 53: courtesy Rockefeller Collection, Yale University 54, 55: T. F. Holte, by kind permission of the Royal Shakespeare Theatre 56, 57: courtesy Theatermuseum, Munich 58: Zodiac 59: Ole Woldbye, Kunstindustrimuseet, Copenhagen; courtesy Teaterhistorisk Museum, Copenhagen 60: courtesy New York Historical Society 61: from *The London Stage* 62: Françoise Foliot 63: courtesy Leonard Leone 64: from *The London Stage* 65, 66, 68: courtesy Theatermuseum, Munich 67, 69: courtesy the designer, Harald Martin 70, 71: courtesy Theatermuseum, Munich 72: Hal Bergsohn 74: courtesy Theatermuseum, Munich

75: courtesy Rod Alexander 76, 77, 78, 79: courtesy Theatermuseum, Munich 81: Martha Swope 82: courtesy Collection, The Museum of Modern Art, New York, Lillie P. Bliss Bequest 83, 84, 85: courtesy Collection, The Museum of Modern Art, New York 87: Martha Swope 88: courtesy Jerzy Grotowski and the Polish Laboratory Theater 89: Ruth Berlau, courtesy Berliner Ensemble 90: Pic 91: Campus Photo Service 92: Hildegard Steinmetz 93: courtesy Michael Addison 94: Dominic, courtesy Royal Court Theatre 95: Ralph Crane, *Life Magazine;* © Time, Inc. 96: Joel Katz, courtesy Yale University School of Drama 97: Martha Swope 98: Dennis Galloway 99: courtesy San Francisco Dancers' Workshop

100: George Ballis, courtesy El Teatro Campesino 101: courtesy Victoria and Albert Museum 102, 103, 104, 105, 106: courtesy Theatermuseum, Munich 107: Percy Paukschta, courtesy Berliner Ensemble 108: Hildegard Steinmetz 109: courtesy Victoria and Albert Museum 110, 111: courtesy New York Public Library, Astor, Lenox and Tilden Foundations 112: T. F. Holte, by kind permission of the Royal Shakespeare Theatre 113: courtesy Theatermuseum, Munich 114: Vera Tenschert, courtesy Berliner Ensemble 116: courtesy Jovan Cirilov, Belgrade International Theater Festival 117, 118: courtesy Victoria and Albert Museum 119: courtesy Theatermuseum, Munich 120: courtesy the designer, Josef Svoboda 121, 122, 123: courtesy Theatermuseum, Munich

125, 126, 127: courtesy Theatermuseum, Munich 128: Percy Paukschta, courtesy

Berliner Ensemble 130, 133: Courtesy Miguel Ortega, Direccion General de Cultura Popular y Espectáculos 131: courtesy New York Public Library, Astor, Lenox and Tilden Foundations 134: courtesy Lee Simonson Collection, New York Public Library, Astor, Lenox and Tilden Foundations 135: Peter A. Juley and Son 136, 137: courtesy New York Public Library, Astor, Lenox and Tilden Foundations 138: Martha Swope 139: courtesy the designer, Josef Svoboda 140: Jaromír Svoboda 141: courtesy the designer, Josef Svoboda 142: Jaromír Svoboda 143: courtesy the designer, Josef Svoboda 144, 145: Jaromír Svoboda 146: Hildegard Steinmetz 147: Jaromír Svoboda 148, 149: drawings by Gerda Becker With; from Kenneth Macgowan and William Melnitz, *The Living Stage:* © 1955, Prentice-Hall, Inc., Englewood Cliffs, N.J. Reprinted by permission

150: print of Shintomi-za, courtesy Theatermuseum, Munich 151: drawing by Gerda Becker With; from *The Living Stage* 152: courtesy Victoria and Albert Museum 153: courtesy Kunsthistorisches Museum, Vienna 154: drawing by Gerda Becker With; from *The Living Stage* 155: courtesy Theatermuseum, Munich 158: courtesy of the Rockefeller Collection, Yale University 159: Thome, Schwetzingen 160: courtesy Theatermuseum, Munich 161, 162, 163: from *Le Lieu Théâtral dans la Societé Moderne,* Centre National de la Recherche Scientifique; copied with permission 164: Herb Nott and Co., Ltd. 165: from *Le Lieu Théâtral dans la Societé Moderne,* Centre National de la Recherche Scientifique. Copied with permission 166: courtesy Minnesota Theatre Company 167: courtesy Mark Taper Forum 168: David Cole, courtesy Festival Theatre 169, 170, 172: courtesy Denys Lasdun and Partners 171: courtesy Nationaltheater, Mannheim 173: courtesy New York Public Library, Astor, Lenox, and Tilden Foundations 174: courtesy Paul List Verlag; from *Daumier und das Theater,* ed. Hans Rothe (Leipzig, 1925)

175: courtesy Paul List Verlag; from *Daumier und das Theater,* ed. Hans Rothe (Leipzig, 1925) 176: Bernand, courtesy Jerzy Grotowski and the Polish Laboratory Theater 177, 178: courtesy Jerzy Grotowski and the Polish Laboratory Theater 179: George Ballis, courtesy El Teatro Campesino 180: Hal Bergsohn 181, 182, 183: Springer/Bettmann Film Archive 184: Wide World Photos 185: Springer/Bettmann Film Archive

index

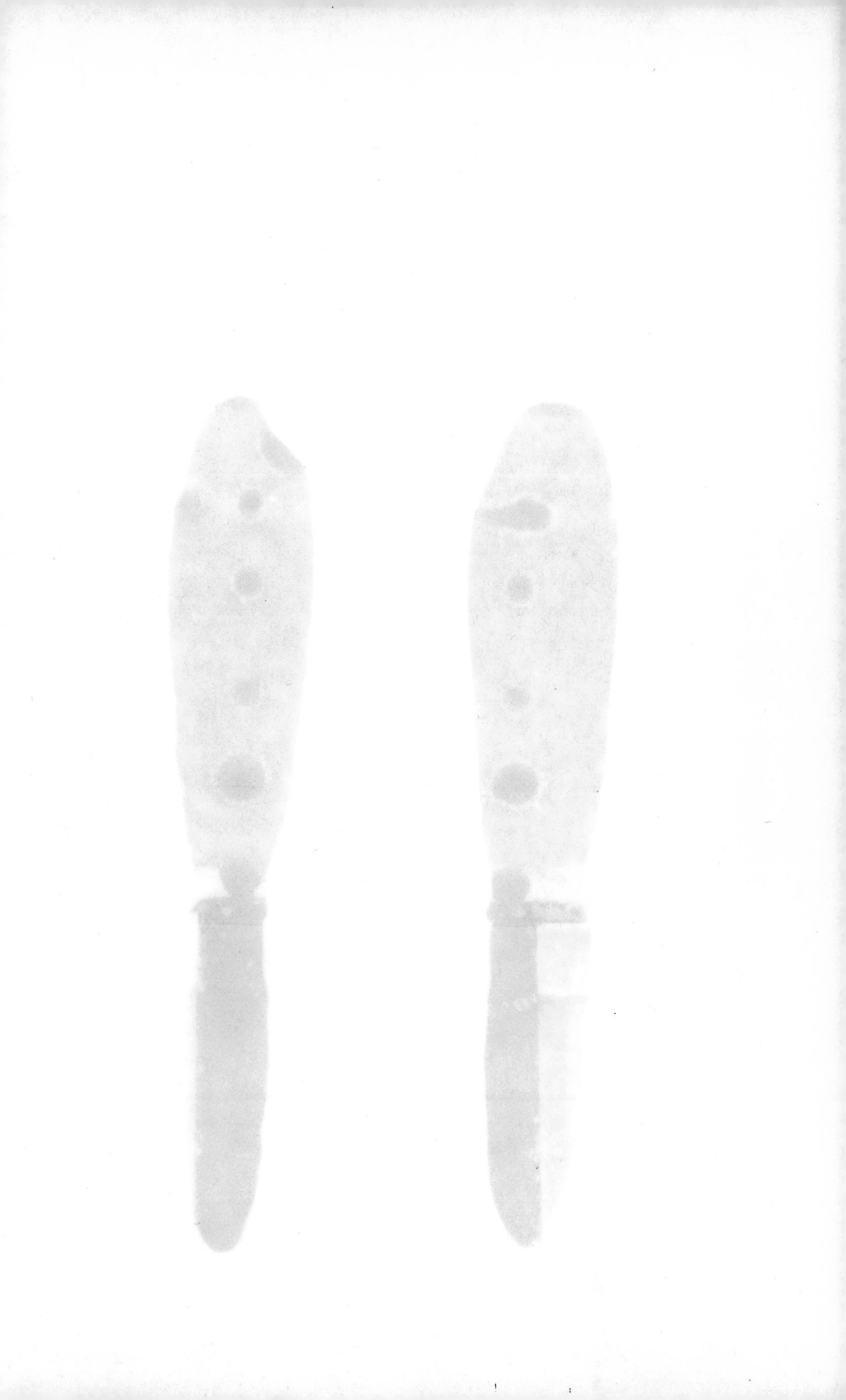